Playing at home

D1584020

From:
'I never thought my life would come out shouting "We are Leeds. We are Leeds" and trying to look ferocious. It has.'

To:
'Hull's fans notice me and start to chant, louder than I thought it possible, as they point at me: "What's it like, what's it like, what's it like to have no friends?"'

Via:
'Another day, another trip up the M1 and M6. Staff at Newport Pagnell service station are now starting to recognise me. I wish they wouldn't.'

It should have been a dream come true for any self-respecting lover of football. Going to ninety-two football matches in one season and getting paid to do it. Well, it seemed like a good idea at the time ...

John Aizlewood lives in London with his wife and two cats.
This is his second book.

Playing at home

John Aizlewood

ORION

For my father, who first took me there in 1970.
And Lorna, who kept me there in 1998.

An Orion paperback
First published in Great Britain by Orion in 1998
This paperback edition published in 1999 by Orion Books Ltd,
Orion House, 5 Upper St Martin's Lane, London WC2H 9EA

Copyright © 1998 John Aizlewood

The right of John Aizlewood to be identified as the author of
this work has been asserted by him in accordance with the
Copyright, Designs and Patents Act 1988.

All rights reserved. No part of this publication may be
reproduced, stored in a retrieval system, or transmitted, in
any form or by any means, electronic, mechanical,
photocopying, recording or otherwise, without the prior
permission of the copyright owner.

A CIP catalogue record for this book
is available from the British Library.

ISBN: 0 75282 642 5

Printed and bound in Great Britain by
The Guernsey Press Co. Ltd, Guernsey, C.I.

Contents

Introduction

Driving south from Crewe on a deserted M6 at 2 a.m. under a full moon, I stopped on the hard shoulder, flashed my hazard lights and sat manfully astride the bonnet of my car. I felt dizzy, unhinged by whatever version of cabin fever turns North Staffordshire into a place of silent, staggering beauty. I sipped from my plastic bottle of Diet Coke (two litre size, sold only to the distressed) until a lorry, last seen in an ITV situation comedy, showered me with a mix of surface water and engine oil. In a roundabout way, that's what *Playing At Home* is all about. And ninety-two football games, from 9 August to 10 May.

It seemed like a logical idea at the time. To take the 1997–98 football season off from my life in order to attend a home league game of every club in the English league. Anyone can do that. So, spurred, I'd like to fantasise, by the ghost of J.B. Priestley, I widened my remit to link football clubs with their locality and people: historically, spiritually and politically. Places have a feel, so do football teams and they are inextricably linked. The result is a snapshot of Britain and British football.

I began as bright-eyed and bushy-tailed as the Barnsley fans I rubbed tanned shoulders with on a scorching August day. Along the way I became depressed – I'll never quite jettison the image of an attractive, seemingly normal woman urinating on a Blackpool pavement in front of me – and terribly lonely. But when my season ended at Villa Park, I went into mourning. I adored almost every moment of it.

That my odyssey often involved me slumped in the corner of some godforsaken pub in Torquay, Cambridge, Blackburn or Middlesbrough, gazing at women and being stared at by men much tougher than myself, is its validation. So is everything I see: the cruelty, the sloth and the magical moments. This is what Britain is like. This is who we are.

And this is why: the brewers – in particular Wetherspoons, but the rest soon followed – have changed Britain beyond recognition. In the mid-80s, those brewers were losing money on town centre hostelries. Boozers rather than pubs, these dark, windowless, male bastions were the province of old bastards smoking roll-ups and young ne'er-do-wells playing pool. Town centres were dangerous. When nightclubbing became a mass activity and dress code deregulation meant pubwear was clubwear, the new generation of clubbers needed places to meet. This atmosphere of non-violent hedonistic anticipation in turn attracted non-clubbers into pubs and town centres.

The brewers woke up and realised that if women could be attracted into pubs, men would follow. So they made their pubs big, open and with glass windows, so women need not fear to enter. Covens of post-feminist women went to pubs, looked fantastic, initiated sex and had a great, drunken time in places that played loud music, sold bottled beer and welcomed all. Men became less violent in this honey trap, the New Lads scam is a sideshow to town centres, from Carlisle to Exeter with all points in between, becoming what they are today. That's the late-90s, it's a social revolution and there's no turning back. I don't know where the old men and the middle aged have gone.

Simultaneously, football changed. It's more fashionable than ever, less violent off the pitch and is attracting the replica-shirt-sporting middle classes, some of them women, in ever-greater numbers. Sky has moved the goalposts, they'd pull them further apart if they could, too. And, obviously, football is more than the Premier League. This much is well known.

What's more interesting – and a half-awake Sunday newspaper ought to have realised this years ago – is that football matches don't take place in a vacuum. Often, the links between town, team, environment and fans are fractured, but no matter how wretched a team like Preston North End can be, they're still a major part of how Preston feels about itself.

Everything I was involved with outside Elland Road was more interesting and significant than Leeds's match against Manchester United inside. Similarly the end-of-season Burnley v. Plymouth Argyle game was unbearably tense – whoever lost was relegated – but the town reacted as though its very existence was at stake, which in a way it was. That's the connection I've made and when the links are absent – new grounds on the outskirts of Walsall, Wycombe, Scunthorpe and Chester – there are reasons for that too and the towns are usually rotten.

As I wandered through the land, I saw several futures for football. Whatever happens it will survive. Rochdale attract 2000 people, twenty-three times a season, no matter how awful they are, and this in a town where rugby league is king and there's a huge immigrant population (football crowds are white, except in London). Famous bands couldn't do that, and cricket and rugby union are rarely on the same playing field.

The watershed won't come until a generation who've seen Premier League football at the closest of quarters on Sky, but never a match (either because they can't afford Premier League or won't go to their local team), come to maturity. In the past, kids were weaned on football, they were admitted cheaply and learned how to be part of a crowd. Like riding a bike, they never forgot. That's gone now, but encouragingly the tide is turning to the degree where only fools and vested interests now argue in favour of all-seater stadiums.

On a practical level, I asked for no help from any club, I paid for all my own ground admission, except where friends lent me season tickets. I adopted a *Field Of Dreams* principle to completion: it will come, even in the dark days around the turn of the year when I couldn't see a way through. In an act of sublime smugness, I finished 3, 2, 1, Premier: in reverse order, just to make me smile.

Lists of names are dull, but dullness is less forgivable than rudeness. These people helped in practical ways or were a shoulder to cry on in the darkest hours. I cannot thank them enough, especially those who demanded to accompany me. I love them all, but not equally – that would be foolish: Mark Blake, Anton Brookes, Steve C, Aaron Cahill, Andrew Collins, David Davies, Tom Doyle, Keith Drummond, Danny Eccleston, Eddie & Ali & Rick, Peter Fiske, Steve Green, Roger Jacobs, Peter Koczerzat, Stuart Maconie, Simon Majumdar, Steve Malins, Tony Nayager, Eleanor Rees, Simon Spanton, Paul Speed, John Stocker, Mark Taylor, X, Zoe Woodward.

1 Barnsley

v. West Ham United
PREMIER LEAGUE
9 August
1-2

> 'It won't all be doom and gloom at Oakwell. I am expecting big things from our lads this year.'

Danny Wilson

Few Barnsley men fought in World War 2. Mining, the town's major direct and indirect employer, was a protected occupation, so almost any local lad eligible for the services was too valuable for mere fighting. Perhaps that's why there wasn't a homecoming parade in Barnsley. Instead, on 20 October 1945, The Band Of The King's Own Yorkshire Light Infantry played outside the town hall to kick off a 'thanksgiving week', which aimed to raise an almighty £40,000 for local causes of worth.

The real festivities had happened on VE Day, 8 May. The pits were given two days' holiday, scant but undeniably real compensation for the war effort. Barnsley celebrated, like it mourned its mining accidents, on its own.

'Flags had appeared everywhere, as if by magic,' gasped the *Barnsley Chronicle*. 'They hung from windows, draped house fronts and sides, were slung in trees, hoisted on flagstaffs and displayed in shops.'

They draped the town hall in the British, American and Soviet flags – not the last time the hammer and sickle would drape itself over Barnsley, the smattering of local anti-Scargillites might muse – a 'juvenile element' burnt effigies of Hitler, while Mayor Alderman A. Jenson JP, presided over a square 'majestically' bathed in floodlights. That night at the local cinemas, George Formby (hugely underrated by the way, but we must press on) was starring in *He Stoops To Conquer*, as was the less venerated Laird Cregar in the X-rated *Hangover Square*.

Meanwhile, Doris Pratt, twenty-nine and single, was reported for swearing on a bus by Mrs Alice McCarthy, who was commended for her 'high sense of public duty'. Things were, it is perhaps obvious to note, different then. Except they weren't, for the local football team were in the old Division Two and their prospects of ascension were as likely as the war-winning coal industry disappearing.

When, at the end of the 1996–97 season, Barnsley were finally promoted to the highest level, it was into the FA Carling Premiership and the coalfields had long gone. Good men, good Barnsley supporters had lived long, decent lives and not seen such a thing. There'd been the occasional cup upset, but more often it would be a home game with Rochdale. Why, as recently as February 1995 just 4733 yeoman stoics turned up to see Barnsley dispatch Millwall. Two years on, they're playing the big boys every week.

Barnsley partied like it was 1945 after they'd beaten Bradford City in April to mathematically leave Division One. Since then, manager Danny Wilson spent the close season signing unproven foreigners and deflecting suggestions his team might be relegated before Easter, overwhelmed in every game they play by a tsunami of footballing sophistication. A team whose supporters have ensured every game at their Oakwell ground this season is a sellout, except when Southampton, Coventry City and Wimbledon can't fill the away end.

Today, it begins. Barnsley town is beside itself with anticipation, but it's a quiet place of a Saturday. There's no loud music pouring out of shops, no traffic because of the pedestrianisation, just hoards of shoppers milling. And shopping. At least a third of them are wearing a red Barnsley FC top and simple, defiant We're In The Premiership window stickers appear to be compulsory. There is fierce civic pride here, not only displayed in the Hands Off Our Green Belt graffiti just off the M1, or the three Barnsley parliamentary seats racking up 85,000 Labour voters, against 16,000 Conservatives. Right now, this swelling of pride is concentrated, to the exclusion of all else, on the football team.

The restaurant-free centre appears to be thriving, everyone seems to know each other. There's the usual high street delights plus Rita Brit-ton's designer boutique and a fire juggler in a black vest on Cheapside, but only 500 yards – yards being the only form of acceptable measurement in Barnsley – from the centre there's a Radical & Liberal Club, a worryingly cheap haberdashers selling faded Manchester United towels and more boarded-up shop fronts than West Belfast.

It is also dizzyingly hot, although as Barnsley was where vines were first grown in Britain, it's surely a freak heat spot. This heat doesn't seem to trouble the huge gang of topless, tattooed, butch men, drinking on the precinct outside Maceys pub. Rednecks may well be the term.

The heat traumatises me enormously. I skulk between shaded areas, feeling slightly conspicuous without a Barnsley shirt, more so trying to eat chips and mushy peas. In any other circumstances I'd slobber on about them, but the heat is so appetite-sapping I can't finish my children's portion. A pint of ice-cold lager seems a logical solution.

All the pubs are guarded by bouncers, but inside they're barely a third full. Only when I've bought my drink from the grouchy Emporium barman, standing in front of a banner declaring 'We're up and we're staying up', do I realise this is because they don't have air conditioning in Barnsley. God help them when global warming comes to South Yorkshire. By the time Danny Wilson has been cheered when he appears on Football Focus to spout one-game-as-it-comes tosh, the trickle of sweat that's been running down my left calf since the chips has evolved into a babbling brook. Time to ooze off.

Oakwell is situated amid the hilly, cobbled streets of cliché. In 1997, the air is clean and the houses are no longer encrusted in grime. Most have satellite dishes, some even have burglar alarms and too many have the ex-council house calling card of latticed windows. Who can possibly speculate what the West Ham players make of it as their coach (Scancoach. Rubbish gold plating on the table lights. Not strictly a Premier League vehicle) glides through these streets? I can. They think nothing about it at all.

Outside the ground I have to take a breather in a shadowy area behind some policemen. A man in sandals, late-50s, decides to speak to me, possibly wanting to encroach on my cool space. He is not one of those many Barnsley souls who still say 'thee' instead of 'you'.

'Well, I hope they do more running off the ball than they did last Friday.'

Obviously I haven't the faintest idea what he's banging on about, although extensive research later reveals this to be Sandalman's dissection of a friendly last week where Pele's old club, Santos, gave Barnsley a 3-0 trouncing. I suggest, with the least pomposity I can muster, that maybe in these conditions, they'd be better letting the ball do the work. He walks off. Nodding I'd like to think. And he was wearing socks with his sandals.

Inside the West Stand concourse, it's cooler still. The beer queue is too long and I feel too sick to join it. Nobody in Barnsley drinks Coca-Cola, so that queue is empty. Alas, the three serving witches haven't got any change, so they form into a huddle, backs turned to punters (i.e. me) and giggle. Gathering what little dignity I have left, I march off to read the dull programme and cute fanzine, *Dizzy Heights*. I sit down, the only person in the place to do so, just as during the game I'm the only person to have a builders' dust arse.

My seat is on the very front row, thrillingly just two seats away from the West Ham contingent, mean-faced but stupefied on an open end by incessant sun they cannot escape. Less of a thrill is the discovery that I cannot see the goal at the far end because of the heat haze and I can't see the goal in front of me because the breeze, which although too gentle to give succour, is strong enough to help the corner flag obscure the whole penalty area. I'm sat next to a young boy in a Barnsley shirt and a couple aged thirty. She has the face of a much older woman. I won't be talking to either of them and they don't want to talk to me.

There's a special atmosphere, midway between mass hysteria and mass surprise. There are forlorn fans who can't get tickets pressed against the outside fences. Those who have made it chant the Barnsley mantra 'It's just like watching Brazil', more wish than declaration, especially with an annoying samba band clanking away beside them. Events will prove to be more akin to watching Torquay.

Apropos of nothing, mascot Toby Tyke leads a community singalong to 'You'll Never Walk Alone', except for the Londoners who simultaneously holler 'I'm Forever Blowing Bubbles'. A huge sack of red and white balloons is unleashed to drift over the old colliery sites. It's a decent stab at spectacle, although too like ice hockey (sport of wankers), slightly tacky and hardly what grown men have yearned for decades to see, but what could Barnsley do, other than assemble a parade of former players who didn't bloom so magnificently as the current crop?

By the time the teams emerge to Emerson, Lake & Palmer's evil 'Fanfare For The Common Man', the Barnsley folk are in such a state of sun-drenched hysteria the all-too-cutting West Ham chant of 'Where were you when you were shit?' is ignored. History will record that Barnsley lost their first Premiership game. It's a poor do, although these conditions would have tested the Ethiopian marathon élite, let alone twenty-two Premiership players, some of whom are called Darren and all of whom may well like a drink or two.

Darren Barnard has Barnsley's first Premiership touch, a chest block which winds him. Because Sheffield Wednesday had levelled Newcastle's early opener up at St James' Park before Neil Redfearn's looping header gave Barnsley the lead and all the other Premiership scores were level, Barnsley led the country for twenty minutes.

A Barnsley man runs on the pitch and scampers beerily towards the West Ham fans, who look keen for what they undoubtedly call a bundle. Their team, though, look morose and disinterested, especially ginger pinkies Steve Lomas and John Hartson, while goalkeeper Ludek Miklosko flaps at every cross. The Barnsley fan is immediately arrested. These teams may well meet again next season, but not at this level. The sun doesn't seem to be setting, instead it shifts around malevolently, with the sole intention of charring my tender white skin.

Half-time and backstage for some shade. The beer queue is still overwhelming – some people have surely missed the whole first half – and there are no cold soft drinks left. Could I therefore have a glass of cold water from the sink behind the serving women, seeing as it's officially 100 degrees out there? No I could not. Looks like Barnsley have really joined the Premiership.

The home side collapse in the second half, the samba band have given up and there are no 'We are Premier League' chants any more. West Ham's Stan Lazaridis, the world's worst forward, is brought on as wing back and snuffs out both Martin Bullock and Redfearn. Barnsley goalkeeper David Watson, too trendy to wear a cap, gifts Hartson a goal and a West Ham fan runs onto the pitch, almost missed by the police who are covertly (small policeman with video camera walks behind larger one) filming both sets of fans. Frank Lampard Jnr scuffs in the winner and it's all over, bar the racist chanting directed at West Ham's Rio Ferdinand. What jet-black Clint Marcelle, so beloved by Barnsley fans, thinks about it only he knows, and he won't be saying.

Afterwards, there is a sense of terrible anticlimax around three sides of the ground. The sun looks like it's up for an all-nighter and it's given me a headache that just won't quit. On the streets outside, it's muted.

As Barnsley fans clamber their way towards the town centre, there's a bastard in a car trying to force his way through. 'Shift,' he sneers, not entirely without malice. He turns out to be a member of South Yorkshire Police (motto: Justice With Courage), too dim to work his siren. Community policing is all the rage round here. 'You're not at Orgreave now,' shouts an ex-miner.

'Tonight,' claimed the *Barnsley Star*'s front page this morning with its unique sense of tense, 'bars were primed for a party – win, lose or draw'. By 5.15, Barnsley was closed. It was like they'd never had a football team in the Premier League and I have to do this ninety-one more times.

2 Sheffield United

v. Sunderland
DIVISION ONE

10 August

2-0

'Oh! Those sleepless nights!'

Nigel Spackman

Sheffield, like Rome the locals proudly boast, is built on seven hills. There the similarity ends. Still, apart from the one blighted by the least-appealing dry ski-slope in South Yorkshire and another infested with slum flats, Sheffield's hills are fine as hills go, undulating southwards towards the Derbyshire moors and northish over the Don Valley, once the most concentrated area of heavy industry in Europe. Until the late-1970s, Don Valley and surrounds were coated in a fine, spongy dust, the colour of the bitter locals still drink in vast quantities. It was the residue of some steel-making process or other, information nobody need know today. Naturally it entered the lungs of the resident steel families and killed them (along with the overwork, the fags, the drink, the lack of money, the bad diet and the hopelessness) just when they'd begun to enjoy their retirement after finishing their sentence of a job for life.

Nothing of this nature troubles Romans, although their air is not for the faint of lung. While Roman families spend their Sunday mornings chattering at cafés or ambling around a city packed with things to do, Sheffield is shut, as if in homage to a German town. This Sunday morning, it's hotter than Arizona. All it needs is tumbleweed and Ennio Morricone in the background and I could have got to Phoenix.

The shops are closed, except for McDonald's – McDonald's isn't allowed that luxury, in case it misses a sale – the streets have already been cleaned (hopefully at council overtime rates) and the people are elsewhere, probably at the ghastly Meadowhall shopping centre just off the M1 which has captured what little imagination the natives here have and which has ensured the city centre is usually ghost-like twenty-four hours a day. Fight back you fools.

I plod disconsolately along The Moor, the pedestrianised high street rebuilt after the Nazis bombed the old one as they missed Don Valley. A construction crew are constructing something which, Rolf Harris-style, I can't yet identify.

Despite everything, there's still occasional evidence of what went before. In 1897, Sheffield was so important that, four short years before she died, Queen Victoria, who didn't get out much, turned up to open the old town hall. A century later, from that very point, she'd have been able to see an Ann Summers shop. Nice one, progress.

It is 11 a.m. The pubs open at 12. The game kicks off at 1. There is nothing to do except go to the ground.

United, Sheffield's inner-city club, are at home to Sunderland. They would be perennial under-achievers if anyone expected anything in the first place. That they're not in the Premier League isn't because of David Hopkin's last-second goal in the play-offs for Crystal Palace, but because United didn't win an away game after Boxing Day. Manager Howard Kendall and his laughable lime-green shirt flicked United a V-sign in the close season and scuttled off to Everton, so the board half-heartedly let Nigel Spackman take over as caretaker. Spackman bought a pair of unknown Greeks and, for £1 million a year, secured the return of Brian Deane, always underrated, played out of position at Leeds and a populist hero round these parts.

Hence the Welcome Home Deano banner some old dears hover around the players' entrance with. Sunderland fans bask in the sun like Wearside whales, perking up only when the team coach (a mighty Moordale, no team coach sign, possibly the most luxurious vehicle in the North East) floats in. A black Sky reporter: Mammon reminding everyone of why we're here at this ludicrous time on the Day Of The Lord, films interviews with supporters in replica shirts. The sun looks like it's here for a while. Great. Just great.

Inside the Arnold Laver (local DIY magnate, recently died, pretended his name was Alan, helped United through financial hard times) Stand, they're selling cold beer and dreadful hot dogs. The PA announces that the PA system isn't working. In the arena, I'm sat next to another urchin, a fat one this time, and a shrieky middle-aged ginger woman. Not an afternoon to make new friends, then.

United's problem is there for all to see: it's the first day of a new season, under new management, against what some might see as glamorous opposition. Deano, their only decent player of the last decade, is back, yet they don't come close to selling out their lovely, refurbished stadium. A third of the executive boxes are vacant. People are simply not interested in Sheffield United; not enough of them anyway. They haven't won the league for exactly 100 years, a record Birmingham City may yearn for, and nobody sentient can remember it.

Bramall Lane was three-sided until the early-70s, when United booted Yorkshire Cricket Club to a park at the posh end of Sheffield. The stand where I sit this lunchtime was ready in time for the 1975–76 season, the one when

United were going to qualify for Europe for the first time. They were as good as relegated from the old Division One by Christmas.

By 1981, they were in Division Four and virtually bankrupt, having been the only club daft enough to let Martin Peters manage them. United's finances weren't in order until the 1995–96 season when ever-strange Reg Brealey, a man with business interests in India and a man not unknown to various police forces, stepped down as chairman in favour of Manchester-based, Manchester City-supporting millionaire Mike McDonald, who installed Howard Kendall, gave him money to spend and, in the positive sense, finished off the ground. A couple of weeks ago, former Vice Chairman Stephen Hinchcliffe sued McDonald for £500,000, claiming the value of his fifteen per cent stake had been misrepresented. 'He sold me the shares. That's his problem,' replied McDonald, who may not be the type to help old ladies across the road.

Some dancers, not all of whom have fabulous legs, wave pom-poms and fail to interest a soul. While Deano, long shirt sleeves and all, is acknowledging the 'Deano, Deano, Deano' chants, nobody is thinking of Wayne Quinn, about to play his first professional football match. The Cornish boy looks terrified, about five years old and full of running. This isn't the climate to scamper around headless chicken style because it's your first time. I really hope Deano pointed this out to him.

As the game progresses Deano plays his usual blinder and little Wayne is holding steady at wing back. He even ventures so far upfield to chance a half-decent shot. Sunderland look lightweight and disjoined and United are soon 2-0 up. The first through the much loathed Jan Aage Fjortoft, who gives the appearance of being uncaring. Perhaps significantly, Deano takes ages to offer congratulations. The second via a spectacular team effort, expertly finished by the excellent Vassilis Borbokis, the only Greek to play. The fat kid next to me starts sneering at the few Sunderland fans who've made the short journey and loudly makes the likely supposition that many of them earn less than his bloated father, who is berating his own team's David Holdsworth as being 'just like an old tank'. What a tough little chap he is. I want to execute father and son.

United's Shoreham End sing their fearsome 'We are Bladesmen' chant, while Sunderland, in a hideous kit the colour of unwashed lemons, never look like pulling anything back and their only chance falls to Lombardo lookalike (alas not Lombardo playalike), Steve Agnew. United, especially Belarussian substitute Petr Katchuro, miss a hatful of chances, but there's no anxiety – Spackman jokingly tries to shove the substituted Fjortoft back on – so feeble are the opposition.

At the final whistle, only new signing Lee Clark and the ever-perceptive Niall Quinn bother to acknowledge the tiny proportion of Sunderland supporters who stayed to the bitter end. Their colleagues are already in the communal bath, far too mature to be comparing penis sizes no doubt.

The United fans are delighted and although their team's propensity to cock up any seemingly favourable situation shouldn't be underestimated, they've looked excellent this morning. The fans chant 'Deano, Deano, Deano' again and 'Deano for England' and twenty-year-old Wayne Quinn, looking not old enough to get served at the players' bar (if they enforce these things), can sleep soundly in the knowledge that, despite being substituted midway through the second half to sustained applause, he's made a fair start and rolled with a succession of elbows in the face from Agnew.

'That's three points towards safety,' chuckles a professional Yorkshireman as the crowd exits in the heat. Nobody laughs.

3 Arsenal

v. Coventry City
PREMIER LEAGUE

11 August

2-0

'We are strong technically and tactically. I believe we are also strong mentally. Now we must see how far we can go.'

Arsene Wenger

The Arsenal Experience begins at Finsbury Park with Arsenal World Of Sport, a not so super superstore, full of official junk. Its outhouse is a shop where, for a lot of money and an infantile sense of humour, you can get SEAMAN on your shirt ...

As the Coventry City coach (Harry Shaw, nothing special, sturdy tables though) pulls in, it's obvious Arsenal are going to whup their Midlands asses, as they don't say in either London or Coventry. Gordon Strachan, a manager who blames his players in defeat for not following his incomprehensible ginger instructions and who takes all the credit on the rare occasions City win, has insisted that on 1997's hottest, stillest evening, every one of these players must make the journey to Highbury attired in shirt and tie. The man is a moron.

Arsenal's victory is confirmed a few minutes later when they arrive in a coach too, a fabulous Hallmark. They must do this all the time, as there's a huge crowd in front of the marble hall of legend to greet them. When the players disembark, some of the crowd scream at these, in effect, pop stars. The foreigners making their home début, Overmars, Petit and Grimandi must know they've lucked into something special. Coventry's new foreigners, Soltvedt and Hedman, sweating beneath their collars, may be thinking slightly different thoughts. Maybe that's why they call Highbury the home of football. Maybe they keep its spirit here.

Arsenal fans have it easy. Their ground is the closest to Central London, it's surrounded by tube stations (there's one called Arsenal for the more stupid of their number) and pubs like The Kings Head where those feeling a trifle tense pre-match can smoke marijuana outside, beneath the gaze of a disinterested police force. Some fools bring their cars, wiser heads use London's public transport – on which it's unusual for someone to be murdered by the way – or they park their cars at underground stations up the line.

Highbury's surrounds are ugly. It's faux Islington, but more accurately it's in grimy Finsbury Park, so down at heel there's a pawnbroker's between Finsbury Park station and Highbury. It's hemmed in by tower blocks and urban ennui. The area comes alive only on match days with mobile programme shops, pedlars peddling all sorts of rubbish and swarms of wardens making sure nobody busts the draconian parking restrictions.

Inside, there's more delights for lucky old Arsenal fans. In the North Bank concourse there's a live band playing Chic covers, there's bars, there's the Arsenal Museum which is otherwise only open on Fridays, there's a bagel shop (smoked salmon £1.90, not bad at all), a closed ticket office, a standard bookies and yet another souvenir 'super' store where you can sign up to the Arsenal internet site for a £10 set up fee, plus a mere £13 a month (+VAT obviously). In one corner, there's a penalty shoot-out at £2 a go for adults, which black kids have taken over. It's clean too, with waves of interchangeable urchins clearing up detritus around the punters.

Until very recently, this would have provided a better evening's entertainment than the team, but Arsenal are a delight these days under wily Wenger. In a horrible irony for their rivals up the Seven Sisters Road, Arsenal have become the new Tottenham, while Tottenham are the new Arsenal.

Meanwhile, once I finally take my seat, again with the unmistakable smell of marijuana hovering, said seat is actually cushioned, with more leg room than Scrubber Class on Virgin Airlines. Then there are giant video screens showing inaudible interviews and literally hundreds of Arsenal goals. It is football heaven, the way it will go unless the bubble bursts and fashion moves on. There's one thing wrong: Arsenal fans themselves.

Arsenal attract whites, blacks, Greeks, Asians, almost any of North London's myriad ethnic groups, save Jews. Unfortunately, they attract the dregs of these races, like the white bloke next to me who mutters 'fucking wankers' on the few occasions Coventry secure possession; like the black man a few rows down who starts on at Marc Overmars, ten minutes into the player's home début. Overmars may indeed prove to be an 'overpaid cunt' and a 'slaaaaag', but the fan's young son doesn't need to know. They barrack poor Ray Parlour, they howl derision at David Platt when he replaces Emmanual Petit, partially explaining why the Englishman wants out. Not once do they collectively give anyone, any of their own players, the benefit of any sort of doubt. It won't be pleasant if the team skid into a bad patch.

Their songs are useless. The chant in all-seater stadiums of 'Stand up if ...' in this case, 'you hate Tottenham', is playground bully and peer pressure writ large. It's football fan as venal moron and Arsenal fans love it, as much as they love their dull litany of anti-Tottenham chants. Mercifully they exclude 'Spurs are on their way to Auschwitz', a result of the clearly visible closed-circuit cameras and the consequential simplicity of pinpointing seated offenders, rather than evolution.

These spoilt, ignorant, flatulent, humourless ingrates were ideal for George Graham's petty, paranoid teams. They don't deserve Arsene Wenger, they don't deserve Patrick Vieira (God, he's a gorgeous footballer), and they don't even deserve Ian Wright, whose two poacher's goals win the game. Just for good measure, he gives his unfortunate marker, Richard Shaw, a torrid ninety minutes.

Coming on the back of an epic victory over Chelsea two days ago, Coventry don't manage to sell out their meagre ticket allocation (couldn't they be relegated, after all this time, after all these years, for this alone?) and they don't have a shot. Arsenal look like world beaters, but Barnsley would have looked like world beaters if they'd played this Coventry side.

Afterwards, there's still no wind and the humidity is still overpowering, even at 10 p.m. There's no joy from the thronging Arsenal fans, just the sure knowledge that they and their team have received exactly what they deserve. That's only half-true.

4 Derby County

v. Wimbledon
PREMIER LEAGUE
13 August
2-1, abandoned

'Be sure of one thing tonight: Wimbledon will want to spoil our party.'

Jim Smith

If, as all right thinking men and women of Derby should, we ignore the official opening by The Queen and her husband, or the pre-season friendly against Sampdoria when defender Chris Powell claims to have spent the evening attempting to secure Jurgen Klinsmann's autograph, this was Derby County's big night. The first proper match at their brand spanking new Pride Park Stadium, so named because once its surroundings are built up, there might be a smattering of pride around the place.

Right now, though, it's a mess. Situated so far out of town, Derby County have to put special buses on – how injured Dean Sturridge gets to work we'll never know, as he claimed he couldn't afford a chauffeur on his weekly £3000 when he was banned from driving in March – Pride Park is an industrial estate without industry, apart from Toys'R'Us. There are no pubs, shops or houses, just impossible-to-police waste ground, ideal for crowd trouble. There's a juicy view of a pair of cooling towers though and in the distance the floodlights of the jilted baseball ground (let's not get sentimental, it was a hole, although before the final game there, the club organised a minute's silence for it ...) stand forlorn and forgotten already. At least the new era means the lucky traveller doesn't have to visit the centre of Derby.

Now that Rolls-Royce and the railway industries are gone, the *Derby Evening Telegraph* (headline: BALLOON HITS OAPs' HOMES) reckons tourism is the future, hence the current but surely ill-fated Feel Welcome In Derbyshire campaign. Maybe the planners are smarter than everyone and see different times ahead as they try to move the centre of Derby south, towards the M1, heartland of Margaret Beckett's constituency.

From 500 metres, Pride Park Stadium loosely resembles Richard Rogers's

Pompidou Centre as it looms out of the dusk. It's an inside-out building. The front entrance is superb, almost like the headquarters of your favourite multinational, with glass fronting, forty-foot flagpoles leaping skywards from a mini-roundabout, manly aluminium girders and women greeters I'd sell what's left of my soul to sleep with. Small-minded small towns like Derby may need time to fully appreciate such grandeur.

It says, like so much of football 1997–98, We Are Important, particularly if you've bought a Pride Park brick, which they've put into the floor, as opposed to the walls, around the stadium. Each brick has a pathos-ridden message, except for the many morons whose brick says Simply The Best, current Derby anthem, and the solitary fertile mind who paid for 'just another brick in the wall'. Even so, there's a feeling of unbridled optimism, which I now know has a sweet smell, a little like vanilla buds. Everyone is smiling, obeying the police and waiting for Wimbledon to make up the numbers.

They turn up, tracksuited, in an impressive Tellings coach which probably costs as much as Ceri Hughes, their sole summer signing. Vinnie Jones stays on board a full five minutes after everyone else, while the crowd jeer him. He ignores it, there's nobody capable of bothering him here.

Inside the Mansfield Bitter Stand, the same caterers of non-distinction as at Sheffield United have the Derby account. There's beer, of course, but the area is ridiculously small, unnecessarily so with acres of untapped space beyond the turnstiles. As there's no smoking in the seats, everyone has a fag in this tiny area, all jammed together in the fug. As there's no ventilation, the smoke stays and lingers. It improves the taste of the beefburger, but it's an eye-watering experience, badly thought out, like much of Pride Park. And they need three times as many toilets.

I gaze lovingly at the roof snaking most of the way round Pride Park, over an unfinished corner which loops up, as if in homage to the corner at Sampdoria. On the pitch, Derby Council give the club some crystal glass to commemorate tonight. Newly passed over for the Minister Of Sport gig, Derby fan Tom Pendry MP hands over a cheque for £3.4 million from the Football Trust towards the ground. It must be hard to cash those six-foot tall cheques though. Even in Derby.

Anyway, the actual match is a fascinating tussle between two sides who might have given Arsenal a game the other evening. Derby take the lead when Ashley Ward neatly tucks in Pride Park's first goal. Wimbledon, as is their way, equalise within a minute. By half-time justice is just about done when Stefano Eranio, Derby's signing from AC Milan (how oddly that reads) pokes them in front.

All is well, even the weather is turning balmy and, happy with my world, I ululate before the cobalt skies. During half-time, an MC and a mascot, Rammie, take over. I adore mascots, especially cuddly, furry ones who slop about: there's something quietly dignified about a grown man dressing up as a ram solely to make people feel better about themselves. Not entirely surprisingly, MC, mascot, and probably the rubbish dancers, too, think The Rams can hang on to their lead.

Wimbledon shove Andy Clarke on at half-time to make a three-man strike force. Then they lay siege, in a strictly footballing sense of course, to Ugly Estonian Mart Poom's goal. The Derby fans have a chant for him and his near-cleft palate every time he touches the ball. It goes 'Pooooooooom', a bit like 'booooo' in other circumstances. We hear it a lot during the second half. The last twenty minutes are looking like they might be special. I'm flummoxed as to who might win.

Then it happens. Wimbledon have a throw-in and there's a loud pop, like a fuse blowing. Turns out it *is* a fuse blowing and darkness spreads across the land. Pride Park doesn't have floodlights, just huge bulbs atop each side stand. At one point, every light, even the safety ones, are down in the main Toyota Stand. Except, that is, for the lights in the executive boxes. They will never go out. Never ever.

Nobody knows what to do. All the socialisation processes a football fan goes through don't legislate for darkness of a non-metaphorical kind. Minutes pass. At five, there's silence. At ten, slow handclapping, helped along by an idiot walking round the pitch banging his huge drum. At fifteen, the DLF (Derby Lunatic Fringe, whose fanzine *Hey Big Spender* proudly boasts had an active hooligan season in 1996–97) stir. They have, with considerable smartness *vis-à-vis* a new ground, positioned themselves next to the away fans. For a moment they stop their anti-Nottingham Forest extravaganza to chant 'Shit fans, no ground' at the Wimbledon few. At twenty minutes, the Wimbledon corner are joining in the Mexican waves – seen as a panacea right now – as the teams mill around gently exercising, trying not to stiffen up. At twenty-five, there's silence again.

After half-an-hour, someone from Derby finally has the grace to make a statement. 'Stay in your seats. The electricians are working on it,' he declares in a most unconvincing manner, the subtext being that if anyone takes a tumble in the murk, guess who might be sued? This causes much jollity and I'm even tempted into a few words with my adult neighbour (the other one is a child yet again, something evil is happening), who doubts this heralds good news. 'Anyway,' concludes the stoic with the firmness of someone who will live in Derby all his life. 'Tonight sums up this club. And we were winning.'

He's wrong. The lights slowly blaze back into life to louder cheers than greeted Eranio's goal. It's magical, a gigantic version of some uncouth amusement arcade worker switching on a pinball machine. Game on. Oh no it isn't. There's another terse announcement, as if everything is our fault. 'The game has been abandoned.' There's no sign of cowardly Rammie.

There's booing rather than Pooming and everyone walks out in an orderly fashion. Nobody is surprised. This, the prevailing mood insists, is Derby County and this is what happens. Exactly the sort of *laissez-faire* diffidence which, thousands of miles away, lets the Macao Mafia control their territory. If the Soviets had invaded during the Cold War (a proposition as remote as Chad invading by the way), Derby town would have turned its industrial base into making Welcome Ivan doormats.

Will they demand entertainment or their money back right now? Oh no, they're off home to watch it on midweek *Match Of The Day* and say they were there the night they didn't sit down in the centre circle and demand concessions. What are mobs of young men for, if not to turn a situation like this around?

Immediately, Wimbledon manager Joe Kinnear is on BBC Radio Derby giving a press conference. He certainly says 'arse', as in 'If we were Manchester United you'd all be kissing our arse in this situation' and I truly believe he said 'fucked' as well, as in 'I dunno, the generator was fucked'. Let's hope so, because it's a) big and b) clever to swear. Especially on BBC Radio Derby.

Useless Derby blamed Wimbledon for the abandonment, claiming they put pressure on referee Uriah Rennie to call it off. That's the same Derby who hadn't put any pressure on Rennie at all by announcing to the crowd that it was his first Premiership game. Kinnear said the referee had given it half an hour and that was that. Pride Park? Hardly. Cute mascot, though.

5 Hull City

v. Notts County
DIVISION THREE
16 August

0-3

'I just ask you to remain patient with us.'

Mark Hateley

Entering Kingston Upon Hull feels like the culmination of a journey to the end of the earth. There's no reason to go there. It's one of life's termini. Literally the end of the line, not a place to be passed through *en route* elsewhere, save for those rash enough to leave the country on a ferry. Even Newcastle's on the way to Scotland.

It's the largest place in England never to have had Premier level football. William Wilberforce, Amy Johnson, some of The Beautiful South and John Prescott, current Hull East MP, have strong Hull links. Philip Larkin showed just how much he disliked people by moving here. Stock of Stock/Aitken/Waterman, *The English Patient* director Anthony Minghella and Everything But The Girl were Hull undergraduates, the latter naming themselves after a furniture shop out Hessle way. In short, nothing happens in Hull and nothing has ever happened.

However, it does have the Humber Bridge, the most beautiful suspension bridge in the world. It towers over the city physically, spiritually and, with its £435 million debt (soon to be recouped by increasing toll fees by 30p, cheers), financially. No wonder the bridge is virtually the sole image on Hull postcards.

Hull has made an effort. The fishing industry has long since shrivelled, battered by the Icelanders during the Cod Wars of the 70s, filleted by EC quotas and fried by the end of the Cold War when the British Ministry Of Defence no longer saw viable reasons for sending pretend trawlers to former Eastern Bloc waters. Once Hull smelled of fish. Now it doesn't. Both working and defunct docks are tourist attractions and container traffic is booming. The signs to the fruit market are in four languages and they've tried to establish a city walk, the Fish Pavement Trail, for tourists. But it's still only the bridge people are aroused by.

I've come to Hull on the train. Just the £60 from King's Cross, no wonder it's so isolated. No more darkness of the soul and not talking to the person slumped next to me. I'm with my friend Peter, so we can gossip like cackly old women.

The Humber Bridge is visible from Hessle station, as are the six floodlights of Hull City's Boothferry Park. Once, the ground had its very own railway station, but there's no call for that now.

Like wayfarers of old, we head for the docks, now partly retrained as Hull Marina. Everyone is northern-cliché friendly (this I like, make no mistake) and while boats are no way to travel for human beings, sitting in the hot sun, talking rubbish, drinking cold beer at The Minerva across from Dagger Street and watching the River Humber is a certain kind of paradise. Low level paradise maybe, but pleasure glands don't differentiate. At least mine don't.

A plump bride with a permagrin is having her wedding reception at Knights, back towards the centre. There's hardly anyone else there yet, but fattening food is laid out and little page boys dressed in waistcoats are running around it. We wave at her. She waves back. It's the greatest day of her life and she'll always remember us. Across the road is Coco's, whose selling point is that every night is *Stars In Their Eyes* night. I'd be Enya on *Stars In Their Eyes*, so I could wear long dresses and go 'aaaah' a lot.

There are no Hull City shirts on display in Hull, but some men do have 'mam' and 'dad' tattooed above each nipple. We trot down Anlaby Road, where City's old ground used to be, before it was bombed to smithereens in World War 2, like most of this place. We're sweltering like squealing porkers, thrilled by some police expertly escorting some topless, handcuffed (presumably the police's, rather than ones the crims were wearing at the time, but you never know) men from a flat. The tower blocks look a touch rough, but it was worse when the fish industry was booming and skinheads were big news in Hull. Not everything makes sense.

This is a big match. Obviously not because Notts County are the guests as no game involving Notts County can be big, but because it's the first home game under new Hull manager Mark Hateley and new owner/director David Lloyd, the former British tennis player who, luckily enough, is now a multi-millionaire through a chain of fitness clubs. He bought Hull City for £2.5 million at the exact point the courts were getting leery at passing yet another stay of financial execution. Terry Dolan, manager since 1991 and with two relegations on his CV, was sacked. Enter Mark Hateley, Richard E. Grant lookalike, but only after talks with Peter Beardsley led nowhere.

Hull City, like so many, are the proverbial sleeping giant. This means there's a groundswell of locals who desperately want them to do well. It means too a decent away support, some of it punchy, and the all-enveloping sense of previous, current and future football-based disappointment. Not today though. After Lloyd and Peter Mandelson-esque chairman Tim Wilby, former professional rugby player turned property developer who resembles a CIA operative and is pictured in the programme wearing the only collarless shirt ever sighted in Hull, have been introduced on the pitch to scenes approaching delirium, the DJ hollers 'this is a new era for The Tigers'.

Oh no it isn't, and while we're at it, the YTS stretcher bearers look suspiciously like Hull City youth players and the worst-dressed ball-boys in the football league have turned up in their own clothes. One has plumped for a tartan shorts and cagoule ensemble. I blame the parents.

Newly relegated Notts County, in such turmoil they're suffering an incoming transfer moratorium (perhaps most of the cash went on their coach, a brown and yellow Hallmark, not as magnificent as Arsenal's but hardly a reflection of the gap between the two teams) after none of their players received promised signing-on fees, are having none of this nonsense.

Ignoring the Kwik Save and Iceland that are part of the ground structure, and against the backdrop of hyped-up crowd and newly painted stadium (the three sides of it that remain uncondemned at least), County don't mind entering the arena to 'Fanfare For The Common Man'. They work as a unit, let Hull puff themselves out in the heat, and never step above third gear.

The home fans don't raise much of a cluck after Matthew Redmile nods in livewire Dennis Pearce's whiplash free kick. By the time County score their third, after some witless defending, Hull still haven't had a shot, look nervous in defence, are overrun in midfield and Scott Thomson, their goalkeeper newly imported on a free transfer from Raith Rovers, is shaky. Ninety-three years of hurt will become ninety-four. According to Chairman Wilby, 'Commitments in the world of tennis have meant David Lloyd has been unable to get up to Hull before today'. He might suddenly find many more commitments in the world of tennis.

The crowd raise a feeble chant of 'Get your cheque book out', pick on random members of the team, notably poor Warren Joyce whose own supporters urge to be sent off after he fouls big Devon White. At nineteen minutes past four, as an advertisement for Bob's Bikes Xmas Club appears on the electronic scoreboard, the first 'Bring back Terry Dolan' of the season is heard. Many new supporters leave *en masse* with ten humiliating minutes to play, some only to return when a Premier League side turns up in one of the cups. Those who remain beg for the final whistle.

County's travelling dozens sense promotion already and while City troop off to the sanctuary of the dressing rooms, County stay on the pitch, warming down. It's the big thing in fitness these days and looks simultaneously professional and ridiculous.

Outside, most of the home support are gathered in front of The Three Tuns, across the road from the ground, watched over by police dogs ready for some woofular action after an afternoon cooped up in sweltering metal police vans. Nothing happens, just like on the pitch.

In Hull tonight, there's none of the mourning there was in Barnsley. It's a rugby city anyway, although with Hull Kingston Rovers in administration (possible buyer: D. Lloyd), and Hull Sharks (chairman: T. Wilby) out of the 'Super' League and a merger in the air, that's slipping away too. The fish'n'chip shops are closed, but the pubs are not. By 6.30, lads are kicking over the bins in front of City Hall and those pubs are filling. The women dress up – inherently a good thing, but how else could a night in Hull become special? – and hunt in packs, always led by a fat one, who's 'a character' but doesn't get the blokes, who all have collars on their shirts. These men bide their time, circling like Yorkshire hyenas. Their time will come, somewhat sooner than Hull City's, but they'll all live in the shadow of the bridge for ever.

6 **Scarborough**

v. Brighton & Hove Albion
DIVISION THREE
22 August
2-1

'We're working very hard to bring success to the club, but with one eye firmly on the realism of the situation.'

Mick Wadsworth

Last night, with a couple of mutual friends, I went out with Chris Evans (I promise to drop no more names). We trawled pubs in Notting Hill and I discovered that, if plied with enough beer, I can croon any verse of Charlie Rich's 'The Most Beautiful Girl'. If nothing else, Chris Evans understands that great moments will happen in pubs and he's at the stage where fame is something to be enjoyed, so he relishes being recognised and writes all the ideas people keep suggesting on his arm in black ballpoint. He also nips out, on his own and unprompted, to buy a sausage-in-batter for each of our merry little band. Nobody's ever done that for me before. His dad was a bookmaker, so he runs a book on our drinking games and at 3 a.m., when I told him I was going to Scarborough in a few hours, he bet me £50 I wouldn't make it. I win, but by the time I reach the York bypass, I've been sick four times.

Scarborough was the first northern seaside resort. It was developed as a spa in the 17th century, but soon the gentry of Yorkshire and Northumberland discovered the delights of sea-bathing machines and promenading. They forgot, or perhaps never knew, that the then-village's natural harbour had supported a fishing fleet for centuries and that since they'd been clobbered by Vikings, the locals didn't take kindly to invaders of any sort. Unperturbed, the gentry built boulevards along the seafront and their seaview mansions on the hill. They hired the locals as servants for the summer. In the winter Scarburghians fended for themselves as the rich went inland, where, as I remember from geography O-level, it's colder. Some things, as I keep seeing, never change.

From the South Bay, looking towards the town, Scarborough is beautiful: its natural curve around the harbour; how it's shepherded by the 12th-century castle overlooking the North Bay; the way the skyline can't have looked *that* different a century ago, despite the funfair that's also beneath the castle. At sea level, there's what looks like a trawler, literally beached. Children's shrieks carrying up from the sand add to this benevolent perfection. This is England and sometimes it's the greatest place on earth. Remember though, that from above, all places, even German places, it always seems as though nothing has ever gone awry.

Down on the seafront, it's different, although the would-be trawler is really a trawler and it's called Maggie M. There's much flesh on display, usually a splendid thing. Here, it's the permanently disappointed who've gone to seed at twenty-five and they're showing too much of their arses. It's pasty-faced working class obesity caused by bad diet, bad lives and holidays in Scarborough, where Scotts Corner provides unpleasant fish'n'chips and there's an ice cream shop every ten yards. Their potential holiday entertainment is Peter Simon's *Run The Risk*, Humphrey Lyttelton, the Scarborough début of the Black Dyke Mills Band, *Spirit Of The Dance* (*Riverdance*-lite) and Frank Carson. The donkeys look the best bet.

Today is Bank Holiday Friday. It's oddly quiet mid-afternoon. There are no tribes of Geordie lads fighting with Leeds nasties, let alone mods or rockers. In fact, there are no gangs at all, just fat couples too young for the three children they all have and older folk, strolling with dignity, especially when they're holding hands, something which always gives me a warm glow inside, more so when they still have things to say to each other. As befits Scarborough, there's a decent proportion of hand-holding old folks today. Physical contact when elderly – that's something to aim for: young couples do think about it, on their wedding day assuming 'we'll be different', but hearts break gradually, through casual lack of maintenance.

Dangerously reckless, I venture inside an amusement arcade. Nothing in the world smells like a seaside amusement arcade, certainly not an inland one. It's the smell of people making big money in small denominations and its soundtrack goes 'piiiing' and then 'whheeeeee'. I chance 2p on the Rio Carnival, which needless to say is neither from Rio, nor a carnival-like experience. It's one of those penny-pushing games, where potential winnings go down side slots (they have to, otherwise Rio Carnival would only break even, so I can't be bitter). Hurrah! I win a different 2p piece. I try again. Boo! It goes to the arcade owners. The cashiers at their local bank must quiver with fright when they stroll in.

The harbour is in reasonably fine fettle. There are two dozen or so active fishing vessels and one, from Fraserburgh, is disgorging its load. All fishermen, several in real waders, are tattooed. All of them smoke (none Marlboro Lights, the cigarette of supermodels between armfuls of heroin) and they have their own patois. Perhaps they're saying 'look at that sad wanker gawping at us'. I don't mind. I'd give anything to be one of them, except I get seasick very easily.

The only unpleasantness is next door on the beach, where local children left to roam by parents working at tourist-snaring cockles stalls are picking on one of their number and, he loudly claims, are shoving a soiled nappy in his face. It does not auger well for Scarborough in a decade.

Scarborough is a football town in a sense. I see Leeds, Sheffield Wednesday, Barnsley, Burnley, Tottenham, Middlesbrough and Manchester United shirts in any given ten-minute period. Anyone, almost, other than Scarborough FC. Once, they were the most feared non-league team in the country. They won the FA Trophy in 1973, '76 and '77, taking half the town to Wembley with them each time. Since they left the Conference in 1987, they've never been out of the basement, attendances have plummeted and the club care so little about anything that they renamed their tiny ground The McCain Stadium, at the behest of a company who make oven chips. Hopefully for a fat fee, but however much they were paid it's a small price for the soul of a once-fairly-proud club, and it wasn't spent on players.

The ground is situated at Scarborough's southern edge, past where the formerly grand Victorian houses are now flats. It's as if neither town nor club wants anything to do with the other. It's past the repeated and typically unpleasant 'You Will Pay Bitch' graffiti, and is set beneath rolling hills, on the edge of a mind-numbingly wretched council estate (estimated hotels: 0), which hasn't been visited by a council official since the football team were last at Wembley. In the little forecourt outside the ground, a bloke dressed as an unidentifiable bird shakes everyone by the hand, even those wearing Millwall or Liverpool shirts.

The McCain Stadium, despite its name, spindly floodlights, unfortunate location and omnipresent sponsor's logo, is quite trim. There's new seating at both ends, plus plenty of oven chips and a bastardisation of Irn Bru, Irons Brew (Scarborough are nicknamed The Boro), for sale. There's a picture of a Scarborough player on the packaging.

This Friday evening – why it is a Friday evening only the local police know – Brighton & Hove Albion have made the long trek north in a London-based Scancoach which, unlike West Ham's, doesn't have lights on the tables. They're accompanied by a few hundred diehards. The only noise to greet the teams onto the pitch, apart from 'Fanfare For The Common Man' again, is 'Brigh-ton, Brigh-ton & Hove Albion' to the 'Go West' tune. It's nice to know they're here and the closed-circuit television starts twitching.

Initially, Brighton look the better team. They're more committed, a tad more skilful and bind like they've done this before, at least once or twice. Scarborough have none of these attributes, although they're ably led by old Sunderland clogger Gary Bennett, who's coaching here too, so at least he's not yet winding his career down before getting that pub. When any of his team make a mistake, especially hapless young full back Colin Sutherland, they're jeered at by a crowd unstinting in its bitterness, a crowd that has no heroes. No wonder there's no Ten Years At The Bottom celebrations, it's not solely because of the overwhelming lack of ambition.

If you happen to be Scarborough born and Scarborough bred, then by turning up here, firstly you're making a statement and secondly you haven't escaped. You've spent your life besieged by outsiders, and those who go down Seamer Road to see Scarborough are saying they don't like it. They probably haven't been to Alan Aykbourn's Stephen Joseph Theatre, a public funding catastrophe. Scarborough fans are stuck here and I'm standing a comfortable distance from eight boys who're throwing used chocolate wrappers and chewing gum at a solitary man stood several rows in front of them.

This continued undercurrent of unpleasantness asserts itself at the end of the first half. Brighton have deservedly taken the lead, but with seconds to the break their dodgy goalkeeper, Mark Ormerod, is flattened in what looks like an accidental collision with Scarborough's Gareth Williams. Before Ormerod surfaces, the ball is crossed and Bennett flings himself between two defenders to head into the unguarded net. The mighty roar that greets the goal is out of context with the home supporters' habitual silence. They're climbing fences, flashing wanker signs and shaking fists at the Brighton fans. It's exactly the sort of *schadenfreude*-topped goal these people want to see. My burger at half-time doesn't taste quite right.

The second half is a cracker. Brighton foolishly sat back earlier and now their support – 'Archer out' or 'If you hate Bellotti clap your hands' directed at their asset-stripping chairman and chief executive being their favourite chants – is bubbling into anger. The referee rejects three strident appeals for penalties, two of which look especially dicey. After the second, Scarborough nip up the field, Steve Brodie is felled and they have their very own penalty. Michael McElhatton, possibly out of sympathy, taps it to Ormerod. Luckily, by this stage Scarborough are winning. At the end of a sparkling move, the previously anonymous Liam Robinson, untroubled by the attention of any defenders, had belted it past the still not properly mobile Ormerod.

There's much injury time, particularly after John Humphrey's vicious foul on Scarborough's John Kay who soon has to flee the pitch. Later, to a general gasp of astonishment Kay is named Man Of The Match. During the added time Scarborough fans howl like dogs for the finish. Then the teams exit in silence, save for the Brighton contingent's frustrated applause and 'The referee's a wanker' chants.

Afterwards, oh yes, it's Bank Holiday Friday in Scarborough, hopefully making Sodom or even Gomorrah look like downtown Riyadh. I want blood running down the street, frisky women cupping my testicles in their tiny hands and drug dealers on every corner. The local police certainly see such a scenario tonight, for as Chief Inspector Keith Moore told the local *Evening News* (headline:

'THE CAT FORCED TO SNIFF GLUE'), 'We're gearing up for extra cover'.

On the walk into town, the football crowd disperses quickly. After five minutes I'm on my own save a trio of fifteen-year-old boys chanting at a couple of girls they know on the opposite side of the road. Yet more unpleasantness, truly the word of the day: 'We're following Sam, she's got HIV' and the golden oldie 'Get your tits out for the lads'. Sam encourages them by waving. Her less attractive friend walks on, head down, wishing they'd chant at her. This mating ritual lasts until we reach the town and I scuttle away, not wanting to be here when all these children are past puberty and unemployed. Scarborough is a place where children are christened Joshua Tetley, because the new mum, one Karen Baker, likes a pint or two at The Albert. If there is hope, it lies in the old and they still like to retire here.

Perhaps the Bank Holiday has been cancelled. There are no police and virtually no people to police. There's nothing happening by the sea, just half-empty pubs with burly bouncers looking frustrated. Couples of all ages saunter up and down, round and about. The old town around St Nicholas Street, packed with pubs and clubs, is virtually dead, I feel like Omega Man all alone after everyone has gone, have a pint of stout (still feeling peaky after that burger) in a rough-looking pub, wander over the suicide bridge at the end of the seafront and go to bed.

7 Bradford City

v. Ipswich Town
DIVISION ONE

23 August

2-1

'I'm sure Ipswich will be in with a shout of the play-offs come May next year. Saying that, I'm sure we will as well.'

Chris Kamara

Bradford is 'a stinking slum littered with human wreckage'. That's the official guide's view. Admittedly it's the 1867 version, but sometimes it's hard to buck history. Bradford has not fared well, never has. It was never quite important enough to cut it as a major wool town in the 14th century, nor did it thrive 400 years later when it embraced worsted. Later still, Jowett cars never cracked a burgeoning market and the remaining heavy industry caused its fair share of pollution, but failed to further Bradford's long-term cause. What the Germans couldn't be goaded to doing in World War 2, the town planners did in the 60s. They hauled the grim city centre down and built less attractive, archetypal constructions of the era with names like Cinecenta, negating the impact of grand old buildings like the city hall. It's impressively pedestrianised in parts, but it's surely no surprise an unbiased survey has just placed Bradford ninth out of ten Yorkshire shopping centres. Cue much wounded local pride. Indeed, the only serious victory the city of Bradford has ever had happened last night when, in front of 17,000, Bradford Bulls won rugby's 'Super' League. No wonder Richard Dunn moved away after Muhammed Ali brushed him aside.

After the bitter partition which created Pakistan out of India's Muslim enclave in 1947, thousands of refugees moved to England, as a second wave would in 1971 when Bangladesh appeared, again through war. Hoards of mainly Muslims settled in Bradford. Why such a bright people should come to such a place is neither here nor there, but they came and they came and they came. Local history will conveniently erase the fact that those who established a bridgehead suffered all sorts of humiliation and resentment, but it might have been the only place they could afford. In 1997, a handsome three-bedroomed detached house will set back Yorkshire folk of any colour just £65,000. Maybe the refugees fancied the glorious moors high above the north of the city. They ought to have done. I certainly do

Now, the city centre is not Asian turf, there are very few mixed couples and even fewer racially-integrated areas, but the mainly white Ravenscliffe estate, where council tenants must fund their own community policemen, confirms the poverty trap is universal. Bradford has some semblance of multi-culturalism and, ironically, because of those racially distinct areas, the city's political machines dare see no colour. Labour won all three Bradford seats, but two of the Conservative candidates were of Asian extraction.

This hasn't filtered through to football. Manager Chris Kamara might be brown, the excellent boy from Brazil Edinho might be coffee-coloured and new signing Jamie Lawrence is undoubtedly black, but there are no Asian names in the first, reserve or youth team line-ups in today's programme. The Asian kids have their own apartheid football leagues, just as they do in the local cricket. They don't come to 'The Pulse Stadium At Valley Parade' either, although it's off Manningham Lane, which runs through their area and still has 1867-style 'human wreckage' strewn between back-to-backs. These young Asians, many in Manchester United shirts, stand outside their brightly coloured homes – lilac is a particular favourite – to stare at the white football fans parking their cars and sprinting past halal butchers to the match. It's as if multi-culturalism never happened.

Bradford City won't give any more of a hoot than they do now if they do manage to reach the Premiership in five years, as is their ludicrous intention. They've sorted the ground out since the disaster in 1985, when the main stand burned down during a match against Lincoln City. That stand has been rebuilt, although wretchedly it's named after a sponsor rather than the Bradford men, women and children who died. The home support have switched ends and now reside on a covered, standing Kop. The away end, the Symphony Stand, has no view from its lower tier so virtually all the Ipswich fans move upstairs when offered the opportunity.

I'm in the Allied Colloids ('caring chemistry', apparently) Stand opposite the rebuilt stand. The beer is cold and pleasant, but the hot dogs are unspeakable and someone is wandering around dressed as a bantam cock, although my detailed anatomical study reveals that he is in fact a woman.

The Queen opened the stand on 27 March 1997. It possibly wasn't the greatest day of her life, for she had to suffer Gerry Marsden doing 'You'll Never Walk Alone', torrents of never-ending rain and had to kip on the Royal Train in a siding at Hellifield the night before. Stylishly, the club have placed the opening plaque on a wall above the livery for John Wood Bookmakers. Somehow I doubt they've mentioned this to Buckingham Palace.

Good news! I'm on the front row. No beer-sodden West Yorkshire blubber mountain to block my view. Bad news! Even my dumpy legs do not fit and I'm seated so low down that the wall comes up to my chin and my eyeline is at players' calf level. Now I know why managers who sit in dugouts have such skew-whiff opinions of games. I'm on the halfway line. This means a linesman with impressively hairy legs will block my view for much of the game. Bring back standing! Everywhere!

There is pre-match entertainment with another loud berk as MC. This must be nationwide League policy. Tragically the Madonna lookalike, Prima Donna, oh yes, is stuck in a broken down car, so it's left to the Bantam Belles (one black, seven white) to throw themselves about to what sounds like a techno version of 'My Darling Clementine'. For the record, I have a soft spot for the fat one who cannot quite get to grips with most of the moves.

The game is a rip-roaring contest. That's why people come to football: it's fabulously exciting. Ipswich Town start off with a three-man defence. This means Bradford's Peter Beagrie – did he really drive a motor bike through a plate glass window while on tour with Everton? – on the left wing bang in front of me, has free rein, with Wayne Jacobs behind him and Edinho ready and willing up front. They're so near, I learn Beagrie is nicknamed 'Beegs' and Jacobs, wait for it, is 'Jakes'.

City soon take the lead, when guile-free centre forward Rob Steiner heads in after some brisk play down that left-hand side. The fans chant '1-0 to the pride of the north' to our old chum, 'Go West'. I've decided against talking to the bloke who can't help but rub his thigh against me or the child, well-behaved at least, the gods of sadism have yet again plucked out for me.

Perhaps because City only just escaped relegation last season, but still increased attendances to their highest average since 1950 (although it was more likely because of the covered Kop), they've sold over 9300 season tickets and the resulting atmosphere is, at times, electrifying. It certainly rattles Ipswich.

Before half-time, Ipswich put on David Kerslake to stop Beagrie and revert to a back four. City though sit back. The visitors, whose tiny, downmarket playing-card-infested coach has only 'Greene King', like their shirts, as identification, seem to take note. Little Mark Stein, on his loan début, establishes rapport with gangly James Scowcroft and away goals seem inevitable.

Early in the second half, Bradford finish it off when they raid down the left again and Jason Cundy soars to scissor-kick home an expert comedy own goal. Ipswich pull one back late on, when elderly City goalkeeper Mark Prudhoe charges out and miskicks, so young Keiron Dyer can slip one in. The howls for the final whistle are Scarborough-esque. Ipswich pile everyone forward, nearly getting caught on the break, but almost scoring themselves. Objectively, a draw might have been a more fair result, but football never had any objectivity.

The Asian kids, four of whom watched the game from outside in the gap between the Kop and main stand, are still in front of their homes afterwards. Maybe one day they'll feel able to go to a match that takes place 100 yards away.

8 **Tottenham Hotspur**

v. Aston Villa
PREMIER LEAGUE

27 August

3-2

'On Saturday your support was very much appreciated. Tonight we need the same again.'

Gerry Francis

It's a twenty-five-minute trot from Seven Sisters underground station to White Hart Lane, home of Tottenham Hotspur, the new Arsenal. Tottenham High Road is not a pleasant place. Stamford Hill, a haven for prostitutes and numerous orthodox Jewish sects, lies to the south, away from the ground. Walk north and West Green Road is on your left. There's a militant black bookshop there, where for years their prize exhibit was Winnie Mandela's autobiography. They seem to have lost their copy. On the other side of the High Road is a poorly stocked Tesco. On top of Tesco there's a car park. On top of the car park is a selection of grim flats with glassed over balconies as a buffer against noise, pollution or suicide. The inhabitants dry their washing on those balconies. Taken whole, the block resembles a prison ship.

I keep walking, passing a 'Global Trade Centre', a World War I monument dedicated to Tottenham's fallen (honourably, the Remembrance Day wreaths lay unmolested) and Philip Lane, where someone was recently stabbed to death outside a faux Kentucky Fried Chicken. The only sound, apart from the traffic blocking the High Road in both directions, is that of police sirens, not bound for the football. Next to the bus garage is The Swan, a public house so scary (moral for life: never go into pubs where you're the softest) I don't get past the first set of doors before noticing that nobody in this unventilated shack has ever thought about going to a football match. Or of leaving. Nor dare I venture into the very-much-open public toilets, helpfully guarded by a white 16-going-on-36-year-old with a mobile telephone.

Floodlight free and therefore invisible from the High Road until the last moment, White Hart Lane, in the days immediately following the Broadwater Farm riot, was adjudged by the police to be too near the estate for a football match against mighty Orient to take place. In truth, it's impossible to even see Broadwater Farm from the High Road and it's over a mile away from the ground. By day, there's more intimidating blocks of flats than Broadwater Farm in Milton Keynes, but none next to so much greenery. The blocks themselves are on stilts, ringed by walkways; the population are multi-racial and in family groups, often toddling off to the community centre. At ground level, there are all sorts of shops, admittedly with the most stringent security precautions, plus carefully tended gardens and speed humps to ensure nobody gets hurt by passing cars. At night, it's the same only darker. And the shops are all padlocked. And the families have been replaced by silent corner boys. And you can't see the gardens. It is no place to linger and it has as little place for football as football has for it.

On and on the High Road stretches. Past more tired-looking flats which don't look as if they have exits and where Haringey Council, priorities never a strong point, have taken the trouble to erect a sign saying Do Not Feed The Birds. Eventually, immediately after the Baptist church, the best appointed building on the High Road, there is White Hart Lane, the reason these well-dressed white folk have been nervously picking their way through since Seven Sisters – and how odd that football fans are now middle-class invaders.

It looks grand, even without the floodlights. Close up, it smells of Arthur Rowe's kick'n'rush side of the early 50s, of Pat Jennings, of stray cat Tony Parks, of Arsenal winning The Double there in 1971, but most of all it smells of Bill Nicholson the gentleman from Scarborough who played 395 games for Tottenham after World War 2 and has just retired as President. More importantly, he managed Spurs' Double-winning team of 1960–61. He, despite Alan Sugar, despite Terry Venables, despite Terry Neill even, is the spirit of Tottenham Hotspur. Close your eyes and he's there, he really is.

In no way paranoid, Tottenham only let ticket-holders into the giant car park in front of the main stand. This means little kids can't get players' autographs (how mean is that) and the Aston Villa team coach, a Flights so space age that Stan Collymore suffers weightlessness inside, is as out of bounds as Alan Sugar's wallet is to Gerry Francis.

Inside, the facilities of the East Stand, where The Shelf was so unceremoniously turned into seating, are primitive, especially in comparison with Arsenal's. There's no beer, nowhere to slouch and what at Highbury is a smart bagel kiosk, is a girl in dirty leggings selling the things wrapped in clingfilm from a grubby tray. The toilets haven't been cleaned since Alan Gilzean was a lad and may once have been painted, while the hot dogs are more dog than hot, and I'm fucking overcharged for them. Not, admittedly, as much as Spurs were overcharged for Jason Dozzell, but the principle is identical.

Inside, there's a big hole where the upper section of the North Stand used to be. The lower section is empty, save for a giant McDonald's advertisement.

Stylish. The hole has its uses, the bright lights of Edmonton (not a place to go without armour, but it looks nice from a distance) shimmer pleasingly and there's a sense that somehow White Hart Lane is the geographical end to proper London. Kindly, Tottenham have installed a huge video screen opposite the hole, which disconcertingly shows the whole game, albeit for the benefit of the murderous population of Edmonton.

There's a bad feeling about supporting Tottenham Hotspur these days, but the crowd are gentle, suffering souls, seemingly much given to unfounded optimism and for every 'that's another terrible first touch, Sinton, get your act together, you tosser', there's encouragement for the lumbering Iversen and the plucky but ungifted Carr. There's an assumption, not that better times are around the corner, but that better times will one day come. The high Jewish presence – skullcaps, chants of 'Yid Army' and a menacing piece of tribal drumming from the otherwise useless band which ends in 'Yeeeeeds' – might have something to do with it. I wish Arabs had adopted a British team ...

Aston Villa come to White Hart Lane having started even more poorly than Tottenham. Les Ferdinand scores his first home goal after five minutes and Villa start arguing among themselves. By half-time it's 1-1, Steve Staunton has hit the bar from a free kick, Dwight Yorke scores smartly and both sides play as if the other is there for the taking. I can't face another half-time squeezed by a tea rush and it's a lovely night so I stay in my seat. Jackpot. Last time Villa visited here, goalkeeper Mark Bosnich, some way from being the brightest tool in any box, entertained the crowd with a Nazi salute after he'd been goaded by the crowd over a shocking foul on Jurgen Klinsmann in a previous game. Tabloid whipped hysteria? Yes. Public apologies? Inevitably. The end of the matter? Oh no. Football fans, even nice Spurs fans, smell weakness with the keenness of Japanese fighting dogs and Bosnich, guarding the net in front of the empty North Stand, spent the first half being booed.

Come half-time, Bosnich, with iron balls the size of planets, marches to the packed Tottenham end with substitute goalkeeper Michael (son of Alan) Oakes. There he stays for the duration, catching Oakes's feeble crosses. The Tottenham fans get tired of booing. The tiny corner (not their fault, only 850 tickets available) of Villa fans are delighted. Testicle tennis: fifteen-love, Bosnich.

For the second half, all the policeman inside White Hart Lane (two) congregate behind Bosnich's goal. Collymore smartly puts Villa in front. Then, a ball trickles harmlessly out for a goal kick. Instead of picking it up and taking it, Bosnich attempts a flash flick up. The ball hits him smack in the face, the crowd laugh viciously and the taunting begins again. Testicle tennis: fifteen-all.

Ferdinand scores again with one of his hanging headers and then Ruel Fox, 'Foxy' to the Spurs fans, slots in the winner. Bosnich, pretends to be unfazed and cups his hand over his ear. Testicle tennis: thirty-fifteen, Bosnich.

The boos don't stop and he's a long way out of the penalty area when Villa press. In the fifth minute of injury time they get a corner. Bosnich charges upfield, the Spurs crowd stop asking for the final whistle to laugh at him. He looks livid. Testicle tennis: thirty-all.

The match finishes. Bosnich takes his time to leave, fiddling with his gloves, staring out the Spurs fans. Testicle tennis: forty-thirty Bosnich.

Then Bosnich blows it again. He doesn't acknowledge the Villa fans who've encouraged his every move. That's breathtakingly rude. I'd fine him if I were Brian Little. Testicle tennis: deuce.

He slopes slowly off, head held high. Nobody waits to shake his hand. No Villa player, no Tottenham player. This after a game without a bad foul. Testicle tennis: advantage the world.

Except that is for the referee, who's obligated to ensure the players leave the pitch. The referee offers his hand. Bosnich doesn't take it. What a wanker. Testicle tennis: game, set and match, the world.

Afterwards, the Spurs fans are delighted. They haven't missed the injured Ginola (who would?), but when Chris Armstrong gets fit, they might start scoring some goals. A new midfield might be useful, too.

After, it's a more jaunty skip back to Seven Sisters for most, buoyed by the glimpses of flair and three points. The white football fans own the area for now, although like a second-rate goalkeeper, it's only on loan. Just off the High Road locals are lurking, waiting for the streets to clear. At the flats with no exit, where feeding birds is an act of rebellion, loud martial music is coming from a darkened window. A figure is moving inside. He comes to his balcony and, to nobody in particular, bellows, at the top of his voice 'Yid Army, Yid Army'. Behind me, scurrying home before the streets are reclaimed, a little boy is quizzing his father: 'Is that a nutter?' he asks. 'Nah,' says the father. 'He's just happy.'

9 Stockport County

v. Birmingham City
DIVISION ONE

29 August

2-2

'I am delighted that we have finally been able to complete the addition to the squad of Eric Nixon.'

Gary Megson

One of the selling points of capitalism and the free-market system is its endless ability to renew itself, contrary to the orthodox Marxist suggestion that its inherent contradictions ensure self-destruction. Clearly this argument would cut little ice in the former pit villages of South Yorkshire, South Wales or those nations which were, literally, banana republics. However, even Dennis Skinner might be impressed with Stockport, as he certainly would have been impressed with the former textile town's once radical workforce, who rioted for better conditions as long ago as the early 19th century.

Essentially, Stockport is Manchester overspill, but it's also on the way to the Cheshire stockbroker belt where Manchester United players cluster. Some of them (i.e. Butt and Beckham), along with minor Oasis members, spend much of their free time at the Elizabethan Hotel just out of town.

Like a plain but bright teenager, Stockport has made the best of itself to become attractive to that 90s industry with a future: personal finance. Times have changed since 1904 when Alderman Giles Atherton laid the foundation stone to the town hall of a town that was already in decline. Now, it's possible to imagine how Stockport looked between the wars, when the Manchester County Bank was taking in cash, The Wellington was a huge corner pub and the Brookfield Hotel catered for a more discriminating clientele. Now, they are an insurance shop, a bingo hall and Brookfield Estates (i.e. estate agents) respectively.

There's a museum and art gallery too, for a touch of soul, although in May 1997, the week after the town received £1.5 million lottery money to build Britain's only hat museum, Christy's millinery closed down, shedding 111 jobs. Still, there's no graffiti on the few tower blocks. Aeroplanes pass low overhead on their way to Manchester Airport, always a hugely exciting 20th-century indicator, unless you live under the flight path. Perhaps that's where John and Emma Hough, who named their child Oasis Ellie and were understandably disowned by their family, live. I do hope so.

The town's team, Stockport County, have never had it so good. They haven't played at the level of the current Division One since 1938 and are finally fulfilling a potential evident when their gates held up during the disastrous years, 1982–85, when they appointed Eric Webster, the groundsman, as manager, a decade or so after Mike Yarwood was a director.

There's early season optimism here, despite promotion-winning manager Dave Jones and two of his team defecting to Southampton. Tonight, sprint-starters Birmingham City are the visitors. These are times to cherish, even the younger County fans can remember, when Doncaster and Hartlepool were perennial visitors.

On Castle Street, a pedestrianised area between railway station and ground, a bunch of Birmingham fans, colours not on display, stand drinking outside the Prince Albert. Only their accents give them away, so the police are nervous and try to usher them into the ground. Inside though, the pub is full of Stockport fans. Maybe hooliganism, if not dead, is in a terminal condition.

In homage to Stockport's past tussles, Birmingham City arrive in a coach Hartlepool and Doncaster might snort at: a garishly liveried, B-reg Johnsons, exactly the sort of transport pensioners on a coach holiday to The Ardennes might use. No wonder Trevor Francis looks so pissed off as he peevishly stops his players from talking with friends outside the ground. Goon.

Like the team it hosts, Edgeley Park has had a 90s face-lift. Luckily for City fans, the away end is standing, but as if to exemplify karma in action, it's also uncovered. Elsewhere, the County fans are seated. Behind the Cheadle End stand, they're selling beer, but bitter has run out and the lager is undrinkable, except by goats. Confusingly, the smoking areas are non-drinking areas and vice-versa. Pie and mushy peas are available for a bargain £1.70. They are scrumptious beyond human comprehension. In a reasonable world, pie and mushy peas would be the future of football, rather than pay for view or David Dein.

The view from the Upper Cheadle (Do they call it that? They must) is further cause for joy and it's not just because of Vernon, the massive bear-mascot with the fixed grin. Waste ground next to the main railway line, owned by The Bit Of Former British Rail Responsible For Waste Ground, gives way to back-to-back terraced houses, which in turn surrender to the moors towards Buxton. As daylight fades, specks of light begin to illuminate those moors, sometimes cars, sometimes homesteads. Again, I feel proud and humbled, tearful almost, to be British: it's breathtaking. And all this despite the County dancing girls, Shooting Stars, and a ridiculous bald MC who may one day learn that invading the field of play is a criminal offence.

The game isn't great. I'm sat next to a warty, balding Stockport fan. My kind of guy! Everyone else is booing Birmingham's Steve Bruce. Warty whispers to me. 'He should be managing this club, don't you think?'

Frankly, I've never previously thought about it, but in my cunning disguise as a Stockport fan, I say that possibly Bruce should but I have a certain amount of faith in Gary Megson. He looks at me as if I've told him he is devilishly handsome and I wish to take him home right now. Repulsed yet intrigued.

Peter Ndlovu misses an open goal for Birmingham in the first minute. Stockport take an early lead, Birmingham get physical, but on the half-hour they substitute full back Michael 'Unmagic' Johnson for forward Paul Devlin to revamp their defensive formation. They are a shambles, with the tactical awareness of any side managed by Trevor Francis, but County, although beaver-like in their eagerness, can't take advantage.

Early in the second half Brett Angell breasts one in for Stockport. The result is settled and the County fans sing cheery anti-Manchester United songs and taunt Birmingham folk, unfairly, about coming in a taxi. They even find time to admire Shooting Stars who, while the game is on, march around the pitch perimeter, led by a trouser-suited ma'am. They wave at fans until the inevitable 'Get your tits out for the lads'. Even Chris Marsden's smacking the ball against the Birmingham bar when it seemed easier to score Stockport's third, doesn't dampen enthusiasm.

Edgeley Park used to be the end of the road for faded footballers like Mike Summerbee or Albert Quixall. It still hasn't fully shed that aura. Enter 34-year-old goalkeeper Eric Nixon. It is his début and he's displaced young Ian Gray, recent signing from Rochdale. Possibly distracted by the way the Birmingham fans have bunched themselves directly behind him, Nixon lets Devlin's innocuous free kick spin through his hands. City are back in it and my new pal sees the future. 'Oooh no. County'll struggle now.' Naturally I don't know, but I agree with him.

Even Trevor Francis has noticed it's time to bring on giant striker Kevin Francis, former Stockport player. He receives a smotheringly warm reception and County fans who jeer are silenced by people power. Idiotically, Francis immediately spoils it for everyone with a savage foul and then scores the equaliser.

The game ends in an almighty punch up in the Stockport penalty area, with a steward in shirt and tie mixing it with Birmingham players. Like the match that preceded it, it's nothing to write home about, but is entertaining. Ultimately, as Kevin Francis milks everyone's generous applause, County fans are frustrated, but they're still in the honeymoon period with Division One, so there's a sense that these two lost points won't matter come May. 'See you again, mate,' says my fine new chum as he skips off. I don't think so.

Afterwards, there's a police operation to rival a Tony Blair walkabout, necessary only for plod overtime. I hover outside the Stockport Binocular & Telescope Centre, as exotic as it sounds, watching as nothing unfolds. Living here might just be tolerable.

10 **Stoke City**

v. Swindon Town
DIVISION ONE

30 August

1-2

'Today's match is surely one of the most eagerly awaited in Stoke City's long, long history.'

Chief Executive Jez Moxey (manager Chic Bates doesn't speak)

Why, then, have city centres died? Why does every family in the land shop at superstores situated close to a motorway, many miles from their lovely homes, instead of popping down the generic High Street to butcher, baker, green-grocer, et bloody cetera? I've no idea, apart from the conspiracy theory about letting property prices slide sufficiently low that inner city land can be bought cheaply and then sold on at massive profit when the area is regentrified. Go to Stoke, home of Eric Bristow, on a Saturday. By the Sunday you'll have I'm Off To Homebase & A Mall, Hang The Pollution car-stickers in the back of your Ford Capri or its 90s equivalent.

Stoke is tiny, which need not be a problem in itself. The centre of the so-called Potteries (nobody mentions the mines for some reason) is Hanley up the hill, with its history of Northern Soul nightspots and its swanky shops of today, some of them designer. However this does not excuse Stoke, which, after all, has the brand name. The place is empty, save for football fans and police, some of them mounted in overbearing preparation for the visit of Swindon Town on the day Stoke City open their new Britannia Stadium. The best, most upmarket of the shops in Stoke is Woolworth's and the most numerous, unsurprisingly, are travel agents, plus shops selling unearthly 'curiosities', or junk as it's more accurately described.

There are the world headquarters of Spode (founded 1770, this is no new town) and Royal Doulton potteries, somehow embarrassed at prospering. Nowhere here has seen a coat of paint for decades and the one café (with its un-attended smashed window) has but one customer. He hasn't shaved for ten days and has no teeth. He catches me staring at him and some of the tea he's trying to drink dribbles down his stubbly chin. I feel like I'm intruding on private grief.

There's nowhere open to buy the local delicacy, oatcakes, but the open-air market is selling underwear for under £1. There are speedbumps on the High Street itself and the tattooist's studio is doing brisk business. The people are white, downtrodden, Dickensian mesomorphs, devoid of hope and posture, muttering to themselves like they were out for the afternoon before returning to their asylums. It's like some shocking experiment has taken place. No wonder the British National Party could field candidates in two of the three Stoke constituencies last time around.

One thing Stoke is not short of is pubs, full pubs. Most of them have a window display of dirty net curtains to dissuade casual customers. I settle on dank, uncheery Cheers, where at least they've stopped the collection for the barstaffer who was hospitalised last year ... Everyone looks at me like I'm a plain clothes policeman. I watch *Football Focus* slumped at the bar, surprised only that I haven't stepped back in time to a 1975 episode featuring John Marsh and Alan Bloor. Then I piss off.

As poignancy would have it, Stoke City's just vacated Victoria Ground is on the way to the Britannia Stadium, named after some building society, luckily not the Bradford & Bingley. Nothing has happened to the forlorn Victoria, apart from the erection of notices to deter vandals. It's impossible to check from the outside, but Stoke claim to have moved the old centre circle to the Britannia. The Sir Stanley Matthews Suite still looks usable and the most recent graffiti declares 'Farewell Victoria Ground, welcome Britannia!'. There must be ghosts, but they're not the ghosts of trophies past.

Like Derby's Pride Park, the Britannia is so far out of town they have to lay buses on for it. I walk and I'm well on my way at 1.45, but it's car chaos already and gridlock next to the neat terraced houses and Michelin factory. Perhaps not without irony, the Britannia has been built next to the council incinerator, or waste-to-energy plant as it's been renamed.

There is, it transpires, only one entrance to the stadium, a narrow bridge over a canal and the railway link to London. Overhead is a 132,000 volt cable, so low-slung that there's a sign ordering mounted policemen to dismount. Apparently the contractors spent the last two months working twenty-four hours a day to meet the deadline and, even then, Stoke's first scheduled home game with Bradford had to be switched to West Yorkshire.

The Britannia Stadium is a sludge-infested construction site outside, but it looks fine, perched atop a hill, well worth £20 million of anybody's money, although Port Vale-supporting local council tax-payers who've subsidised it probably don't agree. The Swindon team coach (Barnes, white, very standard, looks overcrowded) gets lost in the car park outside and a rattled Steve McMahon and his team have to walk through dozens of unfriendly fans to get to the unmarked players' entrance.

Inside, not all the catering facilities are complete and the merit-free pies are devoid of heat. The queue for beer is too long to join, but inside, with local newspaper the *Sentinel*, giving out free souvenir editions, there is the buzz of a genuine event taking place, although at a disgraceful £3 for a programme of less editorial worth than Scarborough's, there ought to be. Stoke City run from one side of the pitch to the other as part of their warm up. They're cheered to the brand new rafters each time.

After dancers, Stoke City Slickers (oh, please), Tom Jones lookalike T.J. Slater arrives in an open-topped Cadillac. This might seem naff, in fact it is naff, but Stoke City's anthem is a faithful rendition of 'Delilah', with a special Stoke-style menacing 'ha ha' after 'she stood there laughing' and a round of applause for themselves, like an old Soviet politburo, afterwards. Tom is slightly behind his own backing track, but he goes down a storm and somebody's remembered to hand out red and white knickers for women to hurl at him. He's accompanied by Hippo 'Potter' Mus, a mascot with a giant sky-blue head.

The official opening to the best building Stoke has ever seen, is performed by Sir Stanley Matthews (standing ovation), the Football League's David Dent (silence) and Graham Kelly (sustained mockery). Sir Stanley's microphone keeps cutting out, but he gets through the ordeal. Then this dignified old man (we'll pass over his apartheid-era South African jaunts) is invited by the preposterous MC to 'score the first goal that will now open up the new Britannia Stadium'. He dribbles from the twenty-yard line and shoots from close to the penalty spot. Summing up Stoke City in one toe-curling moment, Matthews's effort trickles towards the goal, but doesn't quite make it and some tracksuited lackey crashes it in to set off fireworks as a giant sack of red and white balloons is unleashed. The stadium itself is a magnificent beast, similar to the other new grounds in a way that will forever say late-90s, but that's not important right now.

Alas, the team can't complement the ground. I'm at the end of a row, sat next to a huge, shouty bloke with J-O-H-N on each left-hand finger in case he forgets his name. I'm much too scared to talk to him but even he doesn't get too excited when Richard Forsyth's messy goal gives Stoke the lead. It's a tough physical battle. Stoke expects nothing less, but Swindon, a mirror image of Steve McMahon, are not to be messed with, especially Scotsman Scott Leitch who will later distinguish himself with a remarkable goal-line clearance and be carried off in the other penalty area.

At half-time Tom Jones returns. They, whoever 'they' may be, say you should never go back. Good advice, for his microphone and backing track barely work. He shouldn't have worn that Stoke shirt either. Back to the pub circuit then.

Swindon score twice in the second half, well-worked goals which exploit Stoke's leaden defence. A couple of home fans are arrested in the corner next to Swindon's presence, but many more stream out long before the end, realising that the ground's magic hasn't rubbed off. The only noise is from the small percentage of Swindon's impressive turnout who trouble themselves with that singing malarkey.

Afterwards, what previously was one entrance is now one exit and everybody is leaving at once. It's a death trap. Come a frosty or wet evening, let alone a running skirmish, people will be hurt. It takes nearly an hour for everyone to squeeze through, a situation unaided by the thoughtless Britannia Building Society who inflate a huge pink advertising udder, further slowing passage over this bridge too far.

Such is the claustrophobic delicacy of the situation – and only dwarfs can see those tiny bollock-shattering bollards at both ends of the bridge – everyone has stopped talking about how rotten the match was in comparison to the ground. Old men and young kids are united in looking terrified in case they slip. Even here, even in Stoke, this land of crewcuts and tattoos, there is concern and a selfless desire to ensure nobody is hurt. Somehow nobody is. A hard man says to me, 'After you, mate'. In turn, I let a pensioner through, with my best beaming smile on display. 'Cheers, son,' he whispers.

Stoke, at last, has come through. How wonderful hindsight makes Derby's Pride Park Stadium seem.

11 **Luton Town**

v. Millwall
DIVISION TWO
2 September
0-2

'A resounding home win would improve confidence significantly, but we can only wait a certain amount of time for that to occur.'

Lennie Lawrence

It fair takes me back. Football like it used be, in Luton of all places. Outside the railway station there's an Operational Support Vehicle, a longer police van than they usually toddle around in. Chillingly it has no windows and its driver is in full riot gear. Packs of short-haired, expensively dressed young men roam the streets, heads swivelling like alert owls. They are not wearing anything that reveals a football affiliation, but they're only in Luton – twinned with Spandau, soulmates if ever there were – for one reason, and it's not to see Century Plaza 'the largest office block in Bedfordshire' or Luton Airport which will celebrate its fiftieth anniversary in 1998, although it didn't get a concrete runway until 1959. It's said that man has lived in Luton since the Old Stone Age, surely long enough for some people to understand that this is no place for anyone save the undead.

The town is deserted. Sirens howl in the distance. As I wander, frankly lost, along the old Bedford Road past the milliners (straw boaters are the big thing these days) still in existence, it can mean only one thing apart from the undead actually having risen: Millwall are in town.

F-Troop, Bushwhackers and Harry The Dog are long gone, but Luton Town at home to Millwall still has a special resonance. Some matches changed British football forever: Bolton v. Stoke in 1946 where a wall collapsed, people died and the authorities did nothing. Newcastle v. Nottingham Forest in 1974 where anarchic usurpers won and would win for a decade and more afterwards. The disasters at Hillsborough, Valley Parade and Heysel ensured football lost an innocence that the hooligans were somehow part of. Most of all, though, that starry starry night in 1985 when Luton Town played Millwall in the FA Cup was the beginning of the beginning.

Millwall fans and supporters of other London teams addicted to fisticuffs travelled to Luton in their thousands. As the game slipped away from Millwall, Londoners invaded the pitch. A riot followed: sticks, stones and seats flew at policemen, who first retreated, then regrouped and finally – as they invariably did in any football-related incident – charged and restored order. It wasn't *that* bad: nobody innocent was seriously hurt; the game was completed and, without the presence of BBC cameras the fuss would have evaporated by Saturday.

More significantly, in the top flat at Downing Street that very night, Margaret Thatcher, tumbler of whisky in hand, was watching *Sportsnight*. What exactly she was doing watching *Sportsnight* when there was a country to be run has been lost to history, but we must, as ever, press on. The important thing is that she saw the mayhem.

Out of character, she didn't see football trouble as the working class tearing itself apart and thus to be nurtured, she decided that Something Must Be Done. When the smoke finally cleared, things would never be the same. All-seater stadiums; membership schemes; the assimilation into football of the middle class as a powerful, organised force; grown men wearing kits to watch matches, would never have happened had Millwall fans not fancied a barney and a powerful old lady hadn't been watching telly.

Luton's ground, Kenilworth Road, lies in the town's Asian and student quarter. Tonight, there are police on every corner and for a moment of heady nostalgia, it seems as though families don't come to games. Some of the pubs are closed. Ah, yet more nostalgia. There is no trouble.

The ground is cramped by houses along one side and a railway line on the other. Luton Town want to move to the so-called Kohlerdome, a new stadium named after their in-no-way-egotistical chairman David Kohler. On a practical level, this is because there is no room to expand Kenilworth Road, although they'd cram more people in if: a) they hadn't extended the roof over the Kenilworth Stand so far that the now-removed back five rows of seats provided no view at all; b) they hadn't devoted a side of the ground solely to executive boxes so pathetic that there are nets above them to catch the ball when it's hoofed out and c) Luton Town were a half-decent team.

There are gangs of Asian kids loitering just out of the throng, waiting for the game to start so they can break into some cars, hence the warning in the programme (they're not crass enough to say 'Asian kids', but it's hardly likely to be the work of the northern whites who come down the motorway and burgle that middle class estate next to the M1 at the Luton turn off) and guards in the official car park watching over the Millwall team coach, a swish, turquoise Blueways number.

Outside the Oak Road end though, there is a sight to warm my soul as Millwall fans, usually male, usually white, stream in. These are big men, unused to being messed around outside their workplace, where they're ritually humiliated by a dork in Armani glasses and an ill-fitting suit. In their midst are a swarm of Asian boys. Outside the turnstiles in the narrow, terraced street, they're playing a game of football and the Millwall fans are watching them indulgently or dodging out of the way to give them space. Hope can be found anywhere.

Around the corner, entering the wooden, charismatically named Main Stand, is like picking your way through a bombsite. There are warnings everywhere about ducking heads because of low-slung beams. The catering is virtually non-existent. A bewildered but friendly youth is standing at a trolley unable to serve burgers as 'me mate's gone to get them'. More curious than strictly necessary, I wait for Me Mate in an unavoidably crouched position. After seven and a half minutes (pedantic I know, but accurate), Me Mate arrives. The burgers are wrapped in tinfoil and taste like the sort of thing your own mate's glamorous mother – she knows your thirteen-year-old heart races whenever she's near, but she can't cook – might attempt for the school fundraiser. Nobody would eat them, but they'd be really glad she was serving. They are revolting.

I've paid £16.25 to see a Division Two game between a home team who have scored four goals in six games and visitors who are one place above the relegation zone. I cannot get to my seat because there is no room between the end of my row and an exit and I am not a fat man. I have to stalk my seat diagonally from several rows above. When I clamber in there, like Yuri Gagarin boarding his rocket in 1961, my legs, as dumpy as they were at Bradford, simply do not fit. And there's a pillar right in front of me. The weird angle I have to perch at hurts my back and I am sat next to a loathsome specimen. He's bespectacled (not a crime in itself outside the Khmer Rouge's Kampuchea, but I understand what they were getting at), fiftysomething and wearing a pullover around his neck, which is, I believe, definitely a criminal offence.

'You can move if you want to,' he sneers. I would rather have another burger, even when he puts his fat thigh against mine to give himself over half of what little legroom I have. Without over-reacting, may he rot in the burning fires of hell for eternity.

This match actually is hell, but first there is much, and yet little, to entertain us. Luton have a mascot, whom they are too ashamed to name, but he has a plastic – not furry – head and is therefore uncute. There is no MC on the pitch, but at half-time, a Vauxhall factory lackey brings along the World Cup, yes the real one, and waves it about. It is the nearest any footballer playing tonight will ever be to it. It would have been more appropriate if a bloke from the World Cup factory had brought the Vauxhall Conference trophy. The teams enter to 'This Town Ain't Big Enough For Both Of Us' by Sparks. Hurrah! Only joking, it's 'Fanfare For The Common Man' again.

Princess Diana died three days ago, so there is a silence. It's perfectly observed, except for the mobile telephone that trills through the entire minute. She'd have wanted it that way.

The Millwall fans, shirts sponsored by Live TV featuring the unusual slogan *The Weather In Norwegian*, have most of the Oak Road end. Between them and some empty seats is the Main Stand. Cleverly, the Luton mob (mob is a generous term, there are boys younger than twelve in there and two overly made-up women who will spend all the game making wanker signs. Naturally, this thrills me enormously) are in the correct corner for proximity to away fans, without the danger of anything actually happening, especially as policemen are overtly filming everything. The Luton fans have thought up a funny chant: 'West Ham, you all support West Ham', which doesn't go down well at all.

As the teams are read out in silence similar to the one honouring Diana, the problem is as clear as it was at Scarborough. If a team is to do well, it needs heroes. At Kenilworth Road there are none, certainly not Tony Thorpe who scored thirty-one goals last season. Everyone knows he's playing for a move to the Premiership, rather than for Luton Town. Tonight he shows that, if nothing else, his whinging is certainly Premiership quality. Heroes emerge from warm feelings between crowd and players, in fact they cement it. Without heroes football would exist, without the possibility of heroes it would not. Eastern Bloc states, with their Heroes Of The Soviet Union, Etc., understood this perfectly. Without Stakhanovites, everyone else was a worker ant. Without Ian Wright, everyone else is Lee Dixon. Not once do Luton fans chant any of their players' names. The bond has been broken.

Those Luton fans do, however, have a special Bedfordshire welcome for Millwall's new signing Kim Grant, who's just completed his move from Luton. If Luton made a Vauxhall for him, it wouldn't have any brakes.

The first half is a shocker, enlivened only by poor Grant missing an open goal. The quiet is deafening, apart from general groans and mutterings when yet another pass goes astray. There is no sense of potential violence any more. Even fully trained rioters, with degrees in Chaos & Disorder, couldn't raise a fist over this slack-jawed, loose-limbed horror show, so easy to nod out to that it could cure heroin addiction.

People in the executive boxes are watching television rather than the game and I cannot bring myself to feel animosity towards them. Behind me, however, the inedible feast of entertainment hasn't affected three well-spoken boys. They have the fleshy lips, slitty eyes, wedge haircuts and red cheeks of future paedophiles, wife beaters, stockbrokers and alcoholics. Unchecked by adult presence, they graduate from a bashful 'who the flip are you?' in the first ten minutes to kiddy roars of 'caaaaaant' whenever Millwall's porky goalkeeper Tim Carter takes a goal kick in the last ten. It's the future of Britain and it has no compassion.

The second half picks up, although had it wound down the players would be standing still. In front of the away end, Millwall's Brian Law, who once stole a bus while drunk, heads home from a corner more expertly than he handled that bus. Millwall fans go wild. They clamber over the hoardings, worryingly the least secure of which promotes SGC Scaffolding, and a few are hauled outside by a police force who've been itching for something to do all night. From that point a selection of songs from SE16 ring out into the dark, including their all-time favourite 'Let 'Em All Come'.

Skinny young centre forward Danny Hockton looks offside when he scores a second, but as the referee is too fat to catch up and the linesman was asleep, it's 0-2. There are more arrests, on charges of over-joyful celebrations. Some Luton fans, led by a red-faced slob with blonde hair, start chanting at their softer colleagues 'Scared of the Millwall, you're fucking scared of the Millwall'. Poor, very poor.

Thorpe hits a post late on, later still his colleague Gavin McGowan hits the bar and Kim Grant is substituted, but nobody notices and the filming police-men move down the aisles of the Main Stand to further their art. Luton fans, unusually animated, scream at them to move. The police ignore them. Very much like the game, there is only one winner. The three smugateers behind me depart after eighty-five minutes to 'avoid the fighting' and the now-despondent swine next to me has finally removed his leg.

Poetically, Luton Town depart to jeers, Millwall to cheers. In the surrounding streets, Millwall fans are held back by barriers for a while, but the Lutonites have disappeared, cowed and frustrated, back to one of the town's 43,000 households. I shuffle back to the station with 'the Millwall' and half the local police force.

The fans are happy, talkative and eagle-eyed when spotting Luton fans ('Three there, Carl, top of the stairs to your left') skulking in corners hoping to pick off strays. At the station, it's a twenty-minute wait for the next train to London. The platform is jammed with Millwall fans, some of whom embrace the opportunity to take cocaine in the toilets.

Mercifully the train, when it arrives, has enough carriages. Everyone extinguishes their cigarettes and settles down to read the programme. There's no chanting, no drunken destroying of furniture, no loud voices, just a bunch of well-behaved people. At St Albans, a pair of attractive women (visible pantyline, must be Americans) board. There's no wolf-whistles, but pair of beer-gutted Millwall gentlemen smilingly shuffle seats so the women can sit together. Looks like the sons of Harry The Dog are Harry The Pups. What a funny old world it is. Sometimes.

12 **Swansea City**

v. Torquay United
DIVISION THREE

5 September

2-0

**'You can only remind players of the basics and generally we have
done those pretty well so far this season.'**

Jan Molby

Its famous son Dylan Thomas called it an 'ugly, lovely town' but today
Swansea is subdued. Tomorrow they bury Diana, Princess Of Wales, as they
called her round here. In the grounds of St Mary's church ('Wednesday is
refreshment day!'), where they can't have a memorial service tomorrow
because the couple due to get married won't spoil their day, there are hundreds
of flowers, many rotting. A crowd gathers round, silently reading the notes
contained in each offering. Troublingly, every message (mostly Queen Of
Hearts mush, but there's an illogical 'God broke our hearts to prove to us
that he only takes the best'; something scary about shining as bright as a
star above Bethlehem; the occasional dedication to dead Dodi, but none to
the poor driver or the bodyguard who the papers are saying has literally lost
his tongue) is signed Christian name only, as if Diana were a friend. Odd, odd,
odd.

Inside the church, at one end there's a guided tour, at the other an opportunity to sign condolence books with a waiting time of three minutes. I can't
quite bring myself – Diana ought to have been buried under her true love, a
shopping mall – but if I were a Swansea resident I certainly wouldn't be as
idiotic and parochial as Bryan Jenkins of Winch Wen, who contacted the *South
Wales Evening Post* to moan about Elton John calling Diana an English Rose in
'Candle In The Wind'. Buffoon.

Faint praise maybe, but Swansea, named after its Viking – i.e. not Welsh, Mr
Bryan Jenkins – founder Sweyne ('ey' being an inlet in Norse, or Danish, or
whatever language Vikings used) is all right. It's still full of bitter little Welsh
people, the signs are in Welsh – a ridiculous affectation – and the shell-suit
isn't seen as a fashion *faux pas*. Even so, the city centre, bombed heavily by the

Nazis, is smart, the ruins of the castle set off the redeveloped parts as if some thought went into how it would finally look.

There's no trace of the copper mines which Swansea built its wealth on, limited sightings of the coal that sustained that prosperity, but the oil refineries on the east of the city, which prevent mass destitution, are still hard at it. For now.

For the twee in this least twee of cities, there is a Latin American crafts shop, and its customers are no doubt eagerly anticipating the forthcoming Craft & Stitching Festival. Less twee is a bunch of ferocious, unclean *Big Issue* sellers, all with mistreated dogs on strings blocking the entrance to John Menzies. Men and dogs smell that I'm an alien as I scurry past.

The highlight, though, is the marina, close to the beach, miles away from the anti-English locals who live on the hill. It lies across the road from a space-age county hall, with sea-views and all. Good heavens, how could this impoverished area of the British Isles afford such a thing? What wonders there are in the most unpromising of places.

The marina is an unassuming wonder. A one-bedroom flat costs £48,000, a three-bedroom penthouse 'just' £160,000. There's no pubs, so the scum haven't floated in and the absence of burglar bars on the ground-floor flats suggests said scum haven't come of their own accord either. There are Greek letters written in Roman script carved into the sea wall and a dedication 'The more against the less abstract' to William Herschel who discovered Uranus. It might be nice to live here. Seriously.

I wander down to the beach. I feel the presence of God and about bloody time, too. Why hasn't anyone come here on holiday since the Victorians? The sand is hard and firm, ideal for both lounging and beach sports. There's only the barest hint of sand blackness, courtesy of the oil refineries. It's a warm Friday evening, circa 5 p.m., and it's deserted. I walk to the sea at low tide half a mile out. I urinate onto the sand as one mark of respect (dogs know what I mean) and wash my hands in the brown warm sea as a second. There is nobody within a radius of 1000 yards, I can see the ground from the sea and I could cry with happiness.

Back to concrete with a spring in my step towards Swansea West, where Michael Heseltine joined the local Conservatives in October 1951 and launched his political career, to see The Queen's televised tribute to the Princess Of Wales at 6 p.m. I settle on the Rat & Carrot on the coast road. I'm the only customer, except for a gaggle of bar staff (or friends of same, I'm not a census compiler) who leave their positions to watch it on ITV at full volume. With a backdrop of mourners outside Buckingham Palace, The Queen could be a foreign correspondent. She chunters on for a minute or so and then stops. All this is listened to in what I assume is respectful silence.

When it finishes, the women let rip: 'Bitch!', 'She's a fucking hypocrite',

'Any make-up artist could have made it look like she'd been grieving', 'She hated Diana anyway, absolutely hated her'. They change channel to some Grand Prix practice in disgust. I'm dumbfounded, I'd like to marry them all.

Like all the grounds I'm beginning to love, Swansea City's Vetch (a plant suited to temperate climes) Field is in the middle of a terraced housing estate, so swamped by poor people's homes that it's difficult to find the turnstiles, as the Torquay United players discover when they turn up in a Dawlish team coach (not perfect luxury but it does have a television and tables), carrying packed meals in Tupperware containers. How sick must Torquay captain Alex Watson, former Liverpool player and brother of Everton's Dave, feel when he's handed his Tupperware container?

Swansea fans patrol the only road entrance to the away section, wandering between two pubs opposite each other. I'm tempted, but instead settle for a walk around the prison walls which Vetch Field virtually backs onto. The anti-paedophile (modern day witches: is it me or did paedophilia only start in the 90s?) graffiti outside suggests who the locals think are inside, but the walls are so low that only the terminally infirm couldn't hurdle out. There's not much to see, although any idiot knows that's usually the way with the outside of prisons. I go to the ground, feeling slightly foolish.

Inside the North Bank – identical only in name to Arsenal's – it's so dilapidated that it's impossible to imagine Swansea City had glory days, when they were Liverpool Old Boys and finished sixth in the old First Division, as recently as 1982. A lick of paint might help, as would a catering firm who didn't put their lukewarm, squashed burgers in greaseproof paper and forget to cut their onions. Even so, it's not without a certain character, but the club's new owners certainly have much to occupy their minds.

There is one executive box, 'for today's sponsors'. It is empty, save for some tracksuited youth players. Nobody has bothered to paint over the forty-foot HEMELING LAGER stencil on the south stand, unless Hemeling is still in existence in South Wales. The back third of the North Bank has been cordoned off, presumably for so-called safety reasons, more likely to cram everyone together and generate some atmosphere. As if in metaphor, the clock on the opposite side has stopped and, probably not out of forgetfulness, the perimeter fences haven't been taken down. These fences will not be needed tonight, as Torquay United have brought with them thirty-one supporters, who have a whole end to themselves, sufficient room for each Devonian to have brought their car onto the terraces.

There is a perfectly observed minute's silence for Diana once more, although there are those trying to stifle giggles. Like at Luton, the first half is an absolute shocker. When Swansea hit the post, it's so out of context that there's no 'ooh', just the startled 'uh' of four thousand people being jolted awake. There are more black men on the pitch than in the crowd, which means on the one hand 'kill the nigger' directed at Torquay's excellent Rodney Jack and on the other, much chanting of Kwame Ampadu's name, a player some way from being Swansea's finest.

Kids at the front amuse themselves by mimicking all the linesman's movements and running with him up and down the line. The ball-boys (Cygnets to the Swans) turn their backs on the action to chat with mates. The crowd are primarily bunches of older men, young boy- and girlfriends romantically smoking their first cigarettes together, or, much more prevalent, one boy and three girls, which means whichever girl he's trying to pull wants her less attractive mates there for emotional and possibly physical support. I wish I'd known this information when I was younger.

Individually, the older ones shout abuse. They are clearly not chapel-goers. 'That's a load of fucking paedophile bollocks' (that word again, hmmmm), 'you're a cunt, referee' and 'oh fuck fuck fuck' are their favourites. Even the fans who are standing on the outside walls getting a free view look as if this game has ripped them off. Some people leave at half-time, but for everyone the break is a blessed relief. And relief is the issue. There are many gentlemen's toilets at Vetch Field, none of them too disgusting, yet there are at least 100 men pissing against a wall when said toilets are usable and not crushed to breaking point. What a peculiar place Swansea is.

The second half is much better. The Swansea fans start to sing. Loads of anti-English stuff, although disappointingly there's not a balanced chant about how the Welsh economy might suffer if the British government didn't subsidise them, and there's a stirring 'Swansea Till I Die', which may well be adapted from Bryan Adams's '18 Till I Die'. They start to bait Rodney Jack in a non-racist manner and he responds with conducting gestures, as does long-haired (there are no long-haired people in Swansea) Gary Clayton when they taunt him about being a 'gyppo'.

Swansea City swap the long ball approach for a more measured strategy which brings Ampadu and Paul O'Gorman into the game and lets the full-backs bring the ball upfield. Torquay look dangerous going forward and pass the ball along the ground with gusto, but they can't get it to Rodney Jack enough.

O'Gorman scores a splendid individual goal for Swansea. He rounds the keeper like a pro (he may well be a pro, but ...) after beating half the defence, even Jon Gittens who's never been averse to a foul or two if necessary (or just for the hell of it). Torquay push forward and bring on giant, black, ex-Swansea forward Andy McFarlane to generous applause, but Swansea, who somehow conceded seven at Hull last week, stand firm. At the death, Torquay goalkeeper Ken Veysey spills a cross of sorts and Tony Bird who claims in tonight's programme that 'I didn't follow football as a youngster' taps in for Swansea's second. City keep their 100 per cent home league record and everyone goes home semi-delirious, bar the Torquay thirty-one.

The crowd clears quickly and in the centre you'd never know there had been a league football match this evening in Swansea. There is a queue outside Yates's Wine Lodge, as there is outside every Yates's Wine Lodge in Britain, but the men and women from the valleys haven't invaded tonight so there's a feeling of space and of Diana's funeral made tangible by notices in shop windows solemnly declaring that they won't be opening tomorrow as a mark of respect. It's 10.30 now and outside St Mary's, people are still quietly reading the tributes as churchyard serenity blends with the throbbing of Frankie Goes To Hollywood's 'Relax' some pub or club is playing. The silence and the throb are easy bedfellows indeed.

13 Chesterfield

v. Burnley
DIVISION TWO
7 September
1-0

'More big guns are arriving today ...'

John Duncan

There's the old joke about lower level footballers not being household names in their own households. Until last year, Chesterfield players past and present would understand this. Phil Tingay? Colin Tartt? Les Hunter? Exactly. In the mid-70s, these men would have found it difficult to get free entry into The Shoulder Of Mutton, then Chesterfield's nightspot of distinction.

Last year, all that changed, although not for Tingay and co. Had referee David Ellery noticed that Jonathan Howard's effort had crossed the line, Chesterfield may well have appeared in the FA Cup Final. For a few giddy days, the whole country seemed to be Chesterfield fans. Chris Beaumont, Tom Curtis and Andy Morris performed creditably in interviews and it was conveniently forgotten that John Duncan's side were a dour, flair-free ensemble. Results: lasting glory for the market town, a period that boosted the place's self-esteem infinitely; days the folk of Chesterfield will for ever pass down to future generations.

That they blew promotion and that their best players Sean Dyche and Kevin Davies secured relatively lucrative moves to Bristol City and Southampton respectively, seems a small price to pay. Even with hindsight. Perhaps too, like in East London, folk memory excludes the organised gangs of corpse robbers during The Blitz, it will conveniently forget the savage violence meted out to Nottingham Forest fans who dared venture to Saltergate in the glory year.

This season, Chesterfield will not have their moment of cup triumph. Getting promoted is their more mundane task. For the new season, Duncan has bought with typical caution: Ian Breckin from Rotherham, Steve Wilkinson from Preston and Roger Willis from Peterborough. Only Breckin plays today, so it's essentially the same troop as last year, less the departed quality.

It's a sunny Sunday afternoon, the day after Diana's funeral. Understandably, there is little happening in Chesterfield apart from the football. It's a not-quite place. It's not-quite Sheffield, it's not-quite Derby, so civic pride is more civic resentment, a feeling obviously shared by the council who haven't been arsed to clean streets which would disgrace Freetown, Sierra Leone, where it's culturally acceptable for grown men to shit in the gutter.

Picking my way through the detritus, I head for Chesterfield's one place of interest: the crooked spire, or St Mary & All Saints as surely nobody calls it. The floral tributes to Diana have gravitated here, but the church itself is much more interesting. It's not crooked, it doesn't merely tilt, it's utterly misshapen. How did they build it in the 14th century? Was it a joke? Were they trying to create an attraction to this unattractive place? Was it revenge? Did they know it was turning out like that? How (like Coventry City) does it stay up? Whatever, it's fantastic and without it, Chesterfield would wither and die. It's always been a struggle since Roman times when Chesterfield (Open Field By The Camp) was a heavily guarded transportation centre for lead ore on its way from the Peak District to the east coast, and perhaps more so many centuries later when The Black Death killed a quarter of the populace.

Things would finally take a turn for the better in the 17th century when William & Mary's followers plotted the overthrow of James II here, and 150 years on when celebrated native George Stephenson helped the town's railway network chug along.

Chesterfield is in a shell-like state today (Woolworth's has opened for business, a big mistake), but even in its pomp, there would still be nothing to commend it. In the capable hands of smarter people, Ye Olde Crooked Spire pub might have been groomed into a place where outsiders feel welcome. Oh no. There's a sign saying it's opened specially for the Sunday lunchtime session because of the match, but it's empty, apart from a gaggle of fans in Nearly Got To Wembley shirts and three policemen who amble in and ask the landlord 'Where are all t'lads then?' in Python-esque not-quite-Yorkshire accents. It's a disco pub and to celebrate they are playing VH-1 at skullbusting volume. Even Barnsley tries harder and it's no real surprise that, once more, the town hall is the finest building and has a fabulous view southwards over lush hills which were once slag heaps.

Chesterfield, was more a coke (distilled coal, whatever that is) than coal town before the strike. Now, on the outskirts of town are the former pit villages, more barren than the town centre today, populated almost exclusively by those without hope. If ever a town needed Tony Benn as its MP, it is Chesterfield, but in the last election the swing was against him to the Liberal Democrats. This is not a happy town and it doesn't have a cinema. King John didn't intend this when he granted Chesterfield a market permit in 1204.

Today at least, all roads lead to Saltergate, a home Chesterfield are trying to vacate, although it's patently large enough for them. The club shop is a hut, the only stand is a no-smoking fire hazard and Burnley are the visitors. It's not going well for their new player-manager Chris Waddle, despite the magnificent black team coach, with its M3 UFC registration suggesting who else leases it. Burnley haven't scored in five league games to date and eight team changes in today's programme suggest Waddle hasn't got a clue what to do. Still, their away support is holding up for now and there are claret-clad Lancastrians everywhere, ensuring an atmosphere of sorts.

Saltergate is a tip. I'm in the stand, which is wasp-infested and where nobody can be bothered (there's a theme here ...) to print reserved seat tickets. This means that, with so few seats available ('Redevelopment with all that FA Cup money? No way,' somebody might have said recently) friends are parted and well into the game people are still trying to find somewhere, anywhere, to sit. My view is, of course, obscured; a pie shaves another layer of skin off the roof of my mouth and the toilets are a festering open sewer, in which it may well be culturally acceptable to shit.

It's a better state of affairs on the pitch. Last season has resulted in an unusually strong bond between town and team. Ball-boys wander onto the pitch to get players' autographs during the warm up, there's a perfect silence for Diana, and when the teams have tossed for ends, the Chesterfield kop moves *en masse* to the far end of the terraced side, next to the Burnley fans. There's little untoward, for at half-time, except for seven token hard men, they move back. I'm at the end of a row next to a chic couple in their fifties. He can't buy a programme inside and I tell her that's because buying programmes inside grounds is a major cause of hooliganism. She shudders. He mumbles 'It's a joke'. We spend the rest of the afternoon in silence.

Chesterfield score in the first minute when Tony Lormor backheels past flappy Marlon Beresford after a post-corner scramble. Waddle hangs his head, puts his hands on his hips and ambles back to the centre circle. Just like he's always done. Then, obviously lost, he switches wings twice in the first thirty minutes. His underlings look only to him for guidance and inspiration, but Chesterfield full backs Jamie Hewitt and Mark Jules have his measure. It's no fun to see a great man fallen this way, but he's not the first, nor will he be the last. 'You're shit and you know you are,' chant the Chesterfield fans. Waddle doesn't look their way. He's not that sort.

Negative Chesterfield think they've done enough and Burnley are already looking wan. The Chesterfield bench resembles a nightclub for kangaroos. John Duncan is up in the stand, down on the bench, alongside the pitch. He shouts, he points, he shrugs, as does his beer-bellied assistant Kevin Randall. Players respond to him, shouting, gesturing and tactically tinkering themselves. There's still little flair – and once too often Chesterfield will sit back on a lead and get hammered – but there's spirit and organisation. The crowd understand this, even when the game evolves into a question of whether or not Burnley score.

In contrast, the Burnley bench does nothing. Coaches Chris Woods, Gordon Cowans and Glenn Roeder are clearly not leaders of men. They stand in mutual silence, arms folded, offering neither encouragement, nor criticism, nor ideas. It's hard to dispel the impression they don't give a cuss. After one visit too many from Burnley's cartoon physiotherapist Andy Jones – little-legged, red-faced, his tiny steps as he sprints to treat players give the whole ground a chuckle – forces Waddle to substitute himself, there's still nothing emanating from bench to players. They don't even appeal for the throw-ins nearby. The Chesterfield bench, however, choreographed more expertly than the Peter Gordeno Dancers, raise arms as one and shout 'our ball'.

It's a physical game, Burnley carve out a few chances and Andy Cooke will hit the post, but they have problems. Chesterfield fans have seen 1-0 victories like this before, so they're not angry so long as their team is unbeaten and in second place. But there's little joy either and some groans when Duncan moves the bustling Lormor into midfield as part of what now appears to be a 6-3-1 formation.

Nobody speaks up when a scar-faced skinhead steward manhandles a long-haired bloke out of the ground with more force than is strictly necessary and I'm constantly being kicked in the back by a white trash child, who's bored senseless, as are the two men with it who resent the brat's presence ensuring they didn't have a gallon of ale before the game. I would turn round and scowl but they look too tough. Small towns: small minds. I don't say this out loud.

Burnley are still lamely pressing at the end, patient but fundamentally hopeless. John Duncan clenches his fists with delight and shakes his players by the hand when referee David Laws finally gets through the ten minutes of injury time he's somehow noted. Chris Waddle shrugs his shoulders, folds his arms and lumbers towards the tunnel alone.

14 Fulham

v. Plymouth Argyle
DIVISION TWO
9 September
2-0

'Champions and winners are made from an inward desire to succeed, something deep inside themselves, a dream, a vision, a skill and a will to win.'

Micky Adams

Never ones to take an opportunity, somebody at Fulham tipped off one of the tabloids that tonight's game with Plymouth Argyle would attract '18 to 20,000'. Notwithstanding the fact that Craven Cottage has a capacity of under 15,000, potential casual attendees who wanted a real slice of the Diana action were deterred

When Mohamed Al Fayed, Britain's fourteenth-richest man, paid £10 million to become Fulham chairman in May 1997, Micky Adams's team had won promotion to Division Two. By the time his playboy son was killed in that Paris tunnel, he'd barely spared a dime for Fulham and so they were jogging along in mid-table. Maybe for Al Fayed they were an afterthought and his 'I've always supported Fulham' claim evoked merely deep suspicion. After all, Ken Bates claimed he tried Chelsea first.

Tonight will be special. I go with my friend John, whom I haven't seen for over a year. He's thirty-five and has never seen a football match in his life. At school, to escape peer pressure, he'd blurt out that he supported Stoke City because he once saw Gordon Banks on *This Is Your Life*. He grew up in a village in Somerset that football has never reached. When John lived in Tottenham, he'd see crowds going to matches and only wonder why so many of them were wearing white shirts. He is unexcited at the prospect of our evening together and assumes at some point he'll have to sing.

We walk down the Fulham Palace Road, where the family of former Arsenal, QPR, Charlton, Orient and, um, Eire stopper Terry Mancini once had a pub and a boxing accessories shop, although I don't bother explaining this to John. It's quiet, until we cut towards the Thames, past John Brown Publishing, home of *Viz*, past the rows of unthreatening middle class houses, underneath some truly fantastic flats ('apartments' is a more truthful term) with river views, to the Crabtree Tavern where there are hoards of Fulham fans, white males with braying, clear voices without a trace of an accent. There are Plymouth fans too, and we sit outside and watch the river, covered at this spot with bottles, smegma and hair. I don't know whether to be patronising and start explaining the rules, or be uncaring and let the football virgin flounder. We settle on discussing his sister-in-law's sex life.

Craven Cottage, yes there's a cottage on the south-east corner, is London's most friendly ground. John is surprised they play records before the game and sell food. He assumed people would have eaten first (my bank today cancelled both my cheque cards so I can't afford to eat, cheers The Royal Bank Of Scotland, Southampton branch) and wouldn't need to listen to music when they can do that at home. Fulham fans are allergic to physical and emotional violence. Women come here too, older than the usual Beckham groupies and they know they won't be threatened. Some women come on their own, a step forward of sorts. If I didn't know better I'd think romance could begin at Craven Cottage, and then it would be home for vegetarian hot-pot and moderately vigorous sex. Anyway, onto Princess Diana.

The black-bordered programme – proceeds to some charity Diana had embedded her claws in – has surrendered all its advertising to messages to and from the Al Fayeds. A Special Message To Argyle Supporters is especially rum: 'When those Pilgrims bordered the *Mayflower* and left Plymouth for New England, they were seeking a new start to life. Princess Diana and Dodi had just embarked on a new voyage too ... We journey together. Our aims are the same, but above everything else we retain our dignity in battle.' What can they make of that down Union Street?

There's also a page-long letter from one Bill Muddyman, Al Fayed's Vice Chairman. It's as if the pair have never spoken and is a lesson in obsequiousness to all courtiers. It makes no sense: 'For you my friend the tragedy was magnified by your losing a trusted colleague and one being seriously injured, a trusted and very loyal young friend, as well as the Mother of our future King ... I would also like to say how much we admire in you the things that money cannot buy ...' and so it goes on, unintelligibly. It ends 'warmest personal regards', as do the letters my accountant sends me, with his invoices.

There are eight books of condolence around the ground and a real sense of occasion, when Mohamed Al Fayed himself (unseen in public since the crash) trolls down the centre of the Riverside Stand and into the centre circle accompanied by his mouthpiece Michael Cole, plus the Mayoress Of Fulham and a couple of hangers on. The applause is staggering, everyone stands and claps in time for what seems like eternity. It could be one of Nicolae Ceausescu's politburo meetings where each person was terrified to be the first to stop clapping.

Michael Cole attempts to speak, but his microphone cuts out. He tries again. Success. His speech is Dodi-centric. Apparently Dodi wasn't a wastrel who'd never done a day's work in his life, but a fabulous individual. The Al Fayeds, Cole reveals, have had over 60,000 messages of support. Most oddly, today there was a special family memorial service for Dodi in Oxted. The letter-writing Muddyman had 'begged' Al Fayed to come to the match instead. Most oddly of all, he had. Al Fayed makes a brief but dignified 'thank you, God bless you all' speech and walks off with his gang as the players slope on.

I've never seen the value of bagpipes before, but when the lone piper plays 'Flowers Of The Forest', 'a lament selected by our Chairman, Mr Al Fayed', it's more moving than I'd imagined. It's so dignified I feel a lump in my throat for the first and only time over that crash. He must have loved his boy.

'This is history,' says John, next to me in the Hammersmith End. 'Do they do this at every match?' The Fulham players have brought flowers to match the ones pinned to the main gates. The minute's silence is impeccably observed, by the massed Plymouth fans too, not always high up in the decency leagues. It's disturbed only by the clicking cameras of the paparazzi. None of this can possibly have helped the Plymouth players one bit.

The match itself takes a while to settle down and John gets restless. Fulham are big, awkward and mostly white, while Plymouth are small, quick and mostly black. By half-time the visitors should have been two up, but the sweetest moment comes when Fulham's Neil Smith takes a throw-in. He leans right back into the crowd and a fan ruffles his lovely, long, black curly hair, something I'd quite like to have done actually. Smith smiles, he likes it here too. This is a truly nice club, no wonder the writers of *Minder* made Dennis Waterman's character a Fulham fan.

Nice or not, the players depart at half-time to a tirade of boos, not strictly fair for what is a fascinating encounter. John, shocked by the state of the toilets, is sort of enjoying his first match. 'Like Will Smith in *Men In Black*, I don't have anything to compare the situation with,' he explains. Not exactly the ringing endorsement I was hoping for.

Plymouth tire in the second half. Perhaps the ride in their unmarked double-decker coach (a first! I'm beside myself with pleasure. John looks at me like I'm retarded) was too restful, or perhaps the battering they've taken from the uncompromising (i.e. dirty) Danny Cullip has worn them down.

Fulham winger Paul Brooker is a class apart. He roasts the Plymouth defence upon a spit of his own gifts. Brooker crosses, Plymouth goalkeeper Jon Sheffield is barged off the ball and Fulham are 1-0 up. The diehards sing 'Fulham are going up' and everyone else laughs. That, once more, is the sort of club this is.

Plymouth change tactics too late. One of their substitutes, Patrick Wilson, is booked within thirty seconds of coming on and a second, battering ram Simon

Collins, looks like he's spent the rest of the game in a pub. Plymouth press forward, so much so that they give Fulham's Paul Moody the opportunity to seal it with a glorious individual goal. They'll travel back in their double-decker wondering just how they didn't manage to break down Fulham's panicky, cumbersome defence. They have, however, played their part in an evening of rare dignity.

The game finishes and in what may well be a footballing first, Fulham's players walk towards the directors' box (the other side of the ground from the tunnel) and ostentatiously clap Al Fayed and cronies. Then, from the centre circle, they clap the rest of the crowd, even the Plymouth fans. In a sense the game was irrelevant, it was about something else. As we walk back to Hammersmith, past the 'Lewington Out!' graffiti from earlier, more fractious times, John says we must do this again and declares it better than he thought it would be. We don't talk about the game at all when we get to the pub and, because I have no money, he has to pay for all our beer. A fair result in every sense.

15 **Colchester United**

v. Scarborough
DIVISION THREE

12 September

1-0

'It is players who make things work with quality service and then determination and will to get on the end of things.'

Steve Wignall

Colchester's tag-line is The Oldest Recorded Town In Britain. That word 'recorded' gives it away. The obvious truth is that they don't know, they haven't got the balls to call it The Oldest Town In Britain and there's nothing else of sufficient interest to entice weary travellers off the A12.

Colchester is a dormitory town. People sleep here and work in London. Its growth period, post-World War 2, was fuelled by Cockney overspill. This means many things, none of them good. There's nothing in the way of community spirit (although my random car-sticker survey does indicate Essex pride), so there's no need for the council to establish any facilities. Thus, Colchester residents treat their town like a hotel and, worst of all, even second generation residents are not 'from' Colchester, they're 'from' Bow or some other God-awful London slum their grandparents and their grandparents' next door neighbours escaped from, chased by rickets and whooping cough. If that wasn't enough, Colchester is a huge garrison town, as it was in Roman times. Only a fool would be fooled by the air of middle class prosperity.

Layer Road, Colchester United's dingy ground, lies opposite a soulless estate of military homes, where it's all alcoholism and wife-swapping. It nestles in a middle class estate (cheap too, as homes next to a firing range and trigger-happy squaddies from Sunderland ought to be) where two cars are the norm and net curtains the exception.

I peer into those homes like a stalker, the members of posh lads Blur may well have grown up in one of them. Everyone is indoors, even though it's Friday evening, as there's nothing to do in town and for West Ham fans Colchester United hold no sway. Each family set up is identical. Father lies on the sofa clutching the remote control. On the mantelpiece above the stone-clad fireplace, there's a sports trophy of sorts and a gold-plated clock. A child will be running around seeking attention, getting under the feet of its mother who is preparing food for the family as she would if they were still in Bow and bringing it to the father on a tray, maybe with a flash of pudenda, more likely with a resigned shrug. Life in Colchester hasn't changed since the Romans or the 1950s. Except for the television remote control, humankind's great advance of this century.

Suburban Layer Road has the air of a non-league ground. These grounds, refuges of the sad, tend to be in middle class areas: there's less tradition in the Vauxhall Conference, Colchester United's natural home. The clubs of the old Northern and Southern Premier Leagues, the Bishop Aucklands, Lancaster Citys and Worksop Towns have either disappeared or slid into Unibond obscurity. Colchester should be, like Wycombe and Stevenage, the new breed, but it's not working out. They still smell non-league, forty-seven years after joining the biggish boys (apart from that season in the Conference which nobody discusses).

Colchester United beat Leeds United in the FA Cup once. That's it. That's all they've ever done, despite being the only league team in Essex. Southend don't count, as they're Cockney On Sea.

Pin-thin floodlights and all, Layer Road, where ambition is anathema, simply isn't very nice. It's the footballing equivalent of the errant family cousins who don't wash. They're always there, but you don't bother with them. Good news at last – inside there are many food outlets. Bad news as ever – the hot dogs are not even Frankfurters and judging by the state of her nails, my female server hasn't got through the perhaps desirable ritual of washing her hands before handling something which very soon will be stretching my lower bowel. Ugh. And there is a car on the pitch, the prize in some silly raffle, which must delight the groundsman.

Opponents this evening are Scarborough, who are cheered on by twenty-eight noisy supporters. The programme tells us that the son of the Scarborough Chairman is in the squad, as is one Eamon Bazeyla, 'son of Libyan diplomat Mustaffa, who is an Associate Director for the club'. If this isn't an amusing ruse, can there be a more interesting footballer than little Eamon and a person more worthy of detailed investigation than big Mustaffa?

It's an old crowd, world-weary and chiefly up for ninety minutes of moaning. Happily, it transpires that not every game of football will be having a silence for Diana, although the crowd attempt to make up for it anyway. All things considered, why should Colchester United contemplate doing their place up?

Scarborough are here to grind out a 0-0. Colchester are here to try and score, although with big, no-goals-this-season lummox Mark Sale up front, it's a distant prospect. By half-time, Scarborough have created a few chances,

Colchester have not, despite the attempts of skinhead centre half Peter Cawley to soften up Scarborough's tiny teeny goalkeeper Kevin Martin.

I have yards of space in which to bob about in non-committed fashion and I move around at half-time. As the second half begins in the same dismal fashion the first ended, I chance upon The Nutter. He is mid-fifties, clad in shirt and tie and has a crash barrier to himself. He never shuts up. His crusade of irrationality against the poor referee is similar to self-publicist David Mellor's. 'What do you want, ref? Flesh and blood?' he hollers. Bored with that, he turns on the Scarborough fans 'Shut up down there, you noisy lot' and on Scarborough's uncompromising John Kay, 'You short-haired poofter'. Mellor would be a proud man indeed. And Labour finished third in the General Election here.

Scarborough waste time at every opportunity. About to take a free kick, Kay uses a substitution to move the ball a good ten yards forward before the referee notices, but then substitute Neil Campbell creates mini-havoc in Colchester's rickety defence. 'This is bollocks, Wignall,' shouts a frustrated Colchester fan, shattering the silence. Others mutter about there being no competition for places and how half-hearted midfielder Steve Forbes is. As if in retort, goalkeeper Martin flaps at a cross and Colchester's substitute Tony Lock rifles a controlled volley into the top corner.

Scarborough don't waste any of the three remaining minutes, but they won't be scoring. If only that goal had happened three minutes from the beginning ... Time for the Colchester fans – now well pleased – to re-enter suburbia.

I leave Terrace 4, probably christened by George Orwell, and sprint to Colchester town centre, many miles away. It is the wild west 1997 and no place for anyone over thirty, which is handy as there's nobody over thirty about. There are people smoking dope in the streets, gangs of short-skirted, skittish, loud women I dare not gawp at because of the gangs of blokes leering at them from across the road. Under-sixteens are drinking pints in the veranda of McDonald's, in front of ordinary and military police patrolling, the latter leching loudly at anyone female for added vileness. This town centre doesn't give the appearance of being wholly under control, but it is, ironically, somewhat livelier than the Scarborough tonight's away team are returning to on their coach, a Dodsworths without a television but with a self-service coffee machine as found on National Express coaches.

The pubs are dark and their discos are running an informal loudness competition (everyone's a winner to me). I venture uncertainly into the Firkin Brewery. Normally, my solo trips into pubs are times of flaunty, yes-I-have-no-friends-but-I've-got-a-good-book insouciance. I can't wait to leave the Firkin Brewery. It's not bad in itself. There's no disco, just a loud tape, but electricity and its consequential lighting have not reached this dreadful hole. There are no gangs here, but everyone knows I'm an alien and I'm the only person on my own. I slump over a table, one eye open like a cat pretending to sleep. I don't bother to read my programme. Perhaps I've died, mistaken purgatory for the shambles of a match this evening and am in hell. I have an aching longing to go home.

16 **Wolverhampton Wanderers**

v. Charlton Athletic
DIVISION ONE

13 September

3-1

'If you take out eighty per cent of any team, then that team will not be top of the league.'

Mark McGhee

Mysterious things have been happening down Molineux way this week. Chairman Jonathan Heyward has stepped aside for his 74-year-old dad, Jack, whose seriousness at getting his beloved Wolves into the Premiership means he's forsaken the delights of The Bahamas for one of the least appealing places in England. Essentially an extended ring road north of Birmingham, Wolverhampton is a mass of subways, connecting dozens of inhospitable hostelries.

Way back, Wolverhampton Wanderers were at the forefront of the hooligan revolution. A Keyser Sozer-style legend has it that black Wolves fans would hang around those subways which then dominated the short walk between ground and railway station. With a self-deprecating cry of 'Wolves wogs' they'd attack anyone trying to figure out which subway was which and thus not a Wolverhampton resident. They didn't bother going to the games apparently.

News of hooliganism's demise was slow to reach Wolverhampton. There's neither argy nor bargy today because Charlton Athletic, who have no fans, are the visitors. On other days, the sprint to the station is still no fun whatsoever as home fans stand on the far side of the dual carriageway outside Molineux and launch running sorties on away fans.

Within the ring road, Wolverhampton town is a mess: pedestrianised in all the wrong places, enslaved to the car in other, but equally illogical, places, bereft of culture and rammed with boggle-eyed, dangerous men addicted to chips, obviously a legacy of the cholera epidemic of 1832, which killed 193 and led directly to the building of two workhouses which were meant to put the able-bodied poor to communal use, in this case developing Wolverhampton's previously non-existent sanitation.

Fried potatoes, it was said, provided some measure of immunity. It didn't work and by a second cholera outbreak in 1848, life expectancy in Wolverhampton was just nineteen, and the newly built South Staffordshire General Hospital elected not to admit patients with infectious diseases. As late as 1851, the public baths only changed its water once a month. Little has probably changed in the darker areas of Heath Town and Whitmore Reans today, or at St Luke's primary school where brave nursery teacher Lisa Potts fended off machete-wielding Horrett Campbell in July 1996. She resigned when the publicity died down and still gets flashbacks. The tabloids are right: an angel walks among us.

Dragged from village status by wool and then rail (there were vicious Railway Wars in the 1850s here) and canals, Wolverhampton's glory days can't have been that glorious. There are narrow side streets of nothingness off the main drag and little, apart from fighting and student-torturing, ever happens. There's a tradition of locksmithery. Today the Chubb factory is making ninety-five people redundant, a fifth of the workforce.

Thanks to Sir Jack's cash, Molineux, gold and black to garish excess, has been redeveloped into the Wembley Of Outer Birmingham with the requisite car parks and sports centre. A decade ago, Wolverhampton Wanderers were nearly relegated from the old fourth division, with gates so minuscule that for some games they'd only open one side of the ground. Finishing third in the new first division is progress, even to the most bitter, twisted Wolf and there are too many of those.

The team were great in the 50s when Jack Heyward was a young man standing on the terraces, assuming it would never end. His guidance has ensured some sense of history. There's the Billy Wright Stand and an epic sculpture of him in full flight outside the main entrance; the Stan Cullis Stand; as well as ones dedicated to ex-chairmen Jack Harris and John Ireland. Inside the John Ireland Stand, there are bars dedicated to ex-players Johnny Hancocks and Ron Flowers. It's a touch of style and reverence. It almost obscures the taste-free burgers.

I've never been at such an angle to a pitch. I'm in the top corner of the south end of the John Ireland, at a diagonal to the nearest corner. Thus, for me, the game fans out from that corner flag. Perspective? Of sorts.

I'm sandwiched between two big blokes, whose aggression and commitment – like those of everyone around me – know no bounds. It is, though, the aggression and commitment of the nervous, in this, the eighty-fifth consecutive League game with a crowd of over 20,000. If Wolves don't make it to the Premiership this season with their ageing, injury-prone squad, Sir Jack, ageing and injury-prone himself, might just find The Bahamas calling one more time. At least, however, Mark McGhee would be unemployed.

McGhee, all twisty mouth and bad posture, is football's most generally despised figure this side of Ian Wright. As a manager, he walked out on Reading and Leicester City. He blames injuries for his failings at Wolves and was ungracious beyond the call of duty towards Barnsley, who won promotion because they were a better team than his. Sir Jack's return is not a vote of confidence in McGhee. Even the ball-boys, who're introduced as a group to the crowd, look edgy.

No matter, all this – and the one win in the last six matches – is forgotten. Inspired by mercurial Robbie Keane, Wolves go 3-0 up before half-time. Steve Bull, a genuine Wolverhampton Wanderers hero in the tradition of Derek Dougan, John Richards and Andy Gray, notches a brace. He's past his best now, but the way he clips the ball past Andy Petterson for his first confirms he can still finish. It's a strange game though. Charlton Athletic keep having chances. Steve Jones, Paul Mortimer and Mark Kinsella have one-on-ones with goalkeeper Mike Stowell. All fail and a worried McGhee attempts to intimidate the linesman into giving offside decisions that aren't there. Every time Wolves amble upfield they score. Perhaps, like me, Charlton have no perspective and perhaps that's deliberate: there's yards of greenery after the touchline and no halfway line flags to mark it out for unwary visitors. 'Gamesmanship' it's called. The tannoy plays James Brown's 'I Got You (I Feel Good)' whenever Wolves score. Tacky, tacky, tacky.

At half-time, they raffle the match ball. This seems to put the home side off its stroke and the second half is traffic of a one-way bent. Presumably at McGhee's instigation, Wolves cease attacking and let Charlton come at them. They batter the creaking Wolves defence – so depleted they've had to draft in Simon Coleman on loan from Bolton – but somehow they only manage to score one.

By paranoid osmosis, the crowd's uneasiness seeps through to the Wolves players, through the uncomfortable silence, punctuated only by the occasional anti-West Bromwich Albion chant. They daren't criticise too loudly in case Charlton score more. They can't clap them home because there's no air of celebration and a defence including Coleman and Mark Atkins is unlikely to perform heroic rearguard actions. All they can do is sit, wait for the game to finish and boo Charlton substitute Carl Leaburn over some ancient, misty grudge. When the game does finish, the applause stems from pure relief and the result is everything. Three more points towards the Premiership. Ha.

The sound of heads being scratched on Charlton's journey home aboard their plain-clothes Tellings coach (a sub-standard affair) must have been deafening. Wolves fans tend to hang around town afterwards. Everything about their town is stultifying. Because there's nothing, grim pubs rule the town. Nice people stay away, or go to Birmingham, comparative cultural Mecca.

Brushing past the bouncers, I chance The Old Still on King Street, built in 1751, the childhood home of soprano Dame Maggie Tate and a Grade II listed building. The bar staff are pleasantness personified. The customers are barely human. Aside from the occasional football fan, the main group of drinkers are half a dozen black men sprawled over several sofas, with a matching number of white women draped over them. They've obviously been here for some time and whenever anything that isn't R. Kelly's 'I Believe I Can Fly' is on the juke box, their leader figure yells 'Put some fucking decent music on', at which the women giggle like simpletons. It's not yet six o'clock and the town is filling up already. I have outstayed my welcome.

I pay my respects to the statue of Prince Albert mounted – at the behest of Queen Victoria – upon a mighty horse, erected in 1866, unveiled by Victoria herself, and now near one of the downmarket shopping centres. There's a traffic cone on Albert's head. Looks like it's going to be another long Saturday night in Wolverhampton.

17 Crewe Alexandra

v. Port Vale
DIVISION ONE
16 September

0-1

'We are not under siege and our defenders have not fallen apart.'

Dario Gradi

Crewe Alexandra (after Princess Alexandra, whoever she was), have never had it so good. They haven't played at this level of football since 1896 when things were very different. Dario Gradi has managed them since 1983 and they have the respect of their peers for playing sweet football and providing Premiership teams with decent players (Rob Jones, Wayne Collins, Danny Murphy, Ashley Ward, David Platt, Robbie Savage and the rest) at very reasonable prices. They're finding it sticky going at their new level.

There are, in fact, two Crewes. One is the area around the Gresty Road ground and the railway works. It has more fish'n'chip shops per square mile than Scarborough and more pubs than Soho. There's a sense of happening, as there was over a century ago when Crewe was a company town, owned by the Grand Junction Railway Company who cleverly noted that the hamlet was midway between Manchester, Liverpool and Birmingham. When the railway works were opened in 1843, they became Crewe's trusty heartbeat, hegemony unbroken until the Rolls-Royce factory emerged in 1938. Today there's still an impressive vibrancy born of fried food and lukewarm Cheshire beer in a concentrated geographical space. I feel at home.

But, walk north of the ground, parallel with the railway tracks, past the signs to 'Crewe University' (how fabulous that must look on a CV), past a tidy terraced estate, past the Wickes DIY superstore which bravely employs unemployable-looking sixteeen-year-olds and the second Crewe hoves dismally into view. It's a long walk for a small place.

I'm in the town centre. I know this because there is nobody around, although it's not quite six o'clock this Tuesday evening and I've walked past some shops, what looks like a municipal square although it's populated by glue-sniffing types too young to get into pubs, and I'm standing in front of a town hall. The glue sniffers might as well have been pensioners, as what few pubs there are, are closed.

It's a ghost town and as I walk back bemused to Gresty Road. Along the tiny High Street, a fire exit to the Apollo Cinema & Bingo & Social Club flaps open in the keening wind, banging against a wall. The two pubs next to it are both closed. At this point, John Wayne ambling down the road astride his, ahem, 'hoss' wouldn't have shocked me. Unencumbered by customers, the staff of Razzies pizza/kebab (mmm, lovely) emporium rush to the window and stare at me, mouths agape, eyes rolling. I quicken my step and start shivering, although it's pleasantly mild.

Moved from Diana Sunday (although the programme isn't updated), tonight's match is a derby against Port Vale, who haven't changed managers themselves since 1984, and who share with Crewe a deep-seated loathing-cum-envy of Stoke City. I was rather hoping there'd be some violence to warm my chilly insides. It augurs well outside, where police are blocking off roads, stopping pedestrians and only letting ticket holders go through. Port Vale's middling Barretts (apostrophes must wash off coaches in the rain) charabanc stands at the far end of what passes for a car park and the chip shops are doing brisk business to supporters in the red of Crewe or the white of Port Vale. Safe as houses. Most houses, anyway.

Crewe Alexandra are a nice club. The woman who does the credit card stuff in the ticket office might not have taken any address details or ensured that I brought my card when I collected my ticket, but she was good heart personified. Similarly, the ticket-checking police are civil, with copious use of unironic 'mate' appellation. Crewe Alexandra and Port Vale aren't the only teams playing at Gresty Road tonight. What is probably Crewe's training ground next door is being used by community teams. All very cockle-warming.

Inside, there's no covered area to eat hot dogs (yum) and drink tea (there is a black residue of vileness floating in it which isn't a tea bag; I'm scared again, very scared), but there is Bruce Rioch doing a spot of card-marking for Queens Park Rangers who're here on Saturday. Port Vale have sold out their meagre allocation of a ground that only holds 6000, so they've infiltrated the stand I'm in (none of that stand-naming nonsense here). Again it's all very friendly. Even the stewards aren't the usual powerseekers inflated by shiny lemon-coloured jackets. They help crippled old ladies up the stairs and they warn a more selfish punter that the aerial poking from his radio (why, incidentally, do people bring radios into football grounds? Stay at home if you're that bothered about other games) will pluck someone's eye out if he's not careful. If only it was Radioman's own eye.

More disappointing is the fact my seat isn't a seat. It's a red bench on the seventh of eight rows, with a white '31' sloppily painted upon it. It is ridged, which indicates that someone is meant to sit next to me. Not for the first time in my life I regret not having the rear end of a male model. Oh and there's a pillar obscuring one goal, but that is par for the course now.

It's all fun and games on the pitch. As it's a derby, both sides have mascots, Grrresty for Crewe, a rust-coloured lion, and for Port Vale a beast of unknown genealogy who carries a beach ball, lies not unseductively in the penalty area and has mock fights with the less eager-to-please Grrresty. The on-the-pitch MC tries to interview a kiddy team mascot who's having none of it, little horror. He has more success presenting a tankard to a Port Vale fan called Stan who organised a coach to take Port Vale fans to Wembley when Crewe played Brentford there in May. People can have good hearts.

What purports to be Crewe's crew takes its place in the stand opposite me, the Popside. They stand up, which I wouldn't mind doing myself right now, and attempt to taunt the Port Vale fans. Stewards and police wade in and everyone sits down. Crewe play like a polite team, too. They play neat floorbound passing and then find big bad Dele Adebola, who simply isn't up to it. Port Vale, no strangers to a skilful game themselves, are far too wily to get caught out and bide their time, bedding in new signing, right winger Gareth Ainsworth, and breaking dangerously.

The crowd, weaned to be knowledgeable by Gradi's approach, know it will be hard this season. They're not especially passionate, but they encourage youngsters like Colin Little (Port Vale fans sing 'Does your mother know you're here' to this urchin when not copying Manchester City fans' version of 'The Wonder Of You' in the manner Stoke fans approach 'Delilah') who inherently do the right thing. Rightly, Crewe folk are proud of having a player christened Seth. Rightly too, they're less sympathetic to the referee who keeps getting in the way of the ball and who keeps missing the obvious. I hadn't been planning to talk to the youth next to me as he looks retarded, but when I laugh out loud at the referee breaking up a Crewe attack for the second time in five minutes, he shakes his head. 'The worst one yet, the worst one.'

'It'll even out,' I comfort, sincerely.

'Yeah, but if we win, I want it to be right.'

Jesus Christ, it's, well, Jesus Christ himself.

I bite another chunk out of my giant sized Lion bar in supplication. At half-time it's time to squeeze into the toilet, an experience so tactile some may come before they urinate. Through the fence, I watch the football at the training ground next door, as does almost everyone else, before clenching my buttocks for the second half.

Lee Mills scores a scrappy goal to give Port Vale a narrow victory. All their fans in the stand so uncomfortably occupied by me and Jesus go fairly wild. It's all over, despite the niggle that creeps in when Crewe's Steve Anthrobus starts fighting anyone on Port Vale's right-hand side. Bruce Rioch leaves, shaking hands with the nice stewards on his way out, as in a more conspicuous but less friendly manner do a succession of scouts, some of whom have been using Dictaphones. Crewe never look like scoring and the away team, inspired by the excellent Stewart Talbot, know they've done enough.

Outside, all the barricades have disappeared. The Port Vale coaches pick up their supporters on Gresty Road itself. Instantly, Crewe slips back into normality.

18 **Walsall**

v. York City
DIVISION TWO
20 September

2-0

'While the current first team position in the League table does not make pretty reading, it is comforting to note that in the Pontins League we are topping the Third Division table.'

Jan Sorensen

'BING BONG,' screams a hoarding all-too-visible to passengers on trains pulling into Walsall station, although not on Sundays when there's no service, so it's impossible to escape. 'All change for Saddlers' shopping centre.' Ooh goody, another ghastly town with another shopping centre, for which I cannot glean the interest to describe. For the record, it sells mini cans of Coca-Cola, two gulps in volume, at a maxi price of thirty English pence. These cans are guzzled by an endless stream of women, all unattached as a result of physical unattractiveness and a diet consisting solely of lard.

However, of a Saturday lunch-time, Walsall (Hall Of The Welsh, obviously enough) does have a certain charm. Its open market is bustling like billy-o and it's chiefly devoted to quality foodstuffs rather than tat. In the Arboretum Park tonight, Walsall Illuminations will be unveiled, proof of a council making locals feel good about themselves, despite a hefty admission charge.

Unusually for the cultural desert that is the West Midlands, Walsall is having a go. Hardy tourists, welcomed to the library in seventeen different languages ('Witajcie' indeed), can find their way to the lock museum, the possibly unrelated but equally fetishistic leather museum and tributes aplenty to Walsall's own Jerome Klapka Jerome, who handily died seventy-five years ago this year.

Looking to the future, they're building a second town centre by the canal. One day they might even think about cleaning up the Caldmore area, where, while revising for her GCSEs, sixteen-year-old Lucy Burchell used to work as a prostitute before being murdered after being forced to swallow a dose of eighty per cent pure heroin. She passed eight GCSEs and the results were out the day the police found her body. Walsall smells of freshly baked bread and meat pies.

The Town Hall was opened on 29 May 1902, seven years after electricity came here, by no less a personage than His Royal Highness Prince Christian Of Schleswig-Holstein. What can he have been doing in Walsall in 1902? Was he invited? Did he come over specially, for a fat fee, like Sarah Ferguson today when she opens shopping malls in areas close to Schleswig-Holstein? Was he a serial town hall opener? Did he make a speech in English? Did he sign autographs? There may be people alive who can remember.

Public houses are not Walsall's strong point. The Old Court is actually an old court. It plays Bob Marley tapes and only admits over-21s (wouldn't life be better if pubs only admitted over-31s? But, as ever, we must press on). The toilets are through several unmarked doors, up stairs a sober Chris Bonington would need crampons to negotiate, let alone a pissed Brummy at 11.10 on a Friday evening and, camply, they leave a gavel at tables as food-order markers. It smells of new paint and new money.

Alternatively, The Green Dragon, up the hill past the market (ten-pack of Walkers crisps for £1.45) is more boozer than pub. Its decor remains unchanged from the last century, AVFC graffiti and all. In one of the most delectable moments of my life they actually offer a choice of pork scratchings. 'Hard or soft?' asks the barmaid, who has been around the world many times without leaving Walsall, with what I shall claim for the rest of my life was a suggestive smirk.

In The Green Dragon – next to me, underneath the closed-circuit television camera – is the world's most tattooed man. This means spiders' webs on his upper neck and Adam's apple, setting off the unidentifiable symbols on his ears and nose. Presumably he is not a bank clerk, but how does he live his life day to day? He made a decision, possibly in his teens, to drop out until he dies. What's the last thing he thinks about as he slips into unconsciousness each night? If he's proud of himself, I admire him more than any other man whose appearance has scared me too much to strike up a conversation with. If he sobs himself to sleep, I'd shoot him myself as a humanitarian gesture. Time, sadly, to find the football ground.

Opened in 1990, everything is wrong about Walsall FC's Bescot Stadium. Like most newer grounds, it's miles out of town, so far that it's only reachable by train or, much more practically, car. It is literally in the middle of an industrial estate. Once out of Bescot Stadium Station, streams of undignified unlucky punters have to scramble under one of the West Midlands' many motorways (perhaps it's the Walsall stretch of the M6 which the IRA tried to blow up in April), across a caravan site inhabited by tough-looking scrap metal dealers and enter the ground's car park through a gap in a hedge. The so-called stadium resembles nothing more than a minor branch of Iceland and its 9000 capacity shows just how far Walsall's board think their team might one day go.

Although Walsall won at Nottingham Forest in the laughable Coca-Cola Cup this week, they are still third from the bottom of Division Two and judging by the disconsolate mooching huddles, the visit of York City has not aroused the interest of the Walsall public. The visitors have brought two coachloads of supporters and they nestle snugly in the car park next to the Dodsworths team coach, which looks identical to the one Scarborough use, coffee machine and all.

Inside, there is something called a balti pie for sale. Atypically unpompously, I forego the opportunity to explain to the young sales assistant that balti is a fraud, no more a product of Asia than haggis. Anyway, I'm distracted by the notice on the vending hut. Not the one that says they don't take £20 notes, but the one which offers the Bescot Stadium for hire to celebrate your '21th' birthday. I settle on a hot dog which is dwarfed by a roll made for a proper-sized sausage.

This is a horrendous, breeze-blocked place with less soul than a Michael Bolton Christmas record and all the atmosphere of a vacuum cleaner. I totter to my seat, trying to negotiate the hot dog, past the players' tunnel. In said tunnel, secretly watching the players warm up is a tubby man with a haircut which would be spurned by a former member of Mud as too 70s. He is wearing a white shirt and black tie and he's puffing furiously on a cigarette. He is Walsall's Danish manager Jan Sorensen, once of Ajax under Johan Cruyff, but more recently a publican, bowling equipment sales force controller and time-share salesman in order to pay off the first Mrs Sorensen, before he married a West Midlander. I wink at him. He ignores me.

The game is played in front of banks of empty seating in silence broken only by cheers responding to score flashes from Premiership games, despite the main body of Walsall's support being housed in a covered standing end. It's poor fare, enlivened only by the voice of Walsall goalkeeper/captain Jimmy Walker echoing around the ground and a scrap between York's Paul Stephenson and Rodney Rowe, which ends in the former shouting 'twat' at his colleague and the York bench having to calm him down. Before being substituted, Stephenson spends the remainder of the game in winged isolation, muttering to himself.

At half-time there is an announcement that this coming Thursday, for £25, you can 'be entertained' by former head of Manchester CID, Eric Jones, who 'helped' catch the Yorkshire Ripper. He is supported by comedian Johnny Wager. Sometimes, the world doesn't turn how you think it will.

Eventually, the best player on the field, little Roger Boli of Walsall, is left unmarked long enough to score with a firm header. He celebrates like a skipping faun and clearly, he cares. Probably only about himself but that's hardly the point and when he'd had a goal disallowed in the first half, he'd kicked some hoardings over in frustration. That's the attitude that gets people (and maybe clubs) out of Division Two.

York full back Andy McMillan is unluckily sent off when Walsall's Jeff (it's actually Jean-Francois, but seemingly the people of Walsall are too thick to cope) Peron makes a meal of a challenge. The Walsall fans rouse themselves at last, with a chant of 'Cheerio, cheerio, cheerio' as McMillan trudges off, led and conducted unexpectedly by the ball-boy in front of me next to the York dugout. This finally entices York manager Alan Little down from the stand.

McMillan, born in Bloemfontein, showers and comes and sits behind me. He smells of being the best footballer in school and the sort of after-shave the women of York keel over for. McMillan cares too: every time York go forward, without any management nearby to impress, he stands up, egging them on, slumping back into his seat when the service to ex-Walsall forward Neil Tolson doesn't give the poor boy a solitary chance. In the last minute, as York's now-three-man defences tires, John Hodge skips through on his own, avoids goalkeeper Mark Samways's hopeless flop at his feet and it's 2-0. Walsall are out of the bottom three and, in loud celebration, a Concorde flies overhead. Under 3000 people are present.

Saturday night in Walsall. Oh yes.

Oh no. There's nobody there and they can't all be off to the Illuminations. The pubs are struggling, even the tacky-looking Bushwhacker where there is a till at the door, balloons on every table and a DJ booth. It's empty apart from an alcoholic and three bouncers. The Red Lion was opened in 1896 and looks like it hasn't seen a customer since then.

'Is it always this quiet,' I ask the barwoman, all cheery.

'It can get busy you know,' she snarls, noticeably less cheery.

I don't believe her.

19 **Leicester City**

v. Blackburn Rovers
PREMIER LEAGUE

24 September

1-1

'Magnificent though our start may have been, my first inclination later tonight will be to look at the points gap between ourselves and 17th, rather than casting an envious glance upwards.'

Martin O'Neill

Leicester has no appeal, bar that of grim Middle England. Anyway, my only aunt died yesterday and the funeral is tomorrow. The tiny Aizlewood clan will meet for the first time in over a decade. Me and my aunt weren't that close, but I liked her from afar. I'm just worried about my father, her brother. He adored her and I should be with him tonight, but I feel like one of, I think, Jimmy Tarbuck's scriptwriters in the 70s, who had to bury his mother in the morning and in the afternoon write for laughs. Leicester is the right city for me tonight.

It's a foul place with a whiff of malevolence running down its streets. Because they have an eccentric but loveable manager in Martin O'Neill and because they are professional underdogs, Leicester City's psychopathically violent fans are conveniently forgotten, as is their negative football (who can forget Pontus Kaamark on Juninho) and mean-spirited lack of class. That lack of class goes to the top too; right now City fans are livid that last week's trips to Atletico Madrid were organised by travel agents owned by the club's Vice Chairman. Said travel agents had never organised football tours before and the journeys involved hours without food or toilet facilities. Cheaper, unofficial tours had nice hotels, trips round Madrid and nights spent in great bars in one of the world's most wonderful cities. How symbolic of the new age it would be if the club ended up being sued by its own supporters

Like the team, this city of Joe Orton, The Elephant Man and Engelbert Humperdinck, the geographical centre of England, has an overly-high opinion of itself. There is history here, has been since the dinosaurs (the largest in Europe is in the local museum) and then the Romans who built a trading post on the Fosse Way and the Danes who later took over. Reminders of Simon De Montfort, alleged founder of the English parliamentary system and castle chic are on every corner, but Mark Morrison hardly warrants a mention. A merchant and knitwear past has been clumsily grafted onto a modern city with 80s aspirations to money and shopping, via designer boutiques and overdoses of twee. It's sterile, although in the Midlands, Leicester does pass for high sophistication.

Still, it's not all bad news and hasn't been since Richard III spent his last night here. Although J.B. Priestley once declared that it 'seems to have no atmosphere of its own', Leicester might not be such a bad place for a night out and right now the shopgirls are pouring out. There is a theory, one to which I wholeheartedly subscribe, that shopgirls are the highest form of human life. The way they hang their hair, apply their make-up, smoke their cigarettes and forget everything the moment they leave their place of work in search for a good time, none of them on the way to see Leicester City and Blackburn Rovers.

Sick of chic, I loiter just outside the centre. Instantly, the façade of resurgence slips. Shops are shut down, the pristine, bustling, centre streets give way to 'adult shops', the Willie Thorne Snooker Centre, alleyways and empty streets. There's no boom, no designer shops selling lava lamps here, this is the real Leicester.

I am accosted by a man and asked if I would like to buy some drugs. Yes I would! Very much! Right now, I'd like to snort, inject and smoke his wares. This also means, assuming reasonable client observation on the part of drug dealers, I look like I might be someone who takes drugs. Whoo! Fie, middle-age! Alas, he looks too much like a policeman's eye-view of an honest-to-goodness dealer – black, dishevelled, unshaven. I have to send him on his way. I lumber back to the centre, to look for Gary Lineker's dad's market stall, cocooned in my own cowardice. Hello, after all, middle-age ...

Gary Lineker is still Mr Leicester. There's already a Lineker Court named after him and one day he may well be mayor if they can co-opt him onto the council. The open-air market, like much of this city, is under permanent observation ('Smile, You're On 24-Hour Surveillance'), civil liberties organisations' least favourite method of policing, but a logical precaution in this place. By the time I arrive, the market is closing down, the street cleaners (as befits Britain's first Environment City) are hard at it already and I can't find the Lineker stall. Perhaps it only existed for *Football Focus*'s cameras.

Town Hall Square has a no skateboarding notice, so naturally it's full of pimply, anti-social skateboarders, getting in everyone's way, relics of a time when it was almost fashionable. I head for The Last Plantagenet, a refurbished pub full of City fans, oldish and in a state of low tension for Blackburn's arrival.

Symbolically, from the ground, Filbert Street, it's possible to see both the prison and the infirmary. Outside, the club sells chips from kiosks embedded in stand walls to eliminate pull-along wagons, but they've forgotten to develop one side of the ground. Or the residents across the narrow road have complained. Or they think the boom will go bust.

Inside, the pies are, in a moment of uncharacteristic civilisation, served with forks, the in-house DJ seems only to play Oasis or Supertramp and he pronounces the name of Atletico Madrid, who've returned 800 tickets for the return leg, in Manuel-style cod-Spanish. Wanker. I have an unobscurred view of the pitch, but the South Stand is too close to the pitch and too steep for me to see the goal I'm above. The place is full (apart from the away section, Blackburn don't have away support as such, the team's unspecial Options coach from Rochdale being one of possibly three to trundle over the Pennines this evening) and the atmosphere is buzzing.

I'm sat between two women, not something that would have happened ten years ago. One is sulky and pouty and with what I presume and hope is her father. The other is with a boyfriend, but it's very early stages and they haven't got to the point of touching. She will urge City on, he will look uncomfortable and read her programme.

Three mascots circle the perimeter. That's two too many, I'm afraid, and so they are ignored. Once more, we have a dance troupe. Apart from the opening where several hunky men throw one of the women ten feet in the air and catch her, they're dull, dull, dull. They're ignored too, as surely as the invitation (for £24.95) to a Californian Wine Tasting & Appreciation Dinner will be. Never let them claim football is the sport of the working man, when there are executive boxes on two sides to sell these events to. Many more California Wine Tasting & Appreciation Dinners and it won't be the national sport either. Stop this nonsense: send the Leicester players into the Asian areas of the city.

Leicester's Asians came to the Belgrave Road when Idi Amin expelled them from Uganda in 1972, despite the attempts of the local newspaper which announced that 'Leicester is full up'. Let the players see how these people live, find out why they don't go into the city centre – for some of the same reasons well known footballers generally don't – and teach them football skills. They might even enjoy it.

Before the teams come out, the Leicester fans have a right old laugh at a little ball-boy who, as he runs onto the pitch, falls over with a corner flag in his hand. They should meet Scarborough fans some time, they'd get on.

The game is fantastic. Leicester harry and hustle, lacking all-over quality, but Muzzy Izzet, Matt Elliott and Neil Lennon make up for their team-mates, while Blackburn are neat, patient and excellent, especially Colin Hendry who out-muscles Emile Heskey all evening, turning the City player into a great big cry-baby bear. Leicester fans, more than the players, seem to feel this game is a) won and b) irrelevant, what with Madrid to come.

When Chris Sutton (the sort of player heartily disliked by all, except for those two years when he plays for their team) deservedly puts Blackburn in front with a well-taken effort after Izzet uncharacteristically gifts him the ball, the ground seems shocked. If the seemingly uncommitted Martin Dahlin had scored seconds later when he was clean through on Kasey Keller, the game would have been effectively over.

On the touchline, Martin O'Neill seems to be kicking every ball, and disputing every decision with dramatic hand movements when it goes against him. Eventually it dawns on me: he's a fraud. He's as bad as Alex Ferguson. It's a deliberate, conscious attempt to intimidate the referee on a law of averages basis. He'll get away with it because he's a sweet interviewee. In comparison, Blackburn's Roy 'Woy' Hodgson just wears the world's whitest mackintosh.

Just before half-time, with the supporters already becoming unsupportive, Izzet volleys past Tim Flowers and that's the way it stays, despite the introduction of Robbie Savage and his extraordinary haircut, Spencer Prior looking like he'd rather be shopping with Mrs Prior on Granby Street and the referee being anything but a homer. There are clearances off the line, Hendry playing like a god and saggy-bottomed Graham Fenton, Leicester scapegoat, huffing and puffing but short of quality.

By the end, I'm enraptured, but now there's no one sitting around me. This feast cannot last in a club where famine is the norm, especially when O'Neill jumps ship. Outside, the boom-related crush at the junction of the south and west stands is more scary than strictly necessary, with hundreds of people trying to pass through a small corner in opposite directions. The poor people in wheelchairs look small, terrified and very much aware that things weren't so awful when Grimsby Town were the visitors.

They shouldn't worry, those times will return.

20 **Norwich City**

v. Ipswich Town
DIVISION ONE
26 September

2-1

'I know how important this fixture is to our fans. Perhaps you can inspire the team to reach the heights required to take all three points.'

Mike Walker

Opposite Norwich's imposing Thorpe railway station, close to the ghetto where local professional footballers live (like diplomats, players must live close together), is The Compleat Angler, a nondescript city pub. Friday afternoons, it's usually fairly full of workers who, like much of Norwich's workforce, have knocked off for the weekend at four. This Friday things are different. It's cut off from the centre of Norwich by mounted police and a police van stupidly called the Football Intelligence Unit. The police, jittery and traumatised, are attempting to control the 200 or so Ipswich Town fans who've ventured into the territory of their hated rivals Norwich City, have taken the pub over and now stand outside it, drinking and chanting anti-Norwich songs.

In Norwich itself, nobody cares that much. It's a peculiar place, this city of Nurse Edith Cavell, Elizabeth Fry and soon-to-be supermodel Sarah Thomas. As the only metropolis for miles, it has all the facilities the local countryside needs, as it always had, even prior to Tudor times when England was so useless that Norwich was the second city. William The Conqueror's men built the castle, started on the cathedral with real Normandy stone and then metamorphosed into the *nouveau* middle class, benefiting from the trade boost with Europe when Vikings finally stopped invading. Some Jewish scholars reckon anti-Semitism began in Norwich in the 12th century when locals decided that Jews and Satan were conspiring to murder Christian children. Norwich can still round up a posse to run anyone unfortunate enough not to have white skin out of town, although it was Dutch immigrants, 'strangers', who, after 1565, taught the natives of Norwich how to weave – thus halting the worsted industry's decline – and to breed the canaries from which Norwich City take their nickname.

It's a footballing backwater and the dogfight with Ipswich matters little to the outside world. Here though they take it so seriously that even the pig-ignorant local *Evening News*, headlines its front page 'LET'S BURST BLUES' BUBBLE'. So every pub has a Friday afternoon bouncer – a natural occupation for Norwich men in truth – but the gangs of lads looking for trouble, many with mobile telephones, haven't yet acquired the common sense that would lead them to find more trouble than they've bargained for at The Compleat Angler.

An hour before kickoff, police close The Compleat Angler and march the Ipswich fans alongside the River Wensum to City's Carrow Road a few hundred yards away. I sneak in with them, smiling sheepishly at the constable eyeing me as he would a convicted child molester. Slightly drunk, they're high-spirited now, marching, singing about keeping some blue flag or other flying, and congratulating each other for attending the only away game they manage each season. The numbers bring a feeling of power so intense I feel it surge through me as surely as it does through them. They control Norwich for this instant, although it's just one deserted street and they're surrounded by police.

Across the Wensum, at its widest point, is a pub called The Ferry Boat. This is full of Norwich fans standing outside enjoying late summer sun. When they hear the Ipswich fans, they rush to the riverside, unleash their own war cries and throw a few empty pint pots in our direction. Ipswich fans respond with their grammatically incorrect assertion that 'You've never won fuck all' or 'he's only a poor little budgie' in humorous derogation of the home side's nickname. Under the eyes of what is now much of Norfolk's police force (the burglars of Wymondham will have a splendid evening), my new friends move to throw stones at The Ferry Boat.

The police, until now willing to let everyone get all this aggression out of their systems, finally move us on. Norwich fans pound wooden pub tables with unused fists in frustration. Not a punch has been thrown, nor an arrest been made; nobody is hurt and honour is satisfied all round. The Norwich fans hadn't the inclination to walk for twenty seconds up their side of the river to the bridge in front of the ground where the twain could have met. This is RADA fisticuffs. At the ground, I sneak out of the police cordon to watch the fun from the Norwich side of the street.

Surreally, like the climax to a Norman Wisdom film, as the Ipswich fans pass the bridge, a pensioners' ragtime band dressed in Norwich City yellow and green is marching towards them playing a tuneless but loud rendition of 'When The Saints Go Marching In'. A female police officer sprints down the road and clears a path for the not-particularly well-shackled Ipswich fans to march past the band chanting 'Who the fucking hell are you?' to the bemused septuagenarians, while ignoring the solitary, grinning, pony-tailed Norwich fan making masturbatory gestures a foot away.

Inside, I'm in the Barclay Stand. This turns out to be the less demonstrative end of an undemonstrative ground. How quiet it must have been last week when Charlton Athletic won 4-0. Bitter rivalry or not, some Ipswich fans have inveigled their way into this supposed home fans' idyll. They shout foul mouthed abuse for the entire game. Nothing happens to them. On my far right is the rest of the Ipswich contingent, all of whom have taken up their positions thirty minutes before kickoff, as suggested on the tickets. The carnival atmosphere they create could be that of a successful team, not one coming here third from bottom, on the back of a home defeat by Stoke City. They will stand for the whole game. Very few Norwich fans imitate them.

Although the football team didn't arrive here until 1935, Carrow Road is a noble sort of ground close to Jeremiah Colman's mustard mills, with half-decent facilities, full views of the pitch and a relaxed air which means I can't resent the man next to me mumbling nothing sensical all evening or the gentleman with military bearing on my right who tuts at the renegade Ipswich fans without daring to turn their way. Everyone ignores the Norwich cheerleaders who each have to suffer the indignity of wearing one yellow boot and one green one. Delia Smith is a Norwich City director: my pepper-flavoured pie suggests she is not Director For Club Catering.

Inspired perhaps by playing in a kit designed by Bruce Oldfield, Darren Eadie scores early on when he outpaces Jason Cundy. It looks like Mike Walker won't be going back to the skip-hire business he took on with suspicious alacrity when Everton dumped him in 1994 just yet. The Norwich fans go as wild as they ever get, two of them attempt a pitch invasion and all display a shamanistic dance as they croon 'eeeeeedeeeeeee' at their scorer. It turns out their more aggressive supporters have placed themselves in the corner opposite – as opposed to next to – the Ipswich fans. It's the worst view in the ground and the only people they intimidate are the executive box holders, who probably have guards armed with pitchforks anyway, descendants of Robert Kett's 20,000-strong peasant army who so nearly took Norwich for their own in 1549.

Spurred on by their massed ranks, Ipswich look the better side. They're on the verge of clawing themselves back level when gangly forward James Scowcroft collapses in a heap in the penalty area in front of the Barclay Stand. It looks innocuous and the Norwich fans rouse themselves to slow-handclap, but the guy doesn't move a muscle and the physiotherapist shies away from touching him until the doctor runs on. Over six long minutes, it becomes obvious that Scowcroft, still immobile, is in serious trouble. Mercifully the ambulance staff aren't the shoddy shambles of YTS footballers as found at, say, Walsall and they move Scowcroft, now in a neckbrace, expertly onto a stretcher. My blood is chilled and I feel physically sick. I know he's not dead, but he sure looks it. Fundamentally decent, the Norwich fans applaud him off, except for the ones in the wrong corner who sing 'cheerio' at his unconscious torso.

This removes the game's heat and niggle. Footballers might be thick, might never notice poverty around them and might drink more than one gallon of lager some evenings, but when they see a fellow professional in whatever trouble Scowcroft is in, they're shaken. Electronic scoreboards are never shaken, however. Whenever there's been a corner, an advertising slogan beginning 'Ever been in a tight corner?' flashes up. When dumpy Alex Mathie replaces Scowcroft, another slogan, 'There's no substitute for class' appears. Mathie instantly misses the chance of the game. Robert Fleck, petulance personified, gets himself booked, possibly merely for being stupid. Other clubs would not put up with his behaviour. He'll always have a home at Norwich.

This is a Sky game. Only cynical souls could possibly suggest that the first half, extended by the injury, being followed by a half-time so short that the game of rugby in one half (I didn't ask) and the penalty shoot out (prizes to be presented by the mayors of Norwich and Ipswich) in the other, are unfinished when both teams emerge, is a result of Sky's programming schedules. Tsk tsk.

Ipswich carry on where they left off. Every book needs a hero. This book has Jason Cundy. I saw him notch a spectacular comedy own goal at Bradford what seems like aeons ago. Now, Norwich float a corner over, Cundy's central defender partner Tony Mowbray flies to head it out. The ball hits poor Jason and somehow finishes in the corner of the goal. Jason holds his head, the Norwich fans laugh. Maybe it's my fault. He doesn't score own goals every game, only the ones I see him play in. What if I have an accidental hex on him? I cannot deny feeling a frisson of excitement at the prospect. And I will be off to Ipswich itself eventually. What would happen if I met Mrs Cundy? I think she'd quite like me.

As at Bradford, Ipswich pull one back late on, but as at Bradford, they're beaten 2-1, even though Norwich have run out of ideas save playing for time. City fans sing their melody-free anthem 'On The Ball City' and yelp for the whistle. It comes soon enough and, at this rate, Ipswich Town may yet find their way into Division Two.

Outside, there's a steady stream of Norwich fans walking alongside the Wensum. Two of them are of sufficiently excited bent to sing 'We beat the scum 2-1', but only two. The Compleat Angler is still closed and there's too many police – concerned solely with preventing Ipswich fans getting to the city centre – to allow scuffles. There's enough shouting when the Ipswich fans emerge to send the police dogs into bark mode, but nobody is going to start.

In other places, fans would be out in droves singing songs and drinking heavily. Norwich doesn't lend itself to this approach. It's not a city that seems to want its natives to celebrate famous victories, even on such a mild night. Maybe it's folk memory stretching back to the famines of 1666, the bouts of plague, the tradition of vagrancy, the cholera epidemics of the 19th century and the Nazi air raids. Maybe it doesn't feel it can celebrate. The city centre is sparsely populated, the pubs unwelcoming except for The Bell Hotel, where drunk men are dancing on wooden tables outside singing 'stand up if you hate the scum' and 'we beat the scum 2-1' to impress their nubile ladyfolk. It seems to be working.

The pubs close and the city takes on a more eerie, but still soulless veneer. Men piss in the streets and women get into taxis with their chips. In the distance there is a solitary siren. In the greater distance there are The Fens and a special train carrying some Ipswich fans home. Everyone else is asleep.

21 **Leeds United**

v. Manchester United
PREMIER LEAGUE

27 September

1-0

'I can only ask for your patience a bit longer.'

George Graham

Holbeck, suburb of Leeds, is a deprived area of a city, which despite its Harvey Nichols store, its supposed new role as a financial centre and non-existent, but oft-trumpeted renewal, is as deprived as they come. Holbeck is an Asian zone where they string washing out high above cobbled streets like bunting in East Belfast. It has a flourishing tattooist's parlour, betting shops which are not part of a national chain and hoards of fat, white, teenage single mothers, pushing prams bearing the fruits of ill-conceived unions. This, lest we forget, is the city of Peter Sutcliffe; of door grilles, riots and hooded drug dealers in Hyde Park, a mile from the centre; of Chestnut Avenue, the so-called Most Burgled Street In Britain; of Chapeltown where anything really does go; of Swarcliffe where towerblock lift surfers can and do die and of Spice Girl Mel B.

There is a grotty pub called The Britannia on the main road. Outside, mounted police are keeping a triple watch: over the park across from the pub, over their own riot control vehicles near by and over The Britannia's customers. Standing on the policed pavement drinking bottles of designer lager are 150 Manchester United supporters. These are not standard Manchester United fans. None wear a replica shirt, none are accompanied by women or children. All are white, all look like they might be able to handle themselves in a fight and all are completely, utterly, silent. Passing cars seem to slow down out of respect, as if the Mancs were mourners at a wake, soundtracked only by the cackle of police radios or an occasional horseshoe clumping on the pavement.

They have come from Manchester (i.e. not from Basingstoke or Poole or Slough) on the train and walked many miles from Leeds station to Holbeck, half a mile from Elland Road, home of Leeds United.

This is a grudge match, a different league to Norwich City and Ipswich Town. It stands beside West Ham United and Millwall, and the Glasgow derby as British football's nastiest fixture. Why? Stygian depths. Hostilities were in place before Eric Cantona left Leeds for Manchester for a bargain fee in 1992 under still unexplained circumstances. It was happening before Leeds hooligans chanted 'Champions Of Europe' to themselves, instinctively pairing their club off with the biggest in Britain as they were relegated to the old second division in 1982; it was happening before the FA Cup Semi-Final of 1977 at Hillsborough when blood ran down Sheffield Wednesday's East Bank as goals by Steve Coppell and Jimmy Greenhoff sent Manchester to Wembley. Like all tribal wars, its origins don't matter. Generations are raised to hate and this one is undoubtedly the Leeds' fans call. As set-piece hooliganism has declined through the 90s, this fixture has escaped the ravages of time.

Two hours ago, I was in Leeds city centre. Every pub is rammed with monsters. I'm hailed from across the road, by the self-christened Dave Shack, a non-monster Leeds fan whom I know in London. He doesn't seem surprised to see me. I'm shocked, have a swift pint with him and move on.

Mounted police watch over the Scarborough Arms opposite the British Rail Station Of The Year 1995, the pub where Leeds fans used to wait for unwary visitors and chase them around the city before the police got some sort of an act together. Above and opposite, the police are videoing all the fans and a plain-clothes hooligan spotter is assisting with inquiries. He's of Asian extraction (a bad thing in race-relations Stone Age Leeds), unshaven, dressed in a gaudy lilac top popular with the hooligans of 1987, but he has a policeman's haircut, so nobody will suspect. At ground level a police photographer is taking stills of all. Whilst none of his subjects are here to research the nearby statue of the Black Prince statue, just forty-six when he died; drinking beer and looking like Robert Mitchum in the first *Cape Fear* isn't technically against the law. I wave when he photographs me. He doesn't wave back.

Manchester United's only presence is in the centre at the Holiday Inn, where the team are having a pre-match meal. Their coach is the same one Burnley used at Chesterfield, registration M3 UFC and it's guarded by police motor cycle outriders. There are few shoppers around this afternoon and so the population of Leeds seems to be comprised of hard men and a few Goths. A world without women? Without blacks? Without children? Without pensioners? Here we are.

Anyway, after my hike to Holbeck, I walk gingerly past those Manchester gentlemen in The Britannia. I pass several more police vans and turn into a wide, dead end road dominated by The Wagon & Horses, halfway up. My passage is blocked solid by Leeds' élite hooligan wing, waiting. This is not kids' stuff like Norwich last night. These men are dangerous and, while dangerous men can be found outside most football grounds, here there are literally hundreds of them and they're not playing about. It's a gathering of the nuttiest kid from every school in the land, the one who hit teachers, ten years on. Individually, I wouldn't look them in the eye, collectively they are an awesome display of what man can be like. Drink isn't a factor. The tiny pub is too full to cater to these people, so they're talking quietly, spitting absent-mindedly onto the dual carriageway below and waiting, waiting, waiting, as their numbers swell, newcomers arriving by car knowing exactly when and where to come. They've always excelled at communications here, since the city jumped in at the deep end of the late 19th century canal explosion, when Leeds's canal network linked the Ouse and Humber rivers.

Elland Road is over that spittle-covered dual carriageway, a few hundred yards further on. There are two bridges. One – to my left – is away from Elland Road and is a road. The other, closer to Elland Road, is pedestrian only. On that bridge, a black policeman is co-ordinating his colleagues on his radio, beneath him is a battalion of riot police in full gear, shields and all, waiting, waiting, waiting. The law officers are no more playing at this than the fans. The police plan, it seems, is, a) to usher the Mancs through the back streets, under the drying washing; b) then to cut the pedestrian bridge off from Leeds supporters and c) march the visitors to the ground, a brisk five minutes' walk away.

Whilst presumably not especially brilliant at school individually, the Leeds mob has a collective intelligence capable of governing empires, albeit perhaps with an over-enthusiastic approach to law-enforcement. Leeds spies have been working well and as the Manchester fans approach the pedestrian bridge, the men of Leeds swarm towards them, accompanied by pre-hoarded beer bottles and glasses. As the Lancastrians attempt to cross the bridge, they are showered with glass, as, logically, are both the dual carriageway beneath and the riot police. The police shoo the Leeds fans off. Those Leeds fans run back to the road bridge in Ben Johnson time to ensure the battle will be fully engaged across the road.

Once over the bridge, the police, aided by a deafening helicopter to provide a bigger picture, march the Manchester fans towards the ground which lies at the end of the road, past a car park and then over a crossroads.

The Leeds mob catches up with them and I'm in the middle. I never thought my life would come to shouting 'We are Leeds. We are Leeds. We are Leeds' and trying to look ferocious. It has, I am, and the thrill and rush are almost sexual. One day I will be inducted into the Upper Chamber as Lord Aizlewood Of The Flies.

Safe? I'm surrounded by hundreds of men, all tougher than me, all assuming I'm with them. I have never felt so safe and warm. Arrest? I don't fear arrest, sheer weight of numbers will stop that. I look into the eyes of the Mancunians. They're smiling, trying to look smug, making sly wanker gestures and mouthing 'come on' at us, but I've seen that smile before. It's the one Michael Portillo used when he lost his parliamentary seat to Stephen

Twigg. They are terrified and they're outnumbered, by ten, twenty to one as Leeds originals are swollen manifold, the closer the ground looms.

Now things really take off. Police and Manchester fans halt at the car park. To get into Elland Road, they have to pass a second Leeds mob, twice the size of the one I'm part of. There are trees, Leeds fans are climbing and shaking them. There is a pub, The Peacock, which nobody has thought to close and there is that chant again. 'We are Leeds. We are Leeds. We are Leeds.' There are no innocents here. Fathers are putting sons on their shoulders for a better view.

In the middle of the road, hanging on to a traffic light, armed with a camera, as are many of the fighters, is the plain-clothes spotter who was above the Scarborough Arms in the city centre. There's nothing he can do about this, least of all speak with his uniformed colleagues. He might be collecting information or noting faces but from where I'm stood ten yards away, he looks as terrified as the Manchester United fans. I catch his eye for an instant. He's scared of me. Me personally and he knows I – and I alone in the mob – know who he is. It's one of the great moments of my life.

With timing a Sylvester Stallone film would reject for being too hackneyed, two coaches pull into the car park. They are, unusually for vehicles carrying Manchester United supporters, from Manchester itself. Immediately, a section of Leeds fans peels off, runs into the car park and are at the coaches' doors before you can say 'not enough police'. They administer savage beatings to the first fans brave or stupid enough to emerge onto the tarmac. There's no discussion, no 'Come on', they simply wade in, fists and boots flailing. For a few minutes, it looks like the police might have actually lost control. Eventually some constables spare themselves – the riot police are still protecting the Britannia Mancs – and join the fighting, trading punches with Leeds people more effectively than the Manchester coach fans. Both Manchester groups, hard and soft, are now forcibly huddled together.

It's half an hour after the Manchester United fans were halted at the car park, and it is time for a passage to be cleared to walk them into the away end. It's kickoff time too and the PA is pleading with ticket-holders to take their places, but nobody moves. Like unfriendly versions of the 1923 FA Cup Final white horse, the mounted police force back the Leeds fans, who are now screaming 'Who's that dying on the runway? Who's that dying in the snow? It's Matt Busby and his boys ...'

Foot police form a human tunnel through which the visitors pass to the away turnstiles. As they do, Leeds folk, faces distorted with hate, sputum showering on the visitors, chant 'Scum. Scum. Scum. Scum. Scum. Scum ...' until every Manchester fan has passed. It's like those post-war photographs in France, where women's heads were shaven to mark them as having slept with a German and male Vichy collaborators were paraded through cities to be jeered at. For the first time today, I'm a little frightened.

The match is fifteen minutes old when I take my seat in the East Stand. The atmosphere is as poisonous as the chicken and mushroom pie I found time to purchase is pleasant. I'm sat between a young girl, here with her father and girly pal, and a man with unpleasant sideburns and a Paul Heaton face. They are both too hysterical to communicate with. She is chanting 'Scum. Scum. Scum', he cannot bring himself to sit down for longer than thirty seconds at a time. The Leeds fans boo every Manchester United touch of the ball. The whole of the fantastic kop stands – this really is an imposing stadium – and whenever the Manchester end gets a chant going, it's drowned by a vicious, jungly 'LEEDS'. Virtually no away supporters have dared wear replica shirts. In lighter moments, the Leeds fans goad David Beckham with either wolf-whistles or a rousing rendition of 'Posh Spice takes it up the arse'. The girl next to me is disgusted by this one and turns human for a second. She's quite pretty when her face snaps into place.

Leeds United are almost as fired up as their fans, but Manchester United, as ever, don't care. Not as in don't-care-if-they-win, but they don't care what people think, they'll do it their way. Thus Roy Keane, so thick even other footballers must notice, will get himself carried off and booked at the same time, one of the Nevilles doesn't return possession after a throw-in given while a Leeds player is injured, knowing the Leeds fans will neither forget nor forgive, but they really can't get their game together. Maybe they're thinking about Juventus on Wednesday.

Centre half David Wetherall heads Leeds in front after Peter Schmeichel dithers over a cross. The crowd go suitably wild, there's a mini pitch invasion, as friendly as it gets here. The delight is not directed towards the goal, but against the silent Manchester end. It never stops.

At half-time, it transpires the bloke next to me is reading *American Psycho*. It may well be the only book Leeds fans have ever read. This is how they think life is. As distraction, there is a penalty competition where three fat Leeds fans try to win a car. They do this by attempting to place a penalty kick through a barely ball-sized hole in a sheet that now hangs from one goal. None of them manage it. Pele wouldn't have managed it. Ellie, an elephant, is the mascot. He performs a succession of somersaults and has a glamorous assistant. He's ignored. Elland Road isn't that kind of place.

The entire second half is, for Leeds, an agonising wait for the final whistle. To this end, George Graham slings on Robert Molenaar as an extra defender and limits his attacking options to trying to spring Manchester's offside trap via the nippy Rodney Wallace. It rarely works, but Manchester never look dangerous. Obviously Leeds fans don't care how the team plays. Certainly not today, possibly not ever.

For Manchester, it's simply a question of whether they will claw something back. They can't, and when it looks like they can, Nigel Martyn is unbeatable in the Leeds goal. Alex Ferguson brings on Ben Thornley to play where he should have used the absent Ryan Giggs and uses centre half Ronny Johnsen to shore up a midfield where Paul Scholes looks slow and unfit. By the end, Peter Schmeichel is in the Leeds penalty area nearly scoring, Leeds hoof the ball anywhere to gobble up seconds, the referee (on Fergietime) plays seven minutes injury time, the whole ground is on its feet and those Leeds faces are still contorted with tension and hate. The excitement gnaws away at my stomach lining like a boll weevil. I'm stood up like everyone else. It means so much to beat this, well, scum.

Referee Bodenham blows and, after the temporary distraction of the joy of victory, once more the Leeds fans turn towards their guests. This doesn't involve actual trouble in these CCTV days, just 'We beat the scum 1-0', but it lasts for ever. They're probably still doing it now.

Outside, the only noise is from the police helicopter, back in position. On the ground, in position, are the policemen, the Leeds United fans and the Manchester United fans. Here, to coin a phrase, we go ...

22 **Huddersfield Town**

v. Nottingham Forest
DIVISION ONE

3 October

0-2

'I feel we can get out of the position we're in.'

Brian Horton

I'm settling into this now. Wherever I go in Huddersfield, there's a great view. It's a town where nothing happens. A first glance at the flyposters suggests that Val Doonican is coming soon. Look at the small print and it's actually nearby Dewsbury he's playing. Arthur Scargill, leader of the Socialist Labour Party, which didn't field a Huddersfield candidate at the last election, gave a speech in September and Dickie Bird is signing copies of his auto-biography at W.H. Smith on Monday. So it's views, then. Views over the moors, which envelop Huddersfield from the north and west, especially at night, when the occasional car sneaks across them like an electric lava stalking a hatchery.

The stone they build the houses with, northern stone I believe it's called, is pleasing to the eye too. That's that though, unless a holy tomato found by fourteen-year-old Shaista Javed counts. In June 1997 she cut the fruit in half and discovered a message in Arabic saying There Is No God But Allah. That tomato, now preserved, is a tourist attraction. It would be wrong for me to go.

It's the absence of anything great, anything remarkable even, that is Huddersfield's downfall. What is the place for? Other than being close to Holmfirth where *Last Of The Summer Wine* is filmed? Once, though, this textile town, made prosperous by the canals, had a radical tradition. As late as 1813 Huddersfield Luddites were being executed by the state in York, over fifty years after John Wesley preached here.

They've tried to make the centre twee, but one branch of River Island does not a shopping metropolis make. They (presumably 'they' means several generations of Kirklees Council) have blanded out, pedestrianised and dumped modernisation on what should be cobbled hilly streets. What a mess they've made and the one town centre chip shop closes at 6 p.m. on Fridays. People bring decline on themselves sometimes.

This sort of place always has a local sculptor of note: step forward Mick Kirkby-Geddes, whose last exhibition was entitled Junktastic. According to the 44,158th edition of the *Huddersfield Daily Examiner* (chilling strap line: 'It's all you need to know'), Mick is on a BBC2 afternoon programme next month. So that's how they fill their pages each day.

It's not a football town, indeed the Rugby League was founded here, but even so Huddersfield Town are doing little to raise the gloom. Extraordinarily, they were the only club in the entire Football League who failed to purchase a player during the close season to build upon a team who finished an unreassuring twentieth in Division One. This season they have not won a league game in eight attempts and are bottom, in exact contrast to this evening's visitors Nottingham Forest.

The town might be asleep, the team may be wretched, but the ground, the Alfred McAlpine Stadium, is a work of wonder. Situated in a moor-enclosed valley, its three (four in Summer 1998) sides ensured it was the RIBA – that's Royal Institute of British Architects – building of the year in 1995. It's an architect's wet dream with white girders spiralling over each side. Even the floodlights, and they're proper, traditional floodlights, cascade to the ground in a quadruped arrangement. It has roads specially built into its belly. It's football of the future and it's been built for – rather than in spite of – the fans. They even had the common decency to build a dropping-off point for wheelchair users.

Outside, it's relaxed. Sky are filming interviews with children, Nottingham Forest fans, aware of the beer drought in these parts, sit in the car park enjoying the late Autumn warmth. It's so laid back, so comfy, Val Doonican would do well to pop in here on his way to Dewsbury.

Nottingham Forest emerge in an unmarked coach, so luxurious it has blinds and an entrance halfway up the vehicle, which the club owns. They should win tonight, but more importantly the players look like they know they will. They're all in comfortable clothes, Chris Bart-Williams carries a ghetto blaster and even grumpy old Hollander, Pierre Van Hooijdonk, so tall he has to stoop to negotiate the players' entrance, happily stops to sign kids' autograph books, always the mark of a decent human being, beneath the other stuff.

A second team coach turns up, not bad at all with sturdy tables, but not as magnificent as the first. A garish sign reveals all. It is the Nottingham Forest Directors Coach. There's something feudal and pompous about it, but also something quite cute. Do they do this so they can get drunk and not have to schlep back down the M1 in their BMWs? I hope so.

I'm in the Lawrence Batley (no idea, but he is Huddersfield Town President) Stand. Sadly the food, in comparison to its setting, is disgusting. Because I couldn't find a thing in town, I have to have a pie, which is cold, a tea which gives me a dose of Alzheimer's there and then, and a burger so thin it may have been sliced from a greyhound. Instantly, I have my first migraine since puberty, one where I can feel the vein on the side of my head pumping bad blood around. I blame the food. Oh well, you can't have everything: where would you put it?

There is a slight design flaw, in that the Lawrence Batley Stand's seats curl away from the pitch, but that's all. My view is perfect and the seats opposite, either red or blue, make fantastic murals. Nobody ever need get wet in this ground. They might get bored though, as there's no pre-match or half-time entertainment aside from my musings as to exactly who staved Forest's Dean Saunders's head in with a shovel to make him look like a Bash Street Kid.

Huddersfield give a début to Derek O'Connor, a tiny Irish goalkeeper just nineteen, but for the first half he has little to do. I have empty seats to the left and right of me. In front is The Moaner with hair like Harry Enfield's scousers, but without the moustache. He has a comment on everything. Marcus Stewart misses a good early chance: 'You thick bugger, earn your money'. Alex Dyer misplaces a pass: 'You stupid, thick coon'. Forest's Kevin Campbell slightly miss-hits a chip: 'You're a dummy. As bad as that dummy we've got, bloody Dyer'. And so it goes. No wonder I've got a fucking glorified headache.

In a just and fair world, Huddersfield would have been winning at half-time, despite their obvious lack of class, and winger David Beresford's scintillating runs would have been rewarded with a pair of assists, but the world is neither just nor fair. The home fans are well pleased nonetheless. They don't go for songs as such, a result of Huddersfield not scanning with anything, its logical diminution being phonetically identical to udders. So, sadly, the self-proclaimed largest town in England is small scale in Sky's brave new world. This means the referee checks with Sky's touchline person before ordaining the second-half kickoff ...

Maybe too, the lack of atmosphere is a result of another team with no heroes. The main player–fan interaction comes when full back Steve Jenkins gets stroppy with a kid who doesn't throw the ball back quickly enough for a throw-in.

As is the way of these things, Huddersfield are at their zenith when Forest score, Colin Cooper's daisy cutter sneaking in off the post. The Moaner to the whole team: 'Sod off, you're fucking useless'. The large away support sing a handsome rendition of 'You've Lost That Loving Feeling', Town's heads drop and that is very much that.

Dean Saunders scores a lucky second, knocking in poor O'Connor's brilliant parry from the Welshman's own header through the goalkeeper's legs. The Moaner: 'That's it, we're relegated now'. And so it goes. The Forest fans strike up again with a patently half-unfair 'Shit ground no fans'. The Moaner adds 'Shit team as well' and walks out.

Brian Horton, a man who exudes decency and passion, has been standing in front of his dugout urging his team on. For the last ten minutes, like his team, he gives up. The end of his road is in sight and everyone here knows it.

The tiny vein on the side of my head is starting to throb again as Huddersfield are applauded off by those who remain. This ground will look empty in Division Two. With the ludicrous logic of the unwell, I walk out of the ground, past the now-closed car dealership where some Forest fans have had their cars locked in, past the massive cooling tower, past the Ibbotson tower block where one flat has Smith & Wesson graffiti, blacked-out windows and a silhouette of a gunman and into a town centre which is already beginning to smell of vomit. It's badly lit, empty apart from the booming discopubs between which troops of girls (if ever they need Porky Spice, they know where to come) flit and lads humorously wrestle with each other. Now, my head really starts to hurt ...

23 **Rochdale**

v. Scunthorpe United
DIVISION THREE

4 October

2-0

> 'I can take responsibility for a lot of things as a manager, but believe me the players were not instructed to play as they did last week against Brighton. I can only apologise to those of you who made the long journey.'

Graham Barrow

Rochdale and Scunthorpe United. Not, in truth, the more glamorous end of the soccer firmament. No matter, there are those who regard football at this level, not as an anachronism involving clubs who should stop embarrassing themselves and go part time, but as real football, close to the people, where individual supporters really do make a difference.

Rochdale, by whose standards Oldham Athletic are glamorous, upwardly mobile jezebels and Manchester United are on another planet, are a case in point. They have no fans, last spent a season outside the basement in 1973–74 and in the programme of all places, even the anonymous Supporters Club column is spatting with the manager: 'It's a hard fact of life that a manager's performance is judged solely on results. So far, away from home, it's played five, points nil ... my comments angered and upset Mr Barrow at the last home game – tough! Put your teddy back in your pram.' Wow.

As a town Rochdale, logically enough a dale on the River Roch, spanned by what was at one time the widest bridge in Europe, is not beyond redemption. Say what you like about Adolf Hitler, but he had great taste in architecture. He was hopelessly uncreative himself, of course, but he did understand the power and beauty of a massive building. Local legend has it – unable admittedly to explain how Rochdale had crossed Adolf Hitler's eyeline – that when the Germans turned Britain into a slave labour camp, Hitler would have demolished Rochdale's town hall and rebuild it brick by brick somewhere (local legends err towards the unspecific) in Germany. He had a point, there are few more handsome structures in England.

Projected to cost £20,000 when the foundation stone was laid in 1866, on completion five years later the bill presented to Rochdale's struggling millfolk had reached £155,000. It was worth every pound, shilling and pence, especially for the elected representatives of Rochdale who would work there. Today, around the bustling shopping hill, Butts Lane, some people look sufficiently pale and wan to still be paying for it. This is not, by any yardstick, a wealthy town. As I buy a Cornish pasty, the most delectable food I've eaten in months, a little Asian kid asks for one too. He has a fifty pence piece. Although no prices are displayed, the saleswoman, pleasant as sunlight to me, curtly and triumphantly informs him it costs fifty-one pence. Before I can do the decent thing and give him a penny, he's off without a word. I was going to stuff my fat face with a second pasty. I don't feel like it any more. Hmmm.

Groups of schoolboys, in their pomp, walk up and down the hill, through the shoppers and the once-tough-soon-to-be-old men with beer-guts and biker T-shirts, trying to catch the eye of the schoolgirls. In between street cleaners hard at work, stalls sell English sausages or baked potatoes to middle-aged women trying so hard they're still wearing ankle bracelets. The traders at the covered indoor market smoke cigarettes while they bag vegetables and at Quids In, 'your pound goes further'. The boarded up shops, Asian ghettos and 25-storey tower blocks aren't too close to the actual centre. It's a football town, but only if your team is Newcastle or Manchester United.

It's not as if the good times have gone, the good times were never here. Even so, Rochdale always had spirit. It claims to be the home of the first Co-op. The small print admits this wasn't exactly the case, but goes on to boast that Rochdale was where the ideals of the co-operative movement first began to be put into practice. That's better and they have a museum dedicated to the Rochdale Equitable Pioneers Society in Toad Lane to prove it. There isn't, however, a museum to celebrate William Hay, vicar of Rochdale and local magistrate, who sent the cavalry into what became known as the Peterloo Massacre in 1819, arguably the unwitting catalyst for a more representative House Of Commons.

Generous to a fault, Rochdale has made an icon out of the phenomenally untalented Gracie Fields, born at Molesworth Street, and, later, they continued to elect Cyril Smith. There's nothing to do here, it's overwhelmed and under-mined by Manchester yards up the M62, but it has something, something slightly distinguished.

Two miles from Butts Lane, up steep hill and down shallow dale, Rochdale's ground, Spotland, named after the district it and the grand Spotland Church dominate, nestles in a slightly less salubrious chunk of a prosperous area. Outside, it's all busy organisation. The car park is operating with the efficiency of one of Alexander The Great's better campaigns. New stewards are being gently blooded, as Scunthorpe United's basic but presentable coach, a Barnard's (Eureka! Correct English shock! Apostrophe in name of coach firm!) from Kirton Lindsey, wherever that is, is being directed to a space exactly coach-sized. Car spaces for visiting directors are pre-allocated and everyone appears welcome.

However, just when all appears rosy, things take a nasty turn. Outside the car park, on a pavement where the club has no jurisdiction, are three old-style skinheads selling the *British Nationalist*, rag of the British National Party. I'm shocked. I haven't seen this for literally a decade. I watch them for ten minutes. They don't make a sale, but they feel they might and hope always fuels hate.

I trot over to the away turnstiles. There are two more BNP sellers, both over thirty, slouched on a private wall in their black bomber jackets. They're not selling any copies either. Three cheers for free speech. Somehow, I don't think I'd fancy coming to Spotland if I weren't white. I'd certainly be aware that Gary Bergin, British National Party candidate in the last election, polled 653 votes, roughly one per cent of Rochdale's electorate. Not many, but a massive result by their standards.

Inside it seems as though Rochdale's Asian community can take a hint, for I can only see white faces. Oddly, the same applies to Rochdale's squad and has done for some time, although diehards might remember Joe Cooke and Les Lawrence in the 80s. I stand in the Sandy Lane end, watching for racists, but they don't seem to be interested in football. Bastards.

The Rochdale fanzine is called *EGP, Exceedingly Good Pies*. There are no fanzines on sale, and I search with diligence. They've sponsored the match today, so they're probably in the decent-looking executive boxes to my right. More pertinently, the pies are exceedingly average and the peas attending them are watery. This is, in every sense, no Stockport County, but the service is delightful and the woman actually apologises for saying 'bloody' when one of the legion of Spotland wasps attacks her. I wish I could shed the thought of those five skinheads. I'd be so happy.

Scunthorpe, backed by a few hundred loud fans, lie third in Division Three and are a tough test for Rochdale, whose mascot, Desmond The Dragon, is brilliant. He shakes all the kids by the hand when a school trip yelps into the stand; he entertains the kiddy mascot while the players are warming up; he sits and watches the game from behind Graham Barrow's dugout in full costume and, at half-time, joins in the penalty shoot-out, flapping his big old dragony feet everywhere. With great dignity, he ignores the mean Scunthorpe fans singing 'what the fucking hell is that?'. I really want to be Desmond. Deep down, I know it's my vocation. I know I'd be brilliant.

Nippy Alex Russell dispels the home fans' omnipresent fatalism after four minutes when he sidefoots past Scunthorpe's Nosferatu-esque goalkeeper Tim Clarke. To celebrate, Russell stands behinds the goal shaking his fists. At the opposite end to fourteen-steps-deep Sandy Lane is the deserted East Stand. Somehow Rochdale have scraped enough money together to get the impressive thing built and so, on Tuesday, Nat Lofthouse will officially open it before a friendly with Bolton Wanderers, entry just £5. The joy of that occasion will not match Russell's today.

It's an intriguing but niggly game of few chances, and referee Hall, at twenty-six the League's youngest for forty years, is having a stinker, missing all sorts of physical stuff, particularly from Scunthorpe right back Steve Housham, who's on a mission to hurt. Housham's team are badly missing their creative linchpin, David D'Auria and they don't trouble home goalkeeper Lance Key all afternoon.

Rochdale wrap it up midway through the second half, when Scunthorpe centre half Mike Walsh handles on the line. He's sent off and Robbie Painter tucks away the penalty. Scunthorpe player-manager Brian Laws brings himself on to get booked and waste a few free kicks. Somehow Housham isn't sent off for an attempt to decapitate Russell and he's substituted before it gets out of hand. Scunthorpe fans are livid at the home team's subsequent litany of retaliation going unpunished and the Rochdale fans goad them along with limited enthusiasm, preferring instead to marvel at their now-relaxed side succeeding with crossfield passes. At the final whistle a Scunthorpe fan attempts a one-man pitch invasion. Policemen appear from nowhere and carry him out of the ground, still struggling. The Rochdale fans stand and laugh.

It's been that sort of day. Their team won't make it out of the basement this time either, but right now, on a warm October Saturday, there is hope. And that, ultimately, is what fuels football. Just as surely as it fuels the BNP.

24 Exeter City

v. Swansea City
DIVISION THREE

11 October

1-0

'There is a very positive mood at the club and we are all desperate to continue our fine start.'

Peter Fox

The first thing I hear are the pan-pipes. The music of the Andes wafting up Sidwell Street, a sea of red sandstone, like most of Exeter. For all I know or care, it's as authentic as Alberto Fujimori and Tupac Amaru. It's certainly pleasant enough for a bunch of buskers who, to my inexpert eye, look a tad Peruvian in their requisite woollen ponchos. They're drawing a clutch of appreciative locals: Exeter is a place where Saturday shoppers feel they have the time to tarry in the late summer sun and listen to buskers.

The walled city bustles in an isolation where Plymouth, Torbay, Bristol and Yeovil are too far off to compete. Exeter has always stood alone, but it's always had something going for it, since the Romans took over in AD49 after defenestrating the local Celts. The Danes turned up in 976, but Alfred The Great turfed them out a year later. The Normans, led by William The Conqueror himself, sieged in 1068 and after conquering (ironic nomenclature never being a Norman strong point), built a huge castle which still stands today.

In isolation, Exeter survived the decline of its wool industry after Yorkshire asserted itself. It survived backing the wrong horse in the English Civil War, when little Henrietta Maria, wife of Charles I, found herself living where the main post office is today and heavily pregnant. Yet another siege ensued.

Today, Exeter's predominantly moneyed (a city centre garage costs £7500) isolation, means myriad computer shops so Devonians can keep in touch with the outside world, two mainline railway stations and restaurants of sufficient quality to keep villagers in the big city for a few more hours. It means malls, sensible rebuilding after the Nazis did their business during the war, apropos of nothing. This sort of isolation also means everyone is white (bar Trevor McDonald, who has a holiday home at Topsham), a healthy student population including Peter Phillips rugby-playing son of Princess Anne, and some of the most attractive people I've seen in many a place. I know it's a shocking cliché, but the pace does seem slower than in conurbations. Talking of clichés, I buy a Cornish pasty (near enough, near enough) and hover to watch men I've now convinced myself are from Lima. This might be what heaven is like.

It also means that Exeter, with its beautiful cathedral, its redeveloped quay (don't bother, it's full of surf dullards and canoeists, but the apartments on the north bank of the River Exe look fabulous), its acres of parkland and its prison, doesn't care about Exeter City who in their seventy-seven years of league football have meandered absent-mindedly between the two basement divisions.

This season, things look as if they may be different. Only Leyton Orient have lowered their colours in the league and had Exeter scored more goals, they'd be top. Not that St James Park could necessarily take regular visits by Burnley, the much hated and feared Plymouth Argyle, Millwall or the fans of any northern team who make a weekend of it. Local park teams might chafe at playing there. Wooden floodlights grow in the barely used kop end, cables circle the whole ground and there are giant nets to stop the ball breaking the windows of the encroaching houses behind the away – 'end' is too grand a word – steps. I stand on the romantically named Cowshed, from where I can see the narrow, winding roads of old, terraced homes, unbombable by the Nazis, unbatterable by the weather and now too small for whole families to live in.

These are, on the whole good people. Former *World This Weekend* researcher Ben Bradshaw stood as a gay Labour candidate in the election. Sitting Conservative MP Adrian Rogers fought a bitter, bigoted campaign. He lost.

Much has changed for Swansea City since I saw them sweep aside Torquay United at Vetch Field a few weeks ago. Despite scoring as many away goals as Exeter, they have yet to acquire an away point. This dismal record cannot be helped by their Diamond coach, which has just two tables. Many a Swansea player must have died with cramp on the long journeys, since the days of Ivor Allchurch and Wilfred Milne when motorways hadn't reached South Wales.

They harshly sacked Jan Molby this week, and replaced him with Micky Adams, fresh from Fulham and a reported £300,000 payoff. He's obviously taken the first offer presented and, as he doesn't need the cash right now, must surely love football. What a good man and what a shame Swansea supporters are so disillusioned that only one coach load of them has made the trek to see a small slice of their club's history.

My fellow Cowshedders are far from pleasant, although they applaud heartily when the directors present Jamaican-born assistant player-manager Noel Blake with a cake to celebrate his 500th league appearance and they're delighted to have a useful team at last. The casual cruelty of kids leaning on a barrier and playing shoving games is a bad sign: at one end of their barrier there's a frail old man with a hearing aid. He might be a stubborn old cuss who ought maybe to move, but he's not hurting anyone. He doesn't deserve persecution.

I'm stood in the middle of what I take for clean-cut, rugby-playing students, especially when one of them claims to have been in London last weekend and another is going to stay with a doctor friend in Nottingham shortly, but they do come here often and the guy is going to Nottingham when Notts County play Exeter.

Ahead of noisy goalkeeper Ashley Bayes, Exeter are safe in defence, despite Chris Fry having legs so thin Kate Moss's eyebrows are raising right now. Their determination is epitomised by the programme cover, which features centre half Lee Baddeley, unshaven and with the blackest eye you ever did see.

They have a speedy midfield, where Paul Birch, once of Aston Villa and Wolverhampton Wanderers, is a class apart. It's Birch who scores what proves to be the only goal of the game – at which point Exeter fans tumble on me, this is not the sort of physical contact I crave – when he rasps a drive past Roger Freestone, who will save Swansea from a heavy defeat with some expert shot stopping from golden boy Darran Rowbotham, but who gives my season's worst exhibition of kicking. People at either side of the ground cower and giggle when he dribbles the ball out of the area. The players might as well sit down, certainly Swansea's hard-working centre forward Tony Bird doesn't trouble himself to make runs when Freestone has the ball. Not once, though, does one of the goalkeeper's team-mates provide an option for him not to kick. A marauding centre forward, and Exeter would be promoted by March on first-half evidence.

Whatever manager Peter 'Foxy' Fox – a former goalkeeper who first played league football as a schoolboy in 1973, kept a clean sheet and completed ninety minutes despite breaking a toe – said at half-time, I know not. Judging by the second half, it was along the lines of, 'Why don't you stop all the good work, cling on like idiots, surrender possession at every opportunity and watch the crowd getting so nervy they sing the Eng-er-land chant as distraction? Oh, and Birchy, don't touch the ball, eh, son.' If so, his team follow his instructions to the letter. Alas, Swansea are so poor themselves, that despite constant possession and an injection of quality from substitute Richard Appleby, they don't manage a shot. Micky Adams has an Augean Stables of a task. Exeter hang on, but someone along the line will turn them over.

The crowd melts away at the final whistle. As well they might, for this Saturday is a big night in Exeter. England are playing Italy in Rome, a match to which apparently over fifty Exeter fans missed the Swansea game to attend. It's also the city's carnival.

I adore carnivals, they bring families into the streets of city centres at night. For Exeter, they are reminders of times past. Still governed by its medieval layout, and with the totemic Royal Albert Museum up the road, erected in 1869 by carnival-led public subscription, this night wasn't so different two centuries ago, when it would have been just as magical for the children to see gaudy floats drifting by in the darkness. Carnival is a building block of community spirit and there's no room for the mean-spirited, the violent and the killjoy. I adore carnivals, so long as I have nothing to do with them.

It's drizzling heavily, but the streets of Exeter are lined with families. Balloon, luminous necklace and whistle sellers are doing royal business. Little kids are out later than normal, queasy with anticipation for the 130 floats. There's enough room for all, but the pavements are crowded enough to ensure the carnival's success. It's nice and I won't see a second of the parade.

Instead, I'm in The Mint watching a football match from Rome, shown on two televisions. I find it hard to care about England one way or another. All the overtones of racism and nationalism, the pretending to like Paul Ince and Teddy Sheringham, the fact that England (along with fellow non-countries Scotland, Wales and Northern Ireland) con FIFA into actually existing, when others may not field four international teams. This, of course, means three extra votes for UEFA in the intra-FIFA wars against South America and the third world. A simple rule should suffice: a seat at the United Nations means an international soccer team. Easy. I will not be sharing these thoughts in The Mint.

The bouncers on the door say 'Good evening', which implies they're vaguely human and the pub won't get so rammed that people start fighting. The match has attracted a varied clientele. The pair of deaf men, for whom the inaudibility of Martin Tyler's presumably excellent commentary is no problem, sign animatedly to each other and chuckle when they lip read the regulars' 'We're throwing up' chant to the 'it's coming home' part of 'Three Lions'. Everyone else – students (women pretending to be interested in the match), the couples (no pretence of interest there) and the hardish men – must bellow. At the bar, a drunkish man tells me a joke: 'What's the Italian equivalent of an Action Man?' I suspect the answer won't invoke Guiseppe Garibaldi's all-conquering army who subdued Naples and Sicily on the way to unifying Italy, so I shake my head.

'An empty box,' declares my new best friend triumphantly. I had prepared myself to laugh matily, but he's thrown me such a curveball that I can only assume a look of the keen-but-bewildered.

'Because he's a deserter ...' trumps New Best Friend. Good. The playing field is level again. I laugh appropriately and scuttle away.

Appearing in The Mint, by special arrangement, is The Drunkest Man In The World. His role is to wait for Italians to commit some real or imagined offence and then to run to one of the televisions and make wanker gestures at it, while shouting 'You're shit and you know you are' to Gianfranco Zola, who probably can't hear him. He gets a round of applause for the first few times, then no response. Finally he slips away, like a working men's club entertainer on the way to his second gig of the evening.

The fighting in Rome starts midway through the first half. We're all thrilled in The Mint. The England fans are roared on, as, when the tide turns, are the *carabinieri*. I'm quite drunk, on smooth flow bitter, by the second half. My friend Shem says they put in nitrogen to get the smooth flow effect. I don't know, but that smooth flow effect is like cheap cocaine or expensive speed: grinding of teeth, licking of lips and the desire for more and more and more. When England go through to France, the 'Eng-er-land' chant envelops the pub. Grown men hug. I'd rather have hugged some of the women who've turned up for the night club downstairs, but I settle on a huge moustachioed Devonian and head for the city centre.

The carnival is over and the streets have been reclaimed by those who usually walk them at ten o'clock Saturday evening. These streets, of course, are no longer quiet. I go to look at the cathedral, where Sir Francis Drake would hang out rather than in Plymouth. It's bathed in light, an oasis of calm, broken only by 'Eng-er-land' in the background and a busker playing madrigals for tourists. I offer a silent prayer for all the Aizlewoods I've never known and those I have. I must be drunk. I stroll up the High Street. There is real violence now.

On the other side of the street to me, a small but wiry man chases after a group. They, foolishly, ambush him. Now, after politely getting one of the gang he's supposed to be assaulting to hold his coat, he knocks a bigger man clean out with one punch. From the bench I'm slumped on, I can hear the contact of fist and face. I almost stand up and cheer. Leader's group – the girls egging him on as they are wont to do in these situations – finally catch up and half-heartedly join in. Quick as a cobra, Leader knocks someone else over and is finally pulled away by the peacemaker the law requires every street fight to have. One of the vanquished reminds Leader that he's forgotten his coat. He storms off, shouting he doesn't want it. One of his gang, the wise one, snatches it off the bemused coat stand and carries it the twenty yards it takes Leader to realise he did want it after all.

Energised now, I visit The Town House. At the bar, I see another man's penis. As luck would have it, it's about the same size as mine. He was chatting to two women and, mid-flow, had dropped 'em. They spank him and he pulls his trousers up just as the bouncers try to pick their way through the seething masses. I leave into what is now rain, not drunk enough to call in at the Taj

Mahal restaurant, but sufficiently pissed to be resentful for no obvious reason of the Rhode Island numberplates of a car outside. Nitrogen? It all falls into woozy place. In the back of my mind a voice tells me I must visit Birmingham, tomorrow.

25 Birmingham City

v. Wolverhampton Wanderers
DIVISION ONE

12 October

1-0

'When we've been watching Stockport in readiness to play them, Chris Marsden has often been the best player on the pitch.'

Trevor Francis

When I saw Birmingham play Stockport back in August, had Chris Marsden scored instead of hitting the bar when Stockport were 2-0 up, they'd have won. Now, in extra irony, the skinhead former Wolves player is making his Birmingham début, against Wolves.

They all come to Birmingham eventually. Today's big signings like Steve Bruce, Paul Furlong and Gary Ablett. Past mistakes like Alberto Tarantini, Mike Newell, Colin Todd, Neil Whatmore, Howard Kendall, Jose Dominguez and the goons Barry Fry bought. All to a club who haven't won the Championship or FA Cup, although they did manage the Leyland DAF Cup in 1992.

Why do they come to St Andrews where the unironic anthem is 'Keep Right On To The End Of The Road'? Birmingham City has the brand name of Britain's second city and when they stand on the Bull Ring, the city's centre and much pilloried despite being a market for 800 years, Brummies can see St Andrews on top of a hill towards the east. It looks proud and inviting, although no manager, not even Ron Saunders or Willie Bell (now a missionary) stood a player on the Bull Ring and said, 'join me'. No, Birmingham City surely pay well, they are the Rip Van Winkle of sleeping giants and the city has posh bits like Solihull, where footballers like to live.

The walk to St Andrews from the Bull Ring is short and unsweet, evidence that Birmingham (home of the tribe whose leader was called Birm) is a small town which outgrew itself geographically but not spiritually. Today is a Sunday, but the city centre is hard at it. Shopping seems pleasingly multi-ethnic and it's civilised when seventy-five per cent of the shops are open, but only patronised by half of Saturday's shoppers. I thought there might be some confrontation in town, around O'Rafferty's where City's hardcore drink and with Wolves being short on angelic qualities, but there's nothing doing, other than a few mounted police marching past Britain's first Odeon (which, I learn, stands for Oscar Deutsch Entertains Our Nation) and a huge gang of multi-racial Birmingham City supporters – Zulus they like to be called, more conventional loyalists are Bluenoses – scaring a few grannies. And myself.

It's a walk that shows how quickly Birmingham moves from international city to Midlands hellhole. Very much alone, I stroll past Snow Hill station, underneath the signs to the custard factory and the L. Ron Hubbard Dianetics Foundation (I did a Dianetics test once and failed every single personality trait. They did however suggest one potential solution ...), around a cut-price electrical store doing business so robust that cars queue to get in the car park and onto Fazeley Street and the corner of Andover Street, from where UB40 quietly run their multinational operation. It's an industrial wasteland and it's five minutes from the centre. Once the nearby canals (it's oft-quoted that Birmingham has more canals than Venice: the point is they're crap canals) helped ferment the industrial revolution of Birmingham resident James Watt, and Sarehole was inspiration for The Shire in the then-village resident J.R.R. Tolkien's *The Hobbit*. Now, they're a cats' graveyard and where there's muck there isn't brass any more. There's just more muck among Birmingham's six million trees.

St Andrews, formerly synonymous with squalor, has been redeveloped since the *Sunday Sport*'s David Sullivan and the interestingly-mouthed Karren Brady took over. Now Managing Director, she, smile all askew, is advertising some food substitute called Quorn in the programme and pornographers Ralph and David Gold (one or both of them has an autobiography for sale in the club shop) hold most of the power. The car park in front of the new Kop Stand looks ripe for a hotel construction. It's the public face of Birmingham City and an indication as to where the Gold gold has gone. Next to the Kop Stand is the away end, surrounded by ten-foot-high fencing. There is an away car park too, pride of place taken by the luxury Wolves team coach, a Leons of Stafford. It is painted in gold and black and under the tinted windows has Wolverhampton Wanderers Team Coach painted down the side. Ugh. Tacky.

As if in empathy, new houses – constructed with the planned obsolescence of future slums, but at least they're not flats – have sprung up, populated by little criminals who demand/ask to 'mind yer car' for a huge fee. I pay up.

I'm in the Main Stand, the less developed side of the ground. Outside is another car park which the club have forgotten to pave over. Inside, the facilities are primitive, they're selling Dunkin' Donuts, but there's nowhere to stand and eat the things. I'm close to the former directors' box which has now moved to the Kop Stand. As they haven't moved the dugouts or players' tunnel yet, Birmingham manager Trevor Francis, telephone in hand, and his assistants Mick Mills and Ian Bowyer must watch the game from there, unprotected by VIPs.

Things are not as they should be. It's a Midlands derby, both teams have everything to play for, although Mark McGhee did try to get the game postponed because of international call-ups, but it's nowhere near a 25,000 sell-out. Wolves have only managed to fill the upper tier of their end and there are spaces everywhere among the Birmingham fans. Wolves have however brought their mascot, Wolfie. He's brilliant and fights with three little pigs, accompaniment to Birmingham's Beau Brummie, whose body language suggests a rather melancholy adult lurks inside his doggy costume. Wolfie chases an attractive promotions woman around the touch line, lies down in the penalty area and tries to save long shots during the warm up.

Wolfie has less to laugh at during the game. Wolves, as they did at home to Charlton a few weeks ago, look like they don't believe in their tactics. The three centre backs can't function as one and the two wing backs are dragged every which way by Marsden, playing the inevitable blinder, and fast, direct Paul Devlin. Marsden scores what turns out to be the only goal early on, a solo effort aided by dismal defending.

Birmingham, in their exciting kit, very 1973, very Phil Summerill and Stan Harland, then elect to surrender ground, normally a suicide option, but Wolves can't turn possession into chances. There might be a poor turnout, but what supporters there are provide an intimidating atmosphere. When Wolves' Darren Ferguson makes a hash of a shot, they chant 'Savo, Savo' at him in honour of Aston Villa's Savo Milosevic. When their own Martin Grainger does likewise, they do the same again, before launching into rousing renditions of 'Wanky, wanky, wanky Wanderers' and 'Cheer up, Mark McGhee'. It's all done with bitterness rather than celebration, said bitterness epitomised by *The Zulu* fanzine and its 'Aston Arse-Holes' joke page, 'Why can't you circumcise an Aston man? Because there's no end to those pricks'.

So it's no surprise that when one of the half-time penalty shoot-out contestants is revealed as a Villa fan, he's viciously booed, as is Wolfie when he ventures past the halfway line. He spends the rest of the break following divot replacers, impersonating them. I find his hysterically funny. I am alone in this.

A flurry of late tackles ups the stakes during the second half, but the atmosphere is leavened by the dwarf paramedics who rush on with stretchers. Even the Wolves players laugh. Steve Bull, as ever, is the most willing Wanderer, but he fluffs a couple of half chances, cueing the 'Bull! ... Shit!' chant. After those misses he walks backwards, staring at the Birmingham fans. Like them, he's not laughing. Nor are the Wolves support, silent save for booing Marsden's every touch.

At the end, with Birmingham fans refusing to give back the match ball until a new one is in play, as they chant 'On the dole' at the under pressure McGhee.

Those directly behind him run to the dugout and shower him with abuse. Wolves goalkeeper Mike Stowell runs upfield for his team's corner. He succeeds only in kicking Birmingham's Jon McCarthy in the face. A few dozen rows in front of me at pitch side, Mark McGhee raises his eyes skywards and shakes his head. It is, I now know, possible to feel sorry for this man.

26 Carlisle United

v. Preston North End
DIVISION TWO

17 October

0-2

'Let's hope that those watching up and down the country will be left in little doubt why this game means so much to so many!'

Anonymous, like Carlisle's manager

The Auto Windscreens Shield is a nothing competition, but last spring, when Carlisle United won the thing after a penalty shoot-out against Colchester United at Wembley and then won promotion to Division Two a few weeks later, the Cumbrians' future looked so bright Ray-Ban were tempted to invest. This September, chairman Michael Knighton, who believes in UFOs and who once believed so strongly in his capacity to buy Manchester United that he donned a full kit and ball-juggled for the Stretford End, sacked manager Mervyn Day and replaced him with ... well, right now, nobody quite knows.

Knighton appears to be picking the team himself and his club are once more heading towards the basement, a development which will intrigue the Football League if descent turns into freefall. Ominously, there is no league club within fifty miles of Carlisle, hence this so-called derby. There are countless Division Three teams who would relish not having to come this way once a year, as they relish no longer having to compulsarily visit Workington and Barrow.

Down in Botchergate, this beautiful town's less salubrious zone opposite the railway station, among the boarded-up shops and the flats above them, in one of which estate agent's daughter Joanne Tiffen, only twenty-eight, died of an overdose, just seven weeks after her boyfriend Shaun had done the same thing, they're restless. It's where the Border City Firm drink. They're Carlisle's small but vicious fighting fringe, led by Paul Dodd (allegedly banned from every ground in the country, but that's hard to operate when he turns up in Exeter), famous today for being a super-hooligan arrested in Rome last week. The BCF are avoiding the heavy police presence tonight and they're not among those drinkers fingering the unsigned leaflets demanding mass exodus ten minutes from time tonight: 'This is our football club, not Michael Knighton's.'

'You gonna leave early?' asks a youth at the Border Rambler's bar. Like all male Carlisle fans, he has sideburns, lightly gelled hair above the upturned nose and gormless expression that confirms he's from the same tribe as Jimmy Nail.

'Dunno,' offers his mate. 'Depends if we're winning. They're only doing it because Sky's here.'

Their joint gaze turns towards me. I smile weakly, not wishing to speak in this strange land where they were publicly hanging criminals up to 1862, where silly old Bonnie Prince Charlie – many a Jacobite was hanged outside the city walls – is still a tender subject and where any accent from south of Penrith is directly from the tongue of Satan. I've already broken the bar-room etiquette where a new pint is ordered when a third of the previous one is still to be drunk.

From Botchergate, it's a straight trot along Warwick Road, where Abraham Lincoln's father lived, to Carlisle United's Brunton Park, through a flurry of middle class bed and breakfast establishments and large houses, well-maintained since Victorian gentry lived there.

Carlisle's violent history, times when it was part of the Debatable Lands and controlled by the scary Border Reivers clans because neither Scots nor English could get their act together, has given way to a softer feel and, right now, it's doing fairly well. It's the home of Eddie Stobart Trucking, who, as part of their United sponsorship deal, have ensured that the away kit is the colour of the company's livery. There's an Eddie Stobart Fan Club shop in town. It's still a market town and if the men could be Jimmy Nail, the women are moon-faced and ruddy cheeked, exactly how a farmer's daughter might be described to the passing aliens Michael Knighton knows, although omnipresent baggy black leather trousers are an unwelcome surprise. Natives of Carlisle are not the beautiful people and they become parents at an unnaturally early age.

An agricultural hinterland means, as the Irish Republic knows so well, European Community money by the bucketload. A well-preserved castle, a dull cathedral where Sir Walter Scott was married, a plethora of decent restaurants, a life-sized model of George Stephenson's Rocket ('under 24-hour camera surveillance') made out of hedges and Carlisle's selling as Gateway To The Borders & Lakes, ensures tourists will always come here.

Half a mile past the ground, towards the cattle market and M6, lies Carlisle's ring road. Take it south and soon Harraby appears. It's a sprawling council estate, the worst in the area, isolated from the town by green fields and that ring road. It's where problem families are dumped, out of sight out of mind, the ones who didn't buy their homes when Michael Heseltine told everyone to. They're the ones with piles of rubbish outside in their gardens, the ones for whom speedbumps have been erected on every road to challenge the joyriders, responsible for the burnt-out cars.

Invariably, next to the bomb-site houses, and identified by hanging baskets outside front doors, are the trim dwellings of owner-occupied places, bought for a few thousand pounds, heavily invested in and now, owing to location, unresellable at any price. When this generation dies, leaving nothing because their house is worth nothing and their offspring wouldn't live there anyway, the council will have to repossess dwellings they sold off so cheaply. The estate is so self-contained that residents need never head for the big city three miles up the road. It has the components of poor places the world over: pubs, boarded-up shops, a laundrette packed to bursting, a grocery store with a selection of goods citizens of the former Soviet Union would find restrictive, a chemist with security bars across its windows and a bookmakers owned by a local, rather than a major chain who would no more set up a branch in Harraby than in Riyadh.

Back at Brunton Park, there's no sign of leaflet distributors, but Michael Knighton's car has a police guard, as does the Preston coach, a Cosgroves which wouldn't disgrace the Premier League. The away end is out of commission, so Carlisle and Preston fans share the impressive new stand. The PA is inaudible, the food is disgraceful, the servers retarded and surly, and the beer queue long. More sweetly, they have blue and white cushioned bar-stools and tables. Poignantly, the video screens are not playing Sky's coverage of tonight's game featuring Mervyn Day as studio-bound guest, but endless re-runs of April's Auto Windscreen Final. It's not being ignored either.

There's no reserved seating, which is not the cock-up it was at Chesterfield as there's room for all. What it does mean, however, is that Carlisle's more violence-orientated support can bunch as they used to do when there was standing. Beyond an apprehensive looking wall of stewards, Preston have virtually sold their seats out, so the atmosphere sparkles into the night. There's added spice with lanky centre forward David Reeves, former Carlisle hero, making his first return since signing for Preston. Reeves hasn't been in their team recently but Preston manager Gary Peters has done the sensible thing. As soon as Reeves appears, the crowd rise as one to chant 'Judas, Judas' and 'David Reeves is homosexual'. He looks like he doesn't care, but he's betrayed by the ferocity of his early sliding tackles on innocent Carlisle defenders.

Carlisle look uncoached and incohesive, despite veterans Warren Aspinall, recently accused of racially abusing Plymouth's Ronnie Mauge during a match, and Owen Archdeacon. Preston look physically and mentally stronger. They soon take the lead when Gary Parkinson whips in a smart free kick. The Jimmy Nails around me stand up and sing their Carlisle songs, but they know their team is already beaten. Their chanting slips into a desperate 'We want a manager', a dignified 'Mervyn Day's blue and white army' and 'No surrender to the IRA' petty tribalism which speaks too much for this place.

Preston score again early in the second half when Lee Ashcroft taps in after Carlisle's dithery defence fall asleep as one. Preston play out the remaining forty-four minutes in complete control, their fans chant 'Finland's Number One' at goalkeeper Teuvo Moilanen who doesn't have a shot to save to prove it. Optimistic-to-a-man Carlisle fans keep hoping for miracles and to their everlasting credit don't turn on their team, preferring to heap abuse on Judas Reeves. He smiles the smile of the smug and makes a little '2' sign with his right hand and a big round 'o' with his left. 'If he scores, I'll get on the pitch and fucking kill him,' says a Jimmy Nail two rows in front of me, safe in the knowledge that his resolve on this matter will remain untested.

With ten minutes to go, 'We want a manager' echoes around the stadium and Knighton may well have to give himself a vote of confidence, but there is no exodus, just a steady stream of the disappointed ebbing away. Preston fans stand on their seats and holler '2-0 to the PNE' and they'll never collect a more straightforward three points.

Back in Botchergate after the Preston fans have been carefully escorted out of town, it's a quiet Friday night, except, of course at the Yates's Wine Lodge where there's a long queue. The pedestrianised areas are almost deserted and some restaurants haven't opened. In The Cumberland, more boozer than pub, with its tiled floor a reminder of when things were straight forward, customers are making monkey noises and pointing to their no doubt enormous genitalia like gibbons. A favoured regular gets the chance to go to the bar, point at the landlord's beer-gut and sing the 'Who ate all the pies?' song at him. The barman grins like a good 'un. I stay there until closing time.

27 **Darlington**

v. Doncaster Rovers
DIVISION THREE

18 October

5-1

'On a close post-match analysis after the 5-0 defeat at Rochdale, we conceded goals which Jason DeVos agrees were his responsibility. It is, however, very rare that he enters the field of play without a clear vision.'

David Hodgson

There was a moment, after their 4-0 home victory over Bury on 20 April 1996, when it looked as if Darlington were on their way to Division Two. Aided by a magnificent away record – one defeat all season – they finished fifth, before losing to Plymouth Argyle in the Wembley play-off final.

As is the way of these things, the window of opportunity slammed shut. By November the following season, manager Jim Platt had been dumped and the team scattered to the four winds: Matty Appleby, Sean Gregan, Gary Bannister, Steve Gaughan, Robbie Painter and Robbie Blake departed to pastures new. The motley crew of free transfers who replaced them, including John McClelland, born in 1955, finished eighteenth and Darlington were back in the real world. This season, it's worse again and The Quakers (nicknamed more after defensive prowess than religious sect) are now twenty-third, one place and four points above today's opponents, Doncaster Rovers. Thus, today, I'm privileged to witness a match between objectively the worst sides in the country.

Suffice to say, there is little sense of expectation around Darlington. It's a rum little place, far from poverty stricken. The market crackles like one of the steam trains the Railway Centre & Museum – dedicated to the first railway line in the world between Darlington and Stockton – bangs on about: 'here you can see Stephenson's Locomotion, which hauled the first train when the line opened in 1825'. It's less effusive about sculptor David Mach's 1500 tonne, 181,574 brick version of Stephenson's Mallard engine, the largest sculpture in Britain, out towards the A1.

The hillside market square, with a cross dated 1727 which has survived two transplants, has recently been discreetly developed with extra cobbling and granite so passing tourists think they're traipsing around the original. Perhaps too they could revive the tradition, suspended only this century, of agricultural workers coming in to town from the villages and hiring themselves out for a season's work.

Still, an effort has been made. As the wool and rail industries collapsed, Darlington could have died as easily as nearby ghost towns Hartlepool, Bishop Auckland or Consett, but now there are salmon in this stretch of the River Skerne, old blokes' pubs like the Nags Head (nobody under seventy admitted) alongside a café they dare, in the tough North East, to call Il Cappuccino. That the market is selling, ahem, used copies of *Fiesta* magazine; that a shop called What Everyone Wants Discount Superstore is allowed to exist and that the new town hall, replacing the one designed by the guy who did the Natural History Museum, resembles an Eastern European interrogation centre, cannot entirely bully the town of Vic Reeves, Wendy Richard and Wendy Craig into submission.

At the Speedwell pub, both sets of supporters are mingling happily and swapping horror stories. They are not, alas, talking about Arthur 'Darkie' Wharton, the Ghanaian Methodist who won the 1886 AAA 100 yards sprint in a world record time. At the time he was Darlington's goalkeeper. That Darlington were playing the world's best sprinter in goal was a precursor to the rest of their existence.

For today's Darlington, their ground, Feethams (from Fetholmes, a meadow which was part of the 12th-century Bishop's Palace), is the start of their problems, which arguably end with former manager Alan Murray, sacked in 1995, being awarded £35,000 by the county court, which also revealed that his salary was a miserly £28,000 a year. They share site and access, although not actual grass, with the local cricket club, past which self-titled Darlo fans must walk to access Feethams. Redevelopment is finally beginning next Tuesday at the game with Cardiff when this afternoon's raffle winner will blow up the unused East Stand – presumably with help from fully qualified explosives experts, but you never know at this level and he or she may yet end up making the bomb on their kitchen table – an event which the gleeful announcer claims 'some of you have been waiting since 1919 for'. From the rubble of the East Stand, paperweights, car keyrings and the like will emerge, made and sold by the club. By any rational measure, this is a brilliant idea.

The dressing rooms are portakabins, but I'm momentarily infatuated with the woman who proselytises enthusiastically about the pie and peas she's selling me, until she does the same to the less handsome eighty-year-old behind me. Disappointed as ever, I take my place among the uncrushed middle class males on the uncovered South Terrace basking in yet more late summer sun. The two men behind me are talking about the stock market and extra-marital affairs. 'I've got this flat in Leeds,' says one lasciviously, as if he hasn't had this conversation before. 'Janine's got used to me spending two evenings a week down there. I always phone her when I'm in bed with Helen.' Braggadocio, methinks, unless all men really are bastards.

It is Doncaster Rovers, rather than the undoubtedly frumpy Janine, my hard heart aches for. It's silly always being on the side of the underdog, but Doncaster's situation is so without hope, the things I feel for them are beyond sympathy. Like Carlisle United, they have no manager, but Carlisle are Real Madrid by comparison. Rovers have a backer, Ken Richardson, who probably picks the team – certainly he did when Kerry Dixon was nominally manager, until early this season – and who the fans think is running the club down. He won't leave, he won't invest and this week he's turfed the Supporters Club out of their office at the ground. Relevant to today are the facts that their team coach, a Globe from Barnsley (not bad considering they've been using the players' own cars to get to some away games) is only half-full, so team discipline has collapsed to such an extent that players can make their own way to away games and that somehow the club, a full-time Football League club remember, hasn't got a shirt sponsor.

Rovers are padded out with non-contract players. 'I think,' thinks adulterer behind me, 'that we shouldn't have to pay full price to see these players'.

The man in front of me has a radio. As the first half progresses with all the atmosphere of a park game, presumably in homage to Doncaster, he shouts Premier League scores out to nobody in particular. He is a menace to our newly constructed South Terrace society. I try to concentrate on a game where Darlington's dangerous Darren Roberts is head and shoulders above the rest, Doncaster fans sing 'Richardson out' to complement their banners bearing the same phrase and they hang on until just before half-time.

Typically, Glenn Naylor's goal follows a freak deflection off an unsponsored red shirt which presents him with a tap-in. Darlington fans celebrate by singing 'Hartlepool is full of shit. It's full of shit, shit and more shit, oh Hartlepool is full of shit.' Well done everyone.

Less typically, before some of their defenders have stopped holding their heads in anguish, Doncaster storm straight up the field and equalise, Prince Moncrieffe slotting away with aplomb. He celebrates like he's personally saved the western world from the red menace (defunct). Who can blame him? Doncaster's fans are too shocked to go bonkers and when the whistle blows a few seconds after Paul Conlon's long-range effort is brilliantly tipped over by home goalkeeper and Arthur Wharton's heir, David Preece, Darlington are booed off, especially Roberts, on the grounds that this Northampton resident is attracting interest from second division Northampton Town, as confirmed in the programme. They spurn their heroes around here. The only voice I can hear shouts, 'Get off, you're shit'.

Darlington's unconvincing mascot is dressed as a liquorice allsort rather than a Quaker. Another chance missed ... The second half is a disaster for Doncaster, typical for a season that has yet to bring them victory. Firstly Canadian centre back Jason DeVos had entered the field of play with a clear vision, for he scores two identical headed goals from left-side corners. In-between, Conlon is substituted and storms off to the Portakabins, alas his route takes him in front of the North Terrace, and so the former Sunderland and Hartlepool player is jeered to humiliation.

Worse follows. Doncaster captain Harvey Cunningham sets some sort of example by a two-footed assault on Kenny Lowe which is so late, so vicious and so dangerous, that the crowd gasps as one. Even the trees surrounding Feethams, slowly metamorphosing into autumn gold, seem to shudder. Then, twenty of the twenty-two players (Lowe isn't moving anywhere and goalkeeper Preece stays in his goal laughing with the crowd, making camp Dick Emery-style 'Oooh you are awful' hand gestures) start fighting, although what exactly the Doncaster players can be aggrieved about remains unclear. Cunningham joins in the brawling and then leaves the field without checking the colour of the card.

As Lowe, a classy veteran who has spent the whole afternoon shouting at, swearing at ('Hold the fucking middle, lads') and generally inspiring his colleagues, hobbles off, 'Director Of Coaching' David Hodgson prepares to replace him and has Lowe's Number 8 board held up. With only one leg functioning, Lowe starts shaking his fist, demanding not to be taken off. Hodgson, obviously impressed by heroic behaviour, accedes and Lowe returns to continue running the midfield. Hodgson does however give substitute Mario Dorner, one of two new Austrians introduced to the crowd before kickoff, a run out. He looks skilful enough, although he will have tougher opponents than Darren Esdaille. Apparently Dorner and Franz Resch (a full international) were advised by their agent not to come to Darlington. The pair promptly sacked said agent and came. Fools. Dorner scores with literally his first touch, but it's disallowed. There aren't too many perfect moments at the bottom of Division Three.

Doncaster simply give up. There's little resistance when Carl Shutt adds a fourth and even less when right back Simon Shaw ambles upfield to place a fifth past disconsolate Dean Williams, who must regret solving his contractual dispute in the week. Poor Doncaster, poor poor Doncaster.

In fact, I feel so sorry for them, that I must have a solo wake on their behalf. I visit Hogans, the greatest pub in the world. It's opposite Darlington station and its windows are covered by steel blinds to deter unbelievers. Inside, it is paradise of sorts. The huge place, at 5 p.m. Saturday afternoon, is heaving. To get to the bar, I have to brush past handsome fifty-year-old women. The barmaid (forty-ish, ginger, full of life) calls me 'love' and, I believe, means it. There are two televisions, both playing different channels, as loudly as the juke box. All ages are represented and have been here a long, long time, but the atmosphere is perfect. I can't get a seat, so I stand and actually end up talking to people about the match. The beer, proper beer with a head, is eighty pence a pint and were I ever to live in Darlington I would never leave here. At last, then, something to aim for ...

28 **Brighton & Hove Albion**

v. Lincoln City
DIVISION THREE

22 October

0-1

'I have to keep trying. It is not easy in our situation and it does not appeal to some players when they look at our circumstances.'

Steve Gritt

I'll save the delights of Gillingham, Kent for another day, other than to note: a) the town has unequivocally no interest in the twenty-three league games and (probably) one cup game the formerly famous Brighton & Hove Albion will play here and b) a pub called The Pub resembles an alcoholic's front room and has two notices behind the bar. One says '£50 notes accepted'; the other 'Don't ask for a tab, as the answer will be f*** off,' a notice that could have been written by the people of Gillingham for the people of Brighton. This is, in more ways than the eighty miles, a long way from the south coast.

It's a Wednesday evening. European games featuring Manchester and Newcastle United are live on television. Not a soul do I pass from railway station to Priestfield Stadium, five minutes away. There are no parking restrictions because there won't be enough extra vehicles to trouble the natives of these narrow, car-infested streets. It's surreal and, like everyone who makes it here tonight, I feel in exile and unwanted.

Policemen and stewards lurk in the gloom, as does the Lincoln City team coach, a Barnard's from Kirton Lindsey. It's like Scunthorpe United's, only infinitely superior. Lincoln might not be going places, but they travel to places in some comfort.

Tomorrow morning, the day Brighton's bid to move their operation to Woking falls flat on its face, it will transpire that only 1036 people attended this game, including maybe 200 from Lincoln. The atmosphere is deathly. The tenant's attempt to move to another landlord has resulted in an uneasy relationship. Mean-spirited Gillingham's way forward is threefold. Firstly they don't open their Gills Social Club, which in this pub desert is cutting off Kent noses to spite Sussex faces. Secondly, almost rendering the Mister Ham Man hoarding impossible to read, they only use three out of the four floodlights, although luckily neither team will trouble themselves with wingplay this evening, and thirdly there is approximately one steward per twenty customers, none of whom will do anything more dangerous than try and eat one of the scalding pies, sold in its wrapping.

These stewards, idlers of all ages and both sexes, do nothing except prevent punters sitting on the back wall of the Rainham End where Brighton fans stand in tiny, dispirited groups. This, it turns out, is privilege of the stewards themselves. Bastards. The lost fans spend their time looking for matchday magazines to buy, unaware that turnstile operators are surreptitiously moonlighting as programme sellers.

As their former home, Goldstone Ground is turned into a retail park after 1534 games over ninety-six years, it's not going at all well for Brighton & Hove Albion. Were it not for Doncaster's pub ensemble, they would officially be the worst team in the land. They must be haemorrhaging money every day they struggle on and then there is Gillingham, a place that despises them. It's a far cry from that sunny day at Edgar Street last May when Robbie Reinelt equalised Kerry Mayo's own goal to send Hereford United into the Conference, a time when Judith Burke, thirty-three, a Brighton fan living in Barnsley, had a Caesarean two weeks early so she could make the game, a sacrifice she might not be so willing to make tonight. Then, it seemed as if Brighton would prosper once they rid themselves of chairman Bill Archer and his deputy/Chief Executive David Bellotti.

It could never be that simple. Gillingham can never be a permanent home: the club still has offices in Brighton, they train at Sussex University and the reserves play down the road at Lewes. Bellotti has departed but Focus DIY magnate Archer, although no longer chairman, is still one of three directors under new chairman, Wonderbra advertisement man Dick Knight. Worse, boardroom readjustment has removed from public view the two hate figures Brighton fans had bound themselves together against, so there's nobody to vent their anger upon, apart from those who exhaust their spleen on out-of-sorts leading scorer, three-goal Craig Maskell, more out of duty than hate.

Nobody calls for last year's miracle manager Steve Gritt to go, nobody could do it better. Nobody else, apart from perhaps Alan Ball, would want to do it and Brighton fans (no women, no blacks, no children, but no threat) find themselves reduced to singing about Peter Ward, who left for Nottingham Forest in 1980, and that 'the Football League is upside down'. Sad, but not as sad as their harping on about Crystal Palace, as in 'You're worse than ...' when Phil Stant miskicks, an old hatred that is now surely unrequited.

Lincoln City, nicely placed in sixth and fresh from a derby victory at Scunthorpe, must fancy their chances. Nobody fancies playing John Beck's men, or, come to that, watching their long ball game which turns every game into a war of attrition.

Sometimes an encounter between the league's most dispirited and the league's most unappetising teams is a logic- and rumour-defying classic, full of goals, incident and free-flowing football. Not this one. It's horrendous from beginning to end. A few Lincoln fans have taken the trouble to form a samba band and they rattle on during the warm up and the game's opening ten minutes. Then, aware that this is a wake of sorts, the band doesn't play on, even when midway through the second half, Lee Thorpe breaks free and sprints towards Brighton goalkeeper Mark Ormerod, who rashly commits himself, leaving an empty goal for Thorpe to roll the ball into. That's it. That rubbish goal is the only vague incident of semi-note, unless we count the Little Englander announcer contemptuously reading the latest scores of the European games as 'foreign matches' and refusing point blank to pronounce Kosice, or the fairly good-natured baiting of Lincoln goalkeeper Barry Richardson, the gist being that he has 'really ugly' hair. He has his moment of glory late on when he flies through the air looking like an Afghan Hound to deny Jeff Minton and end Brighton's only attack.

Lincoln are better. Their right back Jason Barnett looks fairly capable in the first half and, although they never look like scoring until they do, they never look like conceding one either. As the players troop off, our announcer friend shouts 'Unlucky, Seagulls!' The crowd, too many miles inland, groan as one and slump into the night to prepare for their awkward journeys home.

29 **Reading**

v. Nottingham Forest
DIVISION ONE

24 October

3-3

'The win over Wolves was a joint effort from the team and all our supporters. I know it gave you all great pleasure and satisfaction.'

Terry Bullivant

If Oscar Wilde had been around today, instead of sending him to Reading Gaol, they'd have dropped him in a car trying to escape Reading town centre on a Friday evening. He'd have got out quicker from jail. It's gridlock towards the M4 and Hampshire, towards Caversham, towards Newbury. Conversely, it's impossible there is ever a traffic jam to get into Reading, for it is without soul or character.

It was ever thus. Queen Victoria descended upon the place towards the end of her life, long after the local-economy-boosting monastery had been smashed by Henry VIII, but long before the presumably well-occupied Holiday Inn and Ramada Renaissance (where Reading and Chelsea fans clashed in July after a pre-season unfriendly) hotels set up for business; before the hopelessly planned traffic system, with its inner ring roads and incomprehensible signposting began snarling up the centre; before insurance companies built their enormous tower blocks, ensuring Reading resembles a minor American city. Queen Victoria didn't like Reading one little bit. The good burghers wanted to erect a statue to commemorate her visit. She, ever aware that few knew what she really looked like, willingly acceded. But only if the statue faced where she wanted to be at that moment: away from Reading. And so, close to the railway station, said statue still stands as indictment.

Reading is near enough to London to commute but too far away to do it for a lifetime. Yet it's Silicon Valley, wealthy in its own right, but bereft of culture or feel, less even than the overspill towns of Essex where everyone (or everyone's father) is a West Ham fan. The mix of 12,000 students who are everybody's punchbags and were even when Suzanne Charlton studied here (why not, for a fun game at home, wait until she's doing the television weather and cover the top half of her head with a newspaper or card. *Voilà!* It's Bobby Charlton talking of low pressure and scattered showers!); the Asians (punchbags too, if alone), bitter locals, newcomers from anywhere and The New Posh moving in literally two streets away from those cold shouldered by Reading's economic boom and reduced to applying for 'team leader' jobs paying £12,500 in the newly refurbished George Hotel, makes for all-pervading ennui. When the apathy circle finishes turning, Reading may yet put itself first against the wall.

The football club could be a focus for unity. They've never played at a higher level than their current Division One status and right now they haven't lost since a calamitous 6-0 drubbing at Tranmere Rovers seven games ago. This evening Nottingham Forest and Sky TV are the visitors, but neither concerns the endless stream of Sainsburys shoppers lugging provisions home, or the smattering of punters at the Ship Inn, one of the few pubs in the centre, bathed at one tacky point in sky-blue fluorescent lighting. Somewhere there's an old town and the River Kennet, but I can't find either. It's Friday night and everyone is off home, watched by the closed-circuit surveillance cameras which have displaced crime into the many car parks. I see the way forward: cut crime by making town centres inhospitable, dreary and without facilities. It certainly works in America, where there's no crime at all, oh no. And their McDonald's are 'drive-thru' too.

Reading FC's Elm Park, north-east of the town, sits uncomfortably in the middle of New Posh/oldish poor terraced houses. There's no parking, no room to expand and the unfortunate residents of Norfolk Street spend evenings like these blinded by floodlights shining into their lounges and traumatised by the masses tramping the pavement their front doors open onto. It was the same in the mid-70s, when Reading's only hero, Robin Friday – a maverick from the days when Friday's friend Steve Death kept goal at Elm Park – thrilled what few fans there were. Friday died the other year of lifestyle difficulties and an Oasis drone has co-written a book about him. The PA announces a signing in Reading next week. Everything returns, even the dead.

In their infinite wisdom – this from a club who didn't call security when Uri Geller popped up one day claiming to be a fan and to be able to 'help' them – Reading have decided a 15,000 capacity ground is too small and, after 102 years of Elm Park mediocrity, next season should see them relocate to the Prudential Business Park near the M4 when the Madjeski Stadium, named with American-style egotism after (and by) chairman John Madjeski, is finished. There's an aerial photograph in tonight's programme showing the whole area. There isn't a home in shot. Reading are not a well-supported team, and it's a long way out of a gridlocked town on a snowy February evening in when they entertain Port Vale. This new era might not take quite the form Madjeski assumes.

All the seats (i.e. not many) have been sold tonight. There are a few thousand men of Nottingham on the uncovered East Terrace, home supporters pack out the covered South Bank which runs alongside the pitch and the atmosphere is bubbling nicely under the lights, despite a mascot, Kingsley Royal, who is sponsored by McDonald's and thus more advertising board than entertainment.

I'm on the West Terrace with the more affluent Reading fans, some of whom, in a giveaway for how small this club really is, are wearing colours of Premier League teams. It's not a chanting area, proof again that no seats doesn't automatically mean red hot excitement. Forest score straight away. Big, strong and enormously skilful Pierre Van Hooijdonk takes a direct free kick right in front of me. It takes so long to dribble past goalkeeper Steve Mautone that I actually look away to see where he might place the resultant goal kick. Maybe he was doing the same thing because it ends up in the corner of his net.

Reading fans are not pleased. Affluent or not, they move from silence to 'you lazy cunt, Caskey' – white-booted replacement for injured leading goalscorer Carl Asaba – in thirty seconds. Forest are patently superior and even when Reading start to threaten, Dave Beasant is playing like the colossus of Wimbledon rather than the clown of Newcastle, Chelsea and Southampton. Forest fans chant 'England's Number One' and don't laugh that loudly afterwards.

I always feel sheepish claiming that something is the worst or best ever. It seems ludicrous, especially when football-related, but I've never seen anything quite as spectacular as this. Steve Stone, in his first game since 7 September last season, when his knee tendon ruptured in the home game with Leicester City, has been understandably struggling for pace in the first thirty minutes and he's sprayed a few crossfield passes into the crowd. Then his moment arrives, right in front of me again. He's fed the ball in front of an open goal, with Reading's defence lost in traffic somewhere and Mautone already grounded. From five yards, he sidefoots it high and wide. There is a moment's silence when he realises exactly what he's done before he holds his head and looks up at the crowd, all of whom are laughing uncontrollably. For the rest of the game they will shout 'shoot!' whenever he's in possession. Welcome back, baldy.

I'm sloping around the back of the terrace at half-time (civilised toilets, death-trap steps, but only fifteen more league games to avoid hefty insurance claims) and I bump into Steve, whose Polish surname I could never master. I went to school with him 150 miles away and I haven't seen him for six years. He came to the match as neutral as me, on his own, too, because he had nothing to do. I see this as a sign from a God, with, likewise, nothing better to do than create coincidences to spook me. This is the second time this has happened this season, so the principle must be sound. I had forgotten though that Steve has the world's loudest speaking voice so I spend the second half listening to his tales of house buying, prison visiting, sex scandals at home and what a dump Reading is. As do the entire terrace. Bless him.

The football is enthralling. Immediately after the restart Van Hooijdonk tucks away a penalty and Reading look well out of it, until Martin Williams charges through Forest's defence. He looks to be going nowhere until he falls across Beasant's leg. It is a) a penalty for Reading and b) a red card for the goalkeeper, who is most reluctant to leave and stands there screaming at referee Brandwood for several minutes. Scuffles break out between the players, Steve Chettle goes in goal, smiles and winks at the Reading crowd behind him and gets nowhere near the penalty. 1-2.

This spurs the Reading fans on so much that some (i.e. three) of them next to the Forest fans have a little pitch invasion in order to get themselves on telly. The stewards, as slow to react as Mautone had been to Van Hooijdonk's free kick, let them have their fun and usher them back to their mates. Forest elect to play deep and hit Reading on the break. So cumbersome are Reading's defence, despite numerical superiority, that they let Forest score again. Kevin Campbell, looking atypically sharp, powering in the third.

This would finish most teams off, certainly most teams as poor as Reading, but in their last home league game they gave Crewe Alexandra a three goal start and didn't lose. Now, James Lambert jinks through several bamboozled defenders with skill hitherto undetectable in his game and makes it 2-3 (another mini-pitch invasion, this time the police stir themselves to get involved, albeit peripherally). Lambert's trickery inspires crowd and team. Chettle has stopped smirking now and can't master drop-kicking. He has no chance when Linvoy Primus leaps to head home a corner to fairly wild scenes across Elm Park. It's a wonderful match, brimming with controversy, skill, limitless commitment and unpredictability. Even in the least promising of situations, football thrills.

Still engrossing, the game becomes more chess, less British Bulldog. Chettle is well protected by a solid defence, while Van Hooijdonk and Campbell are starved of service up front, but everyone's happy after ninety minutes, apart from Dave Beasant and Stone. Before a 'record for this season' attendance. Reading have shown their mettle to pull back from the brink and Forest have seen themselves robbed of two – but at least it wasn't three – points, and Sky, well, Sky must be happiest of all, but then again they always are.

Me and Steve pretend we'll see each other again in the foreseeable future in the suspiciously deserted Queen Elizabeth. Outside, the sign says 'No drugs. Drugs = police' and tells us there is a raffle for some meat this Sunday. As we shake hands and go our separate ways, my old friend the Nottingham Forest team coach passes us on its way back north. It will be a long time before any of us returns to Reading.

30 **Manchester United**

v. Barnsley
PREMIER LEAGUE
25 October

7-0

'It's a funny thing in football, but people often take an affection for particular clubs and I have got to say that I have always had an interest in Barnsley's fortunes.'

Alex Ferguson

Fantastic. It is 8.30 on the briskest of October mornings. Exactly twelve hours ago, I was applauding Reading and Nottingham Forest off after the rummest of first halves. Now, I am at South Mimms services on the M25, and already the car park is turning into a swapmart of dubious sort for local traders who look as if they have been up for some time. What exactly they are swapping is none of my business, for I am waiting for the most likely of Monty Python source material, a minibus load of insurance men.

Despite being arguably the best team in Europe, Manchester United haven't sold out all their games this season. A few tickets are available to members (not to be confused with Associate Members who pay £8 apiece but aren't actually allowed to apply for tickets) for each game. A few more, many more in fact, are set aside for corporate hospitality as New United, with considerable success, replace their old fan base of Salford lads, some hard blokes from London and hard-up saddoes from anywhere. Now it's men in suits and rich saddoes from anywhere who spend oodles of money at the club shop.

Corporate hospitality means that men from insurance companies can impress clients by taking them to football matches, any British football match from England v. Germany, Euro '96 and the FA Cup Final downwards. This is not necessarily The Great Satan taking over and when it happens at Rochdale against Torquay it's seen as valuable liaison with business. For Manchester United, it's purely maximising profit per seat, even at the cost of points: a ground full of noisy scum from Ordsall (Old Trafford's version of Maine Road's Moss Side, a place where the ever-harassed Greater Manchester Police fear to tread alone) will create a more inspiring atmosphere than families and groups of men from Basingstoke pissed on cheap red wine. However, a ticket's a ticket and when the van turns up I'm waving like billy-o to attract attention and will remain for the rest of the day puppy-dog-like in my eagerness to appear normal.

They're OK, actually. My friend Steve (not to be confused with last night's Steve), a Barnsley season ticket holder, is driving. Most of the others plead vague allegiance to Manchester United, as southerners who don't really care about football tend to.

One of them has never been to a match before, something which may doubtless endear him to those who have been to a match before and would quite like to have made this one, but it's a technical point, as spurious as claiming that stopping eating hamburgers will reduce starvation in the third world. I sit in the back of the van and read the newspapers' uproar over Dave Beasant's sending-off last night. My new associates talk insurance, not in itself a sin I remind myself, and, anyway it's what they have in common. There's talk of football, occasionally sex and yet more insurance talk. I chip in where necessary.

They take the traffic queues up the M6 like real men and only once, when we speed past a car where the occupants are attempting a crossword is there anything untoward. 'Six down: Jewish baker,' chuckles the Bit Of A Character. It's so quiet my ear drums begin meltdown. 'Hitler,' chirps B.Of A.C. Do I display my moral courage and at least tut, thus creating an atmosphere? I do not. Should there be a heaven, I've failed on grounds of spiritual weakness. Bollocks.

Essentially, corporate hospitality means you get to eat a three-course meal at the ground. For this privilege and the inclusive match ticket (£19), it's £105 per head. We are booked in at the Red Café, which has the advantage of a free car park next to the ground, an advantage somewhat negated by United not mentioning this until we'd left our van at the county cricket ground ten minutes away.

That walk, past Trafford Town Hall, but some way from the rejuvenated Salford Quay ex-docks area, is like stepping into a third world city, without the poverty, crime, dysentery and heat. The surrounds of Old Trafford serve only the ground. The pubs, the endless rows of fast food shops must do minimal business on non-match days to locals. Today, though, thousands of people walk through alleys of stalls selling all sorts of Manchester United junk from programmes to flags and a Scouse-baiting T-shirt which shows a group of 'calm down, calm down' types in wigs and moustaches and a slogan 'Stand up if you've got a job or ever had a job or even seen a job'. The Scousers are, of course, all seated. There's enough Eric Cantona paraphernalia to suggest he'll be back (fat chance), although not the Cantona souvenir footballs which the club was selling as Christian Aid were reporting that blind, eleven-year-old Punjabi girls were making them for 6p an hour. More likely, Cantona's departure caught the vendors by surprise and the only way they can secure a return on their outlay is to make a cult of him. James Dean is not yet rolling in his grave.

The chip shops – including Lou Macari's – are doing splendid business. People like hanging around, that's why they're here 150 minutes before kickoff. It's a place where a home game with Barnsley is an event, indeed every home game is an event, just as it is for Juventus, Barcelona and the truly great clubs. These people saunter up and down Sir Matt Busby Way, picking their way past the legions of touts who're buying not selling and are all from Liverpool. Obviously touting is not illegal or they wouldn't be doing it.

We walk across the forecourt. The sense of occasion is overwhelming. The Munich Clock, forever stopped at the time the 1958 team perished, is a simple, moving memorial. The statue of Sir Matt Busby, however, bestows an air of camp the real thing never had. I met him once, in 1974, when I was nine . His chauffeur-driven limousine was tearing away as I thrust out my autograph book. The old gent stopped the car, wound the window down, signed a lovely, 'Best Wishes, Matt Busby' with his own pen, patted me on the head and said 'Take care, sonny'. I had no time for Manchester United then or now, but my young heart knew it had been touched by greatness. If I were a sculptor, but then again no ... he'd have had a better statue.

The Red Café and its car park are close to the North Stand, opposite where Alex Ferguson and his intimidatory stopwatch sit. Barnsley fan, former Doncaster Rovers player and Britain's first black comedian Charlie Williams, who grins broadly as he leaves his car, seems to have our parking space. Inside, it's lit as harshly as a former Wimpy bar and has ambience encompassing a carpeted Café Rouge and a department store staff canteen. The waitress is pleasant and of the sweetest disposition, but she's not glamorous and worse, she wears a Manchester United top and some jeans she gardened in this morning. Yes, yes, it's terrible how women are judged on appearance, but she wouldn't have got by in a transport café, let alone an establishment where diners are requested to dress smartly. Drinks are extra, apart from the wine, a Cabernet Syrah, more Ralph Milne than Roy Keane.

The clientele are affluent and undiscerning which is probably for the best as there's no choice on the so-called menu or in the cutlery which is red. It's treat time – middle class kids have been brought here to celebrate their birthday and older ones who've done well for themselves have brought their fathers here to show the old man the new, real world in action, very different from when he used to go every week to cheer on Harry Gregg and Maurice Setters. Like a twisted version of 1984, a battery of television screens roll silently and endlessly through Manchester United propaganda, some of superior vintage to the wine. Chris De Burgh's 'The Lady In Red' plays in the foreground. I assume this is a joke.

The food is edible. What more can I ask for in this situation? Everyone in this room knows it exists only to create opportunities for the non-poor to see Manchester United in the flesh, because there's no other way to do so. Capacity Red Café attendance would be guaranteed if they were serving Pedigree Chum. A 'Melon Delight' is a grim starter; a fatty meat, accompanied by a feisty peppery sauce and some droopy vegetables follow. The sweet is too sweet and the coffee is drinkable only by wizened Turkish men no longer blessed with the sense of taste. By some terrible mistake, I have been given a child's portion. So has everyone around me.

Our table is getting gently drunk. Nobody is going to do anything more rash than conspicuously purchase too many lucky draw tickets. I settle inconspicuously on one. It is not lucky. Proceeds are going to charity, but United could cut out the middle man and hand over a whopping cheque if they were really interested. One of my colleagues, who lives in the deep south, tells me about his children and how they love football. I forget who I'm with and declare that it would be terrible indeed if they were to support Manchester United instead of their local team. 'But that's what I want,' he laments. I slurp hard on my coffee.

After the meal, we are given 'a commemorative gift'. The waitresses hands out pens from a bulging sack. They are unbranded except for a Manchester United crest on the top. Thanks, I will always treasure it.

Red Café patrons have their own special stairway to the Stand opposite the one where Ferguson sits. This, I reflect, as we clamber woozily towards the Stand's summit, is a miracle. There are a block of seats for Café users, overlooking a corner flag. They are not the best seats in the house, nor even the nearly best. In fact they are possibly the worst. No matter, they are seats and I am in one. Those from Christchurch who are paying £105 per family member for Timmy's birthday have done their duty. Make 'em support Bournemouth, I say.

Manchester United's marketing people (top quality for football, but hardly Marlboro, eh lads?) call Old Trafford The Theatre Of Dreams. They have a point. It's space age, but not in the design sense that made Huddersfield so special, more the fact that 55,000 people have crammed together in the tiniest of spaces – The Theatre Of Dreams is not for the stout – to pay homage to the superior practitioners of the national game.

The BBC's World Service was, of course, created solely to give exiled Manchester United so-called fans news. They'll be listening in Jakarta (where President TNJ Suhartu's family own the toll road from airport to town), in Lagos (where travellers from America, but not from Britain, are advised the airport is 'insecure') and anywhere where there isn't a decent national league. Barnsley will, for one night only, resonate around the world. 'Temple' is another word the marketing men would like to use. They should.

The teams come out. Giggs, Beckham – collecting glasses at Walthamstow dog track more recently than he'd like to admit, and now on £1 million deals with Brylcreem and Adidas before he kicks a ball – Schmeichel and the rest. Before my eyes, they turn into Best, Charlton, Law, Duncan Edwards and the kids who died at Munich. I can see Matt Busby waving to me after he'd signed my autograph book. I can see Ossie Ardiles scoring that chip for Tottenham, Denis Law backheeling in for Manchester City with his last kick in football, I can see the ghost of David Busst, his leg straight now, but hurting horribly at the darkest point of the night. I look at the faces around me: the insurance men; the Scandinavian woman in front of me with two children I would sacrifice a minor limb to have sired with her; the old guys in new scarves behind me, and I know I'm not the only one who can see these things. There's a lump in my throat the size of Teddy Sheringham's payslip. This – no more, but no less, than a wet evening at Rochdale against Torquay – is what football is about. If I was on my own, I'd have wept over the sheer scale and quality of the experience. I surprise myself sometimes.

I think too of Manchester United fan Vijay Singh who in February 1997 at the age of thirteen, hanged himself after being bullied down the road at Stretford High School. He kept a diary: 'Monday, my money was taken. Tuesday names called. Wednesday my uniform torn. Thursday my body pouring with blood. Friday it's ended. Saturday freedom.' He's worth sobbing for, more so than Duncan Edwards. He never got to see the Red Café and would never, as he so wanted, become the first turbaned Premiership player. I wouldn't think David Beckham has heard of him.

Nobody, save the Barnsley fans in the corner opposite, who cheered their men's rather naff Wallace Arnold team coach into the stadium area, has come to see anything other than a routine home victory. The proportion and volume of replica shirts is staggering. I might see David Busst, but I can only hear the sound of credit card swipers.

Having nothing on the field to ire them, United fans are at war with the stewards who are said to take umbrage at singing, standing or any display of passion. The club noted the seat numbers of those who made wanker gestures at Niall Quinn when he missed a sitter in a recent derby and summon in miscreants for a 'chat' with secretary Kenneth Merrett.

Perhaps this is why the Barnsley fans are the only voices to be heard. Perhaps, too, the crowd sense United don't need encouragement and if they did, in a classic Catch-22, they'd be playing so poorly as not to deserve it. So, United who are so confident of victory they don't bother naming a goalkeeping substitute and give league débuts to impressive Nuneaton-born full back John Curtis, nineteen, and impressively named Manchester-born substitute Ronnie Wallwork, twenty, cruise to a 7-0 victory. People are streaming out at 5-0 to get home to Gloucester and the last few minutes are played out in silence, except for the clicking of cameras almost everyone seems to have. I'm surprised United don't make their own pocket Old Trafford cameras and flog them. Can't be too hard to do.

The guy who hasn't been to a match before must think it's like this all the time. Just before the end, the atmosphere turns nasty for a moment when Barnsley fans sing 'You'll Never Walk Alone'. Self-indulgently and over-sensitively, United fans think the Scouse anthem is directed against them. It wasn't, but once the Barnsley corner realise what's happening, it is.

It's men against boys out there. Andy Cole, who's been seeing psychiatrist Claire Howell about his scoring difficulties, is cheered more than any other player this afternoon except Roy Keane, still injured after the game at Leeds. Cole scores a hat trick before half-time. Giggs and Paul Scholes score goals of world-class quality and Karel Poborsky's isn't far off. Barnsley's fans sing 'We're gonna win 6-5' at 5-0 and enjoy their day in a manner suggesting they won't be around next year, unless they are realising beating Bolton, Coventry, Sheffield Wednesday and Southampton is much more important for survival. 'We won on bloody corners,' says my friend Steve, more morose than I expected. He's right, for despite conceding seven, Barnsley goalkeeper David Watson has hardly had a shot to save. United are just efficient, I reckon.

We try to re-enter the Red Café afterwards. Where two hours ago we were honoured guests, now we are pariahs. The Red Café is doing a post-match shift. Wow. I'm shocked. That's another 200 meals. Another £105 a head. Another £21,000. Plus drinks. That'll be £399,000 per league season. Plus drinks. Before cup games. Before its other, non-matchday, functions. And it's not the only café at Old Trafford. Fact, according to the excellent *Red News* fanzine: out of United's £87.9 million turnover, fans through gate receipts and merchandise contribute sixty-seven per cent, five times that of television.

We amble past the car park they didn't tell us about and through the thousands still staring up at the Matt Busby statue, having their photographs taken, clinging on to the experience for a few more seconds. The stalls are doing a roaring trade. Some of my men of insurance make an investment, £5 for a scarf that might last a whole washing cycle, a little less for some chips to help top up that meal that didn't fill us. We don't talk much on the way home, it's been a long day and darkness always makes it harder to chat. As for me, I can still see Duncan Edwards and Vijay Singh.

31 Millwall

v. Bristol City
DIVISION TWO
29 October
0-2

'There will be days when it doesn't quite go our way.'

Billy Bonds

It's turning cold all of a sudden. Maybe only in South Bermondsey railway station, Britain's bleakest place until I find the next one. It's Wednesday evening and commuters from Central London should be schlepping home while Millwall fans pop off to the match around the corner. Apart from a pair of policemen clocking up overtime, I'm the only person in a deserted station, shrouded in darkness. Not for the first time, I'm relieved not to be a physically attractive woman, dressed in a fairly sexy way. The solitary platform overlooks a travellers' camp and, across a road gridlocked with drivers eager to get to Kent, is a new-slum council estate. It's how Northern folklore might depict the station closest to Millwall. I descend roadwards, along a zig-zaggy path, picking my way past a disabled man trying to reach the platform through the gloom, helped by two more policemen. He looks through me. Please don't let him be the ghost of my future.

Some children, aged about ten, appear from nowhere and sprint through the barbed wire in front of the policemen, back to the train tracks.

'And what are you doing?' asks a constable.

'Going to our estate,' explains an urchin, as if it were the most obvious thing in the world.

'Oh no you're not,' counters plod as the group edge backwards.

'Fuck off,' shouts the leader and they sprint away. The hole in the fence, as the youngsters know well, is too small for the police to follow. Even without Millwall, this would be unpleasant. Brrr.

The Cliftonville, opposite Zampa Road where Millwall's New Den lair lies, is a typical estate pub: harsh lighting, scarred unfriendly bar staff, ghastly beer in plastic glasses and a stage for activities I'm too innocent to picture. Even with an influx of Millwall fans and Russia v. Italy in the Moscow snow on telly, it's only half-full. I must come back some weekday night when there isn't a match.

Outside, The New Den dominates a horrible landscape. Policemen are all around, but there won't be trouble tonight, unlike in the early-90s when, preceding the Feyenoord and Ajax of today, Millwall and Bristol City fans used new-fangled mobile telephones to set up mass brawls away from prying, interfering police eyes. Next to the away end are eight seemingly well-guarded coaches from Bristol, plus the team's high quality, lamp-festooned Peter Carroll transportation. I walk around the ground and they're all unprotected at the back.

It's deserted outside two sides of the unwelcoming New Den. This isn't as it should be on a first team match evening. The car park at the front is busy, made more so by tickets only being on sale from the ticket office there. Mine costs £16. For this, I deserve a centrally-heated seat and attention from bimbos, not October tundra and the twilight of Paul Allen.

Inside, it still feels like a reserve game. One of the few open refreshment bars is selling Cumberland sausage. Mmmmm, surely. Alas no, the server dredges it from a locked vault. Cumberland sausage isn't that sophisticated, even here. It's clot-cold and rather like Millwall themselves, does not travel well. The bread is stale too.

Millwall are dying on their feet. The New Den's capacity is a ludicrously optimistic 20,000 and, although they're fourth, they only fill a third of it. Millwall moved from the old Den on Cold Blow Lane, several hundred yards south, mainly for money, but partially because of hooligan difficulties. Millwall never had the numbers, but they always had the inclination.

Nowadays it's different. Bristol City have a whole end to themselves, which kills what little atmosphere there might have been, for unless it's a major game, away fans are dumped in the top tier, leaving the bottom one unoccupied.

At The New Den, Millwall fans make their own entertainment: charging onto the pitch to attack Derby players in 1994 or a solo assault on Sheffield Wednesday's Kevin Pressman a year later. The fact remains that nobody visits The New Den looking for a fight, but without a decent cup run in years and with visits from Walsall and York every year, the once-élite F-Troop and Bushwhackers are getting rusty.

This is signal disappointment to the group of Germans next to me. They are earringed Teutonic lads, armed with flak jackets, cameras and a basic knowledge of British hooligan tradition. On my other side is a young girl who will giggle throughout the game. For now she has a tray of food with her, although not, I notice, a Cumberland sausage. This is not what the Millwall warriors of the past fought for, nor could anyone fail to be humiliated by a ground which has *The Weather In Norwegian* plastered everywhere. Ironically, it's so chilly the weather is in Norwegian.

The game should be excellent. Bristol City are storming up the league and a win will leapfrog them into third place above Millwall and, for added spice, the clubs will shortly play each other in the FA Cup. There's a quick chorus of the ancient 'Let 'Em All Come', passed through generations of toughs by doughty South-East London griots, as the teams emerge, but it's without the intensity of Millwall fans at Luton in September.

The game is not excellent. City will deservedly win and Millwall, with one league win since August, will barely create a chance.

There is good news on a night when my back is kicked puce by the little shit behind me. He's accompanied by his multi-tattooed granddad, who glares at me with such venom when I turn around and try to scowl, that I let the little prince ensure I'll not be capable of pensioner sex owing to kicked-disc difficulties. The good news is Cockney Geezer a few seats away from Giggling Girl. He looks like Mr Punch, smokes unfiltered fags and blames everything on Millwall's arch-enemies, West Ham, whose Billy Bonds and Pat Holland manage the team and whose Kenny Brown and Paul Allen provide on-field experience.

'It's all down to that Brown,' he bellows, 'Sailor Brown'. Around him, the people laugh, except for me and the apprentice Eurothugs, who don't know what he's on about. City score early on when an unattended Steve Torpey heads home Adam Locke's pull back. 'Rubbish,' shouts Cockney Geezer. 'That was your fault Allen.' Eurothugs photograph both Bristol City fans celebrating and Millwall fans howling at their team.

The home crowd never extricate themselves from their team's back. In this otherworldly hush, the players can hear every word. The fans want it all and they want it now, which given Millwall's history (a second division championship, two Division Three Souths and a Division Four), seems a trifle unrealistic. The veteran Alan McLeary, who beforehand received an award to celebrate his 400th appearance, plays it across the back, seeing no movement up front. 'McLeary you cunt, we're playing the other way,' wails Cockney Geezer. Next time, McLeary hoofs it up field. 'McLeary, why don't you just fuck off,' shouts his tormentor.

McLeary, like the rest of Millwall's defence, has no answer to Locke's wing-back marauding, despite switching full backs Brown and Ricky Newman. Locke is well-prompted by Chesterfield's semi-final skipper Sean Dyche, distinctly unintimidated playing here. Like their newish signing Paul Wilkinson (replacing Danny Hockton who'd scored four goals in the four games prior to Wilkinson's arrival), Millwall are whole-hearted but crap, although Paul Allen's dawdling when Millwall manage a forty-fifth minute corner, suggests all is not well in any department. They are booed off at half-time. 'You shower of shit,' yells Cockney Geezer. People aren't laughing so much right now. I'm getting cold. I have a home and in it there is a bed ...

Bristol City tie it up after the restart when Locke is left unmarked and smartly volleys in Brian Tinnion's cross. Bonds has instigated a rule whereby none of his players can go wide, but after the pace of Michael Black (on loan from Arsenal and how he'll appreciate it back there) contrives a free kick in a dangerous position, the fans rouse themselves to sing that silly 'No one likes us' refrain. The Bristolians, ten times fewer in number but twice as loud, respond with 'You've only got one song'. My hard-earned degree in cod-psychology tells me that the Millwall fans don't actually like themselves very much. Or their club and now they're as bored as their team is wretched.

Millwall's latest arrival, Nigel Spink, is keeping goal in front of the away end's deserted lower tier. The wiser ball-boys have gone home, so whenever the ball whizzes past him he must haul his 39-year-old torso over rows of seats to retrieve it for a goal kick, something the City players quickly learn. This is how once-dignified careers end.

What now passes for Millwall's hooligan element make themselves known in the East Stand, opposite me. They are old blokes and their half-hearted body language suggests they're playing out a tired ritual, which may yet seem less outdated at the November Cup match in Bristol, whose support croon a gloating 'You're just a bunch of wankers', a cheeky 'Is that all you get at home?' and the posturing is over before my German comrades can click their cameras.

'The worst I've ever seen,' bellows Cockney Geezer, unbelievably. 'Shit, shit, shit,' chant the bulk of the fans. 'Come on Millwall,' shouts Cockney Geezer. 'We can still win this.' Our stand laughs as one and he rises to take a deserved bow.

When Millwall are finally put out of their misery, less than half of their support are there to see it. In the toilets, I'm offered a ticket to Saturday's sell-out game at Gillingham for half price. I refuse, adding a gratuitous 'mate' as a personal security measure.

Outside, Millwall fans are singing their way down the poorly-lit streets. Admittedly it's 'Laugh at the caravans, we like to laugh at the caravans' when they pass the travellers' site, but it's something. British Rail, as I still like to call it, doesn't have the common sense to put an extra train through South Bermondsey, so it's a twenty-minute wait. City's fans are let out and some join us on the platform, under the eye of the police. 'There's been a bit of a cock-up on the management front,' whispers a posh yokel, clearly petrified. Down in front of us, the stately convoy of Bristol coaches is being escorted to the M4 by so many police outriders that Salmon Rushdie might feel jealous, and police with dogs are searching two renegade Millwall men who'd been aggressively strutting down the other side of the road from the Bristol fans.

When it finally arrives, the train has two coaches so there isn't room for all. There's pushing and jostling. The police intervene and those Millwall fans who make the train sing the fact-based Harry Roberts ('Harry Roberts is our friend. He kills coppers') song and laugh about it afterwards.

Two minutes later, we are at London Bridge. A trainload, albeit a tiny train, of desultory Millwall fans is an excuse for more police overtime, so twenty of them greet us, accompanied by yet more vicious dogs. It's 10.50 now and just enough time for some cold, dispirited Millwall fans to grab a quick pint at the station. Alas no, for the police have closed the bar early and behind me, their dogs are yapping. Just another Millwall home game, then.

32 **Portsmouth**

v. Swindon Town
DIVISION ONE

31 October

0-1

'I firmly believe we are far better than we have so far shown.'

Terry Fenwick

On 21 August 1979 11,430 people saw Portsmouth beat Torquay United 3-0, the first game of what would prove to be a promotion season as Portsmouth finished fourth in the old Division Four, one place and one point behind Newport County and ahead of Bradford City only on goal difference. There were no play-offs.

Since then, Portsmouth reached the old Division One for a season and now nestle precariously, one place above the bottom of the new Division One. Less people watch them now, indeed only 6827 turned up for their last home game, with booming Bradford City. Portsmouth weren't a sleeping giant, merely an average club a division or two below their level, with a fanatical band of supporters who travelled in large numbers to away games, occasionally in furniture vans for overnight stops up north, but always led by the 6.57 Crew, so named after the train they caught to the north.

Now, turmoil rules. Terry Venables is chairman, having bought what appears to be a controlling stake for £1. As he's in power, he can begin his programme column 'Hi – how ya doin'?', proof in one phrase that he should be stopped. Like anything to do with this man, his relationship with Portsmouth is confused. What does he do? Who provides the money? How can he find time to coach Australia, bring Australian players like John Aloisi and Craig Foster to Portsmouth, do whatever he does at Portsmouth and defend his court cases? And, most pertinently of all, why is he here and what does he get out of it? Search me and search the club mascot, scarily named El Tel; more scarily a bloke with a huge, plastic Terry Venables head. These are odd times.

Fratton is on the northern outskirts of Portsmouth, not quite a town in itself but distinct enough to have its own railway station and competition for Best

Dressed Street. It's not affluent (hence the shop called Cut Price, slogan WE ARE CHEAPER), but there are few vacant shoplots and there is life in these terraced streets once occupied, I'd like to fantasise, by seafarers.

There are a few too many tower blocks around the corner from Charles Dickens's birthplace on Old Commercial Road at Fratton's northern end (the Dickens family moved away before little Charles had had a birthday). These blocks are where shoals of kids on bicycles hang out. Bikes are the criminal's new tool, a modern-day jemmy. A speedy, lightweight bike is handy for all sorts of mischief, from couriering heroin to plotting ambushes and burglaries or escaping from the police. These kids, too expensively street-dressed for flat dwellers, give me the creeps, but a solo Swindon Town fan feels he can walk around playing a Walkman and in a replica shirt – he couldn't have done that in 1979–80 – so it must be okay. I do wish the street lamps were brighter though.

The recent past still echoes. Four Portsmouth fans are due for trial on charges of violent disorder after the match at Queens Park Rangers last season and last night at Landport, around the corner, fire fighters were attacked when they tried to extinguish an unsafe bonfire.

This is a big day for Portsmouth. They're on Sky, which the match programme seems inordinately excited by. More importantly, at 3 p.m. this afternoon, the 4500 capacity, £2.5 million Fratton End stand finally received a safety certificate and will be opened tonight. It's a huge psychological boost. The Pompey Chimes chimed long and loud from this spot until a decade or so ago when the roof was removed and the End's capacity gradually cut to literally nothing. Now, Fratton Park is whole once more and what's left of Portsmouth's support can rejoice. The club are so unconfident of selling out the stand that the tickets are unreserved. They're right, too.

The Fratton End isn't finished, with its prison-like wire fencing where other grounds have walls or windows, and cranes outside for that special building site feel. It's said you can see the Isle Of Wight from here. I can't. It must have moved. There's a smell of wet paint and drying concrete and there are puddles of water outside the toilets, which have been sabotaged by builders who support bitter rivals Southampton and whose graffiti ('Pompey Scum') on the walls makes a different sort of opening present. Portsmouth's idea of an opening ceremony – one which makes Stoke City opening the Britannia look like *Ben Hur* – is to have El Tel (plastic version) parade around the pitch perimeter and a Salvation Army band playing in the centre circle. Rubbish, rubbish rubbish. The pasties are gorgeous, though.

Inside, the PA is inaudible. An unfortunate man – possibly as a form of community punishment – must walk around the ground waving to people while dressed as a sailor. The seat next to me is defective, in that it won't go into a sitting position and leg-room is not generous. The mayor of

Portsmouth, as wide as he is tall, that stupid Venables mascot (he couldn't be inside it himself could he?) and the end's sponsors (a mobile telephone company, for Christ's sake) do the honours. Then, for the benefit of the press photographers, the openers sit in the best seats which have been roped off for them. The moment the cameras depart, they leave to sit in the main North Stand.

The other gimmick is a band in the middle of the stand. This consists of an oaf in top hat, braces and a Lily Savage wig with some cowbells and a trumpet he hasn't quite mastered, stood in front of a drummer. They pursue their tuneless din with the melodic flair of John Cage, conducting anti-Southampton stuff ('Stand up if you hate the scum'), as well as tunes played so poorly as to be unrecognisable, drawing attention to themselves like a fleet of Michael Barrymores. No wonder the dignitaries moved. They sanctioned this embarrassment.

The game is full of promise. An away victory would take Swindon to the top of the league, a home one would lead Portsmouth towards a lesser sense of desperation. Swindon's Mark Walters is mercilessly abused for being an ex-Scummer (i.e. anyone who played for Southampton, even if, like Walters, it was exactly five games). Lord knows what reception Bobby Stokes, scorer of Southampton's 1976 FA Cup Winner, received when he played out his career here, although Portsmouth's own ex-Scummer, substitute Alan McLoughlin, isn't hounded when he comes on.

While I'm Jason Cundy's worst nightmare, I am Chris Hay's fairy godfather. I saw the ubersharp forward score for Swindon at Stoke in August and tonight he does it again in front of the new stand, diving in bravely, hurting himself, but it's a clumsy effort badly defended.

Venables must have been delighted at the coincidence which saw him linking at Portsmouth with his old Crystal Palace, QPR and Tottenham mucker Fenwick. As Hay's header trickles into the net, the 'Fenwick Out' chants begin. The band, for one blissful moment, dare not join in. Venables has a dilemma: friendship and memories of last season's solitary place away from the play-offs; or the immediate present and his shareholding.

Portsmouth struggle forward. Sammy Igoe ('Too small, too lightweight and too crap,' according to one of the increasingly disgruntled fans near me) can't get his crosses in. At the back Adrian Whitbread and Russell Perrett look permanently distracted. McLoughlin, Fitzroy Simpson and Andy Thomson, the three Portsmouth players who live in Swindon, never look like they'll be swaggering around town tomorrow. Swindon show fanatical commitment, looking out for each other in a way Portsmouth wouldn't understand.

On the touchline, Swindon manager Steve McMahon and his coaching staff all wear short-sleeved shirts and shorts and football boots. They look frozen to death, but it must boost spirit. Then, just before the end of the first half,

Swindon's strapping goalkeeper Steve Mildenhall, usually seventh choice, two down from the office cat, and playing tonight because of an injury crisis, is injured himself. He takes an age to recover and then looks unsteady on his feet. The home fans are not sympathetic, even when he can't take goal kicks and has to be helped off the field at half-time.

The second half is a strange business. Swindon have every outfield player in short sleeves, but they have no substitute goalkeeper so Mildenhall, in front of the Fratton End and the infernal band, must play on, although he's barely mobile. Swindon protect him in depth and try to utilise Hay on the break. Alan Knight in the Portsmouth goal, and, amazingly, a member of the 1979–80 side, is in for a quiet forty-five minutes. Portsmouth's sole plan involves giving it to strong, speedy winger Paul Hall. And hoping. They create chance after chance. Mildenhall sways around his area, brave as an ox, tipping over from Robbie Pethick, getting in the way of Craig Foster's shot and just about fisting corners away when surrounded by huge defenders. When he's beaten by substitute John Durnin's drive, veteran Brian Borrows, on loan from Coventry, hacks off the line.

When it becomes obvious Portsmouth would not score past a team of crippled custodians, the crowd turn on their own, singing 'We want Fenwick out' and, more hurtfully, 'Stand up if you hate Fenwick'. The band have lost interest and although Pompey hearts have been played out, the team exit to a chorus of boos. In normal circumstances it would be just one of those nights. Here and now, after the tenth match without victory, it means danger ahead. Outside, Sky's cameras are fuelling an anti-Fenwick demonstration for the twenty people so inclined. It's all a little pathetic. Swindon fans slip away into the dark and I venture into Portsmouth itself, several miles away, for some Hallowe'en fun. I do not find any.

Portsmouth, like its football club, has been a place of violence since 1194 when Richard I granted a royal charter. It's full of submerged history: Nelson spent his last night in Britain here; Raleigh brought back the first tobacco, potatoes and black men England had encountered to Portsmouth, and, Heihachiro Togo the Japanese admiral who destroyed the Russian fleet in the war of 1904–05 (fifteen years before Portsmouth reached the Football League, but fifteen years after Arthur Conan Doyle played in goal for them) and thus paved the way for Lenin, learned naval tactics here.

Sailors, students and deprived locals in for the night from the biggest council estate in Europe a few villages away, make for a volatile night-time mix, chaperoned by a union of local and military police. Like its team, Portsmouth has lost its stuffing and the centre, decimated by the Germans in World War 2 and now dominated by a badly designed Tricorn shopping centre, surely cannot be quieter at 4 a.m. on a Tuesday morning in coldest February.

Close to the High Street, along which, claims the council, every reigning monarch for 800 years (except Mary Tudor) has passed, I pop into The Albany where the bar staff are dressed in Hallowe'en gear, not, their facial expressions suggest, something they do in the privacy of their own homes. They're playing Olive's 'You're Not Alone' – more poignant than I remember – at skullcrushing volume and pissed men are snogging loose women with vodka and cigarette breath. Of course I'm madly jealous. I like it here, but it's not the liking of belonging and I must leave.

When I step outside into the quiet, I can hear the Portsmouth & Southsea station announcer announcing trains nobody will be boarding. I watch empty double-decker buses pass me by as I wait at pelican crossings and I see figures flitting around in the distance, press gangs I fear. The Portsmouth construction group, Warings, have just secured three contracts worth £20 million. Officially, they won't create one more job, but they might secure those already there. Portsmouth's bad times are only just beginning.

33 Wycombe Wanderers

v. Luton Town
DIVISION TWO
1 November

2-2

'We need ALL THREE POINTS!!'

John Gregory

When Wycombe Wanderers joined the Football league in 1993 in place of dour, 19th-century Halifax Town, it underlined a perceived sea change. Here was a new kind of football club, who'd moved to an out-of-town stadium three years previously, utilising their location in one of Britain's most prosperous areas – they even have a Conservative MP now – to become a family club, albeit in the sinister sense that only families seemed to be welcome at Adams Park. They lasted one season in Division Three, sneaking away via a play-off against Preston North End, first winners of the Football League. It was assumed they'd carry on climbing, until they could entertain Manchester United-supporting families, while their 10,000-seater stadium was sold out with nice people and nice people alone. It hasn't quite worked out that way.

Manager Martin O'Neill left for Leicester via Norwich. His replacement Alan Smith, independently wealthy and everything, didn't work out. Last season, John Gregory, once of England (in actuality but never in spirit), guided them to eighteenth and now they hover miserably in mid-table. Wycombe thought they were going to be the new Leicester City. Instead they're the new Lincoln City. Good.

High Wycombe (High Wycombe Wanderers would be much more fun) is a strange, unnatural place. Local folklore has it that bored youths wait on multi-storey roofs and drop bags of cement onto strangers' heads. I find this unlikely in truth, but Wu-Tang Clan graffiti (neatly inscribed, naturally) around the town centre suggests some little boys wish for rebellion. High Wycombe is a mass of A roads, a servant to the M40 and refreshingly free of any traces of character, unless the new Safeway store refusing to employ men with facial hair (this rules out much of the large Asian community funnily enough) counts.

There is an open-air market, but it's the sort where they vend paintings, designer candles and picture frames alongside knickers for a quid. It wasn't like this in the 1750s when Sir Francis Dashwood ran the bacchanalian Hellfire Club at West Wycombe caves and Benjamin Franklin allegedly dropped in for relief. It wasn't like this in the 40s either, when High Wycombe was a glorified village specialising in furniture making, hence Wanderers' nickname, The Chairboys. It wasn't like this until the 80s, when High Wycombe became the quintessential Thatcherite town, breeding Silicone Valley residents and London commuters. On the back of this, it pedestrianised itself, constructed Britain's most incomprehensible traffic system and spawned a culture spoiled by easy money and misplaced sloppy territorialism. Harry Enfield's teenager probably came from here.

The town centre is a building site. This is a county and district councils' joint initiative and they're already admitting these 'Enhancement Works' won't finish until next May. Essentially this means more pedestrianisation (and therefore more night-time crime, but they omit to mention this), a 'revised stall layout' for the open market and – what every town needs – a new taxi rank. Still, if there are no poor people (and the councils won't mention the town centre Asian ghetto in their redevelopment plans or multi-racial Castlefield where buses are ambushed and pubs catch fire), what else can you spend your council tax on?

I've no idea where the ground is. Wycombe and football do not mix, so I visit the tourist office. Surprisingly I'm not the only person there. The woman is suitably helpful, telling me it's an hour's walk away. She also gives me a leaflet, 'an invitation to support your team when they visit Wycombe Wanderers', a leaflet of little use in High Wycombe. It outlines the facilities away fans may find: 'dedicated teabar ... male and female toilets at every entrance ... exclusive use of The Roger Vere Stand ... excellent Wembley-size playing surface'. Whoo! Watch out Paris Ritz! All this is accompanied by a photograph of a stand which isn't named after Roger Vere. They've got this terribly wrong somehow and attendances keep on slipping.

Tourist Woman was right, it's a hell of a trek and unlike, for example, Wycombe's dry ski-slope, Adams Park remains resolutely unsigned. I take the A40 towards Oxford. This major road is lined with huge houses, every one detached, some big enough to be turned into luxury hotels. It is in this moneyed sanctuary, at The White Horse, that I have a new experience: the pub stripper. The first thing I see as I stumble in, exhausted, is a woman naked except for high heels and a G-string, wandering around with a clanking collecting glass.

The naked woman comes towards me, smiling. 'Get it out,' she cackles, as I try to find a shell to crawl into. 'Your change, I mean!' and she guffaws like Barbara Windsor's lecherous niece. Trying desperately not to touch any part of her body, especially her tiny breasts – others are less Christian in their behaviour, but she doesn't appear to mind – I pull out a handful of change and, although I have not seen her act, surrender fifty pence in the hope she'll go away. 'Nah, put it all in,' she bellows. 'I like that.' I think I blush. The spectacles of the policeman next to me (why there is a policeman next to me I do not know, but he's one of a pair) have steamed up. He does not give a penny, being on duty and all.

The lights go down, men gather round a tiny stage at the Oxford end of the pub and 'Claire' is announced. I am on my own, about to watch a stripper at 2 p.m. on a Saturday afternoon. I am the biggest pervert of all. Claire is more fully formed than the previous one. She has a come-to-bed smile, but the eyes of a shark. To The Family Stand's 'Ghetto Heaven', she gyrates lasciviously around a small stage and strips to her shaven pubis. She finds a 'volunteer' from the audience, handcuffs him to a chair, rubs his chest like she cares, puts shaving cream on his head and as a final flourish lights a candle inserted into the shaving cream. Some men applaud, some giggle with their mates, some snap out of erotic trances and pretend nothing has happened, as does Claire, who smiles shyly and gets dressed, losing at once whatever balls make her do this.

Oh, I don't know. It's not right, but nobody gets hurt. What if the women enjoy it? What if they hate themselves every time their underwear drifts towards the floor? What if it stops rape? What if it encourages rape? Oh, I still don't know. I wish I'd felt a little more disgusted though ... I look at the floor and at my watch. It really is time to go. Onwards, ever onwards.

Adams Park is in a dip south of the A40 in Sands, a rare part of High Wycombe that was built Before Thatcher. Here, not all the houses are those of the wealthy, there are some that are merely quite well off. On my return journey, I will try a short cut to the A40 on which there are homes that may house manual workers. It still makes Reading look like The Bronx, though. Sands ends in town-planning disarray: an industrial estate with one entrance and therefore one exit, before the green belt tightens. At the edge of this estate lies Adams Park, in every sense, at the end of the road.

It's poky – ideal for its scale model at Bekonscot, allegedly the world's oldest model village, a few miles away at Beaconsfield – but surrounded by car parks and greenery. Oddly, Adams Park isn't all seated and, at the snappily named Axa Equity & Law Life Assurance End I can stand behind a goal with Wycombe fans, an attraction so appealing that several Bristol Rovers fans infiltrated in the last but one home game. There was no trouble. Perhaps the Bristolians were poisoned as the food is awful, all shiny bread and so-called burgers the thickness of my ticket stub. Now that I'm living exclusively on beer and food served at football grounds, my skin is yellowing and last night's Portsmouth pasty is still tickling my taste buds.

The atmosphere is helped by Luton Town's fans, possibly for the first time in their unillustrious history, selling out not only the 1042 seats of the Reg Vere Stand, but also some of the tiny suntrap that is the Amersham & Wycombe College Stand. They're making noise too, more so than the dreadful team I saw lose at home to Millwall deserve. They lie below Wycombe, just above the relegation zone.

There's enough room for me to stand at the very front next to an old woman so bonkers she wears leggings and high heels which expose her bare feet. Manchester United are playing Sheffield Wednesday and when she hears it's 4-0 to the home side she will spend the rest of the game flashing four fingers at all and sundry, even when they score more. She is annoyed by a video cameraman right in front of us. Silently, I encourage him.

It's a poor game, full of endeavour but with little flair. The Wycombe fans are riled by a Luton child aged twelve in the family area of the Servis Park Stand, so they sing 'Does your mother know you're here?' and he flicks covert V-signs in return. There's little to excite anyone, even though Wycombe have gone ahead through Mark Stallard after a penalty area skirmish. In truth, I must confess I cannot see properly. Stallard might have run fifty yards and chipped over Luton goalkeeper Kelvin Davies for all I know.

I do know that the goal was against the run of play. Luton try to claw their way back in. David Oldfield heads over when it looked easier to score, but eventually (and I can see this really well) the same player does equalise after fine work down the left, a hard low cross and a bit of flapping from chubby Wycombe goalkeeper Martin Taylor.

The crowd become even more apathetic and start talking among themselves, save the woman next to me, who talks to herself. The team's quartered shirts ensure they resemble a rugby team, something much of High Wycombe wishes they were. This is, in effect, a rugby union crowd and they don't give a toss.

You can take the club out of the non-league, but you can't always take the non-league out of the club. The trees which mark the onset of the Chiltern hills outside do look golden and autumnal though, but it's insufficient to disguise a Vauxhall Conference feel to the whole set up: long throw expert Jason Cousins has to shove aside a steward and move an advertising hoarding before he can hurl the ball in.

The second half is similar, except for the young Luton fan moving himself up to the end his team are attacking. Luton make all the running and Wycombe score with their first attack when Steve McGavin thunders home. The crowd seem pleased now and the generous applause they give hard-working black forward Steve Brown when he's substituted for someone christened Maurice suggests there might be something that makes family clubs that touch more decent after all.

Inevitably Luton equalise again when Tony Thorpe (still playing for the Premiership, still some way off) loops a header over Taylor. This sparks a pitch invasion by exuberant Luton fans, partially because it's so easy: they have to walk down onto the perimeter to get to the toilets and 'dedicated teabar'.

Luton fans' excellent timing of 'dodgy keeper' doesn't win the game but Wycombe always seem capable of letting it slip, as the lack of passion on the terraces transmits itself to the pitch, although when Jason Kavanagh louchely passes back with a vista of attacking opportunities open for him, even this most tolerant of crowds briefly turns. In the end, Luton dally so long over taking a corner, that referee Brandwood (the same one who sent Dave Beasant off last week and has now recanted) blows for time. All are happyish and Luton can pootle home in their excellent Hallmark coach with high quality table lights, spirits much raised.

They're probably still there now, ossifying in the car park. Cars and coaches emerge from the ground car parks, from the road verges and from various factory car parks. Nobody moves for forty-five minutes. Although I feel genuinely ill after that burger, I walk back into town, the only person who does so. None of this is right. I pass The White Horse again. A tribute band, Fleetwood Bac, are loading their equipment inside. Fleetwood Bac? I laugh to myself and get out of this place, unnerved, uncomfortable and unwanted.

34 **Oldham Athletic**

v. Gillingham
DIVISION TWO

7 November

3-1

'If we finish above the Gills, I am confident we will be promoted automatically. We must try and avoid the play-offs because they aren't recommended for anyone with a nervous disposition.'

Neil Warnock

Oldham Athletic's Boundary Park is supposed to be the coldest ground in league football. It stands, a lone sentry guarding Oldham from the Pennines, a town twinned with chilly Kranj in Slovenia, but a mere suburb of Manchester seven miles away. This season, Oldham Athletic have got themselves an England international. His name is Carl Serrant and whilst he may only be in the England Under-21s, from where Oldham are counting the sell-on costs, Three Lions are Three Lions. The Under-21s have a play-off in Greece early next week and Serrant may perform. This is enough for Oldham to bring forward their game with Gillingham twenty hours to Friday evening, the only team to do so, apart from Manchester City who have Sky obligations.

So it comes to pass that the Gillingham team, in their lemon-coloured King's Ferry coach without table lamps, must hike up the M2, M25, M1, M6 and M62 on a Friday afternoon as must their two coachloads of supporters after having taken a day off work. What's more, I know Gillingham will lose, because on their lemon-coloured King's Ferry coach, the black players, Dennis Bailey, Ade Akinbiyi and Iffy Onoura, sit at one table, away from the whites.

The poor Gills are probably freaked out by what awaits them as they decoach. Not the cute little programme hut dominated by a huge poster of Jim Morrison or Oldham Athletic's very own travel agency. There are the hangers on (or most loyal supporters depending on whether that glass is half full or half empty) who scrounge match tickets off players. This the players can handle, unlike a man old enough to know better, slightly if not wholly mad, who wordlessly but firmly and with a huge smile blocks the players' entrance. No player may enter until they have signed his scruffy scrap of paper. One of the black players tries to sneak in. The autograph seeker taps him on the shoulder and drags him back to secure a scrawl.

There's another man loitering, more obviously ill, whom I will meet again in Oldham town centre around midnight as he goes into telephone boxes and starts jabbering away without lifting the receiver, his poor, fractured synapses still refusing to connect. He's interrogating the Gillingham coach driver: 'Have you got any international players? How far is your ground from the M25? How far is your ground from Luton?' The driver raises his eyebrows and, to his personal and professional credit, estimates that Gillingham's ground is seventy-five miles from Luton. 'Ah,' exclaims the fan, 'that explains why you get such poor gates.' And with that he walks off. I shudder. I suppose I won't finish my days like that, but it's only a supposition.

Boundary Park is north of the town, close to a hospital and unusually close for a football ground to the better off, bungalowed sector. Athletic had only been there ten years, when, in 1915, Everton pipped them to the League Championship by a solitary point. They still talk about it today. Some kind of fraud I hear. Since then, it's been mostly downhill and even when Joe Royle's team made the top division in 1991 after a 68-year wait, Oldham Athletic were only there on loan. Last season, they were relegated from Division One by five points, despite Warnock being appointed with sufficient time to halt the fall.

Now, things are as they should be, Oldham are at their natural level, pushing for promotion back to Division One, invincible at home but let down by shoddy away form. A win tonight would put them above fifth-place Gillingham, who have exactly the same problem. Boundary Park has changed since the grimmest (but most exciting) day in its history when, in 1980, Sheffield Wednesday fans rioted after their hero Terry Curran had been sent off. Natural tool-makers, Wednesday fans used bricks and rubble, which were handily to hand at the banked, open away end, as missiles. After that afternoon, Oldham began their ground rebuilding earlier than most and the result is an impressive, all-seater, all-covered stadium and if the executive boxes look suspiciously like Portakabins, well that's because they *are* Portakabins, glass-fronted and on loan from a company in Manchester. I like this place. The pie isn't bad, either.

I like the people too, they're not like normal crowds, all gnarled and bitter. They're attractive and a few years older than most. There's a few anti-Blackburn chants, but mostly the feel is positive. Their 'Stand up ...' rallying call ends '... if you love Oldham,' and they're ceaseless in their encouragement, although it's clear from the first minute, when the home side force five corners against the Gillingham giants that there'll be plenty for them to sing about. Fat Gills goalkeeper Jim Stannard is a figure of fun from the outset and he's already been beaten by Paul Reid's penalty – cue a horribly loud snatch of James

Brown's 'I Got You (I Feel Good)' – when he fluffs a backpass and Brian Statham must head off the line from Richard Graham's effort.

By the time Stuart Barlow, nicknamed Barn Door at Everton because he couldn't hit one, scores a second after Stannard ineffectively parries Reid's free kick – cue a horribly loud snatch of 'The Can-Can', not the Bad Manners version – it's carnival time, helped by the occasional post-Bonfire Night firework in the distance. I feel shockingly happy. Shots rain down on poor Stannard and his beleaguered defence, while Reid looks a class above opponents and team mates alike.

At half-time, and in no way suspiciously, the club electrician wins the lucky draw (I buy a draw ticket at every ground. One day, one day soon ...), but when the teams come downstairs (oh yes they do) onto the pitch, accompanied by a horribly loud snatch of 'I'm The Leader Of The Gang (I Am)', Gillingham are a transformed team and not just because they've brought Dennis 'I'm a Christian and once scored a hat trick at Old Trafford' Bailey on. Like Oldham in the first half, they force early corners. Home goalkeeper Michael Pollitt, on loan from Notts County, drops one of them and Guy Butters scuffs in. There's no snatch of any song and the men from Kent have forty minutes to level.

Oldham, as all teams in this position should, step up another gear. Reid weaves his way through what seems like the entire population of the Medway towns to score a third and the appreciation is so noisy I can't make out the tune. A Lancastrian is so overwhelmed he runs on the pitch – he looks mentally ill too, there's too much of this here – and attempts to draw attention to himself. 'You sad bastard', chorus the crowd. Pollitt chases, but is no closer to catching him than he was to that corner he bungled. The intruder is eventually apprehended by the stewards and the solitary policeman in the ground is summoned. Everyone goes home happy, except for the Gillingham fans, who may well need the long journey back home to reflect upon the fact that being outclassed like this too often will mean mid-table mediocrity.

Chilled, but full of silent *bonhomie*, I tramp through the badly lit (lights are dimming across the land) cesspool of a car park behind the, ahem, Lookers Stand and head for a town centre that seems hours away, past husks of what once totalled 320 working mills housing more spindles than the whole of America and thus the reason for Oldham's 19th-century growth and prosperity; towards Tommyfield, the largest outdoor market in Britain, towards the first Methodist chapel in Britain and towards the town hall, from where, in 1900, Winston Churchill delivered a rousing acceptance speech after being elected to Parliament for the first time. I presume it was rousing, but back in 1900 he might have had the public-speaking ability of Deng Xiaoping, whose accent was so pronounced the good folk of China could never quite follow the old fox.

Anyway, it's a centre of two halves. The pedestrianised part is creepy at this time of night and there's nobody about, not even council workers, although as the council is £277.8 million in debt, saving on overtime can but help. In fact it's so quiet, I feel more conspicuous, scared, vulnerable and exposed than I've done all season. Yet, like in that instant shortly after take-off when an aeroplane escapes thick cloud and climbs into blistering sunshine, everything changes.

What seems to be the old High Street is having a party for no reason. There are three types of establishment: takeaways featuring every stratum of junk food from Bab's Kebabs ('High class, traditional cuisine') to the Balti House ('Traditional Punjabi cuisine'); minicab offices and pubs. It's the noisiest street in Christendom and it's in Oldham, home of Eric Sykes and Barclay James Harvest. It's as if the Romans (decline period) were back in control: it's teeming with people, cabs pick their way through the masses and vanloads of police slowly patrol. They daren't go out on foot patrol.

Jacketless lads wander around from pub to pub including the hyper trendy Revolution and the first Yates's Wine Lodge there ever was, shouting babble ('Watch him, he's a copper') and looking at women. My Politically Correct mask slips off and clatters to the floor. Right now, I wish I wasn't dressed for a chilly evening's football match. I fall in love every five or so seconds, not shallow infatuation mind, but deep spiritual love. They're all dressed fabulously, like Hollywood starlets, but with northern accents – I understand the Boddingtons advertisement perfectly now – and if I lived here I'd never have left. My attire is not unpleasing in itself but I might as well be wearing a pin-stripe suit and bowler hat, so I will not join in. And if I did, what then? There is nobody else sad enough to be on their own here and none of these places are ideal for sitting quietly and reading the *Oldham Evening Chronicle*. I retreat with a heavy heart. One day I will return.

35 **Middlesbrough**

v. Queens Park Rangers
DIVISION ONE
8 November

3-0

'The Manager Of The Month trophy seems to have been the kiss of death again.'

Bryan Robson

Where have the people come from? In 1986–87 Middlesbrough spent a season in the old Division Three, entertaining Newport County, Doncaster Rovers and Darlington. Sometimes gates would top 10,000, sometimes not. The game against Port Vale, played at Hartlepool because the Inland Revenue's winding up petition had closed their Ayresome Park ground, attracted 3456 Teessiders. Fast forward, not to now, but to 1994–95, Middlesbrough's first season at the Riverside Stadium, Bryan Robson's first in charge, a season in which they won the Division One title. Sometimes gates would top 20,000, but more often, including the Sunderland derby, they wouldn't. That's the natural order here.

Today, it's different. Robson, who never seemed intelligent enough to notice his club were in danger, took Middlesbrough down last season. The magnificent Juninho has gone and so, in more bitter circumstances, has Fabrizio Ravanelli – did he really strip fixtures and fittings from his club house at Hutton Rudby, the village where he once went to his local and pretended to know darts? Worse, Mikkel Beck and Curtis Fleming have stayed and once more Port Vale and Sunderland will be among the visitors. Yet, the Riverside Stadium is sold out for every game. There are 29,000 season ticket holders and a 5000-long waiting list. This isn't hype. I see it with my own eyes this afternoon. There aren't even touts, for there are no tickets to be touted.

How did this happen? I have to actually break a lifetime's habit and ask a stranger in The Shakespeare. 'Whay aye bonny lad,' he says ... Of course, he says nothing of the kind. He replies in that weird-sounding but geographically logical Middlesbrough accent, part Yorkshire, part Geordie. People, he explains, are so sure of going up that they were scared to lose the chance of seeing Premiership football in 1998–99. If, later in the season, there are doubts, chairman Steve Gibson and his one-man board will buy spectacularly again. Seems more like collective hysteria to me.

Middlesbrough, the steel river town which spawned Paul Daniels and Roy 'Chubby' Brown, needs a break. It's never under-achieved, because it never achieved anything in the first place, never looked like doing so.

How on earth did Emerson not only end up here, but stay on, as the last – but most derided – of the superstar trio? He might have bought Britain's biggest private satellite dish outside London embassies so that Mrs Emerson can receive Brazilian TV, but this isn't Rio De Janeiro, this isn't home. There aren't many Portuguese speakers around and the weather is lousy, but at least the violence is slightly less endemic and there's little chance of a military coup. He's going to blow his World Cup chance and for what? To play against Port Vale and Bury. Idiot, but, bless him, he's so committed now, that alongside Paul Merson he'll be switching on Middlesbrough's Christmas lights later this week. What a guy, although it is the announcer, post-match, who mentions this. Today's programme declares Merson and Nigel Pearson will do the honours. I pray Emerson demanded this, rather than having to be forced. We'll never know, but he did once go for a game of bingo at the River Hall in Stockton, like he'd lived here all his life.

And what of Paul Merson? Does he commute most days on the train from whatever footballers-only Hertfordshire village he lives in? And Bryan Robson? Does he fly up from the Cheshire stockbroker belt most days, still? What was it with Branco? This is a club like no other, a comi-farce-tragedy. Maybe that's why people are hooked and why the club runs guided tours around the Riverside. £3 to you, gullible Teessider.

Football shenanigans are also a splash of glamour in a town so lacking in the stuff that its main attraction is a Transporter bridge, built in 1911. The only other Transporter bridge in Britain is at Newport, Gwent, Middlesbrough's soul-mate. When darkness falls, the bridge is illuminated. Not bad, but Disneyworld is not quaking. Even Eurodisney is not quaking.

Today, it is raining so heavily that I think of poor, friendless Mrs Emerson stuck out in some village trying to tune in to Globo TV, wishing for all the world she were back where the sun shines, where everyone watches Globo TV and where everyone speaks Portuguese. I figure I'm unlikely to bump into her in Middlesbrough town centre, where the pounding rain has sent those not trying to negotiate traffic gridlock scurrying for the shopping centres, of which there are many. What are they like? Exactly.

Having only thirty residents until 1830, Middlesbrough grew by the grace of the ironmasters who turned it into a 19th-century new town. Its population had mushroomed to 90,000 by 1900 as people flooded in from the surrounding villages to build cholera-infested slums for themselves, while finding jobs in the steelworks. William Gladstone had confirmed its potential electoral importance by turning up in 1862, a few years before he first became Prime Minister, to personally hurry along the industrial revolution.

All this means there's no sense of history, no generations of Middlesbrough families stretching back centuries, no shared folk memory of civil war derring-do present in more focused places. Even when it was growing, the best were leaving, like those gangs of Teesside steelworkers who helped construct the Golden Gate and Sydney Harbour bridges. It's a town of foster children, not wholly sure why they feel so angry all the time. Maybe that, too, is why they love the football team, the focal point that doesn't smell of Middlesbrough's other industry, chemicals. What foul, poisonous, Beelzebubbian smell wafted through here before the clean air acts, the Devil himself only knows. I keep looking for people with two heads and no arms. I guess they're hidden in asylums out Redcar way.

Not built by men of irony, the Riverside is indeed by the side of the River Tees. It's close to the town, through acres of waste ground dissected by specially built roads. The tourist board could advertise it as being Great For Fighting and should note that there's more weaponry to hand than in the Pentagon's back garden. It's too wet for all that today and there was a small, non-violent group of Queens Park Rangers fans (including a black man: locals were kneeling at his feet, declaring him Rain God, while offering him trinkets and local delicacies, like chips) nervously slinking around town, but in little danger.

However, football hooliganism is as alive and well here as it was on my final visit to Ayresome Park when some bastard, old enough to be my father, gave me the hardest kick up the coccyx I've yet had. Then he stood there laughing like an in-bred Delilah. I'd like to think he was involved when a Nottingham Forest fan was murdered here in the 80s and that he's now insane with remorse. Last season, there was trouble at several games, the town is usually a no-go area for away supporters and rail passengers who'd dodged the bricks at Middlesbrough station were often ambushed at Thornaby, where there are no police. This season it's been quieter, as it always is against Charlton Athletic and Tranmere Rovers, so Middlesbrough fans made up for it in the otherwise less-than keenly contested Coca-Cola Cup by bricking that beautiful Sunderland Moordale team coach. They don't like strangers round these parts, not entirely a feeling unreciprocated.

The aluminium temple of a ground looms out of the rain as I squelch towards it. It's so beautiful, so imposing, that I forget the hole in my shoe, the dock cranes, the smoke belching from the chemical works that's lowering my sperm count and the moonscape around me. Now I get it: if I lived here (please God no) I'd have to be here every matchday. The Riverside is a symbol of renewal. Middlesbrough didn't have to move away from Ayresome Park, they wanted to. And they wanted, so desperately, to be the biggest team in the North East. Mirror, mirror on the wall, who has the biggest Tyneside, Wearside, Teesside cock of all?

On the far bank of the Tees – looks great, but best not slug a mouthful, eh? – is a shipyard. Glory be, it appears to be in commission. Obviously the MFC stewards patrolling the groundside bank are there to stop the unemployed from swimming over to claim a job. The car park is grand, and although few are without a replica kit, the queue at the club shop is so long that more stewards have to restrict entry. Boom! Boom! As Basil Brush might say.

Middlesbrough are sixth, Queens Park Rangers an underachieving twelfth, but an away win today would see the teams level. It should be an evenly contested cracker and my enthusiasm remains undiminished by a pie topped by pastry incredibly slack and mushy, encasing meat from a species I must not speculate upon.

Inside, the Riverside fair brings a lump to my throat, albeit right now it's a lump of gristle. It's a football marketing man's dream. Red and white fills every seat and almost a fifth of the entire population of Middlesbrough is here. Newly broken windows suggest these people cannot cope with really nice places. *En masse*, they are the council estate family who've moved into a posh neighbourhood. They have a yard while everybody else has a garden, but now they're here they won't be moving in a hurry and they'll do all they can to make their habitat as recognisable and therefore comforting as they can.

Oddly, these Middlesbrough fans don't make the noise I'd anticipated. On the pitch the team are superb. Although his team mates don't want to pass to him, Emerson looks like he's switched his own lights on this afternoon and plays a blinder in midfield. The crowd even chant his name occasionally. Queens Park Rangers, on the other hand, are in disarray. Their fans, bitter and Cockney, boo their captain, poor Steve Morrow, before the kickoff, although he's their best player in a gulch of mediocrity. Middlesbrough fashion a chance so straightforward even Mikkel Beck can't miss to score the first and Paul Merson clearly handles before expertly tucking in a second.

There's even a spot of fighting. Some of Middlesbrough's waiting 5000 have managed to secure tickets at the front of the away section. Middlesbrough score. They cheer. Fighting follows. Stewards and police eject someone. This happens after every goal. These stewards, exaggeratedly polite but finicky, are not a brains trust and they'd rather watch the match than bother with any of this actual stewarding nonsense.

Tomorrow, Robson will say this was his team's best performance of the season, but the crowd are more appreciative than rapturous. The second half continues in much the same vein. Trevor Sinclair, otherwise anonymous, hits the bar with a rasping free kick, the only chance Rangers create, hardly surprising with only Mike Sheron up front and winger Steve Slade unused on the bench.

Soon the loudest noise is from the away corner, next to the highly visible police control module. 'We want Houston out', alternates with 'We want

Rioch out' in case the assistant manager feels he might like a move up the ladder when Stewart Houston does go. At the death, Middlesbrough's impressive substitute Anthony (note how younger footballers seem not to abbreviate Christian names) Ormerod skips through the defence to make it 3-0. Middlesbrough fans are happy but not delighted and after last season's lunatic optimism I can't blame them. On this showing they'll be playing Newcastle United next year. How the fighting men will drool.

Afterwards, there's no real difficulties for the away support, nor for their team's luxury Scancoach with its gold-plated table lamps; it would be like mugging a granny. What is difficult is getting out of the area. The overwhelming majority of the crowd walk into town. The rain has finally stopped, but its puddles and the fencing have made it impossible to go across the waste ground, so everyone must squash together and waddle. My route takes in a railway junction, a narrow underpass, more stuck traffic and newish council offices. The imagination shown in constructing new stadiums seems to stop as soon as customers leave an expertly crafted car park, at which point they are on their own. No change there then.

I'm cold, soggy and miserable. Darkness here seems, well, darker than other places. It's 5.30, the pubs are filling up already with men who didn't wear jackets in the rain. I spurn the opportunity to buy a terraced house for £19,950 on Maple Street, pull my hood over my ears and get out of town.

36 **Nottingham Forest**

v. Birmingham City
DIVISION ONE

15 November

1-0

'Trevor Francis happens to be a very good friend of mine.'

Dave Bassett

Nottingham, formerly Snot Ena Ham (home of the TISWAS-esque tribe of Snot) has everything. A sense of history which gives it character and depth, well-conceived and executed public utilities, loads of pubs and the feeling that, even now, it's a working city, a city where cigarettes are produced, bicycles built and lace fiddled with inconsequentially. We'll forget – but it's hard to forgive – the scab miners.

In 1979 and 1980, Nottingham Forest won the European Cup. Then, Forest represented the smallest city to produce a winner. Decline followed, caused by a sticky smalltown combination of Brian Clough's eccentricity and complacency; a board of dodderers (although Forest fan Kenneth Clarke was recently offered the chairmanship of the club's holding company for £100,000 a year); some rotten signings (Ian Wallace, Andrea Silenzi) and disastrous sales (Roy Keane, Teddy Sheringham). Forest will not be a major force in British (let's not trouble Europe with this one) football for some time.

However, the turnaround has begun. Dave Bassett is an ideal manager to get a team out of Division One and, as I saw at Huddersfield and Reading, Forest look the best team in this division. Plus they have Pierre Van Hooijdonk.

Restlessness is still the order of the day, despite being second from top with a game in hand. Kevin Campbell hasn't shaken off the boo boys; the team were barracked off the field after beating Stoke City the other week and they lost at Bury last week.

Now come Birmingham, who haven't won since I saw them against Wolverhampton Wanderers. Certainly the Nottingham constabulary are interested in this clash and outside the railway station, there's a huge police presence. Birmingham have brought a multi-racial but violence-orientated pack, numbering around forty, into town. To avoid detection they've walked away from both ground and city centre to a quiet pub around the corner from the castle. The police have simply followed them and waited outside, horses and all. As soon as the Birmingham fans depart, the police leave with them, making sure they don't disturb the shoppers. Forest fans are too dim to notice.

Christmas begins early in Nottingham and this the first thing we (I'm not alone, my friend Peter once more ensures rare human contact) hear is Shakin' Stevens's 'Merry Christmas Everyone'. Our hopes plummet, but Nottingham's pavements are wide, its streets have not succumbed to crime-inducing pedestrianisation and the bustle is as positive as the pubs are full.

We head for The Trip To Jerusalem, 'Well known throughout the world'. Founded in 1189, it's allegedly Britain's oldest pub (How do they know? How do people fall for this tripe?) and allegedly hewn out of rock (I'll give them that one). It's a tourist trap but, 'Merry Christmas Everyone' or not, it's still and mild enough to take drink outside. The Trip To Jerusalem was a staging post for the Crusades, of which our combined knowledge amounts to a mismatch of half-truths and speculation. Questions, questions. How come anyone knew there was a problem all those miles away, communications being what they were? How did the Crusaders know to come to this point to join up? Which way did they go? Across Europe and down? Or through France and over? How exactly did chastity belts work and what were the personal hygiene implications? Was anyone, apart from Richard I, religiously moved by this or did they only go for the money? Most importantly, Saladin might have been great, but he never threatened Dover, so why didn't they wait? We both pledge to buy a book on the Crusades.

While Richard The Lionheart was away, Prince John did play. Nottinghamshire was his powerbase and from here he attempted to usurp his brother's throne. Nottingham's castle, built by William The Conqueror in 1068 close to the city centre, was the hub of all sorts of intrigue. The Trip To Jerusalem (it wasn't called that when it was built, now was it?) lies directly under it.

The castle's working life was far from over when John died in a bog near Newark in 1216. Up on Standard Hill, King Charles I raised the royal flag and started the English Civil War. Nottingham paid heavily for backing the wrong horse and Cromwell's stormtroopers pulled the walls down after the war, just in case. Luddite risings in 1811 and 1812 finished the job off. By his time Nottingham was preparing to back the wrong horse again: canals rather than rail and thus lucrative railway works went to the city's mortal enemies, Derby. So that's why there isn't a train back to London after 7.15 on Saturday evenings. Silly old us. We'd thought it was privatisation.

We walk down Castle Gate where, in 1901, D.H. Lawrence was employed as a junior clerk in a surgical appliances factory, towards the mighty River Trent. To do this we have to go through the newish (early 1980s I reckon) Meadows estate. It's not the wealthiest area, so kids on bikes start to appear. It's primarily white (Asians and blacks are packed off to Radford), this year's bonfire (at least they had one) has already been turned into a nascent rubbish tip, there are two pubs and a church. Football fans, the new middle class, have safety in numbers on match days. Things might be different on other occasions. Then, urban jungle safely conquered, The City Ground sweeps into view.

Walking towards The City Ground across Trent Bridge – the cricket ground is further away, maybe the river bends towards it, I neither know nor care – is one of the most glorious, glad-to-be-alive moments in football. It's of its city in the way newer grounds are not. If the football team is geographically part of the community, then that community is part of the football team. Take Wycombe last week: the ground is so far away that town centre shoppers had no idea there might be a game on. Out of sight, out of mind. This, by any yardstick, is dangerous.

The City Ground been redeveloped beyond recognition since the scorching afternoon in 1978 when Osvaldo Ardiles and Ricardo Villa made their British débuts here for Tottenham against the reigning champions, yet another game which marked a new era for British football. Now, as a police launch sits threateningly on the Trent, Forest might not have a truly outstanding team or sufficient fans to fill their 30,000 seats, but they do have a stadium as fine as any in Europe, in an unrivalled setting.

Alas, they don't have a ticket distribution system to match and, obviously not trusting their turnstile operators – the days of '£5 in your pocket, mate, I'll jump over' are sadly long gone – everyone has to queue at four ticket office windows, as opposed to dozens of turnstiles. No wonder the fans are rebelling, the poor sods have to turn up forty-five minutes before kickoff to guarantee seeing the first ten minutes. And those hard-queued-for tickets are £20 each. That's why there won't be many sell-outs this season and why there's dissent in the air.

Inside, the surroundings are sepulchral, the pies fair, the silence deafening and from the misnamed Executive Stand, we can see the stands of the cricket ground, which has only slightly more empty seats. I'm confused, though. It's a derby game, but supporter commitment is more akin to a pre-season friendly. Birmingham fans, despite their hard little bunch, have obviously given up for the season and there can't be more than 500 of them scattered around the bottom tier of the away end. That's fewer than they took to less-than-glamorous Stockport on that Friday evening in August. Trevor Francis might be needing to expand his television punditry empire quite soon and be free to say what he really thinks of Paul Peschisolido, husband of his boss Karren Brady.

If the setting is slightly surreal, the game is more so. Forest are having a collective off-day and Birmingham, playing without the dropped Steve Bruce and Kevin Francis, haven't the nous to take advantage of some pinball defending. Even Van Hooijdonk isn't firing properly. Both sides pussyfoot, too perplexed to create genuine chances. Midway through the first half, Campbell deceives Bruce's replacement, ex-Forest reserve Darren Wassall, and pokes the ball past City's Ian Bennett. Suitably enough for this game, it takes an eternity to bobble over the line.

Forest begin the second half like they mean business, albeit a small grocery business in Worksop, and create a few half-chances. Then they go to sleep. It's a deep, dreamless sleep and Birmingham, hardly bright and breezy themselves, finally cotton on that they might sneak a point. Prompted by the ever-impressive Chris Marsden, their tactic is to go wide and slip over low crosses. This creates one golden chance, but second-half substitute Tony Cottee misses the open goal. They get frustrated: Martin Grainger is booked for an X-certificate challenge on the improving Steve Stone, the players have a fight and Grainger is substituted immediately and, belly still stoked by unknown fires, makes his feelings plain to Francis, not one to forget or forgive. An unhappy club never gets the luck and when Michael Johnson scores, it's mysteriously disallowed.

With one minute to go and one goal down, Birmingham's Martin O'Connor finds himself in acres of space with most of his team-mates in positions to receive the ball. He hoofs it out of play and the Forest fans make the most noise of their afternoon, until they hear that former manager Frank Clark's Manchester City have manufactured a late equaliser at promotion rivals Sheffield United. In a weird way, it's been an absorbing but unsatisfactory game, one so unfocused it's been impossible to plot, but Forest haven't deserved to win and Birmingham haven't deserved to sneak a point.

Over the Tannoy, two minutes after the final whistle, a very serious man indeed barks, 'Stewards, stand down when your area is clear'. He's too late. Crowd and stewards have already gone. Standing terraces, your time is now, your place is here.

37 Chester City

v. Peterborough United
DIVISION THREE

18 November

0-0

'Peterborough come here on top of the league and are sure to present the strongest test to ourselves so far this season.'

Kevin Ratcliffe

Should be a goal feast tonight. Free-scoring, table-topping Peterborough United. Fairly free-scoring, near the top of Division Three Chester City. Jimmy Quinn, Martin Carruthers and Gary 'Psycho' Bennett, the division's three leading scorers.

I'm cheered by this prospect as I try to succumb to Chester's charms. It's an unpleasant place. It's got walls. Big deal. It's too quiet for my liking, a city dedicated to that shining, camera-snappy cash crop, the tourist, rather than Chester's 120,000 actual inhabitants. Chester hasn't prostituted itself to all the six million who arrive each year, only the rich ones fished in by advertisements in the Hamptons edition of *Harpers & Queens*, the ones who stay at the five-star Grosvenor or shop at Laura Ashley, Gieves & Hawkes, Muff's ('The Sausage Specialists!') or Masai Mara, a shop reflecting the fine craftsmanship of the Masai tribe, who have minimal-at-best representation in Chester. Scouse over-spill, Chester's predominant tribe, must love that emporium. How peculiar that it's empty this November Tuesday afternoon.

There's a planning order in force which means, say, Burger King, has to blend in with Chester's faux-medieval fetish, one which presumably isn't extended to sewage collection. The results are twee and quaint for passing wobbly-buttocked Chicagoans in checked slacks, but impractical for lard-arsed Cestrians in leggings.

Chester does have history. The Romans turned up in AD79, built a huge harbour where the Roodee racecourse is now and when they departed in 380, left behind some rubble which is displayed hither and thither. By 1645, when Charles I fled over the River Dee fairly hotly pursued by Roundheads, Chester's status as a major port had withered as the Dee had silted up. By the time the future Edward VII opened the impressive town hall in 1868, a wealth-courting Chester guidebook had been available for eighty years.

As darkness takes over, shop assistants – still the highest form of human life, lest we forget – pour forth and disappear. Not into pubs where trade is abysmal (locals' revenge for catering to tourists when the going is good), or the ubiquitous tea shops deliberately placed out of natives' price range, but home to suburbs which must be more welcoming, even if there's a chance of being stabbed to death on their own doorstep as Alan Gillam, twenty-two, was yesterday in Blacon. It's either that or the squaddies from Dale Camp nearby, who can't be beaten, so they might as well be joined. The display at the local Army office shows a black soldier in Your Country Needs You pose and promises with only the merest hint of disingenuity, 'good rates of pay, world-wide travel, permanent jobs, good career prospect'. The Army must be full of boys from Chester.

Underneath Eastgate Clock, 'The most photographed timepiece in the world after Big Ben' allegedly, there are plenty of tramps on the cobbled streets and crusties with dogs on strings, but nothing in the way of ordinary people, because Chester is closed, the pedestrianisation is the work of madmen and the first tourists won't come until the week before Easter. This, and having Gyles Brandreth as your MP until the last General Election, is what happens when you don't look after your own.

It's a disturbing walk to the ground, past the canal where little Kayleigh Ward was abducted, close to where she was put to an unthinkable death and left by the Dee around the corner. There used to be a small memorial to her and some flowers, but there's nothing now. There are statues in the city centre, there will never be one of Kayleigh Ward. Towns need to collectively forget these things, the tourist board is there to make sure they do. I shudder, mutter a quick prayer for the little girl and press on. Britain 1997. Is, was and ever will be.

Sometimes I could be on a tour of industrial estates. The Deva (Roman name for Chester. Ugh. Tacky) Stadium, as ever with new stadia, lies literally on the edge of the city, at the end of Bumpers Lane, so far away that the Welsh border runs through it. Wales, excellently, is fenced off. All very nice, but I'm sick of Office World (here on the site of the old ground, Sealand Road, and explanation for City's nickname change from Seals to the Blues, which must have taken many great minds many great lunches to plump upon. I suggest The Chests), of municipal tips, of Kwik-Fit, of MFI, of Homefuckingbase, of Halfords and of streets that nobody would dream of walking upon in normal circumstances. The message is unsubtle: Chester City are an embarrassment to Chester city and it's nothing to do with those club-wielding Swansea fans who wandered through the shopping areas before and after last year's play-offs.

Funnier and more numerous away fans than Peterborough's eighty or so often sing at the Chester fans, 'Lego. Your ground's built out of Lego'. They have a point and there must have been a huge breeze-block shortage on Deeside when the Deva went up in the early 90s, a move so badly planned that the team had to play at Macclesfield in the interim. If Millwall's New Den is a victim of overambition, The Deva Stadium, with its 6000 capacity and twelve-step terrace has the opposite problem. The club, like its stadium, is on a road to nowhere. According to the programme, they have one director and seemingly no chairman.

As with all the new grounds, there is a huge car park, in this case more than large enough to accommodate all those who wish to attend. I stand on that twelve-step North Stand terrace, surrounded by bitter Wrexham baiters. They call their rivals and forthcoming FA Cup opponents The Goats for reasons lost in history. It makes me laugh anyway, certainly more than the pies, grumpily served and with stomach stretching heavy pastry. The sign at the counter declares 'enjoy the match and we do not serve hot dogs'. OK then.

Highly toned athlete that he is, Peterborough's Steve Castle has managed to hurt himself in the warm up and doesn't make the kickoff, missing the teams entering the arena to Europe's 'The Final Countdown'. 'We're heading to Venus,' oh yes. Peterborough seem distracted by the reshuffle and in the first minute, they let Bennett sprint through to beat Mark Tyler in the Peterborough goal. It hits the bottom of Tyler's left-hand post and rolls for a goal kick.

The Scouse overspill alongside me – no tourists here – see victory ahead, but it's not to be. Peterborough, fast, gritty and skilful, gird their loins and push forward. Chester's lanky centre half Julian Alsford is caught out time and time again by Carruthers, who in turn is denied by goalkeeper Wayne Brown who goes on to have the game of his life. When not exciting themselves with 'Gary Bennett, you're a wanker' (he's not a former player, just hated by all), Peterborough fans leap up thinking they've scored every ten minutes or so, but there is always Brown to be beaten and he never is. Understandably, little Ronnie Sinclair, who wore Chester's Number 1 shirt until he was sent off last month, has already asked for a transfer.

This is the highest standard Division Three match I've seen this season. Both teams play a mean offside trap, but both have the guile and pacey forwards to spring them. Alongside the skill, there's commitment. Carruthers has a tussle with a less than helpful ball-boy, but Bennett, recently forced to make an out of court settlement to Ian Knight, whose career virtually ended after a leg-shattering tackle, is physically uncompromising. Chester re-re-signed this 34-year-old at the start of the season from Wrexham, where, since his second term at Chester, he'd scored at the Deva and kissed his Goats shirt in front of the twelve-step terrace. He's been forgiven already.

By half-time, it's clear the drummer who's making a nuisance of himself on the twelve-step cannot inspire the Chester fans to anything other than anti-Wrexham fare. Anyway, everyone is absorbed by the game and complimentary about their team, albeit in a grudging 'Even Rod Thomas doesn't look that hopeless tonight' way. They are less appreciative of a bizarre scheme whereby season ticket holders of other clubs can get into the stadium free on match days. Ideally, this would exclude fans of the away team for the match in question. Tonight, a Southend fan – whose team are at Bournemouth tonight – is paraded to vociferous, unironic jeers. 'Daft cunt,' shouts a bloke behind me, who spent the first half planning trips to Everton. 'What the fuck does he want to come here for?'

I know it's going to finish goalless when, midway through the second half, traumatised Alsford leaves the pitch for ten minutes in order to have head stitches and Peterborough don't press home their advantage. They've run out of ideas and their normally substitute-crazy manager Barry Fry doesn't use one. The last portion of the game is Chester's. Substitute Rod McDonald seems well placed to score, being on the edge of the six-yard-box with only Tyler to beat, but he manages to knock the ball out for a throw-in. On ninety minutes, Chris Priest rattles the bar with a fierce drive and that's that. Goalless but excellent. Fine by me.

The fans don't wait to applaud the players off as they should. Instead, ignoring the fat but likeable bloke shouting 'Swansea anyone?' trying to drum up patrons for the away match on Saturday, they sprint for their vehicles as the car park is turned into Le Mans. A special Le Mans where on the first bend there is only room for one car to pass through.

Barry Fry doesn't let his players linger at the players' bar. They're on their mightily crowded Dunn-Line coach within forty-five minutes of Priest hitting Tyler's bar. Fry has a treat for them, a fry up in fact. The Dunn-Line stops at Sealand Fish'n'Chips takeaway, Fry leaps out and, first in the queue, buys his players an evening meal. Such are the realities of life in Division Three, even at its summit. I can smell the coach thirty miles away.

38 **Newcastle United**

v. Southampton
PREMIER LEAGUE

22 November

2-1

'I have nothing but praise for the way our players have fought for the Newcastle cause, often in very difficult circumstances.'

Kenny Dalglish

Occasionally, great moments come absolutely free – financially, emotionally and medically. When it does happen, my eyes mist over and I start thinking of home, like young Irish men in English bars. Then gently, my tight, wrenched stomach muscles unfurl themselves and I bask in the lambent glow of that which feels right. That's how I feel walking across Tyne Bridge. It may be creepy imitating fictional television characters, but when Geordie Peacock did the same thing at the close of *Our Friends In The North* to Oasis's 'Don't Look Back In Anger', it was time to cry and not just because he was heading for Gateshead. Anyway, who couldn't see Newcastle and not walk across Tyne Bridge?

It's green. I'd no idea, a sort of off-khaki and it works. The bridge is – and this is exactly the right word – beautiful. Wonderfully, apart from a few hundred passing cars, I have the entire structure to myself. If I lived here (mmm, perhaps), I'd cross this bridge every single day to nurture my soul a little. I know that like everyone else here except the loathsome 'Richy' and 'Stona', I'd never graffiti this gorgeous structure.

The Tyne is so still and the November sun so bright that, higher than seagulls, I can see the bridge's reflection below me, as I linger over the plaque explaining that George V opened it in 1928 and look east and south towards Gateshead and Paul Gascoigne's manor, Dunstan.

Walking back along the bridge into Newcastle, past another plaque commemorating the architect, R. Burns Dick, who, please God, died a happy man, I look up and see the symbol of Tyneside towering over me like a giant womb. I feel so small, so comforted, so blessed to be here. From a Dunstan hill little Gascoigne could have looked past Tyne Bridge and into Newcastle itself. If so he'd have seen the football ground – not St Nicholas's Cathedral or the quayside they're trying to redevelop – dominating the skyline, a modern-day castle keeping watch over the city. For the young Gascoigne, the five miles from Dunstan to St James' must have seemed as unbridgeable as the Tyne itself once was. Or maybe he never noticed.

St James' Park lies past where the council may allow Damien Hirst to erect a huge DNA helix sculpture underneath the bridge, between the city centre and the third-world tower blocks on Newcastle's outskirts. It's the only building that counts in this strange, oddly coloured, other-worldly city. I stand on Tyne Bridge gazing at the ground and for this moment it's as a million exiled, over-sentimental Geordies claim: there's no place like Newcastle. The hairs on the back of my neck stand up so rigidly I start looking for a comb.

Newcastle has changed, even since *Our Friends in the North*. Newcastle Brown Ale is for the old, for what few tourists drift through and for the naff. It will make a comeback, I'll bet my life on it, unless the brewery goes bankrupt first. More crucially, the football team, Newcastle's barometer of self-esteem since they both won the Football League and, in what was to become their way, lost the FA Cup Final in 1905.

Opposite the lovely station and the Royal Station Hotel where Kurt Cobain once stayed (bet they don't mention that at reception), the pubs are jammed with United fans, the self-styled Toon Army, who are not all they seem. Newcastle is a multi-ethnic city with massive Chinese and Indian communities, not information the all-white city centre proudly surrenders. Thus, even when Newcastle were fielding black players long before Andy Cole, players like Tony Cunningham and Howard Gayle, the jolly old Toon Army were throwing bananas at opposition black players. And that was before they started chanting. Greatest fans in the land, they say.

The Toon Army also liked to go out on manoeuvres, extending a special welcome to away supporters who ventured into this harsh land. Hence pitch invasions against Sunderland (and subsequent banning of away fans from last season's derbys, a ban chiefly broken by Toon Army soldiers desperate for one last trip to Roker Park), the petrol bombs against West Ham United and carnages against Chelsea, Leeds United and Manchester United. It's calmed down now and indeed there are isolated Southampton fans walking the streets unmolested today and away supporters aren't kept in for a further ninety minutes after the match. Anyway – and this is a feature of all-seater, all-season-ticket stadiums – anyone found causing trouble might have their season ticket taken away. All the same, as the fairly pacifist Leeds United fanzine, *Square Ball*, still warns/entices its readers, 'If you don't like violence, then don't go to Newcastle'.

That United are a city-centre club, and that they plan to increase the capacity of St James' Park, links them into the psyche of the city itself. That the decision to stay isn't one of choice is neither here not there. There's no opposition in Newcastle to divide the loyalty or passion and Sunderland don't really count, being the halfwit children down the road. A poster in shops 'Support the Toon, it's your duty' says everything in one sentimental, aggressive, blackmailing but community-minded phrase. This club aren't called Newcastle United for nothing. Black and white stripes, cunningly modelled this season on the design Newcastle wore when they won the Fairs Cup in 1969, are a uniform. Now it's colder, Newcastle fans wear them over their normal clothes. For a laugh, the club put the new design on sale at midnight, although not at all of the nine club shops. The queues stretched for miles. How far can these people be pushed? It's love, to be sure, but it's mightily claustrophobic.

The ground itself has been done up a treat. As Newcastle fans snake up the hill in appropriately Biblical fashion, sacrosanct St James' Park seems to grow, until they reach it, suddenly a world away from the city, 500 yards back down Gallowgate hill. Here, everything is new, smells of money and of Newcastle United being known throughout Europe. That's what the residents of Newcastle take their hubristic civic pride in, although *vis-à-vis* a club where their own lottery winner is introduced by the silly Tannoy man as 'one of oor oon', there isn't much choice.

Inside, it might have been nice if Newcastle had spent a few bob on their catering operation which is sub Division Three standard. My cheeseburger is a) cold, b) virtually raw and c) utterly, utterly disgusting. Taking it back would seem somehow disloyal. Fans don't complain here. They don't go for the burgers much, either.

It's a special day of sorts. Sir John Hall spent money on St James' Park, on Kevin Keegan, on Alan Shearer and saw the club go from near relegation to the old Division Three to the European Cup, albeit by the farcical route which means finishing second is fine now. Today is his last game before he 'steps down' as chairman, whatever that proves to mean. He's given a eulogy so rousing that I'm surprised when a very much alive tycoon emerges to take his bows, to respectful applause rather than adoration. Now is it just me, or hasn't his dream quite worked out for this fascinating man who must know many, many people's secrets and probably has a few of his own?

The Keegan era of flamboyance, style, national attention, grand follies like Asprilla and almost winning the Premiership has been replaced by Kenny Dalglish's more taciturn ways, of never looking like winning the Premiership, of little follies like Ian Rush, Des Hamilton and Paul Dalglish, Kenny's son, a signing hidden from the local press. Newcastle United are looking inwards again, as if Mary Robinson had been replaced by Kim Jong Il. This can't quite have been what Sir John had in mind right here, right now.

Every seat is taken and it does feel like a privilege to be here somehow, a privilege more keenly felt by those who cannot be with us – and like at

Middlesbrough you can't tout yourself in – than those who are, undoubtedly an élite around this city. A working class generation are growing up without ever having seen a match here. Exactly what it is that's been sown, will be reaped. It's just that nobody's quite sure about anything any more.

The Toon Army were less of an élite as recently as 1991 when only 10,004 turned up to see a 2-2 draw with Oxford United. Seems like loyalty and depth of passion are relative. Even Watford rarely went so low in the old Division Two.

Whatever mood Sir John was in surely blackened after five minutes. Baldy Temuri Ketsbaia had nearly scored for the home team when Southampton's Kevin Davies waltzed through a defence comprised entirely of less agile Arthur Mullards and scored a fine individual goal. The Southampton corner goes wild with shock and delight.

The home support take a different view. Many years ago, the Gallowgate end would have roared their team on after an early setback. Now they sit back and snipe at Philippe Albert and Jon Dahl Tomasson, whilst assuming victory anyway. It's like Manchester United without the trophies. Without any trophy, in fact.

Newcastle pummel Paul Jones's goal for the remainder of the half. Jones saves well from John Barnes's header and when the ball spins behind him, the warrior that is Francis Benali is there to make the first of two goal-line clearances. This is played out against a backdrop of black and white striped quiet. They are roused twice. Once to appeal for a ludicrous handball against Kenneth Monkou and, for the second time when Tomasson is clean through and is pulled over by Claus Lundekvam. They scream for the Norwegian to be sent off. A weaker referee than Dermot Gallagher would have acceded. That's the sum total of the fans' efforts.

Meanwhile, Southampton fans squeak their 'When The Saints Go Marching In' continually. A 'You're supposed to be at home', might be silly but it hits home and the Newcastle fans in the dark upper recesses behind each goal try to get a Blaydon Races going with minimal success. The Greatest Fans In Football™ have gotten flabby sitting in those pricey seats. Or they're not the same people with the same traditions.

The pressure is so great that Southampton must buckle eventually and they do after the restart when the outstanding Keith Gillespie – does he bet on himself to score the first goal? – hits the post and wily Barnes playing up front with Tomasson pops in the rebound. Now, the noise unfolds, as if there's a volume control switch. In a wholly covered ground the din is awesome, but the players have still done it on their own. There are a few of the Geordie dispossessed who've acquired tickets for the Southampton corner, too. They're not ejected and the lax security means any Newcastle fan can walk right into the away corner. None dare: season ticket withdrawal fear. Barnes scores again, but it's harshly disallowed. The crowd become unbearably agitated. Spoilt brats.

Finally Barnes heads what proves to be the winner. The noise, finally, is as I hoped it might be. It soon dies down once more when Southampton start to regroup. David Hirst nearly fires a spectacular past Neil 'Shaka' Hislop, but the real chance – and teams like Southampton always create one real chance when they're a goal behind – falls to young substitute Steve Basham when Albert miskicks. He lobs it past Hislop and past the post. Poor Basham looks so distraught that Carlton Palmer, not necessarily the most compassionate man to walk this earth, is moved to cuddle him in sympathy.

That's it. Newcastle fans trot off happily, laughing at Alessandro Pistone's Ken Dodd-esque hair, having witnessed what they always knew would happen. The Southampton fans are let out straight away, but held under police guard outside before being frogmarched to their coaches. This means the Newcastle fans can walk past them: there's no trouble, the wall of police and fear of season ticket confiscation see to that, but there's much ill-natured banter. 'Thanks for the three points,' smiles one bald Geordie. 'Yokel cunts.' The Southampton fans, weight of numbers dictating they're not in a position to reply as they might wish, stand there singing 'When The Saints Go Marching In' and hold their heads as high as yokels can.

Further outside, Southampton have wisely flown up and will fly straight back, which means only a temporary coach from our old friends at Moordale. They leave just after five, all – bar David Hirst – signing autographs for the dozen or so anoraks who've gathered outside to wait, not only for Southampton's players, but Newcastle's too. Odd that, I thought hundreds would try to glimpse their heroes.

As the lights of Southampton's police escort disappear I go back into town, past the statue of Jackie Milburn – not a patch on the Billy Wright one outside Wolverhampton – and go, not to Bigg Market and the old pubs and curry houses or to the quayside with its restaurants and new pubs, but for one last look at the Tyne Bridge. It's lit up now, its greenness shimmering across the still glass-like Tyne. I sigh like a lovesick fool and go home.

39 **Chelsea**

v. Everton
PREMIER LEAGUE
26 November

2-0

'I'm not complaining.'

Ruud Gullit

Two laws, those of averages and geography, dictate that of ninety-two football clubs, there will be one that is genuinely fashionable, that has real glamour. Times will move on and surely football cannot maintain its ultrafashionability, but there will still be Chelsea.

In Britain, glamour itself was invented one day in the 60s. George Best was the first pop star footballer, but he was in the same team as Bobby Charlton, who may still not be aware of pop music, and Bill Foulkes, one of life's bricklayers. And Best plied his trade in South Manchester. Many of that team needed London flats.

Chelsea were different. Before the 60s, Chelsea itself had flirted with the rarefied set. It was mentioned in the *Doomsday Book* and the village was something of a chic Londoner's (Pepys no less) Sunday picnic destination before being consumed into the city during Victorian expansion.

The football club were usually Division One, but never troubled anyone unduly, apart from a Championship in 1954–55. In the 60s, geography placed them parallel with King's Road. In Brian Mears they had a chairman who could mix it with Michael Caine and anyone called Attenborough. Mears saw which way the wind was briefly blowing. Swinging London needed a team and, with Raquel Welch seated in the dilapidated old East Stand, unschooled in the finer points of football but looking like a million dollars, Mears, to coin a Chelsea-type phrase, gave it one.

Chelsea's Jimmy Greaves, Peter Osgood, George Graham, Ian Hutchinson, Tommy Baldwin, Marvin (a footballer called Marvin, times were a-changin') Hinton and David Webb were not teetotallers and thrived upon, without actually understanding, the fact that being a footballer is impossibly glamorous, the key to many doors, few of which have anything to do with kicking a bag of wind around.

When that team broke up, the new East Stand nearly bankrupted the club, the far right took over the supporters' base and Ken Bates took over the club. Chelsea's aura was dimmed but never extinguished. All they needed was money and A Man. The money came through Bates, though nobody quite knows exactly how. Chelsea Village, which seems to own the club is thirty-three per cent owned by the Cecil Lee trust and there the trail goes cold. After Glenn Hoddle left for England, The Man turned out to have dreadlocks, dodgy knees and a carefully contrived laid-back countenance. Devilishly sexy, an acquaintance of Nelson Mandela and a man who takes as much out of London as he put in, Ruud Gullit was made for Chelsea. A foreign legion later, the glamour was back and with it the crowds.

The only losers here, apart from those who can't get tickets, are the moneyed locals. The residents in discreet mews houses where Gabhan O'Keeffe does teardowns for £1 million or more and where net curtains are a *faux pas*, suffer 31,000 invaders walking past their homes, planning burglaries (I am anyway), double parking, shouting, urinating against restaurant walls in full view of the diners, and patronising burger stalls. And on non match days, Stamford Bridge is a building site as both the West Stand and Bates's 140-room hotel (incorporating Europe's largest health club) dream slowly rise over Brompton Cemetery, above which, on the southern side, Leonard Rossiter lived.

At least the short walk from Fulham Broadway underground to Stamford Bridge isn't a battlefield these days. In the 70s and 80s away fans would sneak to their entrance. If there was a queue they were picked off by the home supporters. If not, they'd sprint into the ground laughing with relief. Only to find that to get to their section, they had to walk behind a pen of Chelsea fans. After games, West London stopped as the visitors were evacuated like hostage Serbs fleeing Croatia. The police had the bright idea of escorting away fans to the underground and giving them a special train bound only for the appropriate main line station. Sadly, the police did not board the trains, so when they pulled into, say, Paddington, Chelsea fans would be there waiting, having had an hour's start while the streets outside the ground were cleared. Perhaps the locals are happier now.

There are still undertows of aggression, but diluted by the new breed of Chelsea supporter, making for an uneasy half-yuppie, half-scum arrangement, linked only by their carrying mobile telephones and their beloved 'Chelss'. From the ground I pick my way through the burger stalls and tat floggers that unrestricted commerce brings. Soon, I'm on King's Road. At the Chelsea end, it's exclusively exclusive antique shops which do not need to display their prices, not that Chelsea fans are interested as the stadium sucks them in via pubs it's still warm enough to drink outside of. Glamour by association, that's Chelsea's calling card. King's Road is merely a bunch of antique shops, but it doesn't matter, perception is everything.

'Take care, mate, enjoy the game.' Even Chelsea's programme sellers are friendly nowadays, although he has taken £2.50 off me, so he ought to be. I'm starting to feel claustrophobic at Premiership grounds now, there are simply too many people. That Stamford Bridge is unfinished and, with bars called Tambling's, Dixon's and Drake's, a haven for the corporate, only makes it worse. I don't visit the Chelsea megastore and thus eschew the opportunity to purchase a CFC moped for £2500 or mountain bike for £199. Inside the ground complex there are cars coming at me from all angles and nobody seems to be going in my direction. This might be the big time, but I'm a permanently startled rabbit.

In manner most unmanly I edge to the West Stand. 'Where the glamour stops' could be its marketing slogan. Chelsea's new found popularity is such that it's the only area where I could buy a ticket to this sell-out. It is currently under construction. This means uncovered and unfinished. This means that the toilets resemble the Somme if the Somme had been watered beforehand and this means the catering is primitive, despite distinctly futuristic prices. Worse, said catering is dispensed from stalls identical to those found outside. I wish Bates could have shared my burger.

In fairness, the man at the ticket office did say my view would be poor and 'obstructed view' is printed on my £16 ticket. I'm behind one of the temporary floodlights and I'll miss whole tracts of the game, but I can see both goals. There are people with worse seats than me, but the desperation to see – and be seen at – new Chelsea means that tonight's late purchasers are not the usually disorganised rabble who can't get their act together. They are couples. I'm sat between two women, one moustachioed and one blonde, pointy chinned and obviously great in bed. I smile my most pleasant smile twice. I'm ignored twice. They're typical of the new Chelsea woman though. Hard-boiled but fairly well-off and aware that seeing Chelsea gives them a certain cachet, especially when none of their colleagues can spy them here, getting rained upon, squashed against people like me, unable to see half the pitch, unquestionably second class customers.

There is another complicating factor and he will affect my entertainment as much as the pylon. He's a willowy skinhead with a leather jacket and a packet of Benson & Hedges. As I take my seat, he is in the row behind me singing to himself in slurry, deep throated Cockney. 'In your Northern slums,' he rasps at nobody in particular, getting most of the words wrong, before tailing off into the night. He is a throwback to the hooligan years, but where they used to hunt in their hundreds, now he is alone and pathos-ridden.

This game is crucial to both sides. Everton, who arrived in their specially liveried, specially built Eavesway coach, bottom of the Premiership, desperately need points to save Howard Kendall's job. They haven't won an away Premiership game for eleven months. For Chelsea, this is a game in hand and if they win they'll be third, above Arsenal and London's top team, further proof they can mount a sustained title challenge. Everton parade new signing, Mitch Ward from Sheffield United, Kendall's old club, while Chelsea feel they can afford to leave Mark Hughes (whose wife, pictured in the £2.50 programme, looks like Courteney Cox and were I he, I wouldn't dare let her live alone in a big house in Cheshire while I was in London) on the bench.

Across the pitch, Everton have sold out their ticket allocation too and they're making a lot of noise in the way that teams at the bottom of the league often do. My skinhead friend cannot abide this. He's up on his feet whenever they start. 'Shaaaaat up, you Northern cunts,' he shrieks. 'Cunts, cunts, cunts,' he continues for good measure in case the point was missed. He is the most sweary man in the world. Because nobody is going to tell him to shaaaaat up, he can therefore dominate my area. Nobody can move either because there are no spare seats, enhancing further my all-pervading suffocation.

Sweary Skin is king and his power is absolute. 'Come on Chelss,' he barks. 'We can beat these Northern cunts.' Around him, women – boyfriends intimidated into silence, penises the size of fruit gums – giggle a little. It's a glimpse of a world they can detail at work tomorrow. They've never heard that word spoken quite so often, quite so naturally and quite so loud. Then again, a Cunt Convention, dedicated solely to preserving and extending the use of the word 'cunt', couldn't say it quite so much.

What I see of the match isn't inspiring. Chelsea, with Zola and Vialli struggling, don't have their customary *joie de vivre* and Everton, often with everyone except for Duncan Ferguson behind the ball – although it's him who heads Zola's free kick off the line – are intent only on securing a confidence building 0-0.

Sweary Skin has a challenger, but not on the sweariness front: a drunken oaf of Dudley Moore-esque stature and intonation, a latecomer to the row in front of me. He proceeds to light a joint and stands up to make anti-Scouse remarks. The first one, 'They've sold out their allocation. It must be Giro payday,' draws a chuckle and a 'Nice one, mate' from Sweary Skin. When, however, Dudley Moore does not stop after his triumph, Sweary Skin is bellowing under his breath 'Shaaaaat up cunt,' and trying to start his own chants: 'Fuck 'em all, fuck 'em all, Tottenham, West Ham, Liverpool. We are the Chelsea and we are the best. We are the Chelsea so fuck all the rest,' but everyone is too scared to join in, especially Dudley Moore.

Stamford Bridge is tense tonight. New Chelsea aren't used to stumbling against inferior opposition and the fans have lost the knack of singing their team to a result. Even if Sweary Skin wasn't ruining their lives, the women around me wouldn't be chanting. And their emasculated boyfriends? Well, they're too self-conscious to sing 'Fuck 'em all, fuck 'em all' in front of their partners. Sometimes, the only sound is the whoosh of seats tipping up whenever there's an attack and we all must stand and crane necks. When the half-time whistle goes, it's the Everton fans who're more encouraged. Sweary Skin is apoplectic and lets out a wail Banshees would find spine-chilling, before tailing off into primordial muttering. 'They're cunts, they're cunts,' he says to himself, quietly now. I find this muttering more scary.

The second half is as frustrating as the first. Oh and it's raining, but mercifully my jacket has a hood, so I don't care one iota. Ferguson does force Chelsea's part-palindromic Ed De Goey, a man with the bearing of a 19th-century opium dispenser, into a fingertip save and then appears to hit the post. Gullit takes off Vialli, who runs straight down the tunnel without a glance back, and brings on lanky Norwegian Tore Andre Flo and Chelsea become more direct.

With ten minutes to go, Sweary Skin, temporarily silenced, raises himself for one last rally. 'In your Northern slums' has become 'In your Liverpool slums' but he still fluffs his lines. He's in full flow when Roberto Di Matteo, the Swiss-born naturalised Italian, outpaces Ward, who promptly upends him. Dennis Wise whips the penalty past Neville Southall, who the programme calls 'bin man'. Ha ha. No, really, ha ha.

Everton at last flood forward, but they have nobody alongside Ferguson. It's already too late when, in the last minute the excellent Slaven Bilic fouls Flo, for a less clear penalty than the first. A distraught Croatian is sent off. I think Sweary Skin might have actually come. Whatever, his feelings are surely more orgasmic than anything felt by his girlfriend recently. Obviously I don't know this, but I do know I'm right.

'Bye bye, ya cunt,' he screams at Bilic, whom the Everton fans rightly applaud. 2-0. Everton might feel hard done by, but that is the way of the football world. As they file out, Chelsea fans know their team has played poorly, apart from Sweary Skin who sits alone in his seat oblivious to the rain, shouting that 'we' are the 'greatest team the world has ever seen'. Then he stops, rises and notices me watching him with what I hope is friendly demeanour. He shrugs his shoulders, puts a hand on my shoulders and says, 'Don't worry, mate, it's all part of the fun of the fair'. I could worship him.

40 **Southampton**

v. Sheffield Wednesday
PREMIER LEAGUE
29 November

2-3

> **'We need to be mentally tougher. There's still a lack of concentration at vital stages.'**

Dave Jones

It's nearly pantomime season. This year, for £100,000 over six weeks, the real Dudley Moore was meant to be appearing at Southampton's Mayflower (the real *Mayflower* set sail from here, as, seemingly, it did from several other places) Theatre as Buttons in *Cinderella*. Then he needed a heart bypass and the little fellow had to pull out. Now they have Brian Conley, whoever he may be. That's the sort of place Southampton is: big aspirations, but deep down it's a village.

Its centre has edged north since the 12th century, when it was a walled village on three sides facing the sea, or The Solent at least, which is nearly the sea. It was a major port by the second half of the 15th century, trading with Italians. Later, it was behind only Liverpool and Bristol as a slave port. Long before the QE2 found a berth here and was seen off every time by a top ranking military band, the only southern port to have two high tides a day was packing slave ships off to America on exactly the same route. I search for a monument, any non-cursory acknowledgement. I search in vain.

Drawn like a water diviner to the sea, I head down Above Bar, through the new centre, rebuilt after the Nazis bombed the last one instead of the docks, to the old village down Lower High Street, where there's an archaeological dig with a peephole for the curious. I move on, there's nothing to see.

The quayside has been renovated. Partly a ferry terminal for the Isle Of Wight, it's deserted this morning except for two separate pairs of Southampton fans eating fish'n'chips inside their cars. In summer it's a wanker magnet with ample car parking, large pubs selling bottled beer or cocktails, plus the chance to drink them by water. Even now, there's the skidmarks of recent joyriding.

I go to the end of the quay. It doesn't feel like the end of the country, just like Southampton doesn't feel like a port despite its dock cranes, the navy construction yard and the passing ferries. Maybe it's because the Solent is really a large river.

I sit down and watch the traffic. I'm overwhelmed, always have been, by working non-passenger ships. There's a container ship, *Churruca*, passing by. I can't see a flag, but I can see seamen doing their business. Indeed, were I not seasick whenever I have a bath, I'd envy them. Where can they be going? What are they carrying? Where are they from? Do they have a girl in every port? Or, like whenever an American navy ship lands in Southampton or Portsmouth, do they invade the red light area? In Southampton's case it's Derby Road in inner city St Mary's, where the graffiti screams 'Gay Rights Now' (it's a student area) or is in Hindi (it's Sikh territory, too) and where the council are trying yet another traffic scheme to keep kerb crawlers out.

The warm sea breeze isn't a wind and I'm unlikely to be disturbed, possibly ever over the next fifty-two matches. I luxuriate in deep peace as *Churruca* shrinks towards the yellow horizon. What do I think of? Nothing, not a thing, that's why I feel so at one. There's nothing in my head. I can hear the seagulls, my empty mind sloshing in time with the water and, after fifteen minutes, I can feel the sliver of dribble running down my chin. Time to go, but that's how I'd like to die: sitting on a cold wooden seat staring out to sea, watching container vessels fading away with my life force.

My life force is drained by the climb up to The Dell, through pale Christmas shoppers going about their business with such ferocity baby Jesus himself would have been trading punches with little old ladies. There are fairground rides along Above Bar, sinisterly all playing 'Mary's Boy Child', the Harry Belafonte version.

The Dell lies north, close to where Benny Hill had his milk round. Southampton want to leave this place with its financially crippling 15,000 capacity for a field in Stoneham, near some motorways but little else. The council are less than helpful. The Dell is hemmed in by roads and houses, so expansion is out of the question. Southampton Independent Supporters Association are holding a Rally For The Stadium in a fortnight, 'with the express purpose of demonstrating to the Planning Association the strength of feeling and the unity of ALL Saints fans'. Sounds like a great way to spend a Sunday afternoon, but my bath needs polishing.

There are other factors too. Southampton, although they cannot admit it, are a small club. Before all-seating ruined The Dell, its capacity was an un-Maracana-like 21,900 and only in the most extreme circumstances would they sell it out. Inside, it's cramped and fans almost hover over the pitch. The intimidating atmosphere might not be much, but it's worth the four points a season which prevent Southampton rejoining their rightful home, Division One. Now, there isn't a spare seat in the house, even for Sheffield Wednesday, who arrive in their rather scruffy Dunn-Line (from Nottingham) coach under new management, Big Fat Ron Atkinson, who, in 1991, the day after he celebrated promotion and a Rumbelows Cup victory with the good people of Sheffield, declared he would never leave. Next day, he left for Aston Villa.

Southampton is not a happy club. BBC South's *Southern Eye* recently detailed the club's £6 million merge with Secure Retirement Homes, from which directors – including FA Chairman Keith Wiseman, the first man to demand a wage for such duties – made vast sums of money when one share in Southampton FC was suddenly worth 323 in the new company. Then-chairman Guy Askham rejected a bid for £15 million by an Israeli consortium fronted by ex-manager Graeme Souness. All very odd and Southampton fans know something is wrong and that Sir David Frost is rumoured to be launching a takeover.

The Dell is a dump. My feeling of Premier League suffocation returns at every corner I squeeze through around the ground. Inside, it's little better. The food is revolting, particularly the tea which tastes of grasshopper repellent and is the colour of dandruff. I can't even start to sip it and if I could have gotten out of my seat (more a glorified bench, although there are no grasshoppers to be seen) at the end of the Main Stand, obscured view of course. If this tinder-box goes up, nobody escapes. Still, you don't need to do any more work on the ground than legally necessary if every game is a sell-out, do you?

As I saw last week, they're a decent side, but not today. Matthew Le Tissier is out of form, but untouchable to the crowd as their We're Not Worthy supplications whenever he passes by confirm. Today he'll do nothing apart from rattle the crossbar with a free kick. Instead they pick on goalkeeper Paul Jones (because he came with Dave Jones, no relation, from Stockport, something which at more generous clubs would be a plus point) and Francis Benali, who I just know is the hardest man in the stadium this afternoon.

Both clubs are sponsored by something called Sanderson. Relations between the clubs are cordial, perhaps why Wednesday reserve striker Gordon 'Flash' Watson moved here for a whopping fee in 1995, why they've just signed injury ravaged and non-teetotal Cudworth Cowboy, David Hirst, for £2 million and why David Pleat's last British signing for Wednesday was panic buy Jim Magilton from Southampton. I wonder how the game would go if these teams met on the last day of the season and one needed points to stay up.

There's added spice in that Hirst hasn't faced his old club before, Carlton Palmer used to play for Wednesday (Atkinson is rumoured to be hoping to prise him back to Hillsborough) and Petter Rudi, Wednesday's classy Norwegian snubbed Southampton to join them. The results of this are: a) Hirst is treated like a hero by both sets of fans and responds accordingly; b) Wednesday fans sing 'You've got Carlton Palmer, he smokes marijuana' to the bemused Southampton fans, and c) Rudi is jeered by the home support every time he touches the ball.

This ought to make for a riveting atmosphere, but oh no. The visitors, some of whom are in fancy dress, are noisy enough in their corner, but the Southampton fans in the Archers Road end, mere feet away from the Wednesday support, are shtoom. I'm in the West Stand, which is comatose, apart from the odd bitter comment from supporters who really have no right to any kind of bitterness. Wednesday's Peter Atherton smacks them into the lead following a Rudi corner and the Southampton fans, so encouraging at Newcastle last week, do nothing to help, apart from the occasional anti-Portsmouth jibe, although prolific ex-Portsmouth scorer Guy Whittingham gets nothing like the treatment I saw Swindon's ex-Southampton winger Mark Walters receive at Fratton Park.

Wednesday's pie-eating goalkeeper Kevin Pressman spends half-time warming up, ignoring the excellent, hardworking mascot Super Saint, a most cuddly dog who does his best to gee up the crowd. His falling down dances to Chumbawamba's 'Tubthumping' elicits more response from the Wednesday corner. I chuckle heartily. I swear I hear a tut behind me.

Pressman's dedication doesn't stop him conceding two quick goals. First Hirst cracks an unstoppable volley past him and then, inevitably, Palmer takes Jason Dodd's long ball in his stride to loft it over him from a seemingly impossibly angle. The noise level increases, there are a few choruses of 'When The Saints Go Marching In', but hardly enough to start the adrenaline glands flowing. Wednesday bring on Wayne Collins and a fantastic through ball from Paulo Di Canio, ridiculed for some blatant diving in the first half, sets him up to equalise.

Wednesday's other substitute Benito Carbone (astonishingly not starting) sends over a magnificent crossfield pass which the swarthy but hapless Benali knocks towards Di Canio who sprints through the defence, rounds Jones not once but twice for extra humiliation before scoring. Brilliant and funny. I laugh out loud again. Scowls, scowls, scowls. They've no sense of humour these villagers. They'd like nothing more to put me in a ducking stool to see if I'm a witch. I am, too.

Southampton offer nothing. Kevin Davies is anonymous, save for missing an open goal at 2-1, Hirst is taken off to yet more generous applause (significantly, he returns only the Sheffield supporters') and Wednesday cruise home. The people around me blame Benali and, bizarrely, Jones. Very low key and not as thrilling as a 2-3 should be.

I muse on this as I make my way in the cold November rain to The Cricketers in Southampton's what-passes-for-Bohemian area. It's so Bohemian they've been showing a rugby union international, so it's full of pissed, shouty Hampshirians. I stop musing instantly. In one corner four male and one female Wednesdayites argue with themselves, in another some rugby fans are so drunk they can't argue with anyone. Everyone else is a moaning

Southampton fan. I have a drink and plod back to the station. That's the best thing about Southampton. It's always on the way to somewhere more pleasant.

41 **Blackpool**

v. Plymouth Argyle
DIVISION TWO

2 December

0-0

'I do believe absolutely in taking one game at a time and that's exactly what we're going to do.'

Nigel Worthington

Christ, it's cold. There's no wind pouring in off the Irish Sea, just still, freezing air, hammering my ears, running its chill tentacles through my long coat. I'm also part confused, part frightened. Most of Blackpool's lights are on, as they have been since 1879 when it was the first place in the world to have electric street lighting, but there's nobody home. It's deserted, not just in the sense that seaside towns are supposed to be quiet in winter, but deserted like Whitehaven, 4 a.m. Monday morning. There's the occasional under-ten child wandering around unsupervised, criminals on bikes and two men dressed in orange waders with lengthy fishing rods. I know there are no tourists to diddle, but were the locals run out of town by Frank Carson's summer show? It feels like an American city, St Louis, say, where the streets are empty at night, except for the strange.

I go towards the sea. It's too dark to see, but the tide must be out because I can't hear it. It must have been like this before 1735, when the first guest house was opened for gentrified visitors. When the railway came in 1840, the gentry left, never to return, replaced by Lancashire, Yorkshire and, later, Scottish working classes. The tower went up in 1894 and Blackpool's status was assured for another century. It even rode out World War 2 when hundreds of thousands of servicemen were trained here, thus saving the tourist industry.

This evening the Illuminations have gone, the tower is closed, but empty ghost trams are running up and down the promenade. Some towns need to be invaded by half of Glasgow to get going. Perhaps this is its strength and Blackpool itself has gone on holiday, after a tourist season that lasts through the Illuminations and political conference period to begin again at Christmas. It still feels dead to me though.

It's surreal. Some of the pubs are open, as if it's mid-summer, with music blaring, but there's nobody inside. Between them, Yates's Wine Lodge and Kentucky Fried Chicken can muster five customers. The Christmas lights are up in the town centre. Their motif is blue flashing lights, giving the impression that only policemen are in residence.

Bad things happen in Blackpool, named after a marsh-draining stream, made black by the peaty soil and home of lottery winner Karl Compton, it's in the air. The unnamed ten-year-old who was taught by a social worker to drive cars and ended up in a 90 m.p.h. car chase; the eleven-year-old heroin addict fostered by another addict while her mother and grandmother were in court on drugs charges; the two sisters, one had leukaemia, the other wouldn't donate bone marrow for months and when she did it was a mismatch. Last night Adel Sakly was stabbed to death outside Barney Rubble nightclub. There's a murderer on the loose here, perhaps he knows the sex offender and the Scottish pair of laundrette robbers the police haven't caught yet either.

Fifty yards in front of me are three people wandering, like me but with purpose. This might look bad in a court of law, but the two woman and one man look vaguely young and happening, so I follow them.

They stumble, unsteadily for six o'clock, towards Coral Island, a cavernous amusement arcade that must be run as a winter tax dodge, as it's open and they're running bingo games although only three desolate souls are playing. The trio pass McDonald's where the few diners are arranged around the windows, and to Southern Fried Chicken, whose customers have placed themselves likewise.

There, in full view of myself and the two sets of fast food eaters, one of the women, who I'd noted had a nicely turned ankle beneath her short skirt, pulls down her tights and urinates on the pavement.

As a steaming pool of piss snakes between her legs, I'm transfixed with horror. She's inches away from Southern Fried Chicken and the thought of hiding or doing it furtively seems not to have crossed her mind. Her companions stand chatting, unconcerned by what they're witnessing. Then, business complete, she hitches up her tights, the trio walk on and I have lost all interest in following them. What kind of place is this? Where can they draw a moral line? Never has the town and clapped-out old whore analogy been so apposite.

I need a drink. I return to the sea front, head south and try The Boardwalk, which promises the 'ultimate pub experience'. In a sense it delivers, for there is me, an unnaturally cheery barman and Andrea True Connection's 'More More More' at painful volume. As I drink, he sips his coffee and resumes his interior decoration perched on top of a ladder. 'See you again, mate,' he calls as I slink out. Only in hell, which can be different to Blackpool only in the minutiae.

Thoroughly depressed, my season seeming so long, I head for the ground, Bloomfield Road, which lies opposite a deserted bus station alongside what I mistake for a disused dual carriageway until a car crawls past me. The floodlights are only half the height they once were. The car park, shrouded in darkness, is a series of muddy potholes and I can make out the fading, final admission prices to the disused Kop, £1.50. Stanley Matthews won most of his England caps here, but he still associates himself with Stoke. Now I know why.

I make my way down Graffiti Alley, which links home and away sections. Many years ago, I'D LOVE TO KNIFE A PRESTON BASTARD was scrawled in enormous white letters outside the away turnstiles. It – or the wall it was on – has gone now, but the writings still there tell their own tale. POTTS MUST GO (manager Harry Potts did indeed go, in 1976) recalls an era when Blackpool were a force in the old Division Two. MURPHY OUT NCFC confirms that even Notts County fans get riled sometimes and BFC WE KILL PNE that old rivalries are still intact. At least next to UVF somebody has written SCUM. All very historically interesting, but what sort of place has such a paucity of self-respect that negative graffiti stands for twenty years?

This is another unhappy club. While chairman Owen Oyston serves time in jail for rape, his formidable wife Vicki stands in. There's takeover talk afoot and former Director Of Football Billy Bingham is sueing over scouting and sell-on fees.

There's still no reason why it shouldn't be a decent game. A win would put Blackpool in a play-off position and Plymouth are three points above the relegation places. I'm excited anyway, even if I'm hallucinating puddles of piss and the stewards are wearing British Nuclear Fuels Limited jackets.

Inside Bloomfield Road, like the rest of football from which it seems so isolated, Blackpool has had its revolution. Unfortunately, it's been a backwards one and the place is virtually falling down. The pies are served out of a misleadingly christened hot box through a gap in the railings which means they're lukewarm on this cold night, the empty kop stands guard like a disused lighthouse over a terrible decline. In 1955, over 38,000 people crammed in here to see Stanley Matthews and Stanley Mortensen (when he died they called it The Matthews Funeral) take on Billy Wright's Wolverhampton Wanderers. Now only 11,000 are permitted and that's generous.

I'm in the confusingly named East Paddock South side terrace. It seems like the logical place for the home fans to congregate, close to the away fans (Plymouth Argyle are accompanied by forty-seven Devonians, whose 'Green Army' chant will be the loudest of the evening), under cover, albeit leaky, for maximum amplification and with room for all. Instead they stand behind the goal on a tiny uncovered terrace hemmed in by the rickety South Stand. There isn't enough room for them to stand together, so they're split. No wonder football fans always need to someone to speak up for them.

There is a mascot, Cable Cat, who, bless him, does his best to create some kind of atmosphere, but he's met with puzzled, grizzled looks, except from the children who run forward to shake his paw. I wish I was a kid, things are so much easier. I haven't the guts to go near Cable Cat.

Tonight's game is sponsored by the 'world famous' Palace Discotheque. After the match, in deepest deserted Blackpool, there is 'Christmas Kick-Off' where for £4, Stan Boardman will tell some jokes and an unnamed troupe of silicon-breasted topless women (they're introduced at half-time, they do not bare all) will dance. It is announced that the players will be attending. Players being what they are and having the focusing capacity of hyperactive children, the match is suddenly something to be got through.

Plymouth start better, but they aren't clubbing afterwards. Richard Logan has a free header but misses. Blackpool have a series of dangerous corners but only Tony Butler's flying header causes Plymouth goalkeeper Jon Sheffield serious trauma. The bloke next to me ('next' is a relative term, he's so far away only a feat of spectacular gymnastics would bring contact) has a flask. He's also brought his own mug. Ooooh, steaming hot coffee, home-made, mmmmm. He stares at me smugly and hurls mild abuse at left back (manager Nigel Worthington's position) Ben Dixon, who couldn't get into the reserve team in October and who's gripped by fear whenever he receives the ball. There is a drummer, but he soon gives up, as do the home team and the rest of the crowd, who have no chants whatsoever.

Plymouth's little Lee Hodges is on loan from West Ham. What, he must wonder, is he doing here? He's frozen to death, easily the best player on view, meaning that he's clogged by Blackpool's defence and dragged down by his team mates. Early in the second half, he weaves his way through the defence and, from outside the penalty area, curls the ball past goalkeeper Steve Banks. It hits the woodwork and bounces away. Hodges holds his head, Plymouth fans hold their heads, I hold my head. That's it for the game. Two Plymouth fans take their tops off and swing them around for a while – foolish but hard – and Blackpool fans settle on abusing the linesman who looks less than a twentieth-part Arab. 'Bet you're made up Iran are in the World Cup, colonel,' shouts someone. Everyone chuckles, even the linesman.

Kids are running around squealing and making their own entertainment, while two goalkeepers are getting very cold out there. Worthington brings on Gary Brabin, which raises a cheer. Brabin was arrested on the team coach at Brentford last year after a scrap with the home side's Jamie Bates. This season he's been sent off twice for the reserves and is about to start a seven-match ban. He's built like a Palace Discotheque bouncer, a wide boy in every sense and his first touch is a two-footed lunge into a shocked Jason Rowbotham. Then he disappears for the rest of the game, as, slowly, do the crowd.

'Now,' shouts The Wag, as injury time and the Palace Discotheque beckon, 'they think we're shit, let's hit 'em!' Substitute Brett Ormerod, whom nobody would give a second glance if he sported an 'I Am 12' badge and who wears different socks to the rest of the team, must have heard. He bounds forward and puts over a centre. It lands in the disused Kop, although, as Blackpool had no bodies forward – as ever – a magnificent cross would have been pointless. The referee blows and those of us who are left cluck weakly. 0-0. Abysmal.

I walk back into town, past Gipsy Petulengro's empty shop. She's obviously seen the future and left town, but she did Jimmy Tarbuck's horoscope once. Funland is still open. I don't do fun right now. Depressed by the cold, the match, the ill-feeling, the pissing woman, I look out to sea, over a beach which didn't pass the EU Guideline Water Quality Standard and was condemned by the *Good Beach Guide*. Nobody on earth knows I'm here which is simultaneously lonesome and comforting. If I threw myself in the Irish Sea (unlikely given the cold and the fact that the tide seems to be out and the water being a touch chilly for me) who would really care? I'm so alone.

I go for a drink at The Castle opposite the Palace Discotheque which I haven't the heart to visit. There isn't a queue. The Castle (customers 4; bar staff 3) is showing old Muhammed Ali fights. A Christmas decoration falls from the ceiling underneath my table. I let it lie. This wasn't what I intended or assumed; none of tonight was. Like Stanley Matthews, I'd rather live in Stoke.

42 **Swindon Town**

v. Oxford United
DIVISION ONE
6 December

4-1

> **'I believe we have got character, but the players are the ones who
> have to go out and prove this afternoon that they have got what it
> takes.'**

Steve McMahon

Swindon was a hooter town. Five times in a morning and four in the afternoon, the Great Western Railway company's works hooter would blow for up
to seventeen seconds, marking strategic points in the working day. With a
suitable wind it could be heard twenty-five miles away. Swindon was a
company town and its heartbeat was The Factory, as it was called.

In 1835, Isambard Kingdom Brunel's Great Western Railways had come to
the former canal junction and market town of Swindon – hill where swine are
kept, naturally – midway between Bristol and London. A century and three
years later, the workers – numbering 24,000 at this point, no wonder there were
five cinemas – were given paid holidays, although the company had long since
laid on free trains for the eagerly anticipated Trip Week. In 1986, the hooter
hooted for the last time, the site was sold to Tarmac and Swindon reinvented
itself as a place from where insurance companies, Anchor butter (who sack
workers for smoking on-site) and W.H. Smith's controlled their empires, assisted
by generous land leasing rates. It could have been worse, much worse.

The station itself is a nonentity of which Brunel would be ashamed. Two
working platforms, a waiting room between them, through which everyone
has to pass, but hardly any trains.

Smile! As I exit the station, noting police vans and police horses, I'm
photographed by more police who are snapping and videoing anyone who
might, potentially, be a football hooligan. I'm flattered, until they do the same
to the seventy-year-old man behind me. Clearly, they're not here for
kaffeeklatsch. Lowly Oxford United are the visitors to high-flying Swindon
Town. It's a local derby. This, as Swindonian Desmond Morris might note (it's
obvious enough), is where two tribes clash.

Swindon, so badly designed there were traffic jams in the 60s when there were only 153 cars in the whole of Britain, is oblivious. Down along Regent Street (absolutely no relation), the pedestrianised main drag away from countless roundabouts, walkways, subways and overpowering office blocks, there's no evidence of a football match, let alone a derby. Slit-eyed, down-trodden shoppers are stalking Teletubby toys. Last night demented parents slept outside Toys'R'Us to get them. Special Christmas wishes go to Nikkie (the spelling says so much somehow) Taylor, who made a formal complaint when Mothercare World tried to give some of said Teletubbies to charity.

Jazz and Salvation Army bands are keenly competing to see who can knock out the most awful versions of Christmas carols. The Salvation Army wins with their 'Jingle Bells As Orchestrated By Charles Bukowski'. I want to die.

In an piss-stinking alleyway lies the registry office and outside it in a less than romantic start to married life, couples are posing for wedding photographs. I pause to watch a bald thug marrying a pregnant slattern. They look really happy.

Regent Street is standard smalltown fare but at its ends, where railwaymen's homes built by Brunel as a workers' village still stand, Swindon's roots are exposed. If there's a boom here, it's a shallow one, despite a population explosion that shows no signs of abating. At one end the caravan of the Vale Butcher Of Evesham is parked on some waste ground. The butcher (jolly, red-faced fat man; I'll give him two years before the inevitable) has a microphone strapped to his head and he's selling like a bastard. 'Pork chops, ladies,' he drawls, all rustic burr, 'full tray of steak for a fiver ...' There are no ladies within a fifty-yard radius.

The butcher's recently prised-off Siamese twin is at the other end of Regent Street. He represents Jean Cristian Perfumes and his patter is identical, bar the meat references. The response is identical, too. I cannot look him in the eye. Christ, this is England, this is hard work. I'm with Brunel and Diana Dors (who went to school at Selwood House on Bath Road) on this town. He built railways to take people out of Swindon and she took the first train to Paddington after puberty, both never to return except for a laugh.

I stomp off to the County Ground, on the east side of town, off the childishly named Magic Roundabout (magical only in its idiotic design) which forms the boundary between the small Asian ghetto and the more affluent white area, where rail barons used to reside. Now, it's close to the M4, gateway to civilisation.

I've yet to see anything resembling a mob, or for that matter an Oxford shirt. I encounter the former at the County Ground Hotel which, as logic dictates, is at the entrance to the County Ground. It's so full, I sweat profusely the instant I walk in. Here – instead of in town hunting Oxfordonians – are pretend hard lads. They're all drunk and they're singing anti-Oxford songs: one about going to the Manor Ground and 'pissing up the walls' which I can't quite follow, another concerning Oxford United's parlous financial state, 'Going bust, they're going bust, Oxford's going bust' (the money hasn't been squandered on Oxford's coach, a J-reg Jeffs incorporating what could well be a portable television; good job it's a short journey) and the standard 'Chim-chimernee-chim-chimernee-chim-chim-cheroo, we hate those bastards in yellow and blue'. I stay silent with regard to the fact that Oxford play in yellow and black and return into the sunshine smiling broadly and nodding furiously, as if an Iraqi oil well.

I'm in the Arkell's (local brewery) Stand, which is an endless source of delight. They don't just sell any old hot dogs, oh no. Mine is a Saarlander Hot Dog – admittedly I may have fallen for a cunning marketing scam here – and it's a porky classic (advertising slogans? Piece of piss, but I'm expensive). Better yet, there are free biscuits with the tea! A small thing, but it means a lot. To celebrate, when I'm in my seat I knock my tea over and it dribbles like Blackpool urine underneath the seat in front of me. When the man sitting there arrives, he tries to nick my newspaper to soak the mess. Because he's white of hair and forty years older than me, I metamorphosise Clark Kent-like into Macho Boy.

'Oi, that's my newspaper,' I snarl, so hard of tone I scare myself.

'Well *someone's* spilt it,' he replies, an empty tea cup underneath my seat perhaps giving me away.

'Not me,' I lie, hardness melting under the heat of cowardice as I notice his tattooed hand.

He spits expertly between my legs and turns to watch the pre-match build up.

Perhaps he murdered D. Pennington, the name on the back of my seat. Obviously the ticket office knew D. wouldn't be here to survey matters from his (and it must be a he) personalised perch a few rows behind the directors' box where Associate Director (whatever that means) Willie Carson might be found. Long term, I do hope D.'s OK. Short term, I have his seat level with the halfway line, for just £14.50. Yippee. Hats off to value at football. Never before and never again. Even the view – hills towards the Vale Of The White Horse – is pleasing.

Swindon have slipped since I saw their heroics at Portsmouth and are now fifth after losing their last three games. Oxford are fifth from bottom, have put their entire squad up for sale and are about to go belly up.

'There is something magical about a visit from Oxford United to the County Ground that has magical qualities on the scale of the Cup Final,' claims programme columnist Tony Horne. Perhaps he means the Simod Cup, God rest its soul, for neither side sells out their allocation. However, what they lack in numbers is compensated for in unpleasantness. The contingent from the County Ground Hotel have placed themselves in the North Stand and make themselves known, while the Oxford fans decide not to sit in their seats, something which annoys the home crowd immeasurably. Judging by the amount of police present, all in riot gear, President Clinton is here too, safe and snug among the posh people, I can't spot him myself. Certainly it's the largest concentration of police in Swindon since February when R&K Wise, local bakers, had a staff night out at the Leisure Centre which ended in mayhem, meat wagons and no loaves for Wiltshire the following morning.

The game crackles along merrily. Oxford start better, much to the chagrin of Steve McMahon who today, like the rest of his bench, is wearing a sweat shirt over full kit. They'll pay for winter bare legs in later life when the chilblains kick in. Oxford's Nigel Jemson may be as mobile as the *Ark Royal* but he still has a graceful touch and his linking with Joey Beauchamp (ex-Swindon, couldn't settle there because it wasn't close enough to Oxford, abused by home fans – 'Mummy's boy, mummy's boy, mummy's boy' – for whole match) is balm to my soul.

I was Swindon striker Chris Hay's talisman (if only he knew) but he's suspended today and without him they look disjointed. Oxford should already have been winning – Martin Aldridge's header bringing a flying pig of a save from Swindon goalkeeper Fraser Digby – when they take the lead, Mike Ford, lonesome in the penalty area, nodding in Jemson's cross. Now we can see who's who in the crowd. There's a few Oxford fans in my stand. They stand up to cheer and immediately a few aggressive, very drunk Swindon fans make honour-satisfying noises.

Sat directly behind me is a pompous Scotsman, more Edinburgh than Glasgow. At the hint of any crowd trouble he shouts 'oooo behave yourself, lads'. At the hint of any on the pitch trouble he shouts 'oooo, we've not come to see a rugby game'. At random moments he shouts 'oooo, football, that's what we want to see'. He is a pillock.

The game is frantic, refreshingly open but Hay's replacement Steve Finney hardly carries the same level of threat. Swindon equalise when Brian Wilsterman, Oxford's least accomplished defender, bundles a free kick into his own net, although the PA tries to give it to David Thompson, the Liverpool kid on loan to Swindon. Immediately Beauchamp gets himself booked, further proof fans have an effect. Instantly, Wilsterman (it's not his day, I suspect he doesn't have many days) trips Thompson for a penalty. There are no complaints to referee Frazer Stretton, perhaps they're scared of him: 'Frazer's interests,' declares the programme, 'include listening to his collection of heavy rock music and looking after his beloved Volvo estate.'

This is a signal – apropos of very little indeed – for the police to invade the Oxford end, not once but three times. They wade in like ice hockey players, slugging Oxford fans with batons. The supporters respond with fists and missiles. Mark Walters converts, 2-1. The quantity of Wiltshire policemen earning overtime here needs justification should the same fixture be played next year: the number of arrests they're making – mostly at random, but that doesn't matter – will do this. Who said the police were thick? If I cared, I'd write a letter of complaint, but, in truth I don't. Oh well, sorry.

Half-time is enlivened by what looks like a youth drawn by lots doing the on-pitch announcements and some shockingly poor dancers, only slightly undermined by the otherwise anonymous mascot Rockin' Robin, jiving along with them. As they did at the start of the first half, the dancers turn into cheer-leaders when the teams return. Oxford take the scenic route, electing not to run a gauntlet of fake tans and sportsbras. I would bravely have run that gauntlet.

Swindon look a different team in the second half. As do Oxford, although a much poorer one in their case. Walters weaves some of his old magic and Finney heads in for 3-1.

'If,' booms the Tannoy, 'you want to avoid crowd congestion at the end of the game, please stay in your seat.' This is a euphemism and the last ten minutes are played out beneath the roar of a police helicopter. There's no way back for Oxford and even before Ty Gooden's magnificent individual goal to make it 4-1, the away fans, bidden by some secret signal, leave as one. The police, incompetent as well as overstaffed and vicious, are slow to react, so most of the mob escape in one blob. The police then over-react again, bringing in horses to block the solitary exit.

'Oooo look, they're stoning the police horses,' slimes Scotsman behind me. They are not, they are pressed in a cramped corner and the scared horses are rearing up at them. Oxford's Darren Purse heads against the bar. Nobody flickers and there are few Oxford fans at the death.

It's an extraordinary business outside. Essentially there is one exit from the ground. Literally hundreds of police line the funnel and, every police office has a drawn baton. Without going all Ralph Nader, I stifle my snigger at their stern bearing and take the matter up.

'Why have you got your batons out?' I ask, genuinely interested, nice as the nicest pie.

'Fuck off,' replies the policeman, whose number is oddly not visible. I fuck off.

Towards town, there are even more police (I'd love to see Wiltshire's crime figures for today, up I'd wager), jogging in formation, on horses, in the helicopter and in transit vans. Lights flashing, sirens wailing, helicopter whirring, they're escorting the Oxford fans the back way to the station. There is a gang of Swindon fans picking their way through kids, old people and the traffic the police are too stupid to have stopped, to get to the Oxford fans, but if the United Nations had taken this level of manpower to Bosnia it would have been sorted in an hour. I'm a touch excited now and about to take the back road to the station myself. I'm stopped by a policeman.

'Where are you from?'

I expertly deduce this isn't the time to go into my life history, enlivened with a witty yet poignant anecdote about the time I lived in Caterham where everyone was either a squaddie or from the local mental hospital. I don't know whether 'Swindon' or 'Oxford' is the answer he's looking for.

'Swindon,' I chance.

'Well fuck off out of here and fuck off down there,' he suggests, baton twitching excitedly. This is the angriest set of policemen I ever did see. It's too dark to see his number but he's wearing a fluorescent jacket. Excellent! Sweary policeman. I respect them more.

'Down there,' I'm disappointed to discover is a dual carriageway and a McDonald's. By the time I get into town, the Oxford fans are heading towards Didcot, and Swindon is gearing itself up for a Saturday night of drinking, shouting and vomit. Me? I swear I hear the hooter in the distance, telling me it's time to leave.

43 **Bristol Rovers**

v. Grimsby Town
DIVISION TWO

12 December

0-4

'I don't care what anyone says, we are in mid-table.'

Phil Bater, first team coach. Nothing from manager Ian 'Ollie' Holloway.

Friday night in Bristol. Things could be worse. They could also be better: it could be warmer, I could be with someone, anyone, I could be tucked up in bed. It's infested with posh students (Bristol University is Oxbridge Lite), shoppers and those seeking Christmas spirit. My own spirit is cheered by Bristol Cathedral, bathed in winter lighting – this is an expertly-lit city – looking like the home of the gods of architectural taste. It's opposite the awesome, Georgian council offices, the sort of building which other cities would convert into a museum or railway station. On the cathedral green, there are Orwellian orange and black signs shouting CHEER, SPARKLE and MERRY.

The posters advertising a Mums & Dads Protest Against Paedophilia tomorrow in front of the cathedral unnerves me. What do these people want? Witch trials? Paedophilia is horrible, disgusting and all the rest of it. As the *Sun* might shout, it preys on the innocent and therefore paedophiles can't be left alone like those consenting adults who cheerily nail their scrotums to barbed wire. Yet, yet, yet, it's a sex urge, so being 'against' it can never work. Never ever. It's the same principle as those attention-seekers who wear ribbons 'against' cancer. Nobody is *for* cancer and those *for* paedophilia tend not to have an effective PR machine.

I march in a huff up Gloucester Road, past a bevy of sauna and massage emporiums and a gaggle of drinkers, part of a world where dogs on strings are not yet *passé*. Although I won't be going to Knowle West where the real rough stuff happens, Gloucester Road is close to what passes in Bristol for urban blight. It's where Ciao Hamburgers, 'the best takeaway in town', has a warning poem on the door: 'if you eat on your feet, keep the streets neat!' Wise words indeed.

It's close to St Pauls, where the dispossessed used to riot every summer and where I feel duty-bound to plod through. It's, ha!, a stone's throw from Bristol's business heart (something the rioters were always too linear of thought to comprehend), hardly welcoming and, if the boarded-up but still in use houses are anything to go by, I could buy heroin easier than a loaf of bread, but it's tidy and has its quota of community centres, the legacy of every former riot zone. I don't loiter. Never can be too careful, eh? Especially when I have £250 cash in my pockets.

By the time I reach Bristol Rovers' Memorial (to World War 1 dead – most dignified) Ground, the streets have become middle class, the houses large and robbable. Having hiked for ninety minutes, I'm knackered, my feet have blistered up so much I walk like Dick Emery's drag characters.

Bristol Rovers are only tenants. They've not had a ground since they vacated fire-damaged, unsafe, but sellable Eastville in 1986. Always Bristol City's hick cousins, Rovers' over-developed sense of roving has hardly rescinded their joke status. Tomorrow the rugby club are at home, so Friday night it is, then.

The ground is geared towards rugby union. At least I think it is as nothing (assuming nobody offered sex or cash) could get me to a rugby match. One end is unused because nobody gives a toss about rugby. Bars are everywhere, because the Barbour-wearing toffs need to drink themselves senseless before they drive the Range Rover home and try to sodomize the wife. Really nice toilets. An uncovered end, so the crowd's braying doesn't distract the players. And executive boxes where the afore-mentioned Barbour-wearing toffs can be vile to schoolgirl waitresses. What a shock it must be to the rugby club to host a sport that attracts over 175 paying customers.

The food hutch promises 'Proper Cornish pasties'. I try one. 'Proper' means an onion-swamped sack of pastry doused in pepper. This is an educational evening already. It's freezing too, literally. Despite everything, I'm looking forward to this. Not as much as the hysterical pitch announcer who babbles on about power and passion. Or the Rovers team who go into a huddle before kickoff. Or the handful of Grimsby fans – one mini-coach – who chant 'We only sing when we're fishing' before the home fans (Gasheads being their self-appointed appellation but City fans use it as abuse) can.

Rovers start well. The poetically named Josh Low looks big and pacey on the right wing and Grimsby (an all-white team by the way) centre forward Lee Nogan pulls a hamstring after eight minutes. Obviously the notion of warming up properly in tonight's cold bypassed this outstanding intellect. Rovers' leading scorer Barry Hayles looks electric and surges through the defence time after time, once hitting the post.

Grimsby score when Tony Gallimore curls a free kick past tiny Rovers goalkeeper Andy Collett. A minute later, they score again. Substitute Steve

Livingstone flicks in with the defence still in a huddle. On the bench Nogan must pretend to be ecstatic. The best he can do is to clench his fist and look constipated. Rovers fans are used to this. They encourage their mainly home-grown players good naturedly, mumble the occasional chant about how fantastic it is to be a Gas and wonder how Grimsby, spirited and organised but ordinary, come to be two goals up. Spirit probably: Town centre half Graham Rodger even indulges in Maoist self-criticism after a stray pass is noted by his team mates: 'Yeah,' he bellows, 'you're right, it was fucking shite.'

What Gasheads cannot comprehend is how diabolical Rovers are. Nothing goes right for them. Manager Ian Holloway, almost in front of me, looks bewildered. Next to me, a good father is trying to interest his son in what must be a difficult night for them both. 'Look,' says dad in non-hectoring tones, 'Grimsby are playing good football at the back, they're not giving possession away,' and when débutant Rover Luke (another handsome name, there'll be footballers called Walter, soon) Basford heads off the line, 'You've not seen them lose 5-0 at home, have you? You might tonight, you know.' The boy is almost enthused, what a lovely man and what a fine father. I'd like to be that good.

Grimsby string twenty-six passes together at one point. 'This is what they call taking the piss, Gas,' shouts a wag before settling back to discuss last week's FA Cup tie at Wisbech. 'Like a little, mini-Millwall,' apparently.

At half-time former manager Bobby Gould can't have done much for Holloway's job jitters by presenting a Welsh schoolboy cap to some kid who'll be on the dole in Cynon Valley before he's eighteen, although right now he assumes he'll rule the world before he's seventeen. Gould's reception is half cheers, half jeers. As is the way of honourable people, a better reception is accorded to an old gentleman, 'Seventy years a Gashead', claims the announcer.

Grimsby control the second half. Manager Alan Buckley, a few yards to my left is still not satisfied. 'Fucking hell, when are we going to get this going?' he shouts at Kevin Jobling. After Kevin Donovan makes it three with a blistering individual goal, Buckley smiles, shrugs, sits down and – a rare thing for any manager – enjoys the last ten minutes, safe in the knowledge nothing can go wrong. In contrast, Holloway has brought himself on as an ineffective substitute. Livingstone pokes in a fourth after the ball cannons around the penalty area and goalkeeper Collett elects to turn his back on the proceedings. Middlesbrough, presumably, do not regret letting him go. Nogan forgets to look chuffed.

A 0-4 annihilation, the sixth and worst home defeat of the season. What do the Rovers fans do? Firstly they stay to clap their hopeless heroes off and then sing at manager Holloway, 'Ollie, Ollie, give us a wave'. Head down, hands on hips, walking at snail's pace, he's too upset to respond. The fans try again. This time, he stops, smiles apologetically and gives a wave. They cheer him. I give the poor guy a clap myself. A very human moment.

As Grimsby travel home in their Applebys coach – much better than I'd thought; table lamps and enough space to take their travelling support back too – I return to town, horrified at how poor Rovers were, impressed with Grimsby and delighted by a crowd of decent folk.

Bristol is heaving with good natured gangs. All the pubs are bouncered. When did this start to happen? Like everywhere I end up these days, it's not for the solo traveller, dressed for the football and limping because his new shoes don't fit properly yet (my feet are so wide they go off the measuring scale; shoe shop assistants faint when I unveil).

The Aizlewood Method of gaining entry to anywhere is to march in confidently, never doubling back or hesitating as if I'm a sad git on my own in a place I don't know, nod manfully to bouncers, whilst saying the magical code words 'alright mate'. Wait for inevitable 'alright mate' reply. Enter. This method doesn't work for groups of ten or more. Inside, I walk around, beer in hand, pretending to look for someone and then settle in a corner where I can loll without catching anyone's eye. Taking out a) *The Pirate*, The Official Matchday Magazine Of Bristol Rovers FC, or b) the *Bristol Evening Post*, despite its 'LET'S PARTY!' headline, isn't on. Works every time.

It's nearly midnight. I walk up Park Street, seduced again by the cathedral. A group of students is walking down the hill. I see my second new penis of the season. One of them is waving it around in a most friendly way and his friends are pointing at it. I cannot help noticing that it's much smaller than mine. Then, I cannot help noticing that it's a really cold evening.

I chance upon what I'd like to pretend was a late night shebeen patronised by black gangsters and white molls. It's a late night bar, Brassiere Pierre. Downstairs the lighting is harsh and there are too many people. Upstairs it's darker, there's a mirrored dance floor and a pillar to lean on as I nod discreetly to Blackstreet's fabulous 'No Diggity'. I'm the only person here alone. I look around. Nobody notices me. Again, not a soul in the world knows I'm here. Part of me wishes it hadn't come to this, part of me thinks it's unnatural to glean any enjoyment from this at all and part of me loves it.

I have forty-nine more places to visit in five months – my stomach quivers at this – and God knows how many pubs to launch solo assaults on. I know I'm less sane than I was in August, but, it's not all bad news: I'll be worse in May. I buy another bottled beer. It's 2 o'clock in the morning.

44 Shrewsbury Town

v. Leyton Orient
DIVISION THREE

13 December

1-2

'Throughout my managerial career, I've always placed great emphasis on getting things right defensively.'

Jake King

Shrewsbury calls itself the Town Of Flowers, but I can't see any of the blessed things. It's slumped since Percy Thrower was head of the Town Parks Department. I have a hangover, my feet still ache and I'd like a few more hours of sleep. Oh well. My spirits are lifted once more, but slightly, by Marches town, Shrewsbury (pronounced 'shrew' rather than 'shrow'), seductively looped by the River Severn. On one side is Welsh Bridge, entrance to all things unpleasant, on the other English Bridge, opened by whoever the king was in 1927. Actually, it had been there for centuries, but they took it down and rebuilt it brick by brick with added strength and width. It's not exactly one of the great British bridges, but it'll do me and at the English end of English Bridge is Gay Meadow, home of Shrewsbury Town, in the Football League with no discernible benefit to anyone since 1950.

I walk through the narrow streets, towards the town walls which must have formed an almost impenetrable defence at the neck of the Severn's loop – 'Islanded in Severn stream,' as A.E. Housman's *A Shropshire Lad* put it, although the Tourist Board misspells his name – in addition to the river and hill. These were times when Shrewsbury was much more excitingly called Scrobbesbyrig, before the Normans built a castle in 1083. The Normans, I firmly believe, did nothing but build castles. What canny Normans they were.

Charles I's nephew, dashing Prince Rupert, lived in this royalist town, drapers brought prosperity and, before the railways changed everything, Shrewsbury was a stagecoach town on the London–Holyhead route. Today, Shrewsbury flogs its Tudor heritage as part of a tourist (Ha! As if!) campaign which involves four museums, including one named after Clive Of India who rented a house here and was mayor and MP. All well and good, but then they miscalculate.

Apparently there's a television series, which bypassed me, *Chronicles Of Brother Cadfael*, a medieval whodunit (whogivesatosswhodunit if you ask me, so grumpy that I'm pissing myself off). It's set here, so the tourist board have gone down the Brother Cadfael route, and now Shrewsbury is officially Shrewsbury, Historic Home Of Brother Cadfael and the town's main attraction is The Shrewsbury Quest, a role-playing medieval whodunit. Ugh. Charles Darwin, arguably one of the most important humans, was born and schooled in Shrewsbury, but they virtually ignore him, which will be helpful when the television programme is axed, unless Brother Cadfael is already 'resting'.

The bucolic view from the walls is excellent, I can probably see Wales, twenty miles away. Perhaps, too, the house of Leo, Tony Blair's father. I hurry back to the town centre, suitably pretty, like a more realistic Chester, although it's done no favours by maudlin Christmas carols played by incompetents for a charity too lax to demand an audition. They don't have non-whites here, but that's an accident of history and geography.

I cross English Bridge again and I'm at the one entrance to the ground, Graffiti Road ('Scouse Power & Salop Twats'). Gay Meadow is bordered on another side by the Severn (they used to have a bloke in a coracle to collect lost balls), on another by the railway and on the remainder by meadows, presumably gay ones. The club have not taken the opportunity to expand, although as the ground has only been filled to more than a third of its 8000 capacity twice in the league this season, I take their point.

It's as pleasant a ground as Shrewsbury is a town. Their dwarf mascot Lenny The Lion travels around the pitch perimeter throwing sweets less gently into, more ferociously at, the crowd. People duck, I duck, carefully keeping hold of the hottest pie of the season. Now and possibly forever, the roof of my mouth needs scaffolding. I'm not sure Lenny is as happy in his work as he should be, even though he gets to make paw print autographs for the party of schoolchildren the club have probably let in free. Some people don't know when they're born.

Every record played is a Christmas one, the announcer is superposh, but I enjoy the old duffer. When he reads the team changes out, he gives appraisals (always positive) of each home player. Shrewsbury's that sort of place and Town are the sort of club to carry an advertisement for protecting water shrews in the programme. Unsurprisingly, I have a barrier to myself on the Riverside Terrace. Today, mid-table Shrewsbury are entertaining mid-table Leyton Orient, not technically a glamour game.

Devon White is playing for Shrewsbury. He looked so virile for Notts County against Hull back in August. Now, the big milksop hasn't scored for four games and looks woefully out of sorts, outbustled by Simon Clark. Funny old game, football.

The crowd are stoics to a man (women seem to be barred, except for the model-esque programme sellers who I take a one-way shine to) and there are no police in the ground, certainly not PC Tony Ashton who turned up for work in March, announced he'd had a sex change and was now Claire Ashton. The fans run through some anti-Wrexham ditties, even less passionately than Chester, but they do have a chant that goes 'fuck 'em up, get into 'em' and they make a ner-ner ner-ner siren whine when the St John's Ambulance crew saunters on.

Orient débutant Colin Simpson, signed from mighty Hendon who've just dumped them out of the FA Cup, scores when he bundles in a corner that Shrewsbury goalkeeper Paul Edwards flaps at. This encourages the Orient fans behind him to shout 'dodgy keeper' or 'Get your Grecian out' at the grey-haired custodian. Always shaky, he never gets to grips with the vicious corners, especially when a posse of Orient players stand on his goal line for formidable intimidation value.

Shrewsbury offer nothing, aside from bald of head, huge of arse Lee Steele's occasional burst of speed. They're petrified to go wide. Defender Peter Wilding carries the ball out with the composure of Franz Beckenbauer but can't defend, while the visitors use hands to control the ball more often than feet. Those visitors go 2-0 up when, from another half-cleared corner, Dean Smith smartly deflects in Alex Inglethorpe's shot. That's the first half.

The niceness evaporates as the teams jog off. 'Fucking wankers all of you,' shouts the old man on his own (and I'm not surprised frankly) a few barriers away from me. 'Come on, Town,' he shouts at the restart, 'we can beat this shower of shit.'

All that really matters happens in sixty seconds. Firstly the referee has to stop the game because Orient's left-sided combination of Dominic Naylor and Inglethorpe are fighting each other. Then, with Orient still in confusion, White powers through on his own. Orient's débutant goalkeeper Chris MacKenzie charges like a bison out of his penalty area and handles. He's sent off, despite the Orient players surrounding the linesman claiming White was offside. Centre half Stuart Hicks goes in goal, MacKenzie marches off topless, the crowd bidding him 'Cheerio, cheerio, cheerio' and, with thirty minutes to go, it should be game on.

It isn't. The crowd's next chant is 'We're not very good, we're not very good'. Shrewsbury introduce winger Austin Berkley, a pseudonym if ever there were, but I'll never know how good a goalkeeper Hicks is because he doesn't have a shot to save, with transfer-listed playmaker Darren Currie the architect of all that fails. Steele scores with the last kick of the game for 1-2 and Hicks watches it glide by, so it augers ill should he take over again. Orient's pleasant Travellers coach, with its lamps with shades should rock with laughter on the way back to the hell that is East London.

Me? I have another wander round, past the Abbey Foregate car park full of police after travellers and their caravans have landed. Middle class locals are up in arms about the invasion and if paedophiles are the new witches, travellers are the new Irish and blacks. They do look tough though, these travellers and the council are going to court to evict them on Monday and, in no way anticipating the course of justice, have erected steel gates so more caravans can't drive on site. This also means the caravans can't drive off site ...

I go to the Black Bull In Paradise on St Mary's Street. It is £1 a pint, the lighting is bright and to complete my timeslippage there's a 70s football match on the television. Everyone in here seems to have spent more than a tenner this afternoon and have qualifications in loutishness. A child of eight is at the bar drinking soft drinks. As I settle down uncomfortably, there is a large crash, two men have fallen over in one heap and broken many glasses. The landlord sighs, takes out his bucket and brush and sweeps up around them. The men are fast asleep.

45 **Doncaster Rovers**

v. Rotherham United
DIVISION THREE

19 December

0-3

'After all we have been through in these recent weeks ...'

Bernard Jordan, Programme Editor. Nobody from the club dare speak.

Today, senior Doncaster councillors have been named and condemned by the District Auditor as part of the 'Donnygate' scandal. Trips to Singapore (I adore Singapore by the way: I'm alone on this one, but right), 'considerable private telephone calls', failing to declare hospitality, relationships with developers; all the usual grisly local government fare. The entire district Labour Party has been suspended for some time, shortly after the Conservative opposition had called for an alcohol ban at council meetings, claiming Labour were legless at meetings. The police set up a confidential hotline for Town Hall staff in May.

Corruption – if these people are corrupt – flourishes because nobody cares in the same way they do about paedophiles or travellers. Perhaps they're right. In a sense, it doesn't matter if anyone's on the take. People grab what they can and if there's nothing for them to take, they may find themselves in Doncaster on a sleety Friday afternoon, slumped in AD43 at 5 p.m., fast asleep, about to be gently woken by bouncers.

I'm chirpy today. I must declare a soft spot for Diana Rigg's Doncaster, with its mining tradition – Doncaster mines were as solid as any during the strike: go to villages like Kevin Keegan's Armthorpe or heroin joytown Mexborough to see Thatcher's children living in conditions that Elizabeth Fry wouldn't believe – its pride in being a railway town and the faded early-70s glamour of the Waterdale mall. Now with 10,000 ex-miners out of work, South Korean investment in the disused colliery sites is coming a cropper as the Asian economies implode.

Along the road, Nelsons is having an 'all day party'. This means the street is quaking with Christmas tunes, the bouncers are turning people away for being too drunk and it's not even time for the shops to close.

Influenza coursing through my body, a sleet/rain mix pouring onto it, I move out of town, along Bennetthorpe, a Wembley Way of the north, towards the racecourse, home of the St Leger since 1776. By that time, Doncaster's Quaker tradition was asserting itself and it had been a market town for centuries. Soon, Sir Walter Scott would set parts of *Ivanhoe* in nearby Conisborough castle and those railways and mines would come, unlike immigrants who never really settled here. The houses become progressively more middle class: terraced, semi-detached, detached. It's still raining, but the racecourse, partially lit, stands majestic, the big brother who's done well for himself.

Across the road it's Third World football. Belle Vue is the home of Doncaster Rovers, the worst team in the Football League with the worst ground to match, whose last home gate was 864; who, according to possible manager (nobody knows who does what) Mark Weaver, are heading for the Vauxhall Conference at 'a million miles an hour', who train in local parks, who have had the worst start of any club ever and who may or may not be playing tonight, although kickoff time is an hour away.

This is complicated. Doncaster Rovers' majority shareholders are a company called Dinard, which is connected with Isle Of Man resident Ken Richardson – he claims Dinard are merely friends, but they're registered in Liberia, so nobody knows – businessman and self-proclaimed Rovers 'benefactor', who picked the team, gave team talks and directed operations from the dugout while Kerry Dixon was manager. Richardson is not on the club's masthead although the board is comprised of his pal, his daughter and his niece. Murkier and murkier.

Plans for a new stadium have been rejected by the local council who won't deal with Richardson. Three years ago, Dinard secured the lease to Belle Vue, which is worth more than the club. Dinard refused to spend money on the team, preferring to maximise the value of the lease, but the club still claims Belle Vue will be redeveloped. The Gaza Strip is more likely to be redeveloped.

The floodlights are off, the massive car park outside the ground is in darkness. It's puddle-ridden and I can't see where I'm going. Outside the players' entrance, there is a bare bulb, flickering and forlorn. I assume the game is postponed – my stomach-churning fear for future months – and squelch towards a figure in the gloom. Relief! He is a steward. The game must be on.

Rotherham is a few miles south and, as Rotherham United edge towards the play-off slots, their support will outnumber Doncaster's. Indeed, as the team arrives through the dark in their sponsored Gordons coach – not sponsored enough, no table lights – they are cheered to the dressing room by confident supporters, perhaps the first time this has happened to a Rotherham team.

Someone has a deathwish at Doncaster Rovers. Although tonight will probably be the largest attendance of the season, the club run from

Portakabins have chosen this evening to downscale the programme to fourteen A5, black and white pages for £1. Even entering the stand (I feel like giving the club as much money as I can, despite the people of Doncaster not feeling the same way) is dodgy: turnstiles do not click and therefore register attendance. I hand over a £10 note to the bloke at the door and he doesn't give me a ticket in return.

Inside, it's a non-smoking (largely ignored by this gathering of beagles, which scares me enormously) wooden firetrap. So much so that it burned down in 1995 in circumstances most suspicious. In court 'soon' (the defence keeps delaying it) on arson-connected charges is Ken Richardson.

To get to the catering on the terrace, a steward gives me a cloakroom ticket. There, I'm served by children who were surely in primary school three hours ago (this cannot possibly be legal, unless Doncaster's child labour laws are adopted from Indonesia's robust legal system). Despite tonight's bumper crowd, despite the cold and wet, they've forgotten the pies. One of the girls is chewing gum. While she's waiting for my tea cup to fill, looking me straight in the eye, she pulls the gum out of her mouth with her fingers, stretches it as far as possible and pops it back underneath her tongue. I didn't want a pie anyway.

I mention this Graham Greene-esque scenario to the steward, who explains nearly all. 'You should have been here last week, they were using two electric kettles to make the tea.' The proper catering company, he explains, have recently been sacked, to be replaced by another, whose female head is a very close friend of possible manager Weaver, Richardson's protégé. As a cost-cutting measure they've stopped giving the stewards (down from forty at the beginning of the season to ten at £10 a match and all the abuse they can handle) free tea 'and God, it gets bloody cold here'.

I find a bench seat behind the press box (not a box at all, that's been requisitioned by this most paranoid of clubs for crowd surveillance so they can photograph protesting fans, thus the press have to use seats, less than ideal when, like tonight, it's raining – they do get free tea, though). My seat is a small portion of a small bench, my view is obscured and there are Rotherham fans everywhere.

On the Doncaster bench is pipe-smoking, baseball-hatted former Rotherham manager, 'Director Of Football' Danny Bergara and 'Director Of Youth' Dave Cowling. Neither are actually Doncaster manager, but both have been this season. Bergara resigned after crowd abuse, while Cowling was appointed on a promise of no interference. When, for his third game, he was told what the starting line-up would be, this principled man resigned too. The area behind the bench and in front of the directors' box is cordoned off. Weaver, 'general manager/manager' according to the programme, is probably in the directors' box, but as befits someone who has to hide his car before home games to avoid it being trashed, he keeps a low profile. Confused? I am. Still, at least the rain is helping the lush grass grow on the disused Town End.

The people around me are horrible and blunt. An old man with a Doncaster season ticket asks an arrogant Rotherham fan and his fat pig of a son, who've brought cushions as if the son's rump didn't provide enough padding, to move. The father contemptuously refuses claiming it's not reserved. I think the old man is going to cry, but he shuffles off, knowing it wouldn't have happened when things were different.

Across the aisle from me are more Rotherham fans, none of whom can discuss anything except at shouting volume (I blame city centre pubs for breeding a generation of yellers). They swear so much a fellow Rotherham fan accompanied by little kids asks 'Watch the language, mate'. Response: 'Fuck off'.

Doncaster Rovers, still scandalously without a shirt sponsor (if they're still going next year, I'll do it: £500 for a season of JOHN AIZLEWOOD emblazoned across their manly torsos, perhaps with a picture of a grinning me giving the thumbs down sign too), are even more of a pub team than they were at Darlington with players plucked from obscure teams (Droylesden, Chorley, Netherfield, Worksop Town, Trafford Barons, Hyde United, Stockton) in unknown leagues. The future for them as individuals and for the club as a whole looks more untenable than bleak. The despair is almost tangible.

Unless of course a buyer steps forward, assuming the club really is for sale. The fan-led Rovers Appeal Fund is trying to raise £2 million for a buy-out, but Anton Johnson, new friend of Kerry Dixon, is said to be interested too and allegedly shook hands with Richardson on a deal. This week, the club's value has mysteriously risen to £3.75 million.

Johnson says he would be an adviser to a board led by Doncaster plastic surgeon and former Rovers director John Ryan. Weaver has claimed that Johnson has submitted nothing to the club's accountants. Johnson has a) fallen foul of the law and FA regulations, b) been chairman of Rotherham United when he used to land on the pitch in his helicopter before matches and c) made a single, his version of Bruce Channel's 'Hey! Baby'. It wasn't a hit. Such is the state of things that he's being hailed as a saviour.

Rotherham do the sensible thing and play three up front, including Scott Taylor, on loan from Bolton and victim of such Premier-League-to-Doncaster culture shock that he doesn't touch the ball for thirty minutes. Rotherham are disjointed so Doncaster hang on until just before half-time when little Trevor Berry picks out Andy Roscoe, unmarked at the far post. His cross shot is kindly helped into goal by Doncaster's Ian Gore. Rotherham fans, cold and wet but feeling the unusual swell of being a big club, mercilessly sing 'Donny's going down ... You're worse than Donny Belles' and 'What's it like to see a crowd' before continuing their anti-Sheffield Wednesday selection, 'He's fat, he's round, he's taking Wednesday down, Atkinson, Atkinson'. Doncaster's fans, opposite me on the Popular Stand side-terrace are silent. Outnumbered, they can't even mount their usual protests against Weaver and Richardson. On the field Rovers heads drop. I know it's natural selection, but this is heartbreaking.

There's no half-time entertainment, of course there's no entertainment, there won't be a club soon. After the break Rovers trouble Bobby Mimms (Yes! Him!) once, when brilliant work by Mike Smith sets up ex-Rotherham centre forward Ian Helliwell for a stylishly saved header. Doncaster look so lively that for a moment, I foolishly think they might sneak something, then Rotherham score two in a minute. Lee Glover, having missed several one-on-ones, powers through the shellac defence and thumps home unstoppably from outside the area. Then crafty Steve Thompson's precise through ball sends Taylor out on his own and he shoots through the legs of onrushing ex-Rotherham goalkeeper Craig Davis, who is playing for nothing.

Rotherham, without dominating as they should, have done enough. A cry to manager Ronnie Moore of 'Wake yourself up, get some football played, we didn't come to see this,' is a touch harsh, but these are harsh people, although Rotherham have not had a 3-0 away league victory since Bradford City in 1995. For Doncaster, it's one more game until extinction.

During the match, there'd been an announcement that coaches were being laid on for those who'd travelled by train from Rotherham. 'Coaches' means one double-decker bus, so about fifty Rotherham fans elect to walk along Bennetthorpe, back into town. They are rough, poverty stricken hardmen, but they know what they're doing. So too do a smattering of better-dressed Doncaster fans, who've emerged from nowhere ahead of the men from Rotherham to suggest that a fight is the correct form of South Yorkshire etiquette at this point. Mounted police charge down Bennetthorpe, past the Earl Of Doncaster hotel where a brass band is playing 'Away In A Manger', as the two groups clash. A few kicks and punches later, the police surround the Rotherham fans.

There is a further problem. To get to the railway station, the Rotherham fans have to be marched along Hall Gate, where 'tis the Friday before Christmas and the natives are out in force, queuing to get into pubs and as drunk as they were when Daniel Defoe came in 1743 and noted Doncaster's fine ale houses. This is not a situation into which the police would ideally like to pitch two groups of ex-miners who wish to kick each other into 1998.

The police do well. Two transit vans block off each end of Hall Gate so traffic is stopped, a third zooms to a halt in front of the Doncaster fans. A couple are arrested, the rest shoved back and mounted police ensure the only trouble will come from pissed women trying to stroke the horses. Those arrested may well find themselves in the privatised prison, 'Doncatraz' run by Americans, Wackenhut Corrections Corporation, whose founder has files on three million

Americans and runs a strike-busting operation as a sideline. The Rotherham fans are shoved through to the station.

Now the invaders have been seen off, Doncaster starts to celebrate in a manner that the citizens of Sodom and Gomorrah might consider excessive. I squeeze into Silks Famous Bar, where the central heating is turned up full, ensuring nobody's thirst will be sated tonight.

It's as soul-bolstering as Oldham, with added drink and screaming. This is England at Christmas: Wizzard's 'I Wish It Could Be Christmas Every Day', as loud as God; gorgeous women with bare arms, tinsel around their necks, carrying only a packet of Marlboro Lights, a tiny purse and a rose; Apollo Travel's burglar alarm adding high-pitched treble to the mix; a wheelchair-bound man whizzing around at high speed with a silly grin on his face; vomit running down the gutter and the smell of kebabs and chips. Nobody over thirty-five is allowed out and nobody cares about the local football team. These people do wish it could be Christmas every day, that's why I wish I was part of them.

46 **Wigan Athletic**

v. Brentford
DIVISION TWO
20 December

4-0

'We have a very professional squad of players who always try to play to my game plan.'

John Deehan

The road to Wigan Pier is a dull dual carriageway lined with shops I'll never visit: Tile Mart 'discount ceramic tile centre' and B&Q, run by dark cabals of which I know nothing. George Orwell wouldn't recognise Wigan: the mines (begun circa 1450, expanding to a thousand shafts within five miles of the centre at the end of the last century) have gone and the textiles have shrunk.

The Heinz factory now employs some of the unemployable, but in the mid-1980s the council decided to redevelop the pier sector where, from the 19th century until 1972, coal and cotton were loaded onto the barges of the Leeds & Liverpool Canal. Decline meant dereliction and the area was haven for the usual roll call of the urban forgotten who sometimes shared needles and always charged extra for doing business without a condom. The Queen opened the new tourist attraction in 1986, indication that Britain now saw its future in the heritage industry. Incidentally when Margaret Thatcher came to always-Labour Wigan in 1990, she was only allowed to open the Tidy Britain Group's offices. They haven't started tidying their lobby yet.

Heritage makes me feel queasy, although Doncaster last night may be the future. Winner of 1995's Best Medium Sized Tourist Attraction Of the Year, Wigan Pier has The Way We Were museum (repulsively, live actors perform scenes from 1900 Wigan); souvenir shops; The Orwell pub with its slogan Big Brother We Love You (he lodged in a mining family's canal-side cottage while writing the Wigan Pier book), and, across the road, various mill-related paraphernalia. It's all open, The Orwell promises food, but nobody is around. Why should they be on December 20?

In term time, harassed teachers might fall upon this as a pleasant diversion for their evil little charges, but I give it a miss (and the mining heritage centre the other side of town) to find the football ground, not an easy task in a place where all roads and signs lead to Central Park, home of Wigan rugby league club, on the crest of a slump right now. Who, aside from a few Lancashire Luddites and most of Halifax, would notice or care if rugby league stopped tomorrow? Silly game, although compared with rugby union it's eighty minutes of sex games with all the occupants of Wankworld. I buy the *Wigan Evening News*. There is no mention of Wigan Athletic.

The town where Marks & Spencer began hasn't noticed Christmas is next Friday. There are no hymns, no brass bands working for militaristic charities, no women with flashing reindeer ears, no pissed lads and little overcrowding. It's an odd place, aware of its history but mealy-mouthed *vis-à-vis* the present.

Ever gruff, Wigan disowns its famous. There's no sign of George Formby or Roy Kinnear tributes and Wigan Casino must have been some sort of conspiracy myth, but they boast about the poverty which caused one William Dodd to write in 1841 'I do not remember ever to have seen such misery and wretchedness in so small a compass'.

They revere Wigan's former owner William De Bradshaigh who fought in the Crusades, hopefully joining up at The Trip To Jerusalem in Nottingham. His wife, Mabel, assumed he was dead and married a Welsh knight. On his return, disguised as a pilgrim (the notion of anyone making a pilgrimage to Wigan should have alerted Mabel), De Bradshaigh slayed the usurper and, each week, made Mabel walk several miles into town, barefoot, as penance, to what became known as Mab's Cross.

I empathise with Mabel by the time I reach Springfield Park, via a circuitous route which involves me mistaking floodlights used to illuminate railway sidings as the ground's. It's north-west of town in a park of sorts. Its surrounds are upper working class, i.e. terraced houses but nice ones. The ground, however, is so ramshackle, unpredictable and dangerous, it could form the next government of Sierra Leone all by itself.

The Phoenix Stand is many times superior to Doncaster's last night, but still barely functioning. On the terraces, like all home fans, I can wander between the uncovered Springfield End and covered (where the roof isn't holey) St Andrews Drive Stand. Barriers are in short supply. I reckon that's dangerous, but what do I know about the construction of sports stadia? Not a thing, actually.

Wigan Athletic plan to move to Robin Park soon – perhaps with Wigan RFC, if rugby league is still going – a new ground modelled on Ewood Park. Chairman Dave Whelan, once a Blackburn Rovers player and now millionaire owner of Athletic sponsors JJB Sports has wisely (if the move comes off) neglected the ground, but paid big money to players who would not come here otherwise. Kevin Sharpe, David Lowe and Pat McGibbon were too good for Division Three last season. The same now applies in Division Two to David Lee and toothless Scott Green. If only one attendance this season had topped 6000 ...

Unlike Doncaster, they've remembered the pies. They shouldn't have. It's an unusual concept: meat as semolina. My pie is a special friend for two more days. Today is cold and misty, yet I'm the only purchaser in my vicinity. As she served me, the catering woman said to her colleague, 'I'm off to the toilet now'. I now find this significant.

It should be an interesting game (I always believe this; no wonder life is so disappointing). Wigan have won their last four games, finally clicking into form to take them out of the relegation struggle.

Brentford, on their Travellers coach (possibly the same as Leyton Orient's), are accompanied by one double-decker busload of supporters, reflecting how poorly the team is doing, fourth from bottom and without an away win. They've had three managers this season. Current incumbent Micky Adams has managed three clubs himself. I guess I'm the only person in the world, apart from him, to see Fulham, Swansea City and Brentford under his stewardship. I know it's anoraky, but I'd like it on my gravestone. With all the other stuff. It will not be a discreet gravestone.

Like Doncaster, there's grassed-over, out-of-bounds areas and both ends are uncovered. Unlike Doncaster, there is a mascot, Springy, who tries to raise a docile crowd with the usual antics. During the match, he has a section of unused terrace to himself. He urges the team on, leaps about for goals and looks horror-stuck whenever Brentford attack. He never lets up for ninety minutes. Oh, how I still long for mascothood.

The game is as straightforward as the teams' emergence to Survivor's 'Eye Of The Tiger'. Wigan are excellent, Brentford are physical but dire. After thirty minutes they look to be holding out and the crowd are getting twitchy. Warren Aspinall, thirty-one, is Brentford's latest hope. Wigan-born, he began with Athletic, possibly being their best-ever player. The crowd come to life when Lee incites overrun full back Paul Watson into a terrible tackle for which he's rightly booked. Aspinall leaps in to protest. The crowd chant 'Ohhh, fatty, fatty, fatty, fatty Aspinall'. At this he bears his chest. It's a tanned, hairy chest, quite comforting to nuzzle into I'd hazard. And he's holding it in. This riles the crowd even more, so he makes vomiting gestures in their direction. Everyone laughs. It's a Wigan thing, I guess.

Wigan score one after a corner, some penalty area ping-ping, McGibbon's shoulder and, finally, Lowe's flying header two inches out. Then they score more. Tiny Dutch reserve centre forward Jorg Smeets hasn't had much of a look in. Now, he collects the ball just past the centre circle, runs on and unleashes a staggering dipper which even a trimmer, more agile goalkeeper than Kevin Dearden wouldn't have come close to. 2-0. Fantastic, so much so that I leap into the air and cheer. Sometimes I can't help it.

Before half-time, Brentford have made three substitutions: 38-year-old Glenn Cockerill has hobbled off, David McGhee, young enough to be his son, is carried off and hapless full back Malcolm McPherson is dragged off. The mist descends, the wind picks up and the Londoners want to go home. The dispassionate crowd, white to a man – Steve Morgan's tremendous display does prompt a 'God is a black man' quip – are delighted, as they should be after this.

In the second half, Wigan attack the goal their fans have access to. There's a mass exodus from the covered side, leaving me very much solo in the cold and mist, except for four ruffians who spend the remain forty-five minutes chanting 'Down with the Carlisle, you're going down with the Carlisle' at the snooty but forlorn Brentford fans. One day I'd love to see a team really go for it, despite winning handsomely already. That team isn't Wigan and they only wake up when Carl Hutchings and Leon Townley have nearly pulled Brentford back. The crowd become silent but restive. Brentford over-commit themselves and two identical goals in the last ten minutes – Lee feeds an unmarked Smeets for the third and Smeets feeds an unmarked Ian Kilford for 4-0 – give a slightly unfair tinge to the score, but football isn't meant to be fair. I may have mentioned this before.

I lose my way again on the walk back to the centre, but when I finally get there, past a place where Bonnie Prince Charlie stayed as he slunk back to Scotland – he stayed everywhere, the broke, drunken scamp – the pubs are getting full and lads are trying to kick over construction works in the big square. I take refreshment in the Moon Under Water, or Arse Over Breast, or Students & Slappers, or whatever the town's Wetherspoons pub is called. Jesus, I'm halfway there, forty-six gone forty-six to go. As I sip my pint, alone as ever, face reddening in new heat following a chill afternoon, I look back: that day at Leeds, my despair in Blackpool, Doncaster, the Diana silences, drunk in Bristol and Exeter and the rest, Sweary at Chelsea. Forty-six games left, a whole season outside the Premiership from now to 10 May, including winter. I'm terrified. I've started to sweat too.

47 **Queens Park Rangers**

v. Bradford City
DIVISION ONE

21 December

1-0

> **'I want you to know that I'm relishing the task that lies ahead of both myself and everyone else at the club.'**

Ray Harford

Pies. Yesterday's last food, today's first food. My stomach is saggy, my skin porey and this Sunday morning, the Wigan shocker is still playing havoc with my delicate ecosystem. The Queens Park Rangers pie is a superior beast, although I'm never ready for solids at midday.

I like Queens Park Rangers. Everybody likes Queens Park Rangers. They're harmless and they sacked Stewart Houston and Bruce Rioch after I saw their dismal showing at Middlesbrough. That's two managers (Brian Horton too), I've seen the last rites of. Mid-table nothingnness beckons, as it does for Bradford City, whose bright start should ensure they stay up, and nothing else.

Loftus Road is in a horrible, horrible area. Opposite the ground, White City Estate is tower block Babel for 8000 of the underclass: where in May 1997 a nine-year-old girl was raped by five nine- and ten-year-old boys; where policemen are rarely seen; where widows who've never been affluent enough to move away and who now live to go into a home are mugged, and where BBC employees idiot enough to stray from Television Centre around the corner with bags which may contain a personal computer are robbed. The New Covenant Church – not for whites – is closed.

Shepherds Bush, down the road, is a mixture of slow on the uptake fast food outlets, laundrettes where people drink gin while watching their smalls tumble, 'Information' centres like the Islamic one 'Welcome to the wonderful world of Islam. Read Al Qur'an, The Last Testament' and pubs whose custom is built around the apartheid that naturally occurs when transient, downtrodden ethnic groups are thrust together. Tricky business apartheid, especially when it occurs by tacit, mutual consent. Still, the General Smuts and Springbok pubs and the street names around here – South Africa Road,

Bloemfontein Road – are oddly hip now, legacies of Britain's last privatised war. The names were unchanged during real apartheid.

Up the road is Holland Park, where Richard Branson, Hartlepool MP Peter Mandelson, Van Morrison and other individuals with more money than the entire White City Estate, live. These people are more likely to visit Loftus Road than the immediate locals. It's a clean ground, one where being all-seater doesn't matter because there was no atmosphere while there was standing and a 19,000 capacity that isn't going to be breached in the foreseeable future.

However, Rangers now share their ground with Wasps rugby union club (estimated support: twenty-seven), so wasp motifs are woven into the Ericsson Family Stand and Wasps have a page in the football programme which doesn't mention attendance figures. Even so, this Sunday morning, with banks of empty, closed off seating, may be another future for football if Sky keeps showing unimportant games at difficult times. Couldn't they stop gorging for a moment?

I'm in the Main Stand, right above the halfway line with a pleasingly unobscured view. My neighbour is called Dean. I know this because he's introduced himself and his mate (whose name I don't catch), shaken my hand and we're sharing Fisherman's Friends. Both Dean and his friend are wearing blue and white Santa hats. He's a good man is Dean, he lives in Greenford beyond the North Circular, he's got a kid and can't see Rangers as often as he'd like. I utilise my barely passable Cockney accent, pretend to be a Rangers fan who's been to one game all season ('Middlesbrough away? That's an odd one,' muses Dean) and we're home and dry.

' 'Ere,' confides Dean, as the players half-heartedly warm up, pointing to long-haired centre half Karl Ready, 'Don't you think Ready looks like a puff?' Yes I do, Dean, yes I do. Somehow, I don't think me and Dean will be discussing anything apart from the match. Ready earns £200,000 a year.

It's a wretched game. Sky are shooting themselves in the foot with games like this. Travelling in a lampless Wallace Arnold coach, more suitable, significantly, to a team in a lower league, Bradford have no penetration and Queens Park Rangers don't look like they're out to impress new manager Harford, especially after Hungarian signing (from Bradford ironically enough) George Kulscar limps off half an hour in. 'Bloody hell, £17 for this, know what I mean?' shrugs Dean. I know exactly what he means, 'and couldn't they have given tickets away to schoolkids to help fill the ground?' I'm with him there too, except that schoolkids would be put off for life by this stodge.

The goal that wins it is rubbish too. John Spencer is having a nightmare ('He must have personal problems,' states Dean, gravely) but he entices Chris Wilder into pushing him over in the penalty area. Gavin Peacock takes the penalty. Goalkeeper Gary Walsh makes a fine block, but it spins over him and trickles into the net.

The people behind me are of more unpleasant vintage than Dean. Rangers goalkeeper Tony Roberts is 'a cunt'. They arrived too late to hear the pre-match announcement asking politely for foul language to be outlawed, or they'd never have used that word. More interestingly, Karl The Unready is 'a clam' and they're still talking about 1975–76 when a freak of football life meant Rangers finished second in the whole league. The game plods on and I spend half-time in front of the Wall Of Fame, where for reasons unclear, £26 buys me a brick in a wall with my name on it for the remainder of the season.

Trevor Sinclair wakes up once during the second half to collect the ball on the halfway line, skip through the defence and thunder a drive at the crossbar (as he did at Middlesbrough). The crowd is docile, but understanding of a new regime which has dropped ex-Arsenal players Lee Harper, Steve Morrow and Matthew Rose. They pass the time booing Bradford's on-loan full back Bryan Small for some imagined offence and talking amongst themselves. Their team leaves orthodox winger Peter Beagrie unmarked. Bradford manager Chris Kamara and his preposterous moustache become agitated on the bench. Next door to him, Harford, a touchline dervish, is more animated than his players. Finally, referee Mathieson ends it all and, hurtfully, Dean walks off without a word.

I'm depressed. It's cold and rapidly darkening. I chance an Irish pub (i.e. one full of Irish people, not to be confused with pubs called O'Neills) on the Uxbridge Road. It's so full – Newcastle and Manchester United are warming up on Sky – I have to squeeze against the bar, but as it's London I'm not the only sad case to be drinking alone. The drug doesn't work and twenty minutes later I'm on the underground remembering a school hymn with the hedonistic 'live each day as if it were your last' line. That's not the same as feeling if every day is my last. I know that now.

48 **Wimbledon**

v. Arsenal
PREMIER LEAGUE
22 December

0-0, abandoned

'Rather than harp on, I'd rather keep positive and praise the hard working industrious team.'

Joe Kinnear

Four matches in four days. This isn't great for my state of mind. Neither is stalking South London, where the underground doesn't run, white socks are compulsory and the rest of the worst of Britain begins.

There's talk of Wimbledon moving to Dublin and their fans are demonstrating against it. Whilst I don't want to clamber in bed with David Mellor (how not one but at least three women have done this is a mystery to me, albeit inspiration, too), he's in favour of the move and, unusually, he's right. Everyone benefits except the few Wimbledon fans. Dublin is one of the finest cities in Europe, a £50 flight away for supporters of proper clubs who would love a weekend away. The Irish would go for Wimbledon in a way Londoners have steadfastly refused to do and the club would be saved. Easy, although not as easy as sharing with Fulham, Millwall, Chelsea or Queens Park Rangers.

Wimbledon are tenants. 'Partner/governor' Sam Hammam and his new Norwegian overlords ('partners' officially), Kjell Rokke, owner of Europe's biggest trawler fleet and Bjorn Rune Gjelsten, don't like it. Landlords Crystal Palace don't like it, although they like the money and Merton Council don't seem to want a Premier League club in the borough. They survive every year, ruffle a few over-preened feathers and are the away game fans of Manchester United, Liverpool and the big London teams can attend without a scrap for tickets. Hence tonight, Selhurst, Norwood, Thornton Heath or wherever I am, is swamped by Arsenal fans.

Selhurst Park is in the middle of a soulless but fairly plush area. The Sainsburys – in full flow tonight – at one end makes it a laughing stock and not only are Wimbledon run from Portakabins, but so are Crystal Palace. Outside, Wimbledon fans are preparing yet another protest, giving out leaflets full of sentimental guff 'I could never have imagined that one day someone would try to take my little club away from me' and calling for fan power. A protest is planned, hence the mini-banners saying Back To Merton and It's Time We Had A Home Game. None say Back To The Southern Premier or It's Time We Grew Up.

My celebrity count goes up. I see two former Sheffield Wednesday managers, Trevor Francis and David Pleat, in a minute. Pleat, not a vain man judging by his dress sense, has a personalised number plate, as does Dave Beasant – CP7 BES – who can't keep away from the club he loves. Arsenal, as they did at Highbury in August, arrive in a Hallmark coach so luxurious it could fly me to the moon. The Arsenal headrests are only the start. It's raining again. I could be in *Blade Runner*, except whereas Harrison Ford gets to kiss Sean Young in the wet, I get a rubbish hot dog in the Arthur Wait Stand.

Worse is to come. I bought my ticket from Ticketmaster. The lovely man there told me I was a) in the middle with a view any passing royalty would envy, and b) in a mixed area. I am, a) literally at the end, as I am in relation to my tether, with not one but both goals obscured and, b) as I must concede is always the way here, surrounded by a mix of away supporters and seats the away supporters didn't fill. I make a mental note to burn down the offices of Ticketmaster in the morning. I have to stand up as older Arsenal fans send younger ones to stand on the empty seats in front of me. Bastards. Standing up, looking out across the Arsenal fans, I still loath them, although for every 100 beer-bellied, smug, unfeeling men, there is a truly beautiful, elegant woman. That's a worse ratio than society at large. At least I'm under cover.

Wimbledon, bless them, enter to the *Mission: Impossible* theme. Their supporters wave their banners for the Sky cameras, including a No Ground & We're Sick Of It behind the dugout, behind the Arsenal dugout actually. It's an ineffective protest. Only a small proportion of the tiny amount of Wimbledon supporters have bothered. They deserve all they get.

The game is odd. Arsenal look jittery. Nothing is going right for Ian Wright, disproving the idea that it's impossible to become a bad player overnight; David Seaman is as shaky as he's ever looked; David Platt, expertly described in the programme as having 'the eyes of a man with a pitchfork rooted in his goalmouth', is invisible and even gloved Dakar-born Patrick Vieira looks leaden-footed. Wimbledon potter around, gangly and awkward. Robbie Earle hits the post, the Wimbledon few outsing the Arsenal many with their 'Joe Kinnear's Wimbledon Army' and I'm bored senseless.

Then, thirty seconds into the second half, it happens. The lights go out! There is a huge collective groan, except from me. I am delighted, I am tired and I want to go to home. I am also, I'd presume, the only person here whose only two attempts to see Wimbledon this season have ended in floodlight failure. Ha ha.

As the players slope off in the dark, there is an announcement explaining that the lights won't go on for twenty minutes 'for safety reasons'. The PA booms out soothing drum'n'bass. A Wimbledon player (I can't see who, it's dark) runs on and scores a goal. Soon the lights flood back on and the players warm up once more. Then, the lights go out again, the match is abandoned immediately and we are asked to 'leave the stadium quietly', not something there should be any problem with, despite a quick burst of 'What a fucking shitty ground' from all four sides of it.

Even the rain cannot dampen my spirits, nor the long queue at Selhurst station under the glare of a police helicopter's floodlight beam (four police helicopters and the game could have carried on, but I digress), swollen by those who would normally leave early, nor even the certainty that I'll be back to see Crystal Palace. Inside Selhurst, the police are directing travellers to the wrong platform. I chance correctly and the train stops with a carriage-door right in front of me, so I'm first on, a ball of happiness in a pissed-off world. Opposite me a distraught boy wipes the rain off the end of his nose while his father tries to read his sodden programme. Externally, I'm so quiet church mice are begging me to speak up. Internally, I'm singing a rousing chorus of 'Zip-A-Dee-Doo-Dah', the Harry Nilsson version. My oh my, what a wonderful day ...

49 Liverpool

v. Leeds United
PREMIER LEAGUE

26 December

3-1

'We know it is going to take an absolutely fantastic effort by us in the second half of the season, as well as a slip-up by Manchester United, for us to have a chance.'

Roy Evans

Another day, another slave port. I don't get Liverpool, never have. Today is Boxing Day and the sales haven't begun yet, perhaps because they've been on for the last six months to stave off yet another deepening of the recession that can never leave this place, so Liverpool is closed. Apart, that is, from McDonald's, which covered almost every hamlet in England before it dared come here. It's eerie, there's plenty of shoppers, but nowhere to shop and nobody's buying the *Liverpool Echo*, which really should have taken the day off. There's mawkish sentimentality – hence the mob rule that asserts itself whenever some unfortunate Scouse child is abducted – in the paving stone tribute to a dead busker. What a creepy city this is. It's always like this, even when the shops are open.

The pawnbrokers, Harvey & Thompson, unnervingly close to the city centre, have clearly had a feisty year, but they're alone and Liverpool's 80s veneer is stating to look unkempt, the architectural equivalent of shell-suits. As if there aren't enough problems here, Liverpool now houses 128 destitute refugees which Westminster can't/won't take, dumping them in a special hostel for which Westminster pays Liverpool £126 per week, per refugee.

The finest building in Liverpool is the Queen Elizabeth II law courts. Past it is Albert Dock, the heritage centre packed with museums and a Tate Gallery, which are closed too. Nothing, though, can hide a desperation to give the appearance of giving something, anything, to a city that has nothing other than football. This is a city with five MPs. Last General Election, Conservatives scored four third places and one fourth. Labour's smallest majority was over 18,000. Not the politics of affluence.

I take in the Mersey. It's a good, wide, brown river throwing off a chill wind.

Over in the distance is Birkenhead and The Wirral, where things are better and where Cammell Laird shipbuilders are still in business. I can see the Liver Birds on the Royal Liver Building roof. They need a scrub. Legend has it that if they disappear, Liverpool will sink into the Mersey. The Nazis missed them, although they did hit over 184,000 of 282,000 homes.

To keep out the cold and because I'm alone, I hum my favourite Beatles tune, 'Octopus's Garden'. The fairly-Fabs might have kept the Scouse accent for marketing purposes, but they didn't hang around. And they never came back, thus denying themselves the chance to see Julie Goodyear star in *Aladdin*.

It's a mighty walk to Anfield, which partially explains why there are no football fans in the city centre. Liverpool fans tending not to hail from Liverpool is another. It's a lowering walk too, for Liverpool's flimsy glitz doesn't extend 200 yards from the pawnbrokers. There was a storm last night which killed a woman on Penny Lane, but I don't know whether I'm seeing storm damage or if it's always like this. My odyssey takes me along Great Homer Street, where the library is boarded up, the shops need metal grills and the quiet is a tad too, well, quiet for my liking. I want background noise. A gull will do. There's none of that here. Even the passing cars (and there are not many) are muffled. I could murder someone at random (a long-standing ambition) here and get away with it or be murdered and nobody would know or care.

I buy my *Liverpool Echo* at Denbigh Offie. I knew these places exist, but the reality is a cold shock. It's not like a proper grocery store: the woman – brusque and wary of a stranger – and her stock are protected from the community they feed by a Plexiglas barrier. Nothing is to hand for customers. I scurry away, pausing only to skip round the kids on bikes – all brand, spanking new for Christmas, but these are poor, tough children and Liverpool is the centre of Britain's drug distribution network – who've congregated outside Denbigh Offie while I was inside. Sound idea, Plexiglas barriers.

Imagine – and I'm being stupid now, but doctors say it's good to daydream, although they don't have my daydreams – if Tony Blair decided that the sole task of his administration was to make the woman at Denbigh Offie feel secure enough to take her Plexiglas down. Imagine what he would have accomplished along the way and how, because of one sheet of Plexiglas, the Millennium would be the greatest spiritual renewal Britain has known. Just a thought.

I circle towards Anfield, past blocks of flats, more boarded-up than lived in, and all I can hear in my head is 'Liverpool Lullaby' by Cilla Black (she kept the accent and moved south ASAP: a pattern emerges). I didn't think it would be like this, I didn't think what I thought of as cliché was documentary.

Anfield itself is no Old Trafford. It doesn't have the air of significance. There's not row upon row of chip shops and street vendors for the diaspora that turns Old Trafford into an Old Testament temple. Outside the supposedly sacred Kop is a fence. On this fence, some whore has allowed McDonald's to place several of their corporate letter Ms. There's a statue of Bill Shankly, a fine, noble thing with the slogan He Made The People Happy (great use of the word 'the') on the plinth. This statue is sponsored too. Why don't they just take Liverpool's history, the memories of Shankly and Paisley, all the trophies and burn them on a huge sponsored bonfire? It's disgusting, and the decayed terraced housing (I'd heard the football club had bought the locality up, but it doesn't look like it) subsumed by the ground, whose residents can't afford to see matches, doesn't make it any better. By comparison, the scarf stall playing 'You'll Never Walk Alone' from a ghetto blaster is dignity personified.

The Shankly Gates have an innate decency which the flogging off of family silver elsewhere has lost. Next to the gates is the memorial to the Hillsborough disaster and it's bordered by wooden planks, presumably a precursor to renovation. The names of the dead are on the wall, an eternal flame flickers and there are Leeds and Barnsley scarves among the Liverpool ones left as offerings.

My friend Roger has gone to Australia for Christmas, so I've arranged to meet his matchday companion at the Shankly Gates to use Roger's season ticket. I've never met him before, but like me Paul is early. Fortunately – there's an obligation to make conversation in these often awkward circumstances – he's a splendid human being. He was once in River City People, who had hits in the early-90s and he's now in Speed, who're fine and dandy. He's also seen Liverpool players in late-night drinking dens around The Cavern and has a theory as to why it's usually the YTS players who're caught by drug testing at training grounds. The club nominates who gets tested. Can that really be true?

Our seats are in the Centenary Stand. When he requested his season ticket, Paul asked to be sat opposite Liverpool chairman David Moores. Unusually, the club agreed and so we're on the halfway line, far enough back to be under cover, but close enough to the front to be on top of play. I can even cope with the acute lack of leg room (bet David Moores can stretch his legs fine, thanks), industrial strength tea and a long but microwave-floppy sausage roll. Everyone knows Paul and this means the nice lady behind us will share her toffees with us all afternoon. It makes being alive a little bit better.

Paul explains that Liverpool have been patchy this season, but he's never seen a player like Michael Owen, the game's most striking striker. Two wins on the trot have taken the pressure off Roy Evans, who has a job for life at Anfield. The fans just hope that job isn't manager. Leeds have problems scoring but they're still fifth, a place above the home side.

Leeds's tactic is to stifle. This means wherever Steve McManaman goes, Alf-Inge Haaland follows. Haaland doesn't look for the ball, keep up with play or defend. He just sticks with McManaman who tries everything, but never loses his blonde shadow. The other Spice Boys, Jason McAteer, Robbie Fowler and Jamie Redknapp endeavour to spring Leeds's tightly locked defence. The Liverpool fans are silent, save for barracking Oyvind Leonhardsen, who's not part of the gang. This is another result of all-seater stadiums: a local, working class generation is priced out, replaced by demanding couples from Nuneaton who drive Range Rovers and spend £100 at Liverworld. Payback will come.

The Leeds fans mostly stand, meaning they'll be singing too. They're still going on about beating Manchester United, have an out of character mawkish chant for the recently deceased Billy Bremner and a special song for ex-Manc Paul Ince: 'Shit smug bastard, you're just a shit smug bastard'. I can see their point.

By half-time, Fowler has spurned chances and McAteer has missed an open goal after giving the entire Leeds defence the slip. In the toilet, disorientated by a high pitched wailing sound, designed to subdue asylum patients, I sample some Scouse wit: 'The girls at the bar are better at passing pork pies than Steve Harkness is the ball.' Nurse! The screens! My sides need stitching together.

Within a minute of the restart. Harkness's incisive through-ball sets up Owen, who strikes like it was 1926. 1-0. Haaland still sticks with McManaman, who wriggles free for once and sets up the unmarked Fowler, whose confidence seemed to need a boost. 2-0. The whole outfield team (except Leonhardsen) swamp him with relief. Leeds never look able to respond and Liverpool score a third when Harkness and Owen provide Fowler with a tap-in. There have been moments of red wonder in this game and much as I'm wary of bandwagons, Owen is truly special. Evans introduces Patrik Berger and Karlheinz Riedle for work-permit-securing and ego-cosseting substitute appearances respectively. Haaland pulls one back in the last seconds with a free header, but it's too little way too late and Leeds fans can at least take comfort in the Premiership fixture computer pairing them with Manchester United, as equals. McManaman and McAteer linger afterwards, waving to the crowd, impersonating aeroplanes. The crowd linger too, applauding them and enjoying the moment. Sometimes that bond between players and fans appears unbroken. As we shake hands in farewell, Paul is more confident than he was before the game. 'You never know,' he smiles.

I loiter in the players' car park watching a suspiciously cheery Leeds team board their Wharfdale coach. I'd be cheery getting onto that thing though, it's big and luxurious enough to live the rest of my life in. Liverpool players – there's a deal going on here – specialise in luxury four-wheel drives. Some have personalised number plates, like presumably Ince's CL AI R (his wife's name, without the spaces), although why a 23-year-old kid like Dominic Matteo needs a personalised number-plated, four-wheeled jeep to drive to training is beyond me. Unless he lives on a mountain. Or he's an idiot, driven to drive jeeps by conspicuous consumption. A slave moves some of the players' cars to a side exit, to save them contaminating themselves by signing five or six autographs. Maybe I was wrong about the bond still holding.

I walk back into the city, a slightly different route, past the heavily fortified

Provincial Orange Hall, some waste ground, a few slums and attempts to put middle class apartments into the mix. Personally I'd feel safer in Lagos than being a Scouse yuppy in a legitimate job and living here, in this city of few street lights. Over my two-mile walk I pass nobody, over 40,000 football fans have disappeared, just like that. It's that overpowering *Marie Celeste* stillness again, more frightening in the dark. By the time I reach the city centre, I'm sweating keenly. I still don't get Liverpool.

50 **Grimsby Town**

v. Preston North End
DIVISION TWO

28 December

3-1

'There is much more to football than twenty-two players on the pitch and I know the wiser men amongst you will appreciate that.'

Alan Buckley

There's nothing like a 1 p.m. kickoff to dampen my ardour. The police are blamed, so it must be an overtime thing. If, as the police unconvincingly argue, it was to do with drink, all games would be morning kickoffs. There is self-interest in my bleating. For the first time since I used to stay out all night (i.e. years and years ago) I see 7 a.m. on a Sunday morning. It's fantastically peaceful, even on the A1, where it's only me, some radicals off to church and kids in cars driving carelessly after a night clubbing and drugging.

Famously, Grimsby Town are not in Grimsby. They're in Cleethorpes, a downmarket seaside resort on the Humber estuary, which drains twenty per cent of England. Even today, Cleethorpes with pavements covered in sand, is trying. All the amusement arcades, The Mint, Taylor Made For Fun and the rest, are open – nothing can convince me they're not tax losses – as are gift shops and stalls selling candy floss, which I'd have bought out of sympathy and irony, were the bitter north wind not numbing my face. I could get my ears pierced at Searby's for £2.99. I don't. There's a pretty girl serving at the USA takeaway trailer. I smile at her, she smiles and shivers back at me, pinning herself against the tea urn at the back of her vehicle – not unseductively – for warmth. She's wearing about seven pullovers.

I stroll on the beach, condemned by the *Good Beach Guide*, but 'a site of special scientific interest' from which dogs are banned (good: nasty shitting mutts humans never take proper responsibility for). It's pleasant until the sands turn black. I was going to dig for bait, as you do, but the prospect of a £200 fine kiboshes that particular brainwave. Christ it's cold. The tide's out and I have to walk through mud to touch the brown water.

There's no ground nearer to the sea than Blundell Park. I can see it from the beach and take the seafront walk alongside the railway and across the railway bridge where, with a romantic sigh, I overlook the tiny terraced homes of fishermen and dockers. I like it here and I'm glad it's so cold, it's better this way.

Grimsby haven't lost in the league since November and the impressive performance I saw at Bristol Rovers was the culmination of a run that's taken them from second bottom to the play-off positions. Preston, meanwhile, have been in freefall since I saw them dispatch Carlisle so effortlessly and their uncharacteristically limited travelling support betrays loss of hope.

Around Blundell Park, there's the bustle of a team going up. The women at the ticket office are extraordinarily glamorous in this unglamorous place. The dazzling woman who sells me a £12 ticket tells me I can't sit in the Findus Stand (as, pathetically, I've long fantasised doing) because it's now the John Smiths Stand. Boo. It'll always be Findus to me.

The entrance to the Findus Stand is carpeted. The carpet is sponsored. Two programme sellers are singing in decent harmony while they're selling. Fantastic, unlike the pies which are served at room temperature. I'm going to get food poisoning this season and end up in hospital at the very moment I'm supposed to reach ground ninety-two, I can feel it.

My seat is in row T of the Findus, the back row. I yelp for joy. Not only is my view unobscured and the wind blowing elsewhere, but I can see the estuary sprawling before me and it's trawler rush hour. I'm higher than the seagulls and plumes of smoke billowing from the terraced houses. I want a season ticket here. Dozens of trawlers go by so slowly that all my tension evaporates like condensed milk.

My reverie is interrupted by the old git I'm next to. He looks like the father in *Citizen Smith* and gives a running commentary for ninety minutes. He has bags of sweets which he doesn't share, a bitter catch phrase, 'You lucky lad', and tries to rub himself against me continually in a bid to establish hegemony over our seats. The two mascots have plastic fishermen's heads and seem to be dressed as workers from a nuclear power plant. Not cute at all, unlike the 'William Tell Overture' to which Grimsby come out.

Grimsby are wonderful in the first half, helped by dispirited Preston. They rarely waste possession, although the pitch is of poor quality – salt water induced difficulties, probably – and score three times. Tommy Widdrington and Steve 'Livo' Livingstone set up Kevin Donovan who slots it through goalkeeper Teuvo Moilanen's legs. 'A sloppy goal,' notes Old Git. Then, Kingsley Black rifles in from outside the penalty area with Moilanen painfully slow to dive and finally an unguarded Donovan again, whose shot Moilanen somehow lets through at his near post. Henceforth Preston fans cheer ironically when-ever the Finn touches the ball without conceding. Old Git's thought process is governed by his ludicrous theory that tired-looking centre forward Livingstone is playing to get booked and therefore suspended. Shut up, ignorant old fool.

The crowd do a bit of 'Sing when we're fishing' but in yet another ground which doesn't need to be all-seater, especially the home Pontoon Stand, and which has two wind-attracting empty corners that could easily be filled in, the atmosphere in this sober gathering is polite, rather than passionate. At half-time, I'm four numbers away from third prize for the half-time draw, a less-than-generous entry into another draw for the Grimsby season-ticket I covet for next season. Do I feel lucky? Of course I don't.

One day I'll see a team who really goes for it despite already winning handsomely. I have hopes, but it isn't Grimsby, despite Donovan's hat trick seeking. Preston bring on substitutes including Mark Rankine ('That darkie lad,' notes Old Git), but they're so dismal that the second half peters out and, indeed, 'Peters out' is the chant of the Preston fans, along with a noble 'We're shit and we're sick of it' and a 'Stand up if you think we're shit', to which the whole ground wittily responds. When manager Gary Peters, at 3-0 down, substitutes sole forward Michael Holt, who, without support, has chased everything, the Preston fans are apoplectic.

Having already hit the post, Preston's other trier, Sean Gregan, pulls one back with a wind-assisted free kick. He doesn't celebrate, nobody congratulates him. Instead, he turns around and slouches back to the centre circle, head bowed. Seconds later, it's all over. Grimsby fans applaud politely, the few Preston fans remaining chant 'Greeee-gan' or 'Peters out' and the trawlers are still moving slowly towards Immingham or the North Sea.

I go back into Cleethorpes, past Farringford old people's home. Some of the residents are bunched together in a lounge, silently looking out onto the street. I wave gently to them. None of them notice. All things being equal, that's how it'll end: people once very much like me, sitting in silence with ten others all smelling of urine, too trapped by mental and physical infirmity to wave at someone they were once like, and being force-fed baby-food by contract nurses. There's only one logical and dignified final solution.

Chilled internally as well as externally, I walk down the seafront again, eastwards this time. Overlooking the sea there's a Martello Tower, with a flagpole at its summit, last used in the days when Norman Lamont's mother used to hang out here. When I was much younger, the fragile family Aizlewood used to come here for days out. My favourite thing, even more than playing football on the beach, was to kick a tennis ball up and around this tower with my father. It seemed so big and steep then, the biggest, steepest tower in the world, especially when, typically, I miscontrolled the ball. I suppose I knew those days would end, but I didn't know when, so I can't remember the last time I was here. It's getting dark as well as cold now, but I stand for ten, twenty, thirty minutes next to the rusty flagpole, alone and internally warm again, and wish for all the world that I had a tennis ball with me now. If I have children, I'll bring them here and, as our tennis ball circles round, I won't tell them things will not always be this simple, this joyful.

Mellowed, I pop in to Mr Q's for a reflective drink. It's empty, apart from pool players and Eternal on MTV. I could spend the rest of my life here, I really could. Godspeed.

51 Gillingham

v. Brentford
DIVISION TWO
29 December

3-1

'Let's not forget that prior to our appointment, this club finished in the bottom half of a lower division year after year.'

Tony Pulis

Gillingham again. It is fair to say that my heart is not leaping with anticipation. It's an inconsequential place, unmentioned on the M2's distance signs. There's none of the history and tradition of bordering Rochester and Chatham, but Gillingham does have Kent's football team. It's dark again and it's raining again. The one shop of note, Zebra Kutz, 'Where everything is in black and white!' has closed down and Sir David Frost probably doesn't come back too often.

The ground, Priestfield, is more welcoming than it was when Brighton were at home. Some things, like Dog Turd Alley behind the uncovered end, the awful catering and the gloomy terraced house with televisions tuned to Southampton v. Chelsea, will never change, but all the floodlights are working, the social club and offices are open and doing brisk business. Most importantly of all, the attendance is five times greater than at my Brighton match.

The game augers ill. Brentford (shocking at Wigan a few weeks ago) still haven't won away all season and are in real trouble, while Gillingham haven't won anywhere since October and are in freefall. This however doesn't stop the Tannoy announcer running – 'being forced to run' seems a fairer phrase, but I'm not sure – a competition set by the Scientology cult. The prize is a case of champagne and some books credited to L. Ron Hubbard. If they'd have given a car away, it would have been an L. Reg Hubbard. Scary stuff – and the PA man gives the answer away – but maybe there's a cult competition each match. When Burnley come on Saturday, perhaps there'll be the opportunity to win a Moonie bride. I'm with the Germans and Channel 4 on this one and how dare John Travolta – a man who reads someone else's words out for a living – compare the Germans' attitude to Scientologists with their treatment of Jews in World War 2. The PA man plays a sea shanty. At half-time he will play 'Land Of Hope & Glory'.

The crowd is restless, but at least those of us packed closely together in the Rainham End are dry, unlike the soaked Brentford fans. Dry but unhappy. The Rainham End groans when Brian Statham's name is announced as a team change and whenever he's near the ball, there will be a ripple of terror throughout the ground. They groan again when Michael Sambrook is introduced. He's won a prestigious youth award and he's turned down professional terms with Gillingham to go to university in America. Me, I just wish reserve player Nyron Noseworthy was playing and Priestfield didn't smell of wet coats and post-Christmas flatulence.

Gillingham score early on through Warren Aspinall's own goal, but it's so faraway and the penalty area is so crowded that I've no idea what happened. 'Blow your fucking whistle, ref,' shouts someone, nervousness personified. There's a problem with referee Styles. He's certainly incompetent, but to the home supporters, he's biased too. Taking little succour from Gills' convincing performance in a niggly match, they sing 'How much did you pay the referee'. I learn a new word too, when someone calls Styles a 'titwet'.

Steve Butler should have made it 2-0 when he's alone against goalkeeper Kevin Dearden but poor control lets him down. A few minutes later Butler puts striking partner Ade Akinbiyi through instead. That's 2-0 and the players celebrate like they've won the lottery. The teams go off at half-time, not to cheers but to a resounding 'the referee's a wanker'.

Brentford start the second half with substitute Junior Bent ('Ha,' shouts resident wag, 'the substitute's Bent. And so is the referee') and said referee starts by missing Leon Townley wrestling Akinbiyi, skilful, plus the work-rate of a shire-horse, to the ground.

As play continues, they announce the half-time lottery draw. Again I'm four numbers away from third prize, a less-than-generous 'Gills T-shirt'. By this time, Butler has missed an open goal, a bobbly Guy Butters header has hit Dearden's post, Aspinall – who still appears to enjoy the game in a perverse sort of way – has baited another crowd and Gillingham's committed, aware Paul Smith has begun to dominate from midfield.

Akinbiyi scores a deserved third when he latches onto Smith's incisive pass. Someone sings 'Going up, going up, going up,' and 'what's it like to get three points?' He's silenced by a crowd who remember the last home game when Gillingham led Southend 1-0 after ninety minutes and still lost. To complicate things a little, Brentford's Robert Taylor fires a screamer past Michael Pollitt (who I saw playing against Gillingham in November and gifting them their goal at Oldham) from thirty-five yards. In contrast to Sean Gregan in an identical situation yesterday, Taylor really does celebrate (he must care less), while Gillingham fans, sure of victory, applaud the St John's Ambulance people, who, jolly one and all, wave back. So pleased are team and fans that they spend nigh on five minutes after the match applauding each other. I can sense the bond again.

The rain still hasn't cleared. Gillingham's grim, dimly lit High Street is populated by me, two Transit vans of police and a closed-circuit camera system which flutters noisily as I walk past. The shops are downmarket and facing extinction. A nightclub, The Zone, remains resolutely shut, the pubs are run down and on Eel Pie Island's menu is 'traditional East End pie, mash & liqueur' for £1.95, but no eels. I turn my collar to the cold and damp and pop into the Southern Belle, a pub surrounded by scaffolding. It's virtually empty. There's nothing for me here, except to return to seek and destroy the person who snapped off my car aerial. Bet he uses 'living here' as an excuse.

52 **Southend United**

v. Luton Town
DIVISION TWO

3 January

1-2

'I'd like to wish all Southend supporters the very best of luck this year. I'd like to think we ourselves will get some on the pitch.'

Alvin Martin

Oh dear. I hadn't planned this at all. The weather, my new nemesis, has turned. I got as far as Euston station where plans to go to Macclesfield were thwarted by a fan of visiting Brighton who telephoned his dear old mum and was told the game was off.

A dash to St Pancras. Worthless, except to gawp briefly at its wondrous exterior for calmer karma: the game at Notts County had succumbed and I'd missed the last suitable train to Mansfield. Flailing telephone calls. A result! The man at Southend-On-Sea says the weather is 'terrific' and the game is on. All is not lost. Just.

At least loneliness and despair are temporarily at bay, for I'm accompanied by my comrade, Peter. This means no strange looks in strange pubs, sentient chat and much idle speculation as to exactly why there is an Azerbaijani Air jumbo at Southend's local airport.

The weather in Southend is no more 'terrific', than bowel cancer is 'terrific'. It's a touch breezy, in the same sense that Algeria is a touch dangerous. With the wind we soar at a pace peak-period Carl Lewis might raise a carefully manicured eyebrow at. Against the wind we are bent double in very real fear that one of the many objects whizzing through the air will fell us, causing even more anguish than this tired, uninspiring, unkempt town. Everythings, the everything for £1 store, is having a half-price sale.

The ground, Roots Hall, is on Victoria Avenue, north of what purports to be the town centre. Southend United's clever ruse is not to sell tickets at the turnstiles, but at a tiny ticket office where humiliated customers have to crouch down to shout their request through a crack in a window. On top of the ticket price (only £10 admittedly), there is a compulsory, no doubt interestingly taxed membership scam, where for a further £1 we receive a sheet of paper which has to be given to the turnstile operator who, for reasons unspecified, 'will in turn ensure its return to the Ticket Office via the Accounts Department'. Our turnstile operator ignores it.

Today's match is sponsored by the programme's printers. The programme is three games out of date and printed mostly out of register, rendering much of it unreadable. There are no pies, so I chance a hot dog, the foul taste of which will remain with me for the rest of the day. It's cooked individually. The female chef – not my type, I prefer horizontal mouths – takes an eternity and keeps staring at me, I think, smiling. There's nobody else around. Time has stood still. I'm very scared.

We are in the West Stand, where the view would be excellent if there were not one, not two, not three (I'll stop here), but eleven obstructions between us and the pitch. We're lifted by the fanzine *What's The Story Southern Glory!* where, for £25, a possibly pseudonymous Mr Builder is running a seventeen-seater minibus for the game at Carlisle next week. They leave on Friday, drink on the way, 'head up to my sister's in Huddersfield and sleep on her floor or even in the bus'. On Saturday they see the game, 'go on the piss again, more than likely stopping at a country pub in the back of beyond, possibly ending up staying at my sister's again. On Sunday we head back slowly, yet again on the beer.' He'll even 'pick you up and drop you back at your door' and he can be telephoned 'any time'. He neglects to record how his sister views this arrangement. A true hero.

It's a funny ground, screaming Lack Of Ambition too loudly. Unlike even Doncaster, they've stopped the reserve team, suggesting they will never return to Division One. The home fans are concentrated on a two-tier stand, not dissimilar to the temporary affairs non-league clubs erect when they draw Newcastle in the cup. The away fans – Luton's following is as impressive as it was at Wycombe – have a proper stand, albeit with fences unremoved and when they sing 'You all support West Ham' (the same chant they threw at visiting Millwall supporters in September and still as funny) it's the loudest noise of the afternoon.

The teams are one and two places above the relegation zone. There are puddles on the pitch, the rain is pelting and nobody looks delighted to be play-ing, even Southend loanee Neville Southall. He probably looks dishevelled in a morning suit, but in a football kit, he looks like he slept rough last night. He plays alone with the kiddy mascot during the warm up. Luton score in the first two minutes when the Southend defence stands still and Southall falls over to let Graham Alexander blast home from close range.

Then the sky turns jet black and the rain really starts. I've never seen anything like it. The light is that which illuminated the later Hammer films and the floodlights showcase sheets of rain driven across the pitch by swirling crosswinds. It the sky were to crack open and Lucifer come amongst us, nobody would be surprised. Everything seems to converge on the linesman in front of us. Water cascades down his bald head as his posture hunches and his sopping kit closes in. When he raises his flag, water pours off it like a tyre advertisement. He wants to go home, where fires burn in the hearth and the only moisture on his head is warmth-induced sweat. Alas, his career has culminated in being strapped to a ducking stool in Essex.

Southend equalise. Adrian Clarke's corner swirls in the wind, it hits Keith Dublin's head and Andy Thomson swivels smartly to score. A rainbow appears over the church in a corner. Me and Peter, as one, coo 'aaah'. As we do when Clarke curls a beauty against the bar.

For the second half, everyone changes their soaked kit. Almost, but not completely inured from the wet, we sit and shiver like refugees. Luton soon score what proves to be the winner. Chris Allen, on loan from Nottingham Forest, tries a shot so poor that Tony Thorpe manages to stop it going out for a goal kick. As Southend snooze, he pulls it back smartly and Alexander notches his second.

Southend try hard, but never look like levelling again. Luton hang on in there without mounting another attack. The Southend fans, old around us, break through the torpor to sing 'What a load of rubbish'. Correctly they single out Mark Stimson, who's been around but looks like he's never played before and captain/centre half Andy Harris who may have an IQ of 153 and be in MENSA but plays stupidly, panicking on the ball and is seemingly incapable of starting an attack. They're jeered off, always having tried to do the right thing, but never coming close. That's the price of employing idealistic ex-players trying league management for the first time, as Southend have done with Alvin Martin and his predecessor Ronnie Whelan, now in dispute over £120,000 back pay and bonuses. Recently the idiot Martin spent time at a Southend book shop signing a West Ham history. His first management job may be his last.

As a match, it bypasses me. Every time I sight the ball it disappears behind a pillar and sitting shivering on a plastic seat is far colder than standing, so I lose track of what's going on. I'm slightly excited by the Tannoy announcer, a woman who, worryingly, sounds far more excited than any I've dated and a picture in the badly printed programme of the female Commercial Manager, who I'd commit a shocking crime for (if she asked). People do strange things in Southend, I know this now and I'm not feeling too great.

We head for the seafront. Clearly they put barbed wire on Southend's mud beach during World War 2 to stop people getting out. If the Germans had landed here after sailing up the Thames Estuary, they'd have taken the first ferry back to Lübeck. The town and its two MPs are Conservative (there are seven Labour councillors out of thirty-nine), but, away from the bungalows and wide suburban streets, it's down at heel, like the music hall which thrived in Southend when Nelson's mistress Emma Hamilton performed and royalty visited. Now Melinda Messenger earns £20,000 for a month in pantomime at the Cliffs Pavilion, performing for scummy Cockney overspill.

We try to have a pub crawl, but the wind is working overtime and the pubs are empty. There's an open Wimpy, it has five staff and no customers. Worse is the misleadingly named Hope Hotel with its closed doors. Inside there is an unfriendly old barmaid, Sky TV turned down, four hardened old drinkers trying to flirt with the aforementioned grizzleface and a disco machine *circa* 1968 which still has working flashing lights. Peter and I sit in silence as the five stare at us. When I go to the toilet – outside, through a courtyard of misery – I expect to find them barring my way back in with pitchforks, as they burn poor Peter as a heretic. Close to the Kursaal Ballroom covered in scaffolding ('The magic returns!' screams the lying sign), long decayed since an episode of *The Prisoner* was filmed there, we chance The Minerva, named, misleadingly once more, after the Roman goddess of wisdom. It seems to be a gathering place for skinheads on one side and middle-aged men with mullet haircuts and drink problems on the other. One is trying loudly to squire a woman. 'I'll give you £50 a week housekeeping, I'll take you out every night and I'll throw-in a sack of lugworms.' Laughing, she surrenders. Who wouldn't?

There are buckets on the floor of The Ship to catch the rain that's leaking through the roof. Dispirited, we settle on the one fish'n'chip shop with a queue and sit down for a plateful. It's lovely, but it doesn't obliterate what's gone before.

We go back into town. After months of wittering about loud pubs of hard people, that's all I want now. There isn't one, apart from the Wetherspoons, which is packed with students. It's 11 o'clock. We're pissed. The drink has slightly lifted the depression of Southend, if not the cold and we've started chuntering about relationships. I forget what we decided, but I'll never forget Southend. This is in no way overstating the case, but I'd rather lose a limb – we'll narrow it down to a toe, just in case – than return.

53 **Tranmere Rovers**

v. West Bromwich Albion
DIVISION ONE

9 January

0-0

> **'We have some very promising young players in the reserves, but they are for the future and it would be unfair to put them into the first team. What we need now is experience.'**

John Aldridge

Down the southern side of Albania is the resort of Sarande. Although a southern Albanian himself, Enver Hoxha, and therefore his ministers (not known for their maverick tendencies), took holidays up north at a special government residence in Durres, obscured from local view by dense forest and with a gorgeous private beach protected by armed conscripts. This meant Sarande was neglected somewhat. Its lighting was notoriously dim, its seafront empty, and it had one hotel which served food of, well, variable quality. Permanently visible and a short swim (this wasn't possible, owing to the ever-vigilant Albanian navy's high speed patrol vessels) away was Corfu, glittering with proper lighting, decadence and, if the wind was blowing in the right direction, party noise and the smell of food. For Sarande read Birkenhead; for Corfu, read Liverpool.

I'm standing at Woodside ferry terminal gazing at Liverpool, where, like the Liver birds, I was last week and where, like the Liver birds, I'll be next week. From this side of the Mersey it looks alluring, for Birkenhead is dead and still. It's not even run-down. The pavements and roads are wide, the houses Georgian and the feel boulevard.

Once, there was Birkenhead Priory, the oldest building on Merseyside. Later came shipbuilding and the accompanying working class employment, but as Liverpool expanded into slumcity, Birkenhead and the Wirral further west kept a certain gentrification, but the need for all shops – and the National Westminster cashpoint – to be protected by steel shutters suggests that sometimes the mask slips. I'm curious though, so much so that the loneliness has shifted, if not that nagging feeling in my stomach that ninety-two is a lot of clubs in an unnaturally short time.

Tranmere is a suburb of Birkenhead, but Tranmere Rovers are in neighbouring Prenton, home of the Glenda Jackson Theatre, clearly unvisited for some time by its patron. The ground, Prenton Park, was once a dump of the lowest order and the home support spent many a happy hour chasing visitors around four sides of the ground before some bright spark thought of fences. Now, it's been redeveloped on all sides and seats nearly 17,000.

Rovers, though, are above their station and this season could be their last in Division One. They're fourth from bottom, haven't scored for three games and haven't won since November. The word is that if they don't beat West Bromwich Albion, a place off the play-off positions under the new management of Denis Smith, then John Aldridge and his Scouse muzzy will join the unemployed next week. This might mean returning his company car with its personalised number plates, although as Tranmere can only stretch to an M-reg he won't lose much sleep over it. It's old vehicle night tonight, for West Bromwich Albion's coach is a dodgy N-reg Flights, the sort of thing that might be drafted in as a service coach at Christmas when all the National ones are in use.

It's civilised inside, apart from my hot dog which has a growth on its end I'm too scared to attempt to identify. There's a big crowd tonight, including Kenny Dalglish. 'Obviously not here to look at one of ours,' quips Wirral wit behind me. Tranmere might not be able to afford a new car for their manager, but they have given local schools 2000 free tickets. Common sense (and therefore as rare in football as a caring club) in these all-seated Sky times.

These kids have absorbed every grimace of Ryan Giggs's gorgeous face from Old Trafford to Kosice, but have never seen a live match. Why, objectively, as a ten-year-old, see or be encouraged to see Tranmere Rovers tonight when the game is on Sky? Because going to football is better than watching it on television, always has been, always will be, except at Blackpool. After tonight, they'll return when their parents have to pay. There's always room at Prenton Park – and, kind to everyone, they try hard not to make games all-ticket, even against Manchester City – room even for a gang of scamps trying to bunk in through a hole in the fence. Long term, a few fans will be made; short-term, the kiddie choir will spend the second half successfully putting off Albion goalkeeper Alan Miller when he goal-kicks, without adding 'you're shit' after the 'aaaaaaaagh'.

There's an intense atmosphere, only partially ruined by the silly announcement during the first half for people to sit down. The police arrest a little kid and, quotas satisfied, the ruling is ignored. Albion have brought a large support, who share the steep Kop Stand with a drum-led Tranmere contingent, showing the value of unreserved seating in grounds where there's more than enough seats. The noise never lets up, my view is £11 and just fine. There are good hearts here, I like the mascot Rover who has a huge food bowl with his name on it. (Albion have brought two, one of which grapples with

Tranmere's former Wolves players Andy Thompson – mutual swapping of wanker signs here – and David Kelly, most energetically) and the teams come out onto an almost grassless pitch to *The Rockford Files* theme.

Those rumours about Aldridge might be correct. He's picked himself tonight and judging from the way he shakes his head, puts his hands on his hips and droops his shoulders, he and his Scouse muzzy are riddled with tension, but he gets a let off when to cap a first half in which the visitors have been dominant, Ian Hamilton has a goal disallowed for a dubious looking offside and South Shields-born Rovers goalkeeper Steve Simonsen plays like a man possessed.

This fine game turns in the second half as it moves towards the inevitable scoreline. Tranmere's band play *The Great Escape* theme after Andy Hunt hits Simonsen's post after all the home defence fall over with more co-ordination than they've displayed all evening and the visiting fans jig up and down shouting their trademark 'Boing, boing'. Aldridge slides in at the far post to miss a chance he'd have buried in his prime. He takes himself off for impressive young substitute Andy Parkinson who creates space for himself in a crowded penalty area before blasting over. Only wise John McGreal commiserates with the boy. Finally Kelly, who didn't score in twenty-four Premiership appearances for Sunderland last season, has a chance like Aldridge's but easier. He doesn't make contact either. Both teams are applauded off and surely some of those 2000 kids will come back.

Friday night in Birkenhead beckons. The crowd soon disperses, but not before a young boy, hopefully a free ticketeer, discusses the game with me. 'Great wasn't it, mate?' I agree with him. Soon he and his mute friend have sprinted past me towards town, pressing the stop signals on pelican crossings for the hell of it as they go.

The pubs seem oppressive tonight and I have trouble summoning up the courage to go past the bouncers – especially the ones outside Rockys 'Were you here Wednesday?' 'Yeah.' 'Did you crack anyone?' 'Oh yeah.' – and brazen out drinking on my own. By 10.55 I've stood on the ferry terminal looking out to Liverpool thinking of Albania, I've drunk quickly at The Letters where the bar staff sing along to Prodigy songs and I chance upon Miltons.

Civilisation! Of sorts! It's a late pub, massive, not just for the under-25s and friendly enough to assuage my cowardice. They play Stealers Wheel and Janet Jackson and it's full of my people: women dressed up to go out – that's unusual here, even the dance troupe at Prenton Park wore asexual leggings and scruffy T-shirts – and men in shirts. Tomorrow's newspapers will reveal that tonight is the warmest January day since records began, so underneath my puffa jacket, I'm wearing a smart, short-sleeved Ben Sherman. Cloakrooms aren't needed in places where coats aren't welcome. I stuff my scarf in my trouser pockets. This gives me the appearance of having a hernia which should have been operated on in March. In the toilet I tie it around my waist under my shirt. The effect is slightly slimming.

A woman touches me. Excellent. In fact she grabs my cheeks and moves my mouth into smiling position. It's kind of sexy, but it hurts the third time she does it. It's not easy to explain that I might look glum but I'm happy inside. Her name, she shouts, is Elaine. She is fairly tall, mid-twenties, wears a Little Black Dress, has hair which cascades rather than falls, smokes Benson & Hedges and drinks Pils. My boat has come in and about bloody time too. Sadly, I'm going to push it right back out again.

Her, after minimum small talk: 'Do you want to fuck?' It doesn't usually happen like this.

Me: 'Ummm.'

Her: 'Are you gay?'

Me: 'Um ... no.'

Her 'Don't you fancy me?'

Me: 'Um ... yes.'

Her: 'What's up then?'

I point to my wedding ring. Vaguely. It must have been like this for Jesus Christ in the wilderness when Satan promised him the earth. Had Satan taken the form of Elaine, we'd all be sacrificing goats on Sundays now.

Her: 'Ah, you're married. That's alright.'

Me: 'I can't.'

Her: 'Well what the fuck are you doing here then?'

Perceptive too and she's gone now. What exactly am I doing here, a place where the drink is cheap, they play records which have made no sense before and there's no hassle? I struggle to the bar, unsoiled and unhappy.

There's no time for reflection. At the bar I meet a man and his Aldridge-esque Scouse muzzy. He's not with the woman I assumed he was partnering, so I'm caught. He's unsteadily drinking a pint, the only male in the pub to do so rather than a bottle. He has a small tear in his chinos, through which I can see what I fear are Bugs Bunny boxer shorts. 'I'm on my own me,' he slurs. I can't hear what he's saying properly, so I try to laugh at the right moment. He breaks off his stories every time a woman squeezes past (this happens a lot) and talks to them whilst fondling them. Suddenly, I'd like to talk to him about the bassline in The Jackson Five's 'I Want You Back' that's shaking the room. He's rejected by everyone and, mercifully Elaine does not pass. 'Well you've got to try, haven't you? I don't give a fuck me, I don't,' he smiles, beer snared in Scouse muzzy. His name is John and he's delighted mine is too. If he has taught me nothing else, I've learned that 'We're mates now' is one of the most chilling phrases in the English language. He says we can go 'hunting' as a pair, 'we'll have more chance then.' He and his mates are off out tomorrow. I'm invited and gracefully accept. I go to the toilet, untangle my soggy scarf and don't come back.

Outside, there's a trio of lads drunkenly but expertly singing '(Sittin' On) The Dock Of The Bay' and Birkenhead is more alive than it's been all night, but still as ill-lit. I've discovered things here.

54 Sunderland

v. Sheffield United
DIVISION ONE

10 January

4-2

'Unbeaten in 15 games, progress in the Cup, a sell-out crowd on Boxing Day and even a Nationwide Manager Of The Month award for yours truly. We seem to be flying nicely at the moment, but football can be a cruel game.'

Peter Reid

It's been a few matches since this happened. At 2.55, the crowd are talking amongst themselves, when the roaring PA switches into Prokofiev's 'Romeo & Juliet'. Everyone hushes, stands up and their rumble begins, distant at first but building into a full-throated roar which could never be loud enough to drown the wonderful music. Then, as Sunderland and Sheffield United emerge side by side into The Stadium Of Light, 'Romeo & Juliet' segues into Republica's stirring 'Ready To Go'. That's the moment. My stomach goes, the hairs on every part of my body, especially spine and nape, stand on end. It's so perfect I can hardly breathe. It's worth all the hassle at times like this. This is fortunate because I'm about to get major hassle. As the captains shake hands with the referee, a Sunderland fan arrives at my seat.

'I think you're in the wrong seat,' he says pleasantly, but far too confidently for my liking.

'I don't think so,' I reply, equally pleasantly.

I get my match ticket out, he produces his season ticket. Like some inverted joint orgasm, we have both paid to sit in the same seat. Fuck.

'I'm really sorry,' he continues. 'This has happened before.'

I defer to his more fervent support, tell him it's not his fault and find a steward. Once the steward has forcibly and rudely made the point that it is not his fault either and nothing to do with him, he ignores me. At my pestering, his reluctantly given, Stephen Hawking-like solution, is to find an empty seat and sit in it. It doesn't work like that. There are no empty seats, although despite their lamentable turn out at United's Bramall Lane in Sunderland's first post-Premiership match, the fervent home support is singing 'Sell all your tickets, you couldn't sell all your tickets,' to the United masses and their few untaken seats. I stand in a gangway, abandoned as Roker Park.

Interestingly, I am not alone, like Sting at the end of 'Message In A Bottle' there are hundreds just like me. I have enough time to ponder on the fact that if my £17 seat has already been sold, Sunderland are making £17 profit, which needn't necessarily trouble the Inland Revenue. Multiply that £17 by however often this happens over the season and the whole of Wearside could move to the Cayman Islands, except for programme sellers and blind Sunderland fans, as both groups are too poor after being charged to see matches.

I'm moved on. A boy with crutches is seatless too. Mysteriously, a block of seating on the far side has a few spaces. We're escorted through the Sheffield United fans to those seats – registered unsold – and twenty minutes in, I can watch the game.

The Stadium Of Light (more Stadium Of Light Ale, for everyone is shouting drunk, despite the Louts Keep Out notices in Sunderland's pubs) is a wonder. All views are unobscured, the pies have the crust of the season (hammy cliché, but it does melt in my mouth) and I spot Tyne Tees commentator Roger Tames in the toilets on his mobile telephone explaining to his employers that if Kevin Phillips scores today, he will be the first Sunderland player since Trevor Ford in 1951 to score in six successive games. A news story.

Since long before Ford's day, Sunderland was a byword for Lowry-esque urban misery, generations of underclass with a wariness bordering on violent hostility towards strangers and a massive inferiority complex about Newcastle, possibly stemming from the Wearmouth Bridge, rebuilt by my old friend George Stephenson in 1796, a toy Tyne Bridge. It's the one route from city (as declared in 1992 but this is a town at heart) centre to Stadium Of Light Ale.

The women wear short skirts and have fake tans – Sunderland is Britain's fake tan capital – buskers play bagpipes, possibly badly (how is it possible to tell?), and soon Luke Goss, once of Bros, will appear in a stage version of *Grease*. Sunderland has always suffered, hard times have never been far away. Britain's first cholera epidemic began here in 1531 (meningitis is the big thing now) and thirty-four years later, commentators were noting the 'great decay of buildings and inhabitants'.

The mines have gone, glass-making has been replaced by the National Glass Centre museum, but most of all, Sunderland built ships until the Japanese learned to do it better and cheaper. Now, completing humiliation, it's a company town, effectively owned by Nissan: the Japanese giving back what they took away two generations ago but keeping the profits. As if to maintain sufferation, potentially pleasant beaches at Seaburn and Roker have never been developed. People cannot associate Sunderland with pleasure.

A property developer is trying to establish a marina around the corner from the beach for Nissan high-flyers. It's around another corner from a gaggle of insalubrious tower blocks, which haven't experienced affluence being shoved in their faces since the mid-50s, when, to preserve their record of never being relegated, Sunderland FC spent an astronomical £114,000 on players. I guess the natives may feel different about that marina.

The Stadium Of Light, built without an iota's thought for traffic congestion, is visible from most of Sunderland, despite having no floodlights. It sucks people in from miles around like the almighty hovercraft it resembles. It's surrounded by waste ground on the sides where it's not dwarfing minor Wearside shipbuilders and fans swarm in from all angles, still gazing in rapture at the finest structure Sunderland has seem, a totem – illuminated every night – against an outside world which can only visit under heavy police escort, like the convoy of nine coaches of Sheffield United fans which shoots through the car park at reckless speed. This is a town where in August kids aged three were chased off Sunderland ice rink for wearing Newcastle shirts, where Stadium Of Light bricklayer Ian Bradley was sacked for wearing the same (has he seen the graffiti at Portsmouth's new stand yet?) and where the firm of MP Burke were paying workers sixty-six pence an hour in January 1997.

If the club had spent money on the team instead of the ground, they'd be in the Premiership today. As it is, they're unbeaten since October, defeats by Port Vale and Reading a distant memory, and lie fifth, three points, two places and one game behind Sheffield United, who, like Sheffield Wednesday, travel in a distinctly average Dunn-Line of Nottingham coach. Very strange, although not as strange as the late-70s when both teams used National coaches. Perhaps running a decent coach firm is a prohibited occupation in Sheffield. A funny do, though.

There's the pressure of expectation of 36,000 (plus we the unregistered), a pressure added to by a mawkish north-eastern sentimentality, which means the team are referred to as The Lads in the programme. Ugh. Almost as witless as playing James Brown's 'I Got You (I Feel Good)' after goals. Unfortunately Sunderland do this as well. Most of their fans have taken a brick in a stadium wall with their name upon it. Suckers. I'm relieved they don't break out in tears when Darren Williams wins a throw-in.

I've just taken my seat when United score. Brian Deane heads down and Dean Saunders snaps home. United fans don't sing 'There's only two Deanos,' sadly, but they do sing 'We are Bladesmen, from the Lane' with all the masculine intensity they showed at Bramall Lane.

The Sunderland fans don't stop either and the atmosphere, infinitely superior to both St James' Park and the Riverside, is how football was meant to be. The Roker Roar has been transplanted. It can be done in an all-seater stadium. There's hope yet.

Sunderland soon equalise. United's David Holdsworth and David Lee miss a corner and lanky Niall Quinn scores with a shot, possibly for the first time in his career. My ears tingle and the bloke next to me who patently hadn't wanted me to sit near him moves to give me a hug. No thank you.

At half-time there's an American-style shoot out between a Sunderland and United supporter. First time around, United's contestant, Wayne, is superior. The second go, Sunderland's black cat mascot launches an expert flying tackle to dispossess the Yorkshireman. The ground chuckles. At the end it's a draw, but Wayne won't shake the droopy tailed mascot's paw. Pompous fool.

The second half is even better. United look dangerous on the break and the colossus Deane causes myriad problems for a defence with an average age of twenty-one, especially when he interpasses with Graham Stuart. Territorially, it's Sunderland who look Premiership quality, more so when the ground unite in singing 'Can't Help Falling In Love'. Wise men say Lee Clark exudes class, Alex Rae runs the game at his pace and winger Alan Johnston adds cut'n'thrust. They score when Quinn sets up Rae for a glorious goal. The police celebrate by diving into the United fans, who are not afraid to hit back. Many arrested. More police overtime. When the police finally stop themselves, they retreat to an ironic standing ovation.

Sunderland add a third when United's Alan Kelly brilliantly saves from Michael Gray but Phillips, who's already hit the bar, taps in with the confidence of a striker who can't stop scoring. Within thirty seconds of kicking off from the centre spot brought from Roker Park – this is a wonderful match – United pull one back from gamine substitute Gareth Taylor as Sunderland snooze. United fans had begun their exodus. Now, like thousands of prodigal sons, they return to stand in front of their seats. It's too late though.

On the stroke of full time, Phillips heads in for 4-2 with Kelly hobbling badly and virtually immobile. The scoreboard says Sunderland have had twenty-two shots, United only five, although it doesn't feel like it and more than once the home fans have chanted 'Leeee-on-elll' in multilingual homage to their French goalkeeper Lionel Perez. A game to treasure. I'm out of breath. Newcastle have lost at Sheffield Wednesday and Sunderland fans, Mackems (originally a term of abuse but now appropriated as a badge of pride like rapping 'niggas'), stay on to chant 'The Mags are going down'. Indeed, and the Mackems may yet be going up. Me? I'm going home. Football is great sometimes.

55 Mansfield Town

v. Scunthorpe United
DIVISION THREE

17 January

1-0

'There's 20 matches left and everything still to play for.'

Steve Parkin

It's a morality tale for the collectively greedy. The miners would probably not have won their final strike in 1984–85, what with the NUM forgetting about the massive coal stocks their members had produced at frantic pace, plus their initial fudging of the strike-ballot issue, yet things undoubtedly would have been different had the Union Of Democratic Miners not crawled out of Mansfield, initially conceived and financed by ... well, who knows. An anti-NUM groundswell they claimed, but can people really despise their colleagues so?

Anyway, divide and rule ruled. There would be no illusion of united workers, the Conservatives could laud the UDM-led scab rump as real miners and slowly the battle was won and lost. The Conservatives gave Faustian UDM leader Roy Lynk – how well does he sleep? Are his dreams punctuated by images of his former friends at the coalface? Has he developed a twitch? – an OBE. Then, in October 1992, the very same Conservatives who'd sent him to Buckingham Palace to meet The Queen, closed most of Nottinghamshire's pits. 'They treat you like a soft touch,' wailed Scabbo Lynk, OBE. And while solid strike towns like Rotherham and Barnsley would never be the same again, they did have seven years start on Mansfield in the redevelopment race.

I'm perched on the fence in front of the UDM's isolated headquarters on Berry Hill Lane, past the plush part of Mansfield, miles out of town. The offices – the old NUM ones – have a splendid view over what used to be a mining valley. There's no Vote Conservative bunting to be seen. I could weep for Roy Lynk OBE: his stupidity, ambition and ego, as well as the foolish men duped into following him, who today pick up their Jobseekers' Allowance. Lynk OBE's offices are a 'protected surveillance area', presumably 'protected' from Lynk

OBE's former members as well as NUM stormtroopers these days, but I can't see any cameras and nothing happens when I walk through the open gates up to the door, where a tiny plaque says this is also the offices of Welfare Financial Services Limited, whoever they may be. A sign says Trespassers Will Be Prosecuted. An impossibility under English law, but the UDM was never great with the small print.

The complex is badly maintained, in need of a lick of paint and there are rusty benches outside, one commemorating the Nottinghamshire & District Miners' Pension Scheme's Golden Jubilee in 1989.

Today's Mansfield, a rundown market town whose library opening hours were cut this year, is the UDM's legacy. There was nothing as vibrant as a mining town on payday, now there's no such thing as a mining town on payday. Sleep well, Roy Lynk, Order of the British Empire.

Mansfield is dominated by a railway viaduct built in 1875, so it's only fair that it has a station once more after years of cruel domination by the misleadingly named Alfreton & Mansfield Parkway, almost a marathon's length from Mansfield itself. The town is on the Robin Hood Line now, so at least people can leave.

Mansfield has always been nothing, although it's claimed the outdoor market is the largest in Europe. If I knew what he looked like, I'd go for a peek at Craig McKernon, who apparently works one of the stalls. Three days before Christmas 1989, McKernon, a highly rated Mansfield Town full back, signed for Arsenal, the first great leap forward of a career that would surely culminate in England honours. Two years later, body ravaged by injury and without an Arsenal game to his name, he was forced to retire. Football is a heartbreaker sometimes.

A statue in the market place commemorates Sir George Bentinck, former local landowner and a fair insularity indicator. The Danes came and went and things were so awful by 1823 that Parliament had to pass a special Act for Mansfield's 'improving paving, lighting and cleansing'. Now all that's left is a prominent Ukrainian community (no strangers to collaboration themselves, Roy Lynk OBE could well claim), a twin town of Heiligenhaus (no idea and don't care) and a sad sign in the market square to a better Mansfield, many thousands of kilometres away in America.

The people are ugly, downcast and without pride. The policemen are scary, none more so than ex-PC Michael Hall who stole £180 from a 77-year-old suicide, destined for his widow. Hall is spending his two years in jail studying for a law degree. Mansfield males at liberty are ex-scabs, betrayed by the pot of gold turning out to be a reservation for a lifetime of poverty and self-loathing. Their womenfolk have to support them, but they're stronger. Women are always stronger. Mansfield bitter is a state of mind, as well as the local brew.

Mansfield Town don't help. With Tottenham Hotspur, they spent 1977–78 in the old Division Two. When they met at Mansfield's Field Mill to draw 3-3, the ITV cameras caught Tottenham goalkeeper Daines (Spurs' fans chant at the time, probably in jest: 'He dove, he missed, he must be fucking pissed, Barry Daines') rushing from his penalty area to miskick so Dave Syrett could complete a hat trick.

What the cameras didn't show was Mansfield fans leaving early to pick up bricks and wait on the embankment outside the away end. Tottenham would be promoted and Mansfield relegated, but the North Londoners – both hospitalised and escapees – never forgot their trip to quaint little Mansfield. No Scunthorpe blood will be spilled today, but amid yet another game played in silence, there is a nasty little home posse next to the away end. They stand and stare.

Field Mill has hardly been touched since Spurs came – although New Labour with the GMB union have taken the entire roof of the Bishop Street Stand as advertising. Not something they've done in NUM areas. The crash barriers have been so poorly painted that the spillages underneath look like something Jackson Pollock might have thrown together. Nobody cares and that can never be a good thing.

Last season, Town's reserve team won just one point. There's no mention of them in today's programme. In their centenary season, Town's first eleven are seventeenth, although unbeaten for eight games. Scunthorpe United's early promise has slid into misery and Mansfield's 1-0 victory leapfrogs them over their visitors. Scunthorpe have switched their team coach to a Wrights from Newark, unless the Barnard's that ferried them to Rochdale has broken down. Anyway, it's much nicer, despite a cranky coffee machine.

The goal arrives five minutes after the teams have run out to 2 Unlimited's 'Get Ready For This' and Mansfield's Tony Ford, thirty-nine in May, has been given a bottle of champagne to mark his 900th appearance. Leggy Lee Peacock takes a throw-in while the Scunthorpe defence jog back unconcerned. David Kerr collects it and in one swift movement rounds goalkeeper Tim Clarke and slots home. That, at least, should dampen demand for the guided tours around Premiership grounds Town's Football In The Community department foolishly offers Mansfield children.

The wind blows cold round these parts and I huddle at the back of the North End terrace crouching from icey blasts, peering at the Mansfield Brewery down the hill. The pie – soggy pastry, indeterminate filling – takes another layer of skin off the roof of my mouth and the toilet is an exciting circular stainless steel construction, from times when we thought we'd all be holidaying on the moon by 1989 at the latest. It's been stolen from the set of *Blake's 7*.

The North End is hardly packed. One of them is a thief too, as there's an announcement asking for the return of the club banner which someone 'borrowed' during the trip to Torquay in December. Unlike me, they're not the sort of people to be entertained by a stag mascot and his huge flappy antlers.

The game, not helped by the wind or the early removal of Peacock, easily the best player on display, with what looks like a broken leg, especially after both physiotherapists run onto the pitch to treat him before referee Wolstenholme has stopped play. Later, though, Peacock appears in the dugout, an un-showered ghost, clad only in towels, oblivious to what by then is sleet. Mansfield should have been in a commanding position by half-time, but they spurn a succession of chances.

Town stop attacking in the second half. Scunthorpe try hard and scurry about, but offer nothing save Darryn Stamp's unfeasibly skinny legs and a few crafty touches from Alex Calvo-Garcia. 'Dago wop,' shouts the ex-scab behind me, finally ceasing his berating of Town's admittedly poor Steve Harper. At least his friends don't laugh. I wish I was somewhere else.

I've forgotten the game by the time I've cheerily waved off the solitary Scunthorpe supporters coach who exit Mansfield with a hail of V-signs. I pop into The Swan for a Mansfield bitter. The town might get quite lively on a Saturday evening, for it's populated by those who've spent the afternoon here and won't be going home until closing time. The beer is pleasant enough but their shouting, swearing and unnatural levels of aggression scare me and they sense I'm not one of them. I can't stay in this place a moment longer. Tomorrow it's back to Liverpool and my head's spinning already. In a feeble and futile bid to earn domestic Brownie points, I drive home instead of staying over. Pin me to that cross, centurions.

56 **Everton**

v. Chelsea
PREMIER LEAGUE
18 January

3-1

'What we have tried to do is get into areas where we can get quality service into Duncan Ferguson.'

Howard Kendall

If there is a God, and the objective evidence suggests there is, what can he make of Liverpool? It baffled me when I came here on Boxing Day, it baffled me when I looked at it from Birkenhead and it baffles me now as I walk along Seymour Terrace, towards the Metropolitan Cathedral Of Christ The King. There's a row of the two storey flats, so prevalent in Liverpool, all but one is boarded up, as indeed is the Catholic cathedral itself. Its space age roof is being renovated, but it's still heartstopping, proof that Catholicism (the one true faith, we'll forget the IRA, the inquisition and Polish anti-Semitism for now; anyway this week in this city two six-year-old boys have been suspended from St Anne's Church Of England school for sexual assault) knows the value of spectacle in a way Protestant sects can never understand. I don't think God knows what to make of Liverpool – he can hardly have planned the swagger, the poverty and the gushing sentimentalism – and I know he'd reject the job of managing the city's nominally Catholic football team, Everton.

The cathedral – Paddy's Wigwam or the Mersey Funnel, Scouse wits call it – is open. After all it is Sunday. Its interior is circular, good Catholics are kneeling at the altar, piped music is all around and it's as breathtaking inside as out. It needs security guards though and local tramps – plus me – use the basement toilet facilities. Christian charity, albeit by default. 'A quiet week ahead, at least on the surface,' predicts the pastoral letter, sinisterly. If I knew how, I'd cross myself. Instead I head for Goodison Park via the same route I'd taken for Anfield, past the Adam Cliff Nursery whose snowman in the window is scowling. How very Liverpool.

Goodison Park is past Anfield, across Stanley Park where Liverpool and Everton fans used to fight before and after derby matches at the very moment the press were writing stories about how the locals revelled in each other's company. In fact, all they had in common was a nasty racist streak. After Cliff Marshall left Everton in the mid-70s (because he wasn't good enough, rather than Grand Wizard-convened conspiracy in truth), they wouldn't buy a black player for two decades. When Liverpool signed John Barnes for an aghast Kop, Evertonians used Scouse wit to call them Niggerpool, when they weren't chanting 'Everton are white'. Ooh, ooh, ooh.

Sixth from bottom Everton have brought more coaches to this game than second from top Chelsea and they're all parked in a long line outside Stanley Park, headed by the Chelsea team coach, an R-reg Scancoach with tinted windows, globe lights and enormous wing mirrors guarding the whole contraption like gleaming, white Praetorian Guards. It's better, more expensive and more mobile than my house.

Everton haven't been out of the top division since 1954 and Goodison Park has the atmosphere of a proper ground, especially as it's still a backstreet place. Its hustle and bustle smells of Dixie Dean, George Dunlop, Brian Labone and all the Evertonians who gave the people of this strangest of cities some kind of distraction as they walked alongside the same houses I'm walking past today, although never on a Sunday.

Talk now is of a move to a 60,000 stadium in Kirkby, the dream of much loathed (for tightness) Everton chairman and, so the rumour mill goes, former Liverpool season ticket holder Peter Johnson. There's a sense of history too, not wholly undermined by gormless cheerleaders running around the pitch perimeter waving massive flags, and the centrefold in the programme is 60s centre forward Alex Young. The touts are buying, as well as selling.

'Who ate all the pies?', why Nick Barmby of course and to prove it there are pictures of him advertising hot dogs all over the Main Stand. Obviously I buy one, as does a renegade Chelsea fan, skinhead, over forty, whose order comes to £3.02. 'Do you want the 2?' he asks. 'Ooh yes,' replies smiley assistant. 'Well I haven't fucking got it,' sneers skinhead. He then turns and belches at me. I'm seeing too much knockabout cruelty this season. My heart sinks again, I need refuelling with goodness. People sneered at Rodney King when he asked 'Why can't we all just get along?' I probably did, but he made the most profound point of all.

The hot dog is no consolation. The frankfurter is fine, but the onions are no more onions than the Catholic cathedral's security guards are overpaid: they are the sort of things found in the bottom of crisp packets. I take the taste away with a bar of 'Everton milk chocolate', which is 'finest milk chocolate' apparently. It's no Aztec.

My seat could be worse. If, say, it was facing the wrong way. It could not however be any smaller. At least I'm out of the way of the pounding rain. I'm next to a handsome older woman, over forty but with the look that says 'I'm having more sex than you'. Posh Scouse I silently christen her. She thinks I'm scum at first, but, for once my charm offensive – a posh accent this time, and occasional gentle digs in the stomach, which she started – works. Although we talk of nothing other than the match, she takes my hand and say 'Ooh I'm really excited!' more than once. Twice actually. And she smokes like a teenager.

There's no shots for thirty minutes. Everton are too tense to play properly. Chelsea could do with a little more tension to stop being so sloppy, especially after they take the lead when Tore Andre Flo (ironically Everton's last manager, Joe Royle, resigned when he wasn't allowed to sign him) forces the ball home. This is crisis time for Everton and amazingly they equalise within a minute, Gary Speed, otherwise invisible, slotting in from the narrowest of angles after Chelsea's Dutch goalkeeper Ed De Goey misses a cross. The few Chelsea fans who've turned up stop singing 'You're going down with the Tottenham'. One Scouse wit replies 'You're going down in your helicopter' in evil remembrance of Matthew Harding. I won't see goodness today, however hard I look.

The tension evaporates. The stewards, who have to lay on the pitchside perimeter like lemon-jacketed Scouse Rubens models, roll over with joy, unlike Graeme Le Saux, whose *Guardian*-reading exterior does not conceal his ghastly petulance. Passes start to flow, Liverpudlian voices are raised and football becomes theatre. I'm excited for them.

They're still cheering at half-time, so much so that nobody notices the PA man introducing half-time raffle drawer Jimmy Mulville: 'You can't get much bigger in the celebrity stakes'.

Midway through the second half, after Everton's new signing Mickael Madar has missed a brace of chances, Duncan Ferguson heads down from a corner, De Goey reacts slower than his countrymen did to the North Sea and Everton are in front. Their goalkeeper, the Norwegian, Thomas Myhre runs around his penalty area shaking his fists with joy. Clever man: that's how to make fans forget Neville Southall.

Ruud Gullit brings himself on, delivers a crossfield ball of such genius that fellow substitute Gianluca Vialli could have fallen over, received medical attention and still got to it. Then Michael Duberry makes it 3-1 with a rasping drive past De Goey for a comedy own goal. Myhre slides on his knees to celebrate with the Park Stand and looks like Freddie 'Parrot Face' Davis. Neville who?

The Everton fans, presumably the same ones calling for his dismissal after November's home defeat by Southampton, are singing 'There's only one Howard Kendall'. Chelsea fans sneak off into the wet, cold darkness and don't see Speed hitting the bar or the home fans applauding Everton off the pitch. I bid a friendly farewell to Posh Scouse, nod my head in supplication at the church of St Luke The Evangelist which forms a corner of Goodison Park and which must never have thought Sundays would come to this.

Without irony, I thank God for Rupert Murdoch's Sky TV, without whose manipulation of the fixture lists I wouldn't have the opportunity to visit my thirty-six outstanding grounds. Then, I apologise to God for hating myself so much for thanking Sky, take the hour's walk to the city centre and set off home.

57 **Notts County**

v. Hull City
DIVISION THREE

20 January

1-0

'One way or another, the future looks very rosy.'

Sam Allardyce

A new low. It's half-time this Tuesday evening, the game has been awful, I'm 1356 tickets from winning the half-time prize draw, there's nobody within ten rows of me in any direction, I'm beset by the sharp stabbing pains I get in my guts (surely a stomach tumour) when I think of fitting in another thirty-five games before May 11 and I'm so cold I've lost all feeling in my feet. A few yards from me, in the Kop Stand, behind the goal I'm adjacent to, are the sixty or so travelling Hull fans. Unlike me, they've stood up all game and now they're restless. They notice me and start to chant, louder than I thought it possible for sixty people to chant, as they point at me: 'What's it like, what's it like, what's it like to have no friends?' I don't respond, other than slumping further down my slippery plastic seat, I haven't the heart. It's awful having no friends. I am the loneliest man in the world.

Who cares about Notts County, the oldest club in the football league and among the most superfluous? Certainly not Nottingham people. Before tonight, they were seven points clear of Division Three and with a banker home victory in store. Meadow Lane is a fine ground, all seater, 20,300 capacity, yet they'd be unlikely to fill it were Manchester United the visitors. This evening it's a fifth full and, by comparison, the quiet study area of Nottingham Library is a seething cauldron of decibel-stretching, hot-headed noise.

At least there's some understanding of history in these cold streets, one of which is named after Albert Iremonger, the goalkeeper whose 564 appearances would have been nearer 800 had not World War 1 robbed him of his peak. Chiefly though, Notts County's home since 1910, now in an inner city industrial estate – across the River Trent but a football world from Nottingham

Forest – is the vision of chairman Derek Pavis, who, as County slipped two
divisions since 1995, built a ground that's the envy of most Division One clubs,
let alone the strays of Hartlepool and Colchester.

To honour the old man's ego, I sit in the Derek Pavis Stand. It's a special sort
of person who supports County instead of Forest. They're part middle class
purists, part saddoes but lacking real, heartfelt passion. It's not like Millwall or
Wolverhampton Wanderers, where inferiority towards neighbours breeds
keen, violent support. County are, in a sense, the easy option. Still, they do a
grand tray of pea'n'pies, served by the world's most pleasant woman, to
momentarily keep out the chill even for the loneliest man in the world. A
shame though that the programme from the postponed original fixture hasn't
been reprinted 'given the prohibitive costs'.

They have a point, I grudgingly suppose, but a club that misspells the
manager's name on page twenty-three of that programme is a club that
doesn't care enough, even if manager and assistant manager have P-reg cars
to pose around in. The mascot is presumably a magpie but as the PA is
inaudible and he looks too perished to be interested, he must remain anonymous. That's Notts County, a club that takes £1 off each player to pay for a
meal at the end of training

Hull City are as wretched as August's reverse match at Boothferry Park
suggested and Mark Hateley's frail tendons mean he's a long-term injury. At
least though he and his team have travelled well, on a National Holidays
coach, which sounds horrendous as well as looking yellow and silly, but does
have little globe-shaped lights on the tables. Hull hope. County tentatively
press forward, secure in the knowledge that class will tell. This makes for a
rotten game.

I watch winger Chris Bettney, just twenty and already on the scrap heap after
being dumped by Sheffield United on 'extended loan' to Hull. With his sister's
hairdo, thick lips and spot-infested forehead, he could, like so many young
footballers, be Harry Enfield's sexually frustrated teenager. Unfortunately, he
has the ridiculous temperament of Graeme Le Saux. To complicate matters,
Bettney isn't bad at all. He has a stylish touch, allied with the ability to beat a
man, but the service he gets is a disgrace. His response is to stand there, hands
on hips, marooned and shivering by the touchline, shaking his head slowly,
scowling at the bench when Brian McGinty's lack of elemental skills – they say
he has a shot like thunder: he's more likely to be struck by lightning – ensure
another Hull attack breaks down.

This wasn't how it was meant to be when Bettney was at school in
Chesterfield and his dear old mother was kept busy mashing pots of tea for
scouts from every northern club, trying to camouflage her excitement in
Derbyshire stoicism while they told her that young Chris ('He's a good lad, Mrs
Bettney, or can I call you Betty?') could go all the way. Now, with Matlock Town

and a lifetime of If Onlys beckoning, he must wish he'd taken that apprenticeship at Kwik-Fit.

Early in the second half, after Hull's Steve Wilson makes a fabulous save from Gary Jones's downwards header, Ian Richardson scores a scrambled goal from the resultant corner. Bettney is substituted, Notts County sit back and Hull flap to no avail. I'm bored senseless, but at least the Hull fans are too disconsolate for further Aizlewood taunting. There's even a certain pathos to the way they sing 'And it's Hulllll City, Hulllll City FC, we're by far the greatest team the world has ever seen'. My theories about County not caring quite enough are vindicated when Richardson deservedly wins the Man Of The Match award and the electronic scoreboard flashes up the name Ian Robinson.

Back, then, into Nottingham, which is sub-zero of temperature and disappointingly quiet. My spirit of adventure has buckled under the combined weight of cold, abuse and loneliness, so I shuffle into the Yates's Wine Lodge. Times are tough everywhere on Tuesday evenings, even in Nottingham and so Yates's are having to try. There's a 70s DJ entertaining the scattered punters. Sample joke: 'Saw a comedian last week. I didn't think he was funny, but the old people were pissing themselves'. He's brought along a Rod Stewart impersonator who mimes to 'Do Ya Think I'm Sexy?' in a way that suggests Chris Bettney's prospects aren't as bleak as I'd thought. A female dancing quartet struts along to Toni Basil's 'Mickey' and Cyndi Lauper's 'Girls Just Want To Have Fun'. My crushed libido resurfaces a little as they smoke and drink together like displaced Valley Girls beforehand. That they're hopeless and my favourite one stops when the DJ teases her further fuels my desire to be their evil Svengali manager.

Only when the freezing but still air surrounds me as I leave a slightly livelier Nottingham, slowly cranking itself up for clubbing, through Broadmarsh Shopping Centre which forms a late-night indoor thoroughfare where goods are still on display, guarded by two nervous security men, do I remember that all Humberside now knows that I have no friends. I can't even be an evil Svengali to myself. God, it's cold and I'm too young to feel this old.

58 Plymouth Argyle

v. Wigan Athletic
DIVISION TWO
24 January

3-2

> 'It is approaching half a year since I put the club up for sale and although rumour and counter rumour abound, I have had no offer. If you are a serious genuine buyer, it doesn't take that long to make a decision.'

Chairman Dan McCauley. Nothing from manager Mick Jones

I like the idea of Plymouth. A large, industrial, grey-bricked city, packed with sailors, whores, tower blockers and inbreds, the most westerly point of lovely Devon, so isolated that Exeter is seen as dangerously close to shark-infested London. In times of war, it becomes vital to Britain and local unemployment shrivels. In times of peace it's The Place Where Michael Foot Comes From and too far away for concern.

Reality and theory converge under the closed-circuit cameras of Union Street, a minute away from the city centre and near no residences, except the inner city poor and, as all councils know, they don't count. Devoted to pleasure, like Las Vegas in relation to the rest of Nevada, Union Street is packed with pubs ('Plymouth's craziest fun bar!'), takeaway food emporiums (Ali Baba's 40 Dishes), clubs ('No dress restrictions!') and a Gentleman's Club & Sauna (what happens if, like me right now, a gentleman really does fancy a sauna? Having the spine of a jellyfish in every way, I dare not find out). Next week, one of the pubs promises a 'gentleman's evening: two top London exotic dancers and skimpy waitresses to serve your every need', just £7 in advance. Paradise, of sorts.

Forgetting Plymouth's drug culture, its legion poor areas – try Sutton, but not at night – and the hoards of skateboarders (isn't there a way to make skateboarding illegal? If there is no legal recourse, couldn't drunken, scythe-wielding vigilante posses be recruited in country pubs to kick these idiots to death? Some Plymouth skateboarders are over fifteen, for God's sake), it's a fine city, brimming with history. I'm beside myself with joy, albeit nerdish joy, to find a subway, ungraffitied, detailing the city's history, although it doesn't mention Plymouth's role in the American War Of Independence, when Millboy

Recreation Ground was turned into an internment camp for 1500 American soldiers. Aside from the Armada, Scott Of The Antarctic was actually Scott Of Plymouth and in 1919 Plymouth elected Nancy Astor as Britain's first woman MP. Later, of course they would elect David Owen, so it's not all moral high ground. He doesn't make the subway.

I make my way through the wide, Nazi-bomb created, streets for Plymouth Hoe, where Drake may or may not have played bowls before his wind-assisted routing of Phillip II's Spanish Armada. There is a Hoe bowls club – municipal, too – but it's impossible to see the sea from the green and they'd have let Drake play bowls exactly where he wanted in 1588. Today, under a grand statue of Drake – commemorating not the Armada but his captaincy of mankind's first trip around the world, 1577–80 – parents take their kids for walks, fathers play football with their lads and adults boulevard for pleasure.

I scamper down to the sea and get the break I've been looking for since the teams came out at Sunderland, a moment to cherish, to overturn the lows and the loneliness.

The tide is in, but the sea is accessible. I go to the water's edge to splash holy, turquoise Plymouth water on my face. I sit awhile and fret about finding thirty-four more matches to see. Plymouth is near the equator, so it's always warm. Today might be January, but there are sunbathers on the rocks. Better yet, is the middle-aged couple who're picnicking. They're late-40s, not especially handsome, but they're sat close together and they're talking away like they've just met. They must do this often and it must be better when it's only them, before the tourists – and Plymouth will have a few – come. They look happy, unrestless, at peace. That's enough for me. As I pass them I half smile their way and bend to stroke their cute mongrel dog who licks the salt water on my hands. The couple are so busy chatting and laughing they don't notice me. There's hope yet. I'd almost forgotten that.

Spring well and truly in my step, I head for Plymouth Argyle's Home Park, a long trawl to the north of the city, through the glossy centre full of fair-skinned beautiful people, past the railway station and through the Home Park itself, where a fortnight ago there were running battles between Plymouth and Bristol Rovers fans. There will be none of that today, for moneybags Wigan and perhaps fifty supporters are visiting, the team travelling down in an R-reg Hurst's Of Wigan coach, specially purchased for the club's purposes by Mr Malcolm Hurst himself. It has tinted windows and a coffee machine, although Mr Hurst didn't think table lamps were necessary.

The ground has seen better days. When selling the family home it's customary to give it a quick clean before potential purchasers start coursing through, casing the joint for potential burglaries. The same applies to football clubs. Home Park needs wholesale renovation, very much like the team, the inaudible Tannoy and the tea; although the Cornish pasty is partially edible and the pitch is pristine. I squeeze into the Main Stand, eject the smug slime-meister who'd taken my seat and gaze over Plymouth's far north and eastern suburbs. I'd like to live there one day, trapped in an idyll, sauntering along the Hoe on Saturday lunchtimes and picnicking by the sea with wife, kids and dog.

I'm next to an oldish, jocose, bespectacled man who comes to games on a coach from Penzance and who used to be a rep, so at least he's been to London. Wigan's form has collapsed since I saw them hammer Brentford before Christmas and they languish in mid-table, perhaps the first team I've seen this season with nothing to play for. Plymouth Argyle have everything to play for. They haven't scored in the two games I've seen them and they lie second from bottom in deep, deep trouble. Their next two games are against the teams directly above them, so this match is vital. In these circumstances, perhaps it was a rash idea to show the players – nine with visible pints of beer, one with a cigar – on today's programme cover, during their Christmas trip to Newton Abbot races. They need more than mascot Pilgrim Pete (the Pilgrim Fathers sailed from Plymouth in the *Mayflower* in 1620 to invent America) can give. Silly old Argyle, mascots are animal not human.

Soon, Wigan are 2-0 up, firstly from Ian Kilford and then David Lee, with Argyle's defence sound asleep both times. It's somewhat against the run of play, but hey, goals are goals. 'Criminal, bloody criminal,' sighs Penzancer. The sparse crowd sing loyalty songs, like revolutionaries before a firing squad. At half-time the couple next to Penzancer leave in disgust and he shares his flask of tea with me. A small gesture of friendship, that's all I needed.

Argyle are booed back onto the field for the second half, but it's a nervous booing, as if everyone knows this might be the end. Immediately Argyle press forward. They pull one back when Mark Saunders scrambles in. The response is hardly deafening. Still Argyle press and Penzancer comes into his own. Every time they get in the penalty area, he giggles with excitement. He thumps me in the ribs and points at the two empty seats next to him. 'He he,' he laughs. He's my Bloke Of The Season so far. He gets to giggle a lot as the pressure mounts.

The impressive Martin Barlow makes it 2-2 and I'm on my feet, as I am a few minutes later when Argyle goalkeeper Jon Sheffield makes a fantastic one-on-one save after Roberto Martinez seemed certain to score. Me and Penzancer hug each other when, with injury time approaching, Barlow crosses and big Simon Collins heads home for 3-2. Wigan manager John Deehan looks like he's about to have a coronary, two Plymouth fans are arrested for single-handedly trying to take the Wigan end and 4000 Devonians can make a hell of a din.

It's been a terrific game. I hug Penzancer again as we part after we've applauded the teams off. He hasn't stopped giggling for ten minutes. I walk back, giggling myself, to Union Street. I don't mind leaving, I know I'll return some day. The pubs have been full for most of the day: at the Two Trees, drinkers are sat at the bar lining their stomachs with food before a heavy night on which I'd like to accompany them. Even the barmaid is goodness itself, directing me to beer which is £1 a pint, but only for the next ten minutes. I am buoyant. Sir Francis Drake, knighted at Deptford, over-fond of Exeter, but still a Plymouth man, would understand.

59 Macclesfield Town

v. Brighton & Hove Albion
DIVISION THREE

27 January

1-0

'Next week, we make the long trip down to Torquay. Set off early, wrap up warm, take good care and we'll see you there.'

Sammy McIlroy

Typical. A town waits 123 years for league football and then discovers it doesn't want it after all. Macclesfield Town, in their first season, are unbeaten at home. A win tonight over Brighton – Conference next season but for the grace of Doncaster Rovers – would put them fourth, yet slightly over 2000 diehards turn up. Sure, it's a cold night and Liverpool are live on terrestrial television, but Brighton have found 200 supporters to make the journey. A few defeats and Doncaster's crowds would seem healthy in comparison to Macclesfield's. I propose a swap with Hereford United, right now.

Hardly surprising then that the town of Macclesfield barely registers a pulse. No Women, No Blacks, No Laughter might, for some, be a rallying call for injustice (or a certain type of sauna in Trondheim), but to me it is Macclesfield. The only sounds I hear are my own feet stomping the charnel cobbled streets in search of something I'll never find, not knowing what it is. Anything would do. Macclesfield has always had little to inspire, aside from moderate natural beauty and a steep hill or two. The Normans saw sense and burnt the place down, outlaws (including Will Scarlett allegedly, though greater cynics than myself might doubt that one) hung around the nearby forests and in 1604 Macclesfield passed a local law banning 'foreigners', which presumably meant people from the next village rather than, say, Burkina-Faso.

All was going relatively well until 1 December 1745, when Bonnie Prince Charlie stayed in what had become a butter-making centre on his way to rule Britain. Unfortunately, he brought 6000 of his friends and none of them were in the mood to pay for their B&B. Indeed, they liked it so much they visited again on the way home, albeit without their Prince. Lots of little McBabies were born the following September in a newly bankrupt, dishevelled town. That anti-foreigners law suddenly seemed a theoretical masterstroke, if a practical impossibility. To make up for the Scots, three Fenians were executed in 1867, Britain's last public hanging.

Genuine foreigners, Huguenots, saw Macclesfield as more tolerant than a France ravaged by religious wars with them as whipping sect. In 1768 their skills helped Charles Roe establish the silk throwing industry which led to genuine prosperity until cotton import duties were reduced a few decades later. By the 1820s things were so bad that, according to malicious legend, when a barrel of treacle fell off a dray in Mill Street and cracked open, the locals licked up the sticky goo with their tongues. They still refer to Macclesfield as Treacle Town in next door Congleton. Now, it's a Manchester overspill town, still architecturally ruled by mills, most of them abandoned and turned into mistress flats for Manchester businessmen. It's a melancholy place, the natives don't like to go out here, not even to football.

The ground, Moss Rose, christened to entrap the unwary into assuming beauty, lies on the main road to Leek in front of a housing estate shocking in its unpleasantness in a town which is hardly deprived. Kids on bikes, anti-joyriding (and anti-ambulance) speed bumps, shops with no windows, the whole works. Brighton & Hove Albion are deprived too. I examine their Scancoach more thoroughly than I did at Scarborough. On each table is a big bottle of HP Sauce, plastic knives and forks, plus buckets of salt. A royal feast awaits these professional athletes on the haul home.

Moss Rose is a non-league ground, simple as that, although the end that's seating at the front and standing at the back is novel. Crap, but undoubtedly novel. Macclesfield won the Conference in 1994–95 and Moss Rose denied them admission. It cannot be that different today. In comparison, Hereford's Edgar Street is the San Siro. With heated cushions.

I slouch at the back of the side terrace. I have sufficient space to swing a cat should I so wish (next time, next time), but I'm sufficiently near the scattered punters to ensure they won't think I'm friendless and chant about it. Although as the crowd is entirely old blokes with flasks, smoking roll-ups, they are more likely to commit hara-kiri in the centre circle than chant anything. There's enough room for the mascot, a most friendly Roary The Lion, to come into the crowd and kiss old ladies. It's a homely club – they make tea individually, pouring fresh milk in, removing tea bags, asking 'Is that all right, love?' – and the pies aren't bad either. Cold and hungry, I make a return journey for a teeth-loosening bacon bap. That's OK, too.

Macclesfield (as in 'Oh Maccy Maccy. Maccy Maccy Macclesfield' according to the end, once) play like a competent Conference outfit and that's enough to send Brighton home pointless. Attention-seeking centre half Efetobore Sodje plays in a bandanna and I can smell his amateurism more than the liniment whenever he comes close. Pillock.

As at Scarborough, Brighton give a decent account of themselves. Derek Allen has a header cleared off the line by Town forward Neil Sorvel and the home side have no answer to Peter Smith and his extraordinarily long legs on overlap overload.

Macclesfield step it up in the second half and sneak a fluke winner when winger Stuart Whittaker's cross loops over Nicky Rust. Whittaker is the player of the evening: he's a touch frail, but his speed, skill and awareness of lesser players around him means he won't be at Moss Rose for long. His deserved encomium is to be Man Of The Match. Away players always seem ineligible for some reason. A quick chorus of 'You've come all this way for nothing' to the away support and we're off home.

Nobody is more relieved than the poor steward who has spent all game unsuccessfully trying to shoo off estate urchins whose evening has been spent trying literally to kick their way in. When this fails, they throw junk over the fence. None of the beleaguered official's colleagues bother to help him. More casual cruelty, another modern British tradition that won't be celebrated at the Millennium Dome. More problems in later life for everyone involved. More misery and impotence for me.

I walk back to Treacle Town. Nothing has changed. The pubs are dead; the people, descendants of 'Bonnie' Charles Stuart's ragtag army, are elsewhere. I can take a hint.

60 **Manchester City**

v. Charlton Athletic
DIVISION ONE

28 January

2-2

'The most important task facing us now is out on the pitch and nothing must deflect us from that.'

Frank Clark

Another day, another trip up the M1 and M6. I'm starting to recognise the staff at Newport Pagnell service station now. Worse, they are starting to recognise me.

'Crisis club' is an easy sobriquet, possibly patented by the newspaper formerly known as the *Daily Mirror*. It's all relative though, for Manchester City are not Doncaster Rovers, nor are they Oxford United and only a lunatic pessimist would suggest that they won't be in existence next season. City are fourth from the bottom of Division One, their lowest ever league position, demonstrations are commonplace, relegation is a genuine possibility and they are a laughing stock (the current supporters' campaign is Free The Manchester 30,000), managed by a man often mistaken for a basset hound who has the motivational powers of a stoat.

Maine Road is spooky. It's not in the very worst part of Manchester, but it is on the edge of Moss Side, an area much loved by tabloids and where it might be possible to buy drugs and guns from kids on bikes, or curry from beleaguered Asians in hock to Yardie protection rackets. The latest wave of immigrants are Montserrat volcano refugees.

When City arrived in 1923, it was a typical inner-city ground. The terraced houses that surrounded it were populated by the white working class, who provided the bulk of City's support. Football club and community were one, as was the norm.

Things changed everywhere, but Manchester City were uniquely unlucky. Maine Road's surroundings were not rejuvenated or fossilised by the football club. Gangs moved in, families moved out and City developed Maine Road to its present state, surrounded by a massive car park (nobody dare park in the side streets, apart from me, mainly because I'm too tight to pay; tellingly, 200 yards away, I go back and check it's locked), populated on match days by hundreds of Range Rovers and coach Asa Hartford's R-reg company model. He is the world's worst parker. Pre-designated spaces mean nothing to him. Perhaps his training regime reflects this.

Like the players, City's fans don't live around here and they don't like their four-wheel drives crawling through Markington Street, ten seconds walk from stewarded safety, where every window of the end house, downstairs and up, is protected by thick, black burglar bars. Every street here has a house like this. Every house has a burglar alarm. Manchester City are in the community, but they're alien to it.

White-owned businesses, like Blue Moon fish'n'chip bar, come alive on match days. In more than one fast food outlet, they're playing a video of City's 5-1 annihilation of Manchester United in the tight-shorted days of September 1989. Irredentist City fans, mouths agape with lost pride, watch entranced. It must be on eternal loop around here and City's mindset hasn't evolved from that moment, despite the evidence of league tables. David Oldfield scored that day. Twice. United's struggling manager Alex Ferguson was under enormous pressure. By December, City's Mel Machin had been sacked.

All this also means that few frequent local pubs: tonight's punters seem to appear from and, later, disappear into nowhere, like an army of the night. There are seats aplenty in the cavernous Parkside pub, next to the ground but certainly not at the side of any park. The punters are predominantly locals (i.e. mostly black), they're playing cards and have been for many hours. It must be legal to smoke marijuana in here and the beer is that funny tasting, fizzy, headless stuff that only pubs in poor areas serve. A few City fans mingle around. They don't look nervous because they know nothing will happen, especially as tonight isn't karaoke night, the poor person's entertainment of 1998. It's the fans' secret. I even talk to an Irishman, who chooses to sit with and talk sport with me. He drinks – and I'm counting – five pints to my one. I'm so distracted by this display of powersupping, my conversation is limited to grunts. I nearly applaud when he leaves with a friendly 'Take care'.

Still worried about my car and cross with myself for being so, I venture inside the ground. Chairman Francis Lee, not Frank Clark, not the team (aside from centre half Kit Symons, but there must be one playing scapegoat), is the hate figure round here. Like Mobuto Sese Seko in Zaire, Lee came to power on a wave of popular acclaim and then found he couldn't take the people with him. It's said he interferes in team selection (a believable explanation of Steve Coppell's mysterious departure in 1996 would reveal much); that he has a financial interest in the catering (he certainly doesn't have a gourmet's interest in the disgraceful slop I suffer in the Main Stand); that he hasn't put his own money in and that he holidays in Barbados at crucial moments. Even Lee admits, though, that he willingly employed Alan Ball. Dennis Tueart ('He didn't make any difference as a player, so why should he as a director?' sneers Rodney Marsh, the man whose failure to integrate after signing for City in 1972 cost them a Championship) has just been co-opted onto the board. Tueart is not Lee's man, so the end is near.

It's tense, and the gate, against unglamorous (but third) Charlton Athletic, with Arsenal v. Chelsea on television, is massive, almost a 31,000 sell-out. Adversity breeds a certain stubbornness, and City's replica shirt outsells United's in Manchester.

City's problem is obvious, even after Paul Dickov gives them an early, nerve-settling lead after a fortuitous penalty award. The team are without confidence, spirit and talent. And they're weighed down further by the faith-fuls' expectation. Georgi Kinkladze – he advertises City's Kappa kit in the programme, its 'people on the move' slogan must have a whole new meaning for him soon – is a peripheral figure and has been since he wrote off his £50,000 Ferrari near the M56 in October, but Murtaz Shelia has implausibly manly thighs the size and solidity of oak trunks, while the maligned Symons literally gives blood for the cause. But when Uwe Rösler, contract refusenik, misses an open goal, his own fans jeer him without mercy. When he's substituted, Rösler goes straight down the tunnel. If he cares, I'm a leg of ham.

Charlton, neat and precise, have a serious problem of their own. Their goal-keeper Mike Salmon is injured, possibly concussed, after a corner and spends the remainder of the half stumbling around, unable to take goal kicks. Still City can't score, even after Charlton's Shaun Newton limps off.

Salmon doesn't return for the second half. Charlton don't have a substitute custodian so right back Steve Brown keeps goal. Clark joins the City bench and edginess descends. The couple in front of me leave at half-time after she's spent the whole period demanding to eat and upsetting herself over those in front of her chain smoking through nervousness. Behind me is City's child mascot and her family. She spends the entire game squeaking with her friend and her silly parents elect not to exercise parental discipline.

These people are exceptions. This is a lads' crowd, the same lads who may ensure Manchester keeps its 15–35 male suicide rate at twice the national average as well as having the lowest car ownership rate (a good thing obviously) and the highest schoolgirl pregnancy rate in Britain. They boo their team (especially substitute Jason Van Blerk, Symons having purged himself with his blood), they dress like Liam Gallagher and, were Charlton's fans not so peaceable and few, there would be the crowd trouble that enlivened recent games against Middlesbrough and Sunderland. If City cannot be the best team in Manchester (Greater Manchester if we include Stockport County and Bury), then they're certainly going to have the hardest fans and it's such a long way from Central Manchester to Maine Road.

Brown remains resolutely untested in the Charlton goal, but Shelia getting himself sent off is the watershed. Charlton begin to press and, with their first real attack, substitute Steve Jones fires a wobbly volley past Tommy Wright. 'The referee's a wanker' is the chant of the moment.

The game is due to finish at 9.30. With the clock saying 9.33, Symons rises to head home a free kick. 2-1. Ludicrously, City find time to blow it. Bradley Allen skips around Ian Brightwell, crosses, and Jones, bestowed with the freedom of Maine Road, heads in his and Charlton's second. The clock says 9.35 and even the Charlton fans manage a 'You're not singing any more' while dancing like Cockney dervishes. Clark, patently a decent man, slaps his thigh in anguish and turns round to look at the fans around me. His big Geordie heart has broken again.

The crowds have fled by the time I get out. Nervily, I return to my car, past glassless bus shelters, past kids of primary school age still out on their bikes, past rows of boarded up shops. I don't like the stillness, the cold and the Dickensian mist, I don't like feeling jumpy and I don't like the way a little old lady crosses the road to avoid walking past me.

Having cocked up Maine Road's redevelopment by making it too shallow and small, Manchester City are tentatively planning a move to a bigger 'Millennium' stadium at Eastlands, wherever that may be. That might finish off the double-edged sword that forms Manchester City's character. For now, they're the last great inner city club. And everything has gone wrong.

61 Lincoln City

v. Hull City
DIVISION THREE
31 January

1-0

'I will get it right.'

John Beck

Once it was the tallest man-made structure in the world. Today, Lincoln Cathedral stands on top of the appropriately named Steep Hill and it's still a wonderful example of man's control over nature. Admittedly a hurricane would blow it over (it survived the 1185 earthquake, just), as will three more centuries of rain, but that's not the point and Lincoln isn't on the hurricane trail.

The Romans liked Lincoln. They built a garrison and made it the capital of Eastern England, a tradition that raping and pillaging Danes followed. Later, an anonymous mason would carve an imp into a cathedral wall (hence the football team's Red Imps nickname), wool would bring prosperity and then decline. The world's first tank would be built in Lincoln. Now, nearly 100,000 live here, but it's no football city.

Steep Hill is the only hill in Lincolnshire, probably the only hill in the east of England, so an invading force as canny as the Normans were hardly going to pass up the opportunity to build a cathedral and castle at its summit. How they built it, how they lugged all that stone up Steep Hill (I can barely get myself up there), I haven't the brain power to grasp. Eventually, I notice I'm drooling. Dignity, always dignity.

The result is a well-preserved castle and a triple towered cathedral, which demands a 'suggested donation' of £3 for right of entry and needs £1,750,000 to restore the choir's organs. They're halfway there, despite a ten-year unholy row between the dean and sub-dean. The dean was appointed following the sub-dean's fund-raising trip to Australia in 1988 with Lincoln's original Magna Carta (four survive), which lost over £50,000. Spineless Bishop Hardy boycotted his own cathedral rather than sort it out. Now the dean has left after lengthy financial discussions and the imp's curse has never been exorcised.

Like every cathedral the world over, Lincoln's is being restored and is thus covered with scaffolding. I'm still impressed and from here I can see the edge of the world, over which, just out of reach, are the thirty-one grounds I have yet to visit. Although it's warm, I feel suddenly cold and what seconds ago was tranquil is now foreboding.

I'm with my pal Peter once more. This is benison indeed, for now I can mix with Hull fans with pride as, yes, I do actually have a friend. We can also go by train (easier said than done to Lincoln) and I won't feel like an alcoholic or pervert when I enter a pub. Few of my other so-called friends have bothered to help bail me out of loneliness. This is unbearably discouraging and whilst it's childish to conduct relationships on any principle save Do As You Would Be Done By, I would have accompanied them if the roles were reversed.

Lincoln, however, is not disappointing. Because it's out of the way, it's not sold its soul to tourists as Chester has. There's an open-air market selling Lincolnshire hot dogs. I would gladly kill a distant relative to eat that mix of fresh sausage, fresh bread and lashings of English mustard once more.

There are swans on the canal, buskers sing a cappella arias or play classical guitar, Lynne Franks's autobiography has been reduced to 99p and, for the local youth, there is 999 Night on the first Thursday of every month at Ritzy's. Presumably this means everyone has to dress up in uniform. Failing that, there are duelling pianos 'the latest concept in live entertainment direct from the U. S. of A.' at Mustang Sally's next door, where the 70s and 80s 'quite literally come alive'. This was some people's golden age and those times must never be mocked or we'll lose our souls, but I have a funny feeling that the carny who brought Duelling Pianos to Lincoln might have a local accent.

The ground, Sincil Bank, is south of the city centre, where people like grandmother Lorraine Bowler live. She has twenty-seven rings and studs embedded over her face. Nice. The tourists are steered away from this area, with its cut-price shops, seedy pubs and locals whose chief pleasure is spitting with the zealousness of a mosque-load of spitting imams. It's a pleasant, airy ground and in the spirit of the 999 Night at Ritzy's, there's a Gentlemen's Evening featuring 'stunning strippers Jade, Dani, Sapphire, Gina and Stephanie' (not perhaps all their real names) for a mere £8. What is the world coming to? For the Millennium, Britain might as well have a giant Gentlemen's Evening where thousands, millions, of Danis and Jades strip for millions of drunken, sexually repressed men who each pay £8 and solve the country's New Century Recession at one sitting. Just an idea. I'll be at Ritzy's, dressed as God's very own policeman, James Anderton.

There is dignity at Sincil Bank. We sit in the Stacey West Stand, named after the City fan who died at Bradford's Valley Parade fire the day Lincoln were the visitors. It's a simple gesture, but it warms and humbles us. Unlike my pie (why not use the Lincolnshire hot dog vendor from the town centre?), which was edible, but it was a close run thing. Encouragingly, the serving woman did bat her eyelids at me and, assuming she doesn't have a tick, I'll register that as an invitation.

It's a ground which has been substantially redeveloped. The Stacey West's middle third is seated and everyone has the option to stand or sit. Disappointingly, most people sit given the choice. Even more disappointingly, we sit. The Linpave (I no more know what a linpave is than a sincil) Stand down the side is impressive, although there aren't enough seats for the Hull City (sleeping giant etc.) fans and the jittery police have to fold some tarpaulin and reduce the size of no man's land to accommodate them.

Lincoln City are not a happy club. An unbeaten run of eighteen matches has sloughed into a winless ten and what was once a no-one-likes-us-we-don't-care attitude has evolved into an incipient rebellion where a smattering of fans wave placards saying We Want Football, placated by the suspicious public disclosure that John Beck's contract runs out at the end of the season and is less likely to be renewed than Frank Clark's. Locals are claiming the conveniently unemployed Brian Horton and/or Mervyn Day have been seen at Sincil Bank this week. Lincoln are eleventh but as Beck – who will patrol the dugout in shorts and boots like a cut-price Steve McMahon – explains, only six points behind third placed Barnet and his team have a game in hand. That's seventeen points and eleven places better off than Hull City.

Another poor game. Lincoln's fans are divided – they were fighting each other at Peterborough last month – between the purists who would rather the team's sole aim was not to win throw-ins, which in Terry Fleming's capable hands are more like corners, and the realists who favour a more craft-based approach. Peter and I do not give a toss either way, although in Steve Wilson, Hull City have a Dracula goalkeeper (i.e. afraid of crosses, an old gag to be sure but it gets me every time).

Fleming has already hit the bar by the time Wilson drops a corner at the feet of Dean Walling who scores easily. Hull centre half Rob Dewhurst makes punching gestures towards Wilson, emphasising how much spirit they have. The rest of the team glare at the forlorn goalkeeper, who stares hard at the grass. The Bosman Ruling was not designed to benefit goalkeepers freed from the third worst team in the land. If, as is likely, Wilson knows nothing else, he knows this.

Hull are awful and for the third time this season I will see them fail to even look like scoring. Seeming to understand what a lost cause this is, manager Mark Hateley sends his team out a full five minutes early for the second half. At least they can hear the PA man's record collection: 'Silver Machine', 'Ace Of Spades', 'Paranoid' and 'Smoke On The Water' at full volume. Crikey, they'll be playing that new fangled punk rock next.

Lincoln are delighted with 1-0. Steve Brown looks a fine player, out of place in a match played without midfields, although he misses an open goal when Wilson miskicks. Lincoln's band – stop the bands, those instruments are dangerous – keep trying to inject some atmosphere into what, after all, is a derby. Hull's fans have stopped singing 'What's it like to see a crowd?' and cannot believe what they're seeing. Lincoln's are happy to stand and point in a vaguely menacing manner. Is that all there is? Yes, that's all there is. Lincoln doesn't need football any more than football needs Lincoln.

We go back into the city, which looks like it might be a fine place to spend a Saturday evening. Alas, the primitive train service means this is not possible, although when the last connecting train to London leaves, we are the only two people on it. I blame privatisation, but it feels knee-jerk. We do, however, have time to scramble up Steep Hill again to check Lincoln is gorgeous in the dark (it is) and to a bubbling Yates's where a hen night is taking shape. Two girls – not to be confused with women – are wearing L-plates: 'My name is Sarah and I take it up the Gary Glitter' and 'My name is Sue and I take it up the passage of poo'. They both have a drink in each hand and they're already giggling loudly. We have to sprint for that last train.

62 **Leyton Orient**

v. Peterborough United
DIVISION THREE

6 February

1-0

> **'We have won six of our last nine league games and that's the sort of points return I would like us to keep achieving between now and the end of the season.'**

Tommy Taylor

Leyton High Street is exactly how anyone born outside the sound of the M25 might imagine London to be. It's dark (this is because it's a Friday evening in February), cold (ditto) and filthy. All the stereos of passing cars work only at distortion volume; a so-called 'gardens' is locked; the only shops are dodgy-looking flat rental agencies or scum-sucking fast food outlets. The mobile-telephone wielding populace may be multicultural, but you wouldn't take them home. You wouldn't take them to anyone else's home. It's not even especially run down, although muggings are rife, despite last Wednesday afternoon's (white boy on Asian woman) being foiled by an alert (white) car valeter. Perhaps for the one and only time, the word 'shitty' is perfect.

Leyton High Street has bred Leyton Orient. A team despised by nobody, loved by a very few and bereft of passion inside or outside the club, except for the groundsman, one Charlie Hasler, who has it written into his contract that he attends all home and away games. He even saw his team play in Stoke the day his daughter married. Parenting may very well be a cesspool of difficult decisions. Not in the Hasler household obviously. Still, he rolls an expert pitch.

Lonely and depressed, I visit the barn-like Coach & Horses. The pub is full of Peterborough fans (now there's a phrase that's rarely used) singing anti-Cambridge songs, none of which I can follow. The locals watch, bemused. They're not going to the match.

Leyton Orient have been in the news this week and not, alas, for sneakily changing the name of their Brisbane Road ground to Matchroom Stadium in homage to chairman Barry Hearn and director and well-known football fan Steve Davis. There's been a survey of football clubs' catering and Orient finished bottom.

Now, having consumed nothing but pastry, hot dogs and tea at football stadiums since August, I immodestly consider myself to be an expert on this matter. The mighty Stockport are nowhere to be found, so the whole enterprise is flawed. Tonight I have a burger, the most maligned food at the worst caterers. It's not something I'd wish to eat again, it's not something I'd like my cat to eat. For food at a football ground it's average, although the 'tea' is a liquid which I have never previously encountered, an uncomfortable blend of sewage outflow and lavender. I'll monitor my guts tomorrow. Surreally, while the match is taking place, the police will notice a man in the ground behaving strangely, arrest him and charge him with possessing cocaine. He turns out to be Orient's catering franchise man.

The ground is three-sided now with no sign of building work at the demolished South Terrace and needs investment badly, like the team itself who loiter four points behind the play-off positions and eight behind second placed Peterborough. The last financial year saw Orient lose £657,283 and pay an astronomical wage bill of £1,300,000. Last week 34-year-old goalkeeper Paul Hyde, father of two autistic children, broke his leg in two places at Exeter. It won't be a prosperous future for the family Hyde. This week's solution is to sign Billy Turley, Northampton Town's reserve custodian, on wages of three felt tips and all the burgers he can eat. He looks nervous, not least when the jolly PA man invites fans to send Get Well Soon cards to Hyde.

They've never gone for atmosphere at Leyton Orient. Hearn's latest initiative is a band, which are too close to me in the East Stand. Obviously they're all keen students of Karlheinz Stockhausen (later of Stockhausen, Waterman) as they're so experimental some people close to me think they can't play a note to save their lives. Me, I embrace the atonal.

Although dispassionate, Orient fans are friendly – the woman at the ticket office is goodness personified – and refreshingly unbitter. After all, they made the choice not to support West Ham and they didn't do it for kudos or fighting. Thus Orient encourage and laugh at their own, even when the play-offs are in sight. I'm sandwiched between a short-haired, chunky 'geezer' who correctly moans about Orient having no width and a man with dribble running down his chin and pungent body odour. I'm in front of a posh Range Rovery couple. He's patronisingly explaining how football works, she's wishing he'd do it a little quieter. They leave at half-time, something which is happening too much right now. Perhaps it's me, perhaps it's my own body odour.

It's not much of game. Peterborough fans boo their former player Carl Griffiths, Orient fans jeer the band and sing 'we've got the worst pies in the land'. My attention wanders towards Canary Wharf, flashing in the distance. It might have been Thatcher's substitute phallus; it might be impossible to get to by public and private transport; it might symbolise the gap between rich incomers and poor British National Party-loving Isle Of Doggers, but it's an inspiration and all Ayn Rand would have needed to prove that architects shape our world.

Peterborough's David Farrell's mazy run sees him beat all the home defence and set up Martin Carruthers who somehow doesn't score. Turley dislikes crosses but is fearless in crowded penalty areas and a fine shot stopper. Five minutes before the end, Orient substitute Joe Baker, who has the gait and body of a *Hard Times* orphan, shapes to cross, but slices. The ball sails over Mark Tyler into the top corner. 1-0: money for Barry Hearn, a mini-pitch invasion by children, relief for Sky, misery on the Peterborough bench for Barry Fry and Phil Neal (Phil Neal? Oh yes). It might be me: two Peterborough games and I've yet to see the division's top scorers score.

I return to the Coach & Horses. A group of hard-faced, old Peterborough fans are scaring everyone with a quiet bout of low, demonic chanting. Unlike the Orient fans, they're bitter. That's how the world divides.

63 **Hartlepool United**

v. Darlington
DIVISION THREE

7 February

2-2

'I've never said we would get promotion, but it is a realistic possibility.'

Mick Tait

During the Napoleonic wars, the ever-vigilant seafaring folk of Seaton Carew were never complacent enough to assume their hardy coastal village, now subsumed into Hartlepool ('the place where deer drink'), would not be Bonaparte's bridgehead for his inevitable invasion. These suspicions were confirmed one stormy night when a French ship ran aground. All hands were lost, except for the vessel's mascot, a monkey whom the amusing Gauls had dressed in military uniform. The little chap was taken to Hartlepool, tried and hanged as a French spy. The rest of Britain found out and laughed. Hartlepool has never recovered its self-esteem. Never forget, though, that the monkey was guilty.

I like Hartlepool, birthtown of Wayne Sleep and Ridley Scott. Germans like it too, for it was the first place their warships shelled in World War 1. It's only existed as a borough since 1967 when ancient Hartlepool (still the area to tread carefully in) around The Headland merged with the larger, Victorian boom-town of West Hartlepool to form one large, social-services stretching entity. Despite the collapse of the local shipbuilding industry, the sea air is bracing and Hartlepool is making an effort (I adore effort: dullards need all the help they can get; the average become above average and the brilliant become combustible with genius), trying to transcend a potentially fatal mix of deprivation and ridicule. So plasterers spend a hard-working Saturday lunchtime opposite the railway station, stuck up rickety scaffolding like 21st-century ragged-trousered philanthropists, a tribe whose number is inexorably growing. I'm fine, last night's Orientburger hasn't made a reappearance.

No, there's more, much of it under the EC-funded, cinema-free Hartlepool Renaissance umbrella. An art gallery housed in an old church has an exhibition of cartoons, mainly by 81-year-old Reg Smythe, creator of obvious fellow-Hartlepudlian Andy Capp. Smythe, bless him, still lives around Caledonian Road. There's a museum where it's only slightly patronising to be invited to lift sacks like real workers used to do. And instead of surrendering Hartlepool's quay and focal point to gangs of the dispossessed roaming the waste ground circling the quay's southern side, it's been rejuvenated with historical displays, ideal for kids' school outings, some shops and been given a sheen that a place like this needs so badly. If it doesn't work – and all this might still not be enough – they have tried. In a town with nothing save the scramble to get out, it is something. Individually built detached houses cost just £71,000 and it's illegal to drink alcohol in the streets.

Tony Blair's Sedgfield constituency is the other side of the A1 and Peter Mandelson is the town's MP, a Labour politician's job for life. It's an uneasy marriage. The locals tell one story, probably apocryphal, but the broadsheets print it from time to time and it's the new monkey-hanging legend. In a rare constituency visit, MP and handsome entourage go to a chip shop. Mandelson orders and then points at the mushy peas, saying 'and some of that guacamole dip, please'.

The football team are hopeless, of course. Always have been, always will be. In 1956–57 they finished runners-up in the old Division Three (North) in the days when only champions were promoted. In the January of that season the Busby Babes came to Victoria Park in the FA Cup. Oh, and Brian Clough began his managerial career here. That's all.

Today though is as special as it gets. Darlington have arrived in their N-reg Atkinsons of Northallerton coach, which has two lampless tables and the ubiquitous lower league coffee machine. Fine for a short hop north east, less so for Exeter.

There are many large ugly people both on the streets and in the packed Yates's where I take a pre-match beer. This might be Hartlepool's usual face to the world, but the police have not made this game – one which is more likely to feature Alan Shearer as a Darlington substitute than sell out – all ticket for nothing.

Victoria Park is to the north of the town, overlooking the refurbished quay and North Sea. From the Town End, my natural bounce is further lifted by the North Sea at rush hour and the sweary, shouty crowd. They sing 'Stand up if you hate Darlington', always funnier on a standing end. I laugh like a drain. Outside, clawing at the gates, there is a mass of under-twelves who have never had a full meal in their brief, unhappy lives. The pie upon which I munch sticks to its foil tray as if, perhaps, it had been overcooked. More than once.

It's a mid-table scrap, but Hartlepool have yet to lose at home (they have lost money at home though, a programme seller was robbed before the Macclesfield game and his wares sold cheaply in town; turnstile operators have also been targeted), while Darlington have not won away. Victory for either might ease the dulling pain of Division Three mediocrity. Darlington have sold out the 740-capacity Rink End (any rink is long gone). Ignoring the pie-eating competition between a fat bastard supporter of each side goaded by a minor local radio celebrity, Hartlepool fans sing 'The Rink End is full of shit', Darlington reply with 'Where's your monkey gone?'. Behind me, at the back corner, are a trio of old, silent skinheads, dressed in black Harrington jackets, the uniform of the far right, wearing no insignia save St George's Cross badges. To amuse themselves, and themselves alone, they set fire to a Darlington scarf. If only it hadn't been them ...

The first half runs to form, as predictable as the teams running out to 2 Unlimited's 'Get Ready For This'. Hartlepool, with Strongarm upon their breasts, have the game's best player, Ian Clark, who inspires Jan Ove Pedersen to stroll through a dopey defence and tuck Richard Lucas's smart pass home. Clark himself scores the second in much the same way. There's a mass on-pitch brawl, which everyone enjoys, except the two booked Hartlepool players. All looks well by half-time, when a local theatre group brings a man dressed as a dinosaur into the centre circle and then promptly shoos him off.

I know things will be different in the second half from the moment unnervingly breezy Darlington goalkeeper David Preece places his Lucazade Sport bottle in the corner of his goal in front of the Town End. A young kid, ten at the most, has spent his half-time saving up spittle. He showers Preece with hepatitis-ridden phlegm. Those behind him laugh rather too keenly and taunt Darlington's boss, 'Hodgson, give us a wave'. He doesn't.

Clark hobbles off and the game alters course in a minute. Paul Connor, on loan to Hartlepool from Middlesbrough, is felled in the penalty area. Referee Cain waves play on. The ball falls to plump substitute Stephen Halliday (nickname: Jabba) who smacks it at Preece when it was easier to score. Dreadful Darlington rush up field and Darren Roberts heads in Simon Shaw's cross.

The celebratory atmosphere is replaced by tension. The chants switch to 'Fuck off Darlo' and, last heard in 1982, 'You're gonna get your fucking heads kicked in'. Everyone assumes an equaliser is coming and, with thirty seconds remaining, substitute Carl Shutt crosses low and Roberts pounces again to drive home. The Darlington players collapse in an orgiastic heap near their dugout. When the whistle goes, Preece looks up at the Town End and, half smirking, shrugs and claps as if to apologise. The spittle pours down on him and this time everyone (not me, obviously not me, it's disgusting) joins in. A steward escorts him away.

There is only one route, along Clarence Road, to the town centre and station. The police have blocked the road off in order to shepherd the Darlington fans back to the station. Hartlepool's fighters, 150 at the most, gather where Clarence Road meets the town centre. It's here that I finally understand the urchins outside the ground and spittle shower boy, for the oldest of these Bugsy Malones is no more than seventeen. Some of them, I swear, aren't at secondary school yet. Hartlepool is planning for the future in every way.

I've had to hang back, too old and therefore too conspicuous to mingle. Mounted police prepare a passage for the Darlington fans by attempting to break up the tots, who scatter through the Middleton Grange shopping centre, traumatising pensioners with carrier bags and mothers with young children like it was the late-70s all over again. They regroup around the art gallery where, for once, the police have not planned ahead and stationed personnel. The teenies follow the chuckling Darlington fans towards the station, picking off strays and dawdlers along the way, but with insufficient venom to trouble local hospitals or juvenile courts. The laughing policemen at the railway station do the rest. In ten years, the youths will have realised fighting at football is more addictive than crack cocaine and Hartlepool will be a different proposition.

Before I depart, I sample Bikini's Fun Bar. There are no bikinis, it is not, in any way 'fun' and my dream of combining the two and finding Peter Mandelson in a bikini is a non-starter. An unfortunate couple seem to have held their wedding reception here this afternoon and some of the scraps of food they managed to afford remain uneaten. Evil children are ruling the place, drinking lemonade, playing pool and screeching at the top of their unbroken voices while their impotent parents sip cans of lager, smoke Embassy Regal and slyly stroke the top of each other's thighs. They're all married, but not necessarily to each other. I don't understand their rules and so I must leave them. They don't notice.

64 **Watford**

v. Gillingham
DIVISION TWO
8 February

0-2

> **'I do not always get a chance to read the club's programme and when I do, I usually skip the manager's notes because my wife Rita says they are a load of rubbish.'**

Graham Taylor

I thought I'd dream about Bikini's Fun Bar last night, but no, I dreamed about Vicarage Road, Watford, a ground I've dreaded visiting, the dullest place in the land. I dreamed I'd met a school girlfriend – one I'd never slept with – on the way here. I'd gone out without wearing any socks, which she found hilarious. While I'd gone to buy a pair, I missed the last train to Watford and thus the match. A good job I can't believe in dream interpretation.

I don't miss any trains this Sunday morning, although the line between Wembley and Harrow is down, like my heart. Watford is, well, quite pleasant. That's the best I can do, but, in memory of when things were different, the local Labour Party offices are next to Trade Union Hall. I stare like a community care madman at a short skirted, chicken-legged assistant at Maplin, a High Street electronics shop. What is she doing, spending her Sundays trying to sell some useless gadget to the permanently ungrateful? London is twenty minutes away and she might as well be in Jarrow. Watford: Where Only The Dregs Are Left is its slogan.

Vicarage Road is west, through the town centre. I merge with flaccid-chinned, middle-aged men in corduroy trousers, with their precocious sons and middle-aged women in home made yellow, black and red scarves. Watford share their ground with Saracens, a rugby union team. The crowds will be similar, only twenty times as small. The pitch is, of course, a disgrace and the blue rugby markings serve only to confuse linesmen, players and supporters.

My Vicarage Road Stand hot dog is so average it could get its own programme commissioned by Carlton Television and there's no milk to go with the tea. Watford might be top of Division Two (a level where even Jason Lee looks competent although he hasn't scored since 1 November) and the division's best supported team, but there's a basement club trying to get out. Luckily Gillingham, in tenth place and rising fast, have brought a huge band of noisy Kent men, so there's some vim in the Rookery Stand at least.

It's not all bad, despite the PA announcer screaming 'Let the millions hear us' when the players enter to the *Star Wars* theme. Excellent mascot Harry The Hornet is chanted at 'Har-ee, Har-ee' and performs a mad dance in the centre circle with four kiddy mascots, later he will patrol the touchline being given offside from time to time. Whenever Gilllingham's ex-Watford skipper Andy Hessenthaler secures possession the crowd sing 'You're just a short greedy bastard', showing at last, anger and, humorously, 'There's only one Lennie Lawrence' for the hapless manager of local rivals Luton and 'Taylor for England' for their own. Edge? Almost.

Gillingham seem fired. Watford goalkeeper Alec Chamberlain has already made a world-class save from Steve Butler and Gillingham's Paul Smith has fluffed a one-on-one, when Watford's dithery Richard Johnson loses out to Nicky Southall on the halfway line. Butler picks it up and feeds Ade Akinbiyi who neatly scores a goal similar to Hartlepool's pair yesterday.

Watford fall apart. It can't usually be like this and their fans sing 'Shit on the telly, we're always shit on the telly' as explanation; 'We're supposed to be at home' after a long silence punctuated only by a grim band and 'We've had a shot' after Peter Kennedy's slice worries the corner flag. Then, these Mellorites settle on the last refuge of the useless and blame blameless (but fat) referee Furnandiz: 'You don't know what you're doing'.

Watford flurry briefly in the second half. Tommy Mooney hits the bar and when Gillingham goalkeeper Mark Walton takes a goal kick, instead of 'Aaaaaagh! You're shit!', the Watford fans go 'Shhhh' and then a brief 'Aaagh!' as foot and ball connect. By the time substitute Iffy Onuora sets up Akinbiyi for 0-2, the ground is half empty. Nobody seems to care, Watford are still top and Fulham are still sixteen points away in third.

The green paint has run on the war memorial which once displayed three heroic figures; the footpaths are numbered; the hideous shopping centre is at half-flow, populated by the worst dressed shoppers this side of Sofia; but the pedestrianised pub/club area near the town hall (which proudly boasts that Watford has had clean air for the last 720 hours) looks like it might be fun if I'd surrendered my mind to cheap drugs and expensive beer. I have a wheat beer (I know, I know) in the Moon Under Water (I know, I know) and nurse what is a substantial misery-induced headache. The staff are breathtakingly rude and there's a group of bespectacled Watford fans talking to a group of bespectacled Gillingham fans. They're making plans to meet, although their teams have played each other twice this season.

I cannot shake the mantra, 'London is twenty minutes away' from my befuddled brain. Up the road is the headquarters of Camelot. I turn the other way and go home. Watford's skyline is dominated by the local YMCA and the big local story this week features the white residents of North Watford trying to prevent local Muslims building a mosque there. I won't be back in a hurry.

65 Crystal Palace

v. Wimbledon
PREMIER LEAGUE
9 February

0-3

'I think you can see the players are trying as hard as they can.'

Steve Coppell

Four games in four days. Watford and then Crystal Palace. Even medieval serfs didn't visit two such places in two days and not because of transport difficulties either.

Still, Wimbledon are playing and I haven't seen them complete a full game in two attempts. Going to a match hoping the floodlights fail isn't perhaps the right attitude, but it's the only one I have. Selhurst Park is as grim and gridlocked as it was when I saw Wimbledon, although at least there are no Arsenal fans. Crystal Palace fans like coming here, it's their home and has been since 1924, although they haven't won a league game here all season (they defeated Wimbledon in their away game here, but that doesn't count). Takeovers from within are in the air and the Italians Lombardo and Padovano will be injured until their country crumbles into warring statelets again. Tonight, for one night only, Wimbledon can't resent Selhurst Park. This is a proper away game. To celebrate, they nearly sell-out their section.

Pretty girls are handing out Rice Krispies Squares, i.e. Rice Krispies glued together with marshmallow. Slipping into mental decline, I amuse myself by repeatedly walking past them. Although unrecognised by the prettiest for the fifth time, I gradually fill my pockets. All my twelve squares are lovely, but tomorrow my pockets will be marshmallow.

Disappointingly, my £25 ticket doesn't buy me a Crystal Palace player (I'd want change if I splurged on Valerien Ismael), but it does grant admittance to the sparsely populated Glaziers Bar underneath the Main Stand. Here the beer is cold, the punters talk of knowing the team, but not well enough to secure entrance to the players' bar. I lean against a post and look quizzically at my watch regularly in passable impersonation of waiting for a friend. Like an idiot

I eschew Glaziers' handsome fast food in favour of the slop offered to those in the cheap seats. I forget the pie instantly. My tender digestive tract has a longer memory.

I'm next to an old man. He scowls at me. I scowl back. My view is fine, but the Main Stand is filthy. My seat is covered in rubbish and an oozy substance I'm not qualified to identify. Don't Crystal Palace have apprentices or trainees or whatever they're called? Not if the first team is anything to go by.

Anyway, Palace are in deep trouble, so deep that Tomas Brolin (like Doncaster's Craig Davis) is allegedly playing for nothing and Wimbledon are sliding down the table like they've finally been found out. There is a disastrous attempt at Premier League glitz: the cheerleaders are ignored; the unlovable mascot's plumage isn't right; the crowd are mainly South London petty gangsters and coming out to Dave Clark Five's 'Glad All Over' pushes the bounds of irony too far when Palace fans are outsung by Wimbledon's. 'Let's will them to win,' shrieks the PA man. Let's not, eh? At least they don't turn on their team, unless apathy counts.

Sky's viewing figures must have plummeted during the abysmal first half. Now I understand why Palace print the Division One table in the programme. They are shocking – ineptitude thy name is Dean Gordon – and Wimbledon bide their time.

For the second half, Wimbledon winger Michael Hughes wakes up, realises he's quite good and thus provides three goals in ten minutes. Carl Leaburn bundles in the first and nods in the second, seemingly through goalkeeper Kevin Miller. Jason Euell's third, after the post has been hit twice, leads to a 'What a load of rubbish' from the home fans and a 'It's just like watching Brazil' from the dazzled away support. 'Do something, Coppell, you berk,' shouts the man in front of me. Coppell looks haunted. The Wimbledon substitutes, homoerotically tactile, stage mock fights with each other.

'Once again it was not to be,' trills the more-buoyant-than-his-team PA man to a hail of boos. Wimbledon manager Joe Kinnear puts a comforting arm around Coppell. The Glaziers Bar is deserted. I don't bother.

66 **Northampton Town**

v. Wycombe Wanderers
DIVISION TWO
10 February

2-0

'No one in this division has had more difficulties than us.'

Ian Atkins

Five games in five days. As I showered this morning I stared hard at my penis, now shrivelled to the size of a thimble for people with unnaturally small thumbs. This sorry sight confirmed my wary suspicions that I'm going mad. Not in a wacky sense, but deep seated, slowly creeping, penis-reducing madness. I live on pies, tea and extra large Mars bars. I can taste them twenty-four hours a day, I probably smell of them. I'm overdosing on mediocre football, ennui, road blindness and isolation.

I haven't seen my few remaining friends in months. I haven't had a conversation with my wife over the same period. She might have taken a lover; how would I know? What's more I don't care, for my thimble led sex-drive is now nil. She might have moved on, evolved personally. Again, I wouldn't, a) notice and b) care. And at the end of it all, I might not see ninety-two clubs. What then? I don't know. That ubiquitous unpleasant tickling sensation in my gut is kicking harder.

Back in August, in the warm, I saw many things ahead, but I failed to see that I'd be consumed like this. The house could be falling down and I'd merely shrug. More to the point, the house *is* falling down (subsidence, London clay, people making tunnels) and, yes, I merely shrug. Northampton, then ...

Northampton Town are known exclusively for George Best scoring six against them in the FA Cup Fifth Round in February 1970 and for zooming from fourth to first and back again in successive seasons. This last fact isn't quite true, but nobody minds. Town shared the County Ground – as very much the secondary party – with Northamptonshire County Cricket Club until 1994. They moved mid-season to the newly built, council-owned 7653 capacity Sixfields Community Stadium. Few noticed, but extinction was averted. Few noticed either, at first, that as part of the rent arrangement, the council pays the club's electricity and gas bills, policing and pitch maintenance. The council gets twenty free tickets for each game. Naturally Northampton's Conservative opposition pretends to be livid ('no such thing as society', etc.), but town and team are bound together. A bright future beckons.

Sixfields is miles out of town, north towards the MI, my current home. Disconcertingly, I will be able to see the evil thoroughfare from my West Stand seat. It's on an industrial estate (or 'leisure area'), populated by 'diners', Burger King, family pubs (what do families want to go to pubs for? Don't they have living rooms?) and a cinema. I hate it and the person in front of me on the trek to the ground who has BIG TEL sewn into his pullover. I don't need to pay to go in as I can see most of the pitch from a grassy bank adjacent to a theme restaurant.

The Exchange Bar Diner opposite the ground isn't a family pub, it's a family restaurant with a bar area. Needs must. I don't last long and skulk back across the car park. The sponsored car is the ultimate status symbol of lower league players. So, even if it's an M-reg Peugeot, Northampton Town goalkeeper Andy Woodman (Gareth Southgate's best man) will willingly have his name plastered over its doors. Cheers Andy, may your parents be proud of you and may you never go kerb crawling.

Cleverly, Northampton Town, who scraped up via the Division Three playoffs despite having four directors christened Barry, have manoeuvred themselves into seventh. The reasons are clear, for in only one league game this season have they conceded more than two goals. The programme's three pictures of a recent game against Oldham all show Town players fouling badly.

Wycombe Wanderers, who've arrived in a bizarre Motts Of Stoke Mandeville double-decker – two tiers being sensible for Plymouth who need supplies of Kendal Mint Cake and a squad of thirty for away games, but it must crush team spirit on a quick M40, M25, MI jaunt, especially for upper deck passengers who have no tables – might get caught in the relegation mêlée if they're not careful.

It's a non-league ground, which could feasibly be hosting Everton or Tottenham Hotspur next season. It's one future of football: a viewing gantry where, while eating a disgusting hot dog (but no chocolate, they don't sell it) I can watch the punters beneath me strolling past Woodman's car. It's a future where traffic gridlock will ensure Sixfields' capacity will never be allowed to reach 8000 without Northamptonshire grinding to a halt. Not a bad thing in itself admittedly, but business would chafe.

Inside I can look down over the reasonably numerous away supporters. I'm in the midst of what passes for Northampton's hardcore, although I strongly suspect paper bags would remain untorn if these people tried to punch their way out of them. Their abuse is delivered solo, mostly against Wycombe's

Northampton-born, ex-Town midfielder Steve Brown, in the local mangled accent, part Birmingham, part Nottingham. They haven't the perception to go for Wycombe manager and former Northampton player John Gregory, who, wearing hooped shirt and beret, appears to have a fetish for dressing as a French onion seller. The advertisement hoarding for some ghastly prep school sums Sixfields up.

The couple in front of me leave after forty minutes. Again. I wish they hadn't, I can't be innocent in all this. I'm getting more Kurtz-like, but without the charisma. Maybe it's the horrendous game. 'We can't and they won't,' muses the man next to me (dirty fingernails, good tattoo, dainty shoes) into the silence. The fans argue among themselves. 'Get it on the floor,' shrieks a woman. 'If you came here often enough, you'd know we don't do that,' sneers Dainty Shoes. And so it goes. Like those schools where pupils can smoke cigarettes, inject themselves with heroin and go to lessons, but only if they fancy it, Wycombe appear uncoached, apart from little Maurice Harkin, who's on a mission to maim.

I stare into the distance, possibly drooling, gazing longingly at Northampton's sole landmark (unless the Carlsberg brewery counts), the gigantic Express Lift Tower. There, they test lifts. Is there anything more exciting than a tower with the sole function of testing lifts? There isn't. How do they do it? Phenomenal speeds, like an overgrown particle accelerator? Do they drop the lifts with a mighty crash, waking the burghers of Northampton in the middle of the night? Can people be lift testers? How do you qualify? When I've finished being a club mascot (not at Northampton, council involvement or not, this club of Barrys doesn't reach out; the camel and Mr Blobby at half-time are a commercial enterprise, not Town's vision), I'll make the move into lift testing.

The atmosphere should be electric, despite the football, for Northampton are well above their station. I cough loudly and it echoes around the stand, but my cough does begin a brief chant, 'Get into 'em, fuck 'em up'. Mercifully, Northampton take the lead. Nippy forward Chris Freestone is bundled over in the penalty area by a brutish defender (Wycombe's shirts are yellow and navy quarters, so their numbers are illegible) and David Seal scores the penalty. Wycombe attack at last and Harkin even forces Woodman to make a save, but when Freestone springs an amateurish offside trap and saunters through to make it 2-0, Harkin returns to savagery with a frightening foul on elderly substitute Kevin Wilson.

There's enough time for a 'You're shit and you always were' chant to Steve Brown and for Woodman to please his car sponsors further with a flying save from Jason Kavanagh's well-struck free kick.

I'm so tired and it's so far into the centre of this long, spread-out town. It's brimming with interesting stuff: Thomas à Becket was tried here in 1164; the marvellous All Saints church is dedicated to Charles I, who gave 1000 'tun' of timber for its construction; Cromwell, it's said, slept in Hazelrigg House the night before Naseby; the Victorian town hall is a wonder and even the war memorial was designed by Lutyens. This means nothing to the philistines of prosperous Northampton (multinationals Coca-Cola and Barclaycard base their British operations here: must be the road network and low rates, not the barely functioning railway), birthplace of Des O'Connor, home of quality cobbling and where the gunpowder plot was planned. The town centre is deserted, apart from a clutch of beggars sleeping in doorways, guaranteed, if nothing else, a decent night's sleep.

I've walked miles to do another Omega Man impersonation, to see pubs without customers other than diehards sprinkled around the bars, and to tread empty streets. I've braved yet more kids on bikes in grim and police-infested Doddridge, the occasional stranger who doesn't make eye contact and a shouting, seventy-year-old drunk who calls me a bastard. That's without going near the Spencer estate or the pleasingly named but unpleasant Lumbertubs. Tomorrow, Wednesday, I shall not see a football match.

67 Cambridge United

v. Lincoln City
DIVISION THREE

13 February

1-1

'The Club must be praised for the various initiatives which have been offered to encourage the number of children and new supporters attending this evening's fixture.'

Roy McFarland

Hailing from Cambridge plays tricks on the mind. Life's lottery will have ensured you're not sufficiently bright or well bred to attend the local university. Yet every year your city is invaded by students who know that, under your nose, they can drink, fuck and drug their way through the best years of your (but not their) life: loudly, as is the way of braying toffs. Then they depart to rule the world. These conditions would have turned Mahatma Gandhi, let alone a fiftieth generation fensman, into both a machete-wielding maniac and an ardent supporter of Cambridge United.

Football isn't on Cambridge's agenda. The poky Abbey Stadium, impenetrable as Urdu, has been cast out of town, far from the gleaming spires of Oxbridge cliché, to a zone where the pubs aren't open (except for The Seven Stars which is populated exclusively by bikers who glower at me when, like the nancy boy I am, I read a newspaper while I drink), dominated by industrial estates and dual carriageways.

Education arrived in Cambridge by mistake. It was already a thriving commercial centre by 1209, when there were town/gown wars in Oxford. A bunch of intellectuals fled to Cambridge and started their own establishment under the patronage of Henry III, who saw the value to his own survival of harnessing brains trusts. Soon, scholars had the legal power to set local traders' prices. The inevitable riots followed, but the university would never lose its influence and today Trinity College is Britain's third largest landowner after crown and church.

Cambridge United are bumbling along in the middle of Division Three harming nobody, but the hot news – seven programme pages, pitchside presentations, the unusual glow of winning – round these parts, is that

United's catering won the same food survey that Leyton Orient did not. Bacon rolls made the difference. I buy two. Essentially, these £1.60 delicacies are slices of fairly fatty bacon shoved into a hot dog roll. Not bad at all, but as ever, no Stockport County. Neither is the team.

It's a misanthropic Abbey, despite the mascot Marvin The Moose (if United were nicknamed The Moose, the world would be a better place, only by a smidgen, but it all counts) and his cheeky pink tongue, the pitch perimeter jugglers and the man on stilts. Doncaster Rovers won at local rivals Peterborough this week. The Tannoy plays a radio recording of Rovers' goal and the crowd overdose on grisly *schadenfreude*, 'The scum are staying down'. The 'Sky TV wank, wank, wank' chants make me smile, being tricky to edit out of tonight's live broadcast, but they'll have been noted. Meanwhile, under beleaguered former Cambridge manager John Beck, Lincoln are still edging towards the play-offs, but their away support is sparse and includes an inept band.

It's a poor game. On a rare excursion forward, Cambridge full back Ben Chenery shapes to cross. His slice weaves and swerves everywhere before landing beyond visiting goalkeeper Barry Richardson. 1-0. 'Becky, what's the score?' howl his former acolytes.

When they're not gloating, the Newmarket Road End indulge in a spot of homophobia, bordering, as it always must, on homoerotic. Apropos of nothing they sing 'Colin Alcide's a homosexual' to Lincoln's winger. For the second half Barry Richardson is in the goal in front of them. As I swooned at Brighton and Lincoln, Barry has lovely swept back hair, part supermodel, part hound, blow-dried for supporters' enjoyment. I'd love to run my fingers through it, were the top section not coated in gel. A Terry Thomas moustache completes Barry's toilet.

The Cambridge fans begin with a cheery 'gyppo' and 'where's your caravan?' and Barry waves and grins like he's a *Play School* presenter. By the time Lincoln have equalised when Alcide heads in Terry Fleming's long throw (even Lincoln's goals are dull) and Barry has delayed a goal kick to cup his ears and thus elicit more abuse, the chant has changed to a more charged 'Ladyboy, ladyboy, ladyboy'. Everyone seems happy with this arrangement.

The game withers, despite Cambridge's giant, black (cue 'Bruno' chant) substitute Trevor Benjamin putting the wind up Lincoln's stern defence and his striking partner Jamie Barnwell (formerly Jamie Barnwell-Edinboro, don't want anyone thinking we're posh, do we?) missing a chance so simple it was Paul Gascoigne's intellectual inferior.

Cambridge has its Buddhist Centre – where they perhaps quietly reflect that Buddhism is more hobby than religion – its Soul Café, its Irish Sandwich Bar and a city centre devoted to bicycles which are used generally, not just by aspirant criminals. It's different in the suburbs close to Cambridge's green belt, where heroin costs £80 a gram, its use is second only to cannabis and also where town meets gown – two groups united only by their apathy towards Cambridge United – but students rule here. In a sense they'd be better staying, for life expectancy in always cold Cambridge is the best in Britain and high-tech industries – Microsoft's first non-American research facility – are flooding in, despite the Luddite campaign, Cambridge Is Full.

Short of time after strolling back into town, I skip over the puddles of vomit outside The Castle into The Prince Regent. Everyone is beautiful, self-assured, ten years my junior and trying to pack a lifetime's worth of decadent memories into however long their degrees take. The girl at the bar next to me, long blonde hair (not as nice as Barry's), the shape of a goddess (Greek not Roman) has been to finishing school where she's been taught how to smoke, drink vodka mules from brown bottles, rub against her blonde rugby-playing boyfriend and swear in a posh voice. Twenty years after the Millennium, she will be Minister Of The Interior and be sanctioning MI5-planted stories in the *Daily Telegraph* about her former left-leaning tutors. I think I love her.

68 **Barnet**

v. Cardiff City
DIVISION THREE
14 February

2-2

'We are all members of the same team.'

John Still

Valentine's Day. Suffice to say, the postman did not find himself troubled with a hernia after delivering my post. Two minutes' saunter from my crumbling house is a Number 34 bus stop. Ten minutes aboard the 34 (not technically a bus, more a coachette), I'm in Barnet, hence a full night's sleep for the first Friday/Saturday since the week before Barnsley v. West Ham. Joy to the world.

Barnet is the end of London. Afterwards lies the green belt, the A1 and, ultimately, Scotland. It's a long way to proper London but Barnet hasn't had its own identity since it became the termination point of the underground's Northern Line. There are five dispersed Barnets – Chipping, High, New, East and Friern – to confuse the unwary. Its (sort of) centre is High Barnet, at the summit of Barnet Hill. It's typical Far North London: depressed High Street despite Barnet's plethora of large houses (not as large as Mike Tyson's mansion in Farmington, Connecticut, recently offered for sale in the *Barnet Advertiser*); multi-ethnicity starring wealthy Greeks and Jews rather than blacks; a village green with pond and some grotty pubs designed to enjoin the drift south to Whetstone, where serious money and the soap stars who have it reside.

Even when it wasn't London, Barnet was never more than a stage coach stop (the Battle Of Barnet in the War Of The Roses was in nearby Hadley Green where David Livingstone lived), until World War 2 when the Maw's factory made artificial skin to aid the recoveries of burns victims. Moreover, those Barnet pubs were gossip magnets as Jews and European political refugees migrated here after fleeing the Nazis. Handily, the Crown & Anchor, next to High Barnet's Baptist church ('fight truth decay!'), looks like it hasn't been decorated since World War 2. Silly old fear of football violence means it's the only pub that has opened. When Cardiff City came to Barnet last April they lost

3-1, endangering their play-offs place. Their fans rearranged High Barnet, but not permanently. The street sweepers seem to have neglected to turn up for work since that day.

If Mike Leigh owned a pub, it would be The Crown & Anchor: ill-lit, smoke-filled, populated by women with no make up (subtext: 'I don't care any more'), single fathers drinking while snapping at their bored senseless children, old people who look as if they'll die at any moment and a young couple who're arguing for the last time. I could stay here all afternoon.

Instead, I walk past the sunbathers (global warming alert: this is mid-February) on the grassy bank next to Barnet Hill and head for Underhill, Barnet's correctly named ground. Barnet and football don't go together, except as a second club for Arsenal or Tottenham fans. They've only been in the league since 1991 and should soon be back in their customary non-league habitat sharpish, as Underhill is more Ryman League than Nationwide League and an unsupportive council, backed by local NIMBYs won't help the club move. Underhill is a charmless dump in a charmless housing estate. The pies are served in wrappers by insolent youths and the tea could strip the Great Wall Of China. I stand on the tiny North West Terrace so I'm not staring into the sun like the rest of the ground. Throughout the match, the North West Terrace will be distracted by two birds trying to have noisy bird sex inside the Tannoy.

Admirably, Barnet's troubles haven't filtered through to the team or the cuddly bee mascot, who dances like a fool, making everyone's day that little bit more special. Despite severe financial limitations, Barnet lie second, unbeaten in 1998. They're sponsored by *Loaded* magazine, a peculiar arrangement for both parties.

Cardiff, still swayed by old nostrums, sacked manager Russell Osman the day before their fourth round FA Cup game a fortnight ago. They're sixth from bottom, give thanks each night for Hull, Brighton and Doncaster and have nothing to play for, not even a new contract-issuing manager unless he's hiding in the crowd. Acting manager and Osman's 'Director Of Football', Kenny Hibbitt, is incapacitated after an implausible-sounding 'fall' at home.

All the more surprising then, that Cardiff are 2-0 up in fifteen minutes. Jason Fowler – two divisions too good for this match – sambas through the defence and sets up ageing skinhead Andy Saville for a tap in. Then, after a short corner routine with Craig Middleton, Fowler himself unleashes a grass cutter through the confused Barnet defence which comes to rest in the far corner of Lee Harrison's goal. It looks like the journey home to South Wales on their managerless, unmarked, M-reg white coach – a few tables but no lamps – will be a party on wheels. The fifty or so fans who've bothered to follow City sing some horrible Welsh songs and '2-0 to the sheepshaggers' into the great wide open. High Barnet will be safe this evening. Phew.

Barnet are as shell-shocked as those burns patients Maw's gave solace to. John Still, dressed in a romper suit for reasons unclear, substitutes floundering full back Michael Harle instantly and his team paw their way back. The man next door to me says 'for goodness sake' a lot and rightly moans when Barnet pull everyone back for Cardiff corners giving no outlet for clearances, so allowing City to push men forward with impunity. On the stroke of half-time, City goalkeeper Jon Hallworth clips Barnet's Eire B forward Sean Devine (born Lewisham) and Paul Wilson scores the penalty.

It's a passionate game, but there's no supporting passion. The people carp at South African Warren Goodhind ('you pillock'), at new signing John Doolan ('lazy Scouse git; 60,000 quid? I wouldn't pay 60,000 pence') and at Cardiff's niggly Chris Beech ('he's got to be a bighead'), despite the East Terrace's funny rendition of 'Twist & Shout' ('oooooooooh') and a swift 'We heard you ran from the Swansea' to the Cardiff few.

Barnet equalise when Scott McGleish twists to head Greg Heald's goalbound header following a corner. McGleish does a few cartwheels and Cardiff must wonder how they let it slip away. The mascot dances once more, alone and unencouraged, except by me.

I slip back into High Barnet. The Crown & Anchor's personnel remains unchanged, although the single fathers with children have been replaced by single mothers and different children. There's a meanness of spirit to Barnet. It's not just the plastic glasses only rule at the Sceptre & Mitre or the gangs of sixteen-year-olds flooding into proper London, or the isolated ignored old drunks singing war songs to themselves, perhaps in relatively new skins. Nobody cares about Barnet, the place or its professional football team, so long as there's nothing untoward in their back gardens and the green belt is never unbuckled.

69 **Oxford United**

v. West Bromwich Albion
DIVISION ONE
17 February

2-1

'I have always had a great fondness for Oxford United.'

Malcolm Shotton

There must be a difference between Oxford and Cambridge. As a sixth former of willing but hardly Hawking-esque intellect, none of my teachers found it necessary to tell me. If I'd needed to know, I would have been ambassador to Chad now (N'djamena is quite warm this time of year), a keen member of MI6 like all ex-Oxfordians and a finer human being.

As I lean on 226-year-old Magdalen Bridge, where a few months ago thirteen students in evening dress were arrested after a ball when they leaped into the Cherwell with its punting station and adjoining deer park. Unnerved by the sinister hum of bicycles – why aren't bicycles taxed? – ridden by the beautiful, I'm jealous of all I found heartening in Cambridge on Friday, especially when they're showing their proud parents around; parents who've always known it would culminate in this. I'm comforted by the prospect of Saudi Arabia's King Fadh funding The Oxford Centre For Islamic Studies close by, designed by the Egyptian architect Abdel Wahed Al-Wakil. It won't be too Olde Englishe.

Tramps sleep in doorways, Blackbird Leys – where children are reared by wolves and know their handbrake turns – is twenty minutes away on a 52 bus. But here, for as far as I can see, is where some of the world's destiny is shaped. And I might as well be in downtown N'djamena or Blackbird Leys for all the difference I can make. I feel like an oik. As with Cambridge, I cannot grasp how locals cope, perpetually humiliated since the Scholastica's Day riots of 1355, in this pub-strewn academic playground, with only distorted car stereos to keep them sane. At least I will miss tonight's wacky student comedian, Dan Geron, 'there's danger in his name'.

Oxford United is a flag of convenience. They were Headington United until

1960. Two years later, the Football League were seduced by the Oxford name and the team were elected to Division Four. This means another long walk, from the spires, towards London, past something in Headington which calls itself Oxford Brookes University (i.e. a polytechnic or worse). It will look good on many a CV, especially in far-off parts where intricacies of the British education system remain as big a mystery as the popularity of scientology and Deepak Chopra. Technically, these students have been to university. In Oxford.

Oxford United are a shambles: constrained by their tiny Manor Ground (not that they fill it as a rule) with its five stands, all virtually derelict. They're losing £70,000 a month, meaning players like Bobby Ford and Nigel Jemson are offloaded for trinkets. Work has halted on a new ground and they don't switch the floodlights on until kickoff. Relegation looms so large that the table showing United a mere three points clear of second bottom Bury (scandalously, Jemson's new home) is omitted from the programme. The Butchers Bake pies are stodgy but edible, but the world's slowest service, as displayed here, would have given Princess Diana (God rest her soul, she was perfect) hunger pangs. The tea might be tasteless, but there's gallons of it.

Tonight has extra thrill potential. Ex-manager Denis Smith, who jumped Oxford's ship around Christmas, makes his first return. He's unpopular round these parts, chiefly for almost begging Manchester City to employ him and for musing that he was surprised to not be considered for the England job, both on national television. The main chant is a robust 'Fuck off, Denis Smith', but there's also a more complex one which suggests he 'sucks lots of penis' and ends memorably 'Denis Smith is a horse's ass'. After a torrid time under caretaker Malcolm Crosby, Oxford have wheeled in former centre half Malcolm Shotton, presumably because he'll do the job on the cheap. Two loanees, Barnsley's Steve Davis and Sheffield Wednesday's O'Neill Donaldson, plus exchange signing, lanky Kevin Francis, make their débuts on a wonderfully preserved pitch.

The cramped Manor and West Bromwich Albion's again impressive turnout – they're still sixth – makes for a rip-roaring floodlit atmosphere. It's a fine game too, especially when Oxford's Joey Beauchamp, at home here if nowhere else, takes control. Soon, Oxford centre half Phil Gilchrist is left alone in Albion's penalty area and he heads in easily. Smith stands up and waves his arms around, wishing he'd had a defensive strategy.

The sweary Manor ('Swindon Town is falling down, falling down, falling down, fuck off Swindon'), a haven from students, responds with a 'Sit down yer cunt' and a cheeky 'Smith out'. Shotton meanwhile, leaves his seat only to impersonate a martial arts expert whenever Beauchamp is felled. He does this often.

At half-time a pub singer, helped by embarrassed ex-Chelsea Football In The Community mandarin Peter Rhodes-Brown, sings a dreadful pro-England dirge (sample lyric: 'We're going to win in France/We've got every chance'). The Manor is having none of this drivel and drown him out with 'What a load of rubbish'. Surprising pockets of uncompromising intensity make everything better.

Albion sort themselves out for the second half. They give a game to substitute Franz Carr who misses an open goal with his first touch and equalise when the implausibly ginger Lee Hughes, rampant down the right, crosses for Bob Taylor to head home, as unmarked as Gilchrist was in the first half. The Albion fans sing 'boing boing' and bounce up and down.

Now the crowd get tense. Where once there was a cheery 'You're not very good. SHIT' whenever an Albion player made a mistake, now the swearing is mumbled and individual. There's a kind of impassioned hush and massive relief when referee Taylor misses United's Martin Gray taking an off-the-ball kick at Richard Sneekes, although he also misses Gray being yanked off the ball by Shaun Murphy in the penalty area a few moments later, so justice is done. At the death, the see-saw tips Oxford's way and right in front of me Kevin Francis – a folk hero already – taps a low cross home. 2-1. I'm crushed and during the following week this brave soldier will flaunt the grey patch across his ribs.

As I walk back into town, buoyed by the game, the swearing and the white trash at play, there's a hungry police helicopter whirring in the distance, its searchlight blinding the residents – both peaceful and warlike – of some council estate where students have never trod. This is an unhappy town.

It's a quiet town too this Tuesday. The football fans don't make it back to the centre, the council estate marooned can't afford to leave their hovels and the students are laughing like hyenas with Dan Geron. Oxford turns out to be a Mecca for mobile fast food vans – Hassan's Cuisine, Ahmed's Bar-B-Q Bar – none of which I dare sample. The pubs are empty, even the student-friendly Fuggle & Firkin, but the Queens Coffee House, sweating with students discussing Channel 5 and *Thunderbirds*, is doing brisk late-night business. In a few days, Alice Walker and John Mortimer – not together, alas – will be giving talks to some lucky students. If I thought they were stopping off at Ahmed's Bar-B-Q Bar to sample a kebab, I wouldn't feel so deflated.

There's a word in Afrikaans for what goes on in Oxford, a word which explains Oxford's posh north towards Summertown, originally built for dons and its deprived east (some of the 20,000 former car workers), which explains both John Mortimer and Joey Beauchamp, the tramps and the college balls (£86 a ticket at Wadham) and which explains the loud music in cars and the proud but ungrateful parents. Apartheid it's called.

v. Norwich City
DIVISION ONE

21 February

5-0

'Today is the day that I know many of you supporters have been looking forward to all season.'

George Burley

It begins, like the best football days, at the railway station. There are more police than travellers on the platforms, many with video cameras. Cleverly, the Station Hotel opposite is only admitting supporters who have a ticket for the away section of Portman Road, home of Ipswich Town. This cold and wet Saturday, a tiny, drab, dormitory town is hosting the East Anglia derby and it will come to moderately unpleasant life.

I press on. It's a plastic market town and has been since AD550, always too busy making money from heavy cloth (Russian and Turkish merchants were regular medieval visitors), shipbuilding, beer, cigarettes and underwear, to build upon the community spirit fostered by a noble tradition of non-conformism, killed off by endemic 18th-century civil corruption.

Centuries earlier, Ipswich was founded at the lowest crossing point of the River Orwell by a tribe of Swedes, led by Gippa (a silent 'G' and we're there ...), who, somehow appropriately, was renowned for his yawning. Cardinal Wolsey was born here and Dickens based *Pickwick Papers* here, it's claimed. Since then, nothing, only Ipswich Town and an irrational hatred of beautiful, backward Norwich.

All the pubs are heavily guarded by bouncers. Being solo, I roam freely and use the Aizlewood Method of gaining admission. The Swan is full of shouting, pissed (it's not one o'clock yet) Ipswich fans singing 'He's only a poor little budgie, his face is all tattered and torn; he made me feel sick, so I kicked the cunt in and now he don't sing any more'. A small group comes in chanting 'We've stirred the Norwich up', which sets this fools' gathering arguing. Non-singers – older – explain that it might be better to sup up, stop singing, take to the streets and start actually hunting down this possibly mythical group of stirred Norwich fans. Now.

We all leave The Swan at 2.40, ranks swollen by other groups of Ipswich fans until we are 500 smalltown smallminds. We march down Princes Street endlessly singing – not me by the way – the song of the day: 'There's a circus in the town (in the town), Mike Walker is the clown (is the clown), Delia Smith? Well she's a fucking slag, Norwich City's going down (going down)'. We meet no Norwich fans, although when we pass a sports bar outside the ground, a pixilated figure appears making wanker gestures, before the police – as confused as myself – stop him. 'I'm Colchester United's top boy, basically,' he explains helpfully. He is wearing dungarees.

After being handed a leaflet pleading BE COURTEOUS TO YOUR FELLOW SUPPORTERS PLEASE REMAIN SEATED, I'm in the Pioneer Stand, where the food has surely been prepared by vengeful Norwich fans. The ticket office person had explained my £18 (+ 50p 'admin') view would be obscured. She was right. No matter, I can hear the circus song. Ipswich, for once, feels like a football town.

There's objective interest too. Ipswich are unbeaten in the league since Boxing Day and are hurtling towards the play-offs, while Norwich are heading slowly but resolutely in the other direction and, insanely, City manager Walker has predicted a heavy defeat for his team.

Only a minute has passed when Ipswich's Alex Mathie collects a throw-in outside the penalty area. In one movement he collects the ball and fires it past Andy Marshall. 1-0. The ground erupts to point at the disconsolate clutch of Norwich fans in the corner of the Cobbold Stand (named after the former chairman and brewer who wouldn't let the club turn professional until 1936) to drunkenly bawl 'Fuck off if you're 1-0 down'. The second comes soon enough. Mick Stockwell's through ball catches out the naïve Norwich offside trap and Mathie strides through. 2-0.

The crowd turn their attention to City's Robert Fleck, who's having a nightmare and has already skied a simple chance. 'You fat bastard,' they goad. When City scramble a corner, Fleck picks the ball up in front of the North Stand and stands there, looking for a fight. 2-0 or no 2-0, the Ipswich fans are easily riled and move as if to kill him. He swiftly exits, chuckling maniacally. Shortly afterwards, in that North Stand, a steward has what seems to be a heart attack. As play continues, paramedics try to revive him, after twenty minutes he's taken away on a stretcher. I don't know what happened to him.

By half-time, Mathie has completed a hat trick. Gus Uhlenbeek (car registration number: an attention-seeking GUS 7) feeds Stockwell who crosses. City's Craig Fleming falls over and Mathie taps in, through Marshall. 'Who's the shit of Anglia? It's Narrrrrich. Narrrrrrich is their name,' croon the Ipswich fans, ungrammatically. I know that this afternoon I will not see Jason Cundy score an own goal for the third time. Ipswich are sensational, Norwich are riddled with defensive peculiarities.

The rout climaxes in the second half, despite Mathie's non-reappearance. Bobby Petta, the Ipswich winger, so awful at Bradford in August that he was substituted before half-time and dropped for six games, scores twice. Once after a wonderful solo run which bamboozled poor Fleming and Daryl Sutch, plus another when Matt Holland confuses City's Danny Mills and sets up Petta for a weak shot which Arthur Marshall, let alone Andy, should have saved. 5-0. Hysteria.

'Can we play you every week?' taunt the Ipswich fans as they conga around the North Stand and 'On the dole, on the dole' as the fool Fleck is substituted.

At the final whistle the Ipswich players celebrate with every section of their crowd. The humiliated, dispirited Norwich players clap their humiliated, dispirited fans, who've been prevented from escaping by the police, and sink to the turf, heads in hands. None of them will chance going out in Norwich tonight.

Outside, the police seem to have been replaced by press-ganged innocents plucked off the street at random. In theory, it's a simple task to escort the Norwich fans a few hundred yards from ground to station, where a Football Special departs at 17.13, in fifteen minutes' time. We are, lest we forget, in Ipswich, not, say, Drumcree.

A few Ipswich fans – replica shirts manufactured by Punch and it says this on their throats – have gathered to taunt their seething visitors. The fighting starts on Portman Road itself where Norwich fans try to push a mobile burger stand (they'd probably purchased one before the game) onto their Ipswich taunters, led by a fat, ruddy cheeked buffoon. They only succeed in making a scared little boy cry. The hopeless police panic and leave the fighters to it, regrouping on the bridge betwixt town and station, over which a lone woman driver is trying to guide her car as fans assault each other around her nice new motor. 'I shouldn't have come this way,' she wails to a disinterested constable.

Like a twat out of hell, a man in glasses (there's a certain type of spectacle wearer prone to excessive violence), early twenties, no club colours, shouts 'Fuck you!' at a policeman who is so shocked he actually says 'Pardon?'. Speccy does it again and four police lunge towards him. He runs away only to turn and sprint into a steel fence. Over he goes and the Keystone Cops arrest him roughly, oblivious to the mini-mayhem around them.

Colchester United's 'top boy, basically' is there, as are some drunk Norwich fans singing 'City 'til I die', sat on a bench outside the station looking for more fights. The Special leaves on time, it doesn't have a buffet and Ipswich returns to normal.

I return to Portman Road, to watch the Norwich players board their coach, a lampless P-reg Ambassador from Great Yarmouth. It's a handsome vehicle with special Norwich City livery, already enhanced by 'WE BEAT THE SCUM 5-0' graffiti, fingered in the dust on its flanks.

The City players are greeted by a couple of autograph hunters, some family, a girl who wants a photograph with gorgeous Darren Eadie and four Ipswich fans who've come to shout. The black players Adrian Forbes and Darren Kenton bond. All the players use mobile telephones, in exact inverse proportion to the number who are reading books. Walker keeps everyone waiting for over an hour, Fleck for slightly less. The coach leaves with a swoosh of the automatic doors, drunkenly jeered as it turns towards home.

I descend further into Ipswich. It's quiet now, like this afternoon never happened. I take vicarious pleasure in these lonely streets, where McDonald's is the busiest place and courting couples wait for each other. I visit the Cock & Pye, where beer is ninety-nine pence and the drum'n'bass is loud. It's to here that the Ipswich fans have retired, in order to consume yet more beer. People clutch each other in celebration of the great battle that has been won. Then, the music stops and that song starts again: 'There's a circus in the town (in the town) ...' and so it will ever be.

71 York City

v. Bristol City
DIVISION TWO
24 February
0-1

'Players in Division Two need time to adjust to team mates and formations.'

Alan Little

If nothing else, York has a great set of walls. At the narrowest point of a corridor between Wolds and Pennines, it's been strategically important since the Romans made it their northern capital – Emperor Constantius Chlorus died here it's claimed – and used it as a staging post for nearby Tadcaster quarry. Edward I had those well-preserved walls built and for three months in 1644 they withstood a siege by parliamentarians, giving the inhabitants time to build York's oldest pub, the suspiciously named Ye Olde Starre Inne.

Today, it's a romantic city, hence disgraced ex-MP Piers Merchant taking his lovely mistress Anna Cox on a city shopping trip during their affair. She managed to find an in-no-way-tacky, crotchless, fake leopard-skin body suit. The walls may have ears, but they protect the city centre and its overpriced, twee Peter Rabbit & Friends Shop (opposite The Teddy Bear Shop) from the ravages of cars, from York people – employed once more in heavy industry, for an American company is building 2500 rail freight wagons here, two years after the old carriageworks factory closed – from the council estates littering York's outskirts and from the football team. Only the beggars get through, but then they always did, probably from caravan sites like the one where Christopher Smith, aged seven, recently died in the cab of a pick-up truck, while glue sniffing.

York is history. The railway; the coach stop (four days to London in 1706, 'if God permits'); Dick Turpin, who was hanged at Tyburn, outside the walls on Pontefract Road; even Guy Fawkes who plotted here (what a well-travelled plotter he was). York has always disowned its underbelly, so when sociologist Joseph Rowntree (of the Quaker chocolate family; major employers here since 1767) surveyed his city, he found conditions as desperate as London's East End, although it had avoided the industrial revolution. Now it's a place where employees of the local Job Centre gave themselves jobs as extras in an Asda television commercial.

Most of all there is the fire-prone Minster, the Anglo-Saxon centre for evangelism properly known as The Cathedral & Metropolitan Church Of St Peter In York. The passion still burns and a few months ago, three evangelicals were arrested for 'aggressive preaching' when they blocked a city centre road and withstood a medieval-type mob pelting them with eggs. Even covered in scaffolding, the Minster is as Gothic as Bela Lugosi tending a graveyard, more so this Tuesday evening, when it's as if tourism never happened. A tourist was shot yesterday lunch-time by a city centre sniper, so perhaps they've fled *en masse*. York is empty.

As they attract no tourists, York City are eschewed by York (Yorkshire pronunciation of the Viking Jorvik) city. Logically, the club should be a rallying cause for the York that tourists and students recoil from, but it hasn't worked out that way. Their ground, Bootham Crescent, lies off Bootham, the road which eventually took the Romans to Hadrian's Wall. It's a genteel area, spoiled only by Territorial Army barracks, where grown men may play at soldiers and not be hauled before local magistrates. As ever, York City are pottering along in mid-table, safe from promotion and relegation. Bristol City, meanwhile, managed by former York boss John Ward, have brought minimal support but lie second, ten points ahead of third place Northampton Town, seemingly assured of automatic promotion, although trembling slightly of late.

I'm in the Shipton Street End, next to a well-to-do but ignorant ('People like George Graham don't drive, they get others to do that for them'), Barbour-clad quartet and an extra from *Taxi Driver*, who has a deep voice and uses it to terrify me with his 'ooohhhhhhhh' drone. The pie-vending cubby-hole opens just before kickoff, but the food is fair and the service delightful. The ground is dead, apart from York City's contribution to football culture: a chant of 'Bastard, bastard' in perfect stereo. The York mascot first appears when he runs out with the team and then disappears. I wouldn't behave like that if his job was mine.

The first half of this Channel 4 sponsored (what an odd use of funds) game is unspeakable, but it's an absorbing second period with York looking ominous. Graeme Murty, the gutsy, skilful left back rattles Bristol whenever he surges forward. The turning point comes when York's Gary Bull heads over when he appears to be actually under the bar. The crowd do not let him forget. Bristol, outclassed, sense this may be their night. Scott Murray charges through the home defence, goalkeeper Mark Samways brings him down and Mickey Bell blasts in the penalty.

There's time for an equaliser, but it's a bad night to conclude a bad day for the Little family, as Alan's big brother Brian left Aston Villa this afternoon.

Bristol's Shaun Taylor heads off the line from Murty's vicious corner, but worse comes when substitute Jonathan Greening tears into the penalty area and already booked centre half Louis Carey uses both hands to block the cross. Referee Coddington gives a corner. Greening is unstoppable. He charges into the penalty area again and is mauled by two defenders. No penalty again. Psycho next to me roars so loudly the crowd, for once, stops chattering and the players turn round. I hope everyone thinks I'm his friend. His best friend.

Without tourists, York's spine has been sucked out. My footsteps are the only sounds on streets differently cobbled to those in Macclesfield. I wander out of the city, along silent Walmgate where twenty police launched a fruitless dawn drugs raid less than twenty hours ago. Past the city walls, I settle on The Exhibition, where tourists do not care to venture. It's empty, apart from a darts match that was started at the beginning of time. Too tired to think, I leave my body and float off, above the darts players, to hover under the nicotine-stained ceiling. A man with no neck scores a treble 20, a single 20 and double 6: 92. I know I can do this thing now. This is where joy begins: I could be anywhere in Britain, I'm more anonymous than a Shadow Cabinet member and my happiness is complete.

72 **Rotherham United**

v. Leyton Orient
DIVISION THREE
28 February

2-1

**'There is no real leadership on the pitch, someone to organise
without myself having to scream at them all the time.'**

Ronnie Moore

Everyone has a home town, I guess mine is Rotherham, but I always felt like a Sheffielder. I can't view it objectively, although it's been transformed from what I might laughably (but no less genuinely, mind) think of as My Day. I don't visit other than to see my father, but every day I think of those I once knew. I wouldn't want to meet any of them and embrace mutual disappointment: a typed list of everyone's occupations, marital status and an indication of general happiness would suffice. I can remember all their names, sometimes I dream about them. We never said we'd be friends forever, any of us. I wish we had now.

My father doesn't feel like going to the match. It's so cold that the afternoon will be pock-marked with snow flurries, but he's over seventy and cutting corners in his life now. If I sire a son, the cycle will repeat itself, but I'd love to be a good enough father for him to care as much as I do now when he can't make it to a match for the first time in both our lives. In a gesture of fatherhood, he insists I take a packet of pineapple-flavoured Dried Fruit Snax. I eat every last one.

In the mid-70s, Rotherham was a bus town. The newly formed South Yorkshire County Council decreed that the entire bus network would be subsidised, meaning less traffic, working class mobility and hundreds of buses chugging along, packed to the gunwales. Rotherham had two cinemas and a mesmeric bookshop, Harpers. Years later there would be clubs, kissing anyone who'd have me until my lower jaw ached, under age drinking and the post-last-bus sway home, but the Rotherham I compare today's version with, the town I compare everywhere I go with, is Rotherham circa 1974.

Now, both cinemas are closed, Harpers is still a handsome looking bookshop with a new name but Rotherham doesn't use double-decker buses, instead favouring glorified taxis owned, profited from and run by private companies, rather than the community.

Some things never change. Firstly, there was nothing here, there is nothing here and there will be nothing here, but it's a friendly town where middle-aged women's handbags are decorated with Barry Manilow keyrings and courtly old folk greet strangers as a matter of course. Secondly, Rotherham is as much of a drinkers' town as it was when there were mines. So, despite being redecorated to reflect England's homogenisation in time for the silly Millennium, pubs like The Angel, even on this nondescript Saturday afternoon, are full of sad-eyed men from the generation after my father.

Rotherham, home of Paul Shane and Peter Elliott, was never going to make much of itself. The Romans tarried for a while; iron smelting came and went; in 1483 someone built a chapel-on-the-bridge, which is almost (a very Rotherham word) unique; the Puritans were ascendant during the Civil War; my forebears were digging coal out of the slag heaps to prevent starvation during the miners' strikes of 1921 and 1926; Northern Soul came and lingered; Thatcher destroyed the mining industry and that's all.

Today, there is a restaurant in the town centre, the bus station's WELCOME sign is repeated in eight languages and, in the face of competition from Meadowhall, sinister shopping city on the way to Sheffield, Rotherham has gently redeveloped, trying not to follow Doncaster, Chesterfield and Mexborough into remorseful gloom. The forces of darkness haven't been totally vanquished, but they are on the run, for now.

Appropriately, Rotherham United are owned by Ken Booth, the elderly scrap metal dealer whose yard is at the bottom of the Railway End, in full Big Brothery view of the home fans standing on the Tivoli (after a long-lost cinema) End. It's handy when they get uppity and forget who bankrolls who. I spurn the non-animal mascot Dusty The Miller Man, who is sponsored by a private healthcare firm and resembles a riverboat pilot from a Wilkie Collins novel. No doubt he'll be attending the 'Gentleman's Evening' featuring Bernard Manning in April organised by the club's commercial department. Instead, I munch my pie – fine but not warm enough – sip my disgusting tea and convince myself I'll see a familiar face. I don't and I know I've lost something somewhere along the way.

In front of a few hundred Leyton Orient supporters and their wretched band are the comforting advertising hoardings of Aizlewoods Building Materials. I don't know them, but they turned me down for a summer job once. Someone has started a dirty protest in the toilets.

Today, United are in their natural position, just beneath the Division Three play-off places. Orient are level on points and have a game in hand. 'Everything to play for' is the phrase, but it doesn't feel like that.

Rotherham fans – so white that anti-racist leaflets are needed today, after recent abuse directed at Exeter City's Noel Blake – adore manager Ronnie Moore (there's a Saddam Hussein-esque mural of him outside the crumbling Millmoor ground: he appears deranged), but dislike their team, notably winger Andy Roscoe who is jeered to the echo. Rotherham goalkeeper Bobby Mimms has already saved expertly from Alex Inglethorpe and brilliantly tipped over from Dean Smith when, shortly before half-time, Matthew Joseph's cross is headed back by Dominic Naylor. Mimms palms weakly and Carl Griffiths heads into the open goal.

And that's the way it stays for another fifty minutes. Stupid Orient sit back and Rotherham plug away gracelessly against the snidest of backdrops. Then, as if life were written by Hans Christian Andersen (it is, occasionally), from twenty yards Roscoe chests the balls down and thumps it past a slow-to-react Billy Turley. Rotherham fans do not look sheepish when they cheer as Roscoe's name is read out over the Tannoy, nor when they sneer 'You're not singing any more' to the Orient end.

Amazingly, with the clock showing 4.50, Rotherham score the winner. Turley flaps when big centre half Alan Knill challenges him for a cross and Mark Monington scuffs it home, the ball crawling over the line, chased by disbelieving yellow-shirted defenders. The final whistle follows immediately, Rotherham fans stand around, shaking their heads and laughing, particularly at those who left early vowing never to return.

Afterwards, the contrast in emotions between both uncomprehending sets of supporters leads to mini-scuffles outside, but I head off to the Yates's, delighted and unnaturally proud that such civilisation has come to a town even McDonald's ignored for much of the 80s. I'm the only person there, but the beer tastes of nectar. I'm still mentally lost though and, watched only by EC-funded closed-circuit cameras, I stumble from pub to pub, half-hoping to see someone I went to school with, but only finding a man sound asleep and snoring in The Horse & Hounds. Where are they all? Jilted? Prematurely aged? Without hope? In America? Parents? Child molesters? Red faced? Ashed faced? Content? I give up, walk across Clifton Park in the pitch black to prove to myself that I dare and return to my father with fish'n'chips. At last, I understand what the cliché Home Is Where The Heart Is really means, but I'd still like to show Rotherham to a child of my own.

My father has decided, much to my delight, that we are to patronise a Working Men's Club. This is where the spirit of Rotherham lies. The glass and cannon making, the mines and steelworks are no more, but this informal network of subsidised beer and free entertainment for the former working class goes on. It's not all Yates's and 'fun' pubs yet in our brave new Millennium.

The East Dene Club is packed with couples who've made the effort to observe the ritual: she sups halves or soft drinks (twenty years ago it would have been Hague's – as in William – local lemonade) and looks her best; he gulps pints and pats her on the wrist as a display of affection. Everyone knows everyone else. My father is greeted like Martin Frobisher returning from Baffin Island; I, 'young John', am gravely nodded to. Men talk to men, women talk to women. Smoking is compulsory. Swearing is frowned upon and fighting is something that happens on other planets far away from here.

The beer is sensational, the acts – who each perform two sets of forty minutes – less so. Mandi G is plumpish but fairly attractive, from Chesterfield, under twenty, as alone as I was in York and her backing tape keeps letting her down. To sustained indifference she sings 'It's Raining Men' and 'Don't Cry For Me Argentina'. Then she goes back to Chesterfield. What a way to spend a Saturday evening. A summer season in Filey may be slipping from her grasp.

Domain are a different proposition. Their singer's costumes – tiny glitter bikini, thigh-length white leather boots, micro mini-skirt – raise a few disapproving eyebrows. That's not quite the done thing here, overt sexiness, but I'd follow her to the ends of the earth, or Stoke where she lives (tomorrow's trip encouragingly). She's backed by bozos with 70s haircuts, albeit competent bozos. By the end of their second set, men and women who've lived for longer than fifty years are frugging along to fairly current dance hits like 'Sunshine After The Rain'. I catch my father's eye and we smile at each other. For a moment, I belong here.

73 **Port Vale**

v. Stoke City
DIVISION ONE

1 March

0-0

'The situation we are in may not be resolved until the last day of the season, so all guns must be kept blazing!'

John Rudge

Burslem is little more than a hamlet, a dirty industrial village of shabby pubs, third world public transport, buffeted terraced houses (one of which housed a young Lemmy of Motorhead fame), downmarket shops and an imposing, out of character, town hall. If Burslem were a dog, it would have been put down in 1919. Since 1950, when they moved from happening Hanley up the road, Port Vale have played in this hideous place, once the largest of the six towns which comprise the city of Stoke-On-Trent, but now a backwater, even in this backwater.

This Sunday morning is special and not because it's the revolting countryside march (and where do they choose to have this march? The biggest city in the country. They don't understand how we like to live our lives etc. etc.). Burslem is crawling with policemen, the pubs are closed and Stoke City are in town. Stokies simply hang around, wearing Burberry jackets, the new hard lad uniform, discretely hunting Vale fans. There don't seem to be any. I'm looking for the singer from Domain. She's isn't here.

These are trying times in the Potteries. Port Vale are bottom of Division One. Stoke are a place and a point ahead. In the mid-table comfort zone lie the other local team, all-conquering Crewe Alexandra. Desperation and despair are all around. Once capable of holding 50,000 (pointless for Port Vale naturally), Vale Park was modelled on Wembley Stadium. This much is still true today in that the slippery seats are cramped and a long way from the pitch and the food is beyond redemption. For the first time this season, my pie is so revolting I cannot finish it. The tea has been flavoured with lard.

Apathy is a close cousin of desperation and despair. Stoke City are a big club, if only in comparison to Port Vale. This means they travel in a luxurious P-reg

Leons Of Stafford coach (John Rudge has an R-reg company car), they sell all their tickets and have a presence outside the ground during the match. They even cause a little trouble when they infiltrate Vale's paddock. Port Vale's end, meanwhile, is a little over half full. What is wrong with these people?

Port Vale have a doggie mascot. Stoke fans have a huge banner which almost covers their Hamil End. Trying to beef up the atmosphere, Stoke players run up to that end and applaud the fans (as they did at the Britannia), but there's no 'Delilah', merely tension and endless run throughs of Elvis Presley's 'The Wonder Of You' to accompany the players' entrance. I'm sat between an oldish man whose nervous tic is to keep pulling his jacket collar over his ears and a young girl shaking with excitement.

Within fifteen minutes, she has stopped shaking and the crowd is stunned into silence. It's an appalling match between two awful teams, devoid of skill, thought and passes. It's like watching two elephants taking forty-five minutes to die. Twice, with a fifteen-minute break in between.

There isn't an incident of note, apart from a twenty-man punch up which referee Rejer lets go. Stoke's on-loan goalkeeper Neville Southall (uniquely, I suppose, I've seen him play for three clubs this season, they might all be relegated) must have had busier afternoons catnapping. Tic Man turns out to be a Stoke fan. 'We're down,' he whispers as City players and fans applaud each other, more in ritual and relief at not having lost, than jubilation.

Afterwards, police swamp Burslem, clocking up overtime, and ensuring barely a punch is thrown. Good work. Therefore, although Stoke monsters are again on the prowl, there's nothing for them to do apart from look threatening, avoid Staffordshire Constabulary Alsatians and amble home. I charm the bouncers at the Duke William, which had given out regulars' cards for today, into letting me inside. Inside, I see some Port Vale fans at last. They are falling-over drunk. One spots me reading the programme and staggers over. 'At least the scum didn't beat us,' he slurs. I smile, nod and look for an escape route.

74 **West Ham United**

v. Arsenal
PREMIER LEAGUE
2 March

0-0

'I'm aiming to finish in the top six and qualify for Europe.'

Harry Redknapp

These are funny times and perhaps I'm behind them to think like this, but this evening an Arsenal fan can walk along ugly, bruised Green Street from Upton Park underground to Upton Park ground wearing a replica shirt and be in absolutely no danger. It wasn't always thus. It is of course A Good Thing and a sign of better times that people – Arsenal fans even – can walk the streets unmolested, but I'd like more edge. Once, visiting Upton Park was a fearful experience, the footballing equivalent of Mossad spies operating out of Damascus pretending to be Arabs: assuming native characteristics, drawing no attention, betraying no loyalties and living in perpetual fear of discovery. Now, Upton Park is just another Premiership ground and Mossad bungles its killings in Switzerland of all places.

I take refuge in the Queens pub along the way, where at least beer is served in plastic glasses and there's a notice on the wall politely asking customers not to sell stolen goods on the premises. It's packed with West Hammers (plus, surely, plain clothes Arsenal fans) and black men playing dominoes in the corner as they've been doing all afternoon. Where once the police would abandon the area to West Ham mobs, now they're everywhere on overtime, gossiping about passing out parades at Hendon.

Inside, the former seething cauldron of East End frenzy (Oswald Mosley acolytes, rather than the multicultural East End: by the late-70s West Ham were British National Party, Chelsea preferred the National Front and the goon twain never did meet) is now home to the Hammers Dog, 'a delicious jumbo Frankfurter freshly cooked and served with a selection of relish and pickles' and delicious it is too. The PA was better at Rotherham and I'm more lissom than the pre-match dancers. If Upton Park were a market stall – and it nearly is – it would vend old men's underpants, £1.99 per pack of three.

I'm in the West Stand lower tier, out of the teeming rain, close to the Arsenal fans. The timid mascot, with a hammer-shaped head, won't go on the pitch. I'm surrounded by a disparate, insular bunch, united only in their love of gaudy jewellery: upmarket couples; fathers and sons, like the pair next to me and older, balder, harder men who will threaten the people behind them after being asked to sit down. With a new type of team to match their new breed of supporter – flatulent *en masse* judging by the vile odour – West Ham are unbeatable at home. Arsenal might be second in the league with games in hand and these teams might meet again in six days in the FA Cup sixth round, but the atmosphere is deathly. I want to be more tense, not part of a sanitised zone.

Here, more than anywhere I've been, the transition to seats hasn't worked. The Hammers are not happy: a bond scheme was a fiasco which alienated core support forever; they lost £5.5 million last year; they charged full price for an FA Cup match with Emley and in November Eyal Berkovic slapped team mate John Moncur in the face during a match with Chelsea and told the tabloids 'he is one of the most jealous people that I have ever met in my life'.

It's a cagey match. Arsenal, subdued without Dennis Bergkamp and Ian Wright, are content to slog it out for a point. West Ham – like Doncaster Rovers, unable to secure a shirt sponsor, possibly the most extraordinary fact of this entire season – with John Hartson again freezing against his old club, have only Berkovic providing guile, but after his early drive is well saved by Alex Manninger, he disappears. Martin Keown hurts his head, has it bandaged and carries on. Even that doesn't seem heroic tonight. More out of ritual than intent, the home fans chance a few choruses of 'I'm Forever Blowing Bubbles' and a few affectionate 'Abooooooooou's to substitute Samassi Abou. Nobody seems interested, although there's a mass exodus to the bar five minutes before half-time.

Near the end, Arsenal substitute Luis Boa Morte has a simple chance. Frenchman Bernard Lama, West Ham's débutant goalkeeper, saves with his feet, hardly bothering to dive properly.

Afterwards, everyone shuffles off into the rain, past the collectors' buckets in aid of the Bobby Moore Fund For Imperial Cancer Research. He wouldn't recognise Upton Park now. I head back to the Queens to avoid the lengthy, saturated but beautifully ordered queue at Upton Park tube. Two stinking 0-0 draws in two days. God help me.

75 **Preston North End**

v. Luton Town
DIVISION TWO

3 March

1-0

'We need to continue picking up as many points as possible to ensure our position in the Second Division.'

David Moyes

Four games in four days again, but, after York, my stomach-tugging has lifted, despite two 0-0s and bloody Luton Town again. Twice now I've set out to see other teams. In January, I ended up at Southend in weather to welcome Armageddon. Today, a few specks of rain in Burnley means their game with Blackpool is off, so I divert to Preston, home of superior quality groundstaff.

No matter, this should be a desperate encounter. After that fateful December day at Grimsby when they played with zero spirit and the fans sang 'We're shit and we're sick of it' with more pathos than football deserves, Preston sacked manager Gary Peters and, presumably unable to pay him off (scandalously a rugby team plays at the ground too, in front of 400), have demoted him to Centre Of Excellence Manager, a move akin to Nikita Khrushchev being sent to run that electricity generating plant in Siberia the day after he was deposed from leading the Soviet Union. Since Grimsby, Preston have won once and are eighth from bottom, but fourth from top of the attendance league. Luton are a point and two places worse off. Brentford, rock bottom, are a mere four points shy of Luton.

Preston's street-lighting is woeful and it's easy to understand why Prestonian Nick Park set *Wallace & Grommit* here. The public buildings are as grand as any Lancashire weaving town and even on this dead Tuesday with rain hurtling down upon the home of the temperance movement, the pubs have bouncers. The men are tall and strong and the women are beautiful, it's not yet seven o'clock and Preston is halfway between Glasgow and London.

Preston North End's Deepdale is at the north end of town – nothing gets past me, oh no – past the Hollywood Bar 'Preston's premier fun pub'. Its windows are whited out and its chief attraction is drag artist Lady Muck. The prison is on the way to Deepdale, too. Tonight, the inmates will be tortured by floodlights shining through the rain. Every day, they are further roasted upon the spit by the County Arms pub across the road, in full view of some cells. Poor prisoners, especially the innocent ones.

Deepdale is opposite Moor Park, at the edge of Preston's Asian ghetto. The football crowd is a healthy mix of Asians and whites, plus a few blacks ensuring Preston's racial demographic is represented accurately. Only joking, ho ho: it's exclusively white.

Preston have played at Deepdale since 1881, before the Football League began, when this area was reasonably wealthy. Only Burnley have played league football at the same place from day one to now, but nobody has waited so long to follow a championship. They haven't won it since 1890 and the ghosts have been rattling ever since. Football runs deep here, perhaps deepest of all. Preston is where the National Football Museum is to be sited and rightly so.

It's an old-style ground, a labyrinth of dark, pot-holed alleyways, but it's going through partial redevelopment. The seats of the new Tom Finney Stand – someone forgot to put a television gantry in – form a mosaic of the great man's face: hearteningly, his plumber's van is in the car park outside. The Fulwood End is under construction but the Pavilion Stand and Paddock, where the drenched few from Luton must stand, look like they haven't been touched since 1946, when Finney scored the first of his 187 league goals. The players' entrance is draped in shrubbery and PNE is etched on the iron gates. Lovely.

I'm on the similarly olde worlde Town End, packed and noisy. I feel young again and celebrate by having a burger. This is a mistake, as it tastes of baby sick and came from one of those trailers right-thinking folk avoid like the appropriately titled plague. Cunningly, the trailer had been smuggled into the ground. I have to try a pie from the proper outlet, which sits in a hard-to-find corner: it's local, it's Ashworth's and it's scrumptious.

Deepdale Duck is the Preston mascot. He has a huge smiley beak, carries an umbrella, wears a boyish sailor's cap, shakes everyone's hands and orchestrates chants like a mascot should. And this team need all the encouragement they can get.

The game is riddled with tension. Having finally offloaded Tony Thorpe, Luton are sharp. As at Wycombe and Southend, they seem too classy to be in such a mess. Dwight Marshall and Mitchell Thomas are causing Preston right back Gary Parkinson all sorts of problems, but at least Preston goalkeeper Teuvo Moilanen looks safe after his Grimsby farrago.

The crowd are tense too, an elegiac 'If you still hate Blackpool ...' raises spirits, although not as much as a heartfelt 'You're just a soft southern bastard' to Luton's David Oldfield when he's felled by a Colin Murdock challenge which would have floored prime-period Mike Tyson. I'm wedged in between a mutterer wearing a child molester's woolly hat and a fifty-year-old with a giant earring, neat beard and comedy glasses. A straw on the shorter side I feel. Soon, poor Parkinson is getting slow-handclapped.

The expectation is still huge here, even the programme is at it, commenting on 'the apparent lack of effort that the players showed' in the last home game, a 0-3 against Carlisle. The management have circulated route maps to Hartlepool among the players, to make the point. At half-time I watch the drenched slave labour kids (players change kits at half-time, these children do not), pulling heavy trolleys of steaming coffee around the pitch perimeter and wonder why these Preston people care so much and why I envy them so.

Preston attack towards us Town Enders in the second half and the passion swells. They're trying to make a hero out of Habib Sissoko who looks like Paulo Wanchope, but plays like Paula Yates. Thing is, he seems to care too.

Luton's teeny tiny goalkeeper Kelvin Davis beats out a shot from Lee Ashcroft and, pushed back, Luton start to play offside, a rule Sissoko seems not to have experienced before. Whenever referee Coddington notices, he's jeered with a 'You're not fit to referee' or 'You don't know what you're doing'. This new sport of referee baiting is exclusively David Mellor's responsibility after his ridiculous mob-inflaming campaign on 606. Generally, they're fine.

Excitingly – and I've yearned to see this so explicitly – ancient links are strong here. When Sissoko gestures for yet more support, he gets it and when captain Sean Gregan does the same thing, I can't hear myself think. The goal comes twenty minutes from time after a frantic spell of Preston pressure. Davis slaps at a cross and full back Ryan Kidd, with presence of mind his dad Brian would have appreciated, lobs into the top corner right in front of me. Everyone goes wild, even I jump about a little. 'You're going down with the Burnley,' swagger the home fans after 'the whites are staying up'. I almost join in when they sing 'Can't Help Falling In Love' and those hairs on the back of my neck make themselves known again. When someone cries 'we can still make the play-offs!' we all choke with laughter.

Then, Luton abandon the offside business and begin to press heavily. The more they swarm forward towards the empty end, the worse it gets. My stomach is trying to punch its way out. Gregan is inspirational, Moilanen saves spectacularly from Phil Gray. Deepdale Duck sneaks into Davis's goal to mop his furry brow and when home substitute John Mullin fails to make it two after a rare breakaway, the whistles for time begin. I stop being objective and join in.

In the last minute Parkinson nearly scores an own goal, there's a mass brawl – somehow Luton's Darren Patterson isn't transported straight to Preston jail for his role – and Luton force five successive corners. When the whistle goes, the roar will have stopped traffic in Blackpool. Substituted Sissoko does his own lap of honour, the rest of the team haul themselves to the Town End, hold each other and applaud the rapturous throng. They've done it and nobody present quite knows how. I feel cleansed. This is what I've been looking for. Town is team, team is town. Today's Preston North End might be a shower, but old links remain unbroken. They can be and that's all I need to know.

The rain still hasn't stopped, but I skip back into town, rejuvenated. Like its team, Preston ('town owned by priests') is full of history, although the Romans ignored it. It was once the richest town in Lancashire until Robert The Bruce's McArmy burned it down. It's claimed Dickens based *Hard Times*'s Coketown on Preston, certainly Richard Arkwright developed his Spinning Jenny beneath the Red Lion and, much later, after Butch Cassidy's father moved to America, the Miller Arcade was backdrop for some of *A Kind Of Loving* and Britain's first Kentucky Fried Chicken. I'll wager few broke the solidarity of 1854's local General Strike after millworkers were locked out, a time when Preston had the country's highest mortality rate. Karl Marx reckoned the revolution would begin here.

I go to the Wall Street pub with its giant video juke-box screen. It's not crammed, but business is brisk and the atmosphere is keen. I slip to The Varsity where there is an advertisement for another drag act. It's less full and too brightly lit, but some of the women have tattoos.

Outside the gents I meet the nicest man in Lancashire. We chat about the game and I bluff my way through by talking about the Grimsby experience. 'That's where Peters lost it,' he reflects. As I make to leave, he shakes my hand. I'd like to shake everyone in Preston's hand. There's no weirdness here, everything seems right. This place has a good heart, tonight I shall sleep soundly and Preston North End are the healthiest football club in football.

76 **Sheffield Wednesday**

v. Manchester United
PREMIER LEAGUE

7 March

2-0

'It must be a nice old feeling to be able to concentrate on Europe knowing that the title is virtually in the bank.'

Ron Atkinson

I'm a Sheffield Wednesday fan. Have been since 21 March 1970 when my father – from a generation which supported all the local teams, depending on who was at home – took five-year-old me to our nearest ground to see Wednesday beat Nottingham Forest 2-1, a rare victory in the season which saw them leave the old Division One for fourteen seasons, my hardcore years. By the time Wednesday sunk to the old Division Three in 1975 we had season tickets. When they returned to the top, I'd moved away. One day I'll move back and get another season ticket, perhaps with my own son – cycles of abuse are supposed to repeat themselves, surely cycles of devotion can do the same – perhaps not. Whatever, Sheffield Wednesday will be the longest running non-familial relationship of my life.

Today, my wife is with me. She too is a Sheffield Wednesday supporter, something I claim untruthfully to have been a condition of our marriage. With the zealousness of a new convert, she refers to the team as 'we', whereas I have never been able to. Regrettably, she does not share my interest in going to rough pubs and staring at tarty women and hard men. Thus, we must eat at the Fraternity House, a 'nice' place (this means no pies later on, but Wednesday's were always light of meat, heavy of pepper and delicious of pastry) where service is slow, beer is smoothflow (for extra hangover value and a nastier pissed), burgers crisp and customers dress like Londoners. I'm horrified to fit in.

Sheffield, Britain's fifth largest city, isn't this sort of place deep down. It's where Karl Marx, to his dying day, thought he'd been underpaid by local newspapers and where, in 1928 when it was ruled by tossing ring (coins thrown into the air, bets taken as to how they'd land) gangs, one Sir Gerard Du

Maurier decided 'Sheffield streets are hideous. Everything that is interesting, entertaining or amusing is shut down and there is nothing for the poor Sheffielder to do but amble about trying to make his own amusement or waiting with a thirsty throat for the pubs to open'.

Things change, but they don't. Sheffield might have The Shires Health & Fitness Club, but it is attached to The Shires pub and Roy 'Chubby' Brown can sell out two nights at the City Hall. 'See Roy's helmet part the curtains,' is his loveable sales pitch.

Hillsborough is three miles north of a city where traffic is so bad that walking is the only option. Having escaped from near bankruptcy caused by the council's decision to host the ridiculed World Student Games in 1991, they ripped up Sheffield's roads to build a Supertram system, a far better idea. It doesn't make money yet, although it's an answer to any city's transport problems. We walk for miles (this is not going down well domestically), along West Bar, scene of 1864's great Sheffield Flood which drowned 300. This area used to be part of the steel, cutlery and toolmaking heartland. Now, it's closed-down shops and a McDonald's 'drive-thru'. After seventy-six games, I miss my first kickoff, by seven minutes. I would forgive her if she didn't blame me in the first place. I've missed Wednesday's Ozzie Owl mascot (poor, although I want the job too much for objectivity) and laughing stock of a pitch announcer – a Bladesman, claim Wednesdayites.

We're towards the back of the North Stand. Dozens of rows further down is where my father and I sat in Wednesday's lowest post-war crowd, a match against Colchester United. The club tried to credit the only goal to unpopular midfielder Phil Henson when everyone knew a Colchester defender had poked it in to his own goal.

Wednesday have always been in denial. The heart of a great team was ripped out when Peter Swan and David Layne weren't replaced after the bribery scandal of 1964. More pertinently, I'm ashamed to the depths of my soul that there's no commemoration of the 1989 disaster which took place at the Leppings Lane end, beneath another stand where my father and I had season tickets. There are two memorials, but they're away from the ground and unsigned. The issue is one of common decency.

Last season, according to their fanzine, *Red All Over The Land*, Liverpool fans were not allowed to lay wreaths at the turnstiles in case it upset the Wednesday stewards. This season, to gasps of disbelief, the Liverpool match was sponsored by the *Sun*, whose coverage of 1989's events was so widely (unfairly maybe, but that's not my point) reviled on Merseyside. Sensitivity was never Wednesday's forte.

This is a peculiar match: Hillsborough looks full; there's a proper atmosphere, despite Wednesday's universally reviled band. On a disgraceful pitch, Wednesday are playing with a spirit and passion that eclipses lethargic United, albeit the reserve team they've put out after allegedly being tired following a game in Monaco several days ago. I too would be knackered if my workload had gone up from one-and-a-half to three hours a week.

Whatever the circumstances, whatever the outside factors, my heart swells whenever I'm inside a packed Hillsborough. It's my home, or at least one of them. I've always wanted to avoid dying during the football season in case Wednesday make it to the FA Cup Final or, a statistically more likely occurrence, they need to avoid relegation on the last day of the season.

I'm sat next to my wife and an old man who smokes a succession of filterless cigarettes. Since Wednesday fans rioted at Oldham in 1980, resulting in a four-match away game ban (obviously I went and sang 'we're not here' with my coal-mining friends after we'd all chipped in to send someone by train to Derby, Grimsby, Bristol Rovers and Swansea to buy advance tickets), it's been an unthreatening kind of club. Today, Manchester United fans are everywhere. Like sulky cats not really wanting confrontation, Wednesday fans tut and mutter about the poor lambs being tired after a journey up from Gloucester, but do nothing. It's a grumpy passion, being a Wednesdayite.

Flying pig Kevin Pressman has already made a wonder save from malevolent pixie Ole Gunnar Solskjaer when, after a short corner, Benito (I always wonder about Italians called Benito; Adolph died out as a German Christian name after 1945 ...) Carbone crosses from the left wing (damn!) and Peter Atherton soars to score with a fine header. For once, the crowd drowns out the band.

Manchester heads drop and workmanlike Wednesday harass them as all teams should. My wife stands up to scream abuse at referee Jones when United's David May miraculously escapes a booking for clattering short-shorted Paolo Di Canio. I shuffle uncomfortably in my seat and make small talk with Smoking Man.

When United's second-half substitute Paul Scholes hits the bar shortly after the restart, the crowd know it's going to be a famous Wednesday victory and probably enough already to stave off relegation for another year. For these – for us – stoics, beating Manchester United is a welcome reminder of South Yorkshire football's pecking order. Anyway, if Wednesday were on Manchester United's level, nobody would have anything to moan about. Being on Leeds United's level would be welcome though ...

To make the day special, Wednesday hit the bar twice in a frantic scramble and in the last minute Carbone crosses, Guy Whittingham heads across goal and Di Canio's overhead kick leaves United's reserve goalkeeper Raimond Van Der Gouw flat-footed. They are hard-working these Italians. My wife and I clasp each other, Smoking Man leaves and some of the silent Manchester United fans must wish they'd elected to follow their local team instead. There's even a chant – an unusual thing at Hillsborough – of 'Who the fuck are Man United?'.

The hike back along Penistone Road into the city is more leisurely. There's no sign of any away supporters – it's hard to get to Hampshire and Kent from Sheffield by train at this time of the day – so it's a quiet but upbeat throng. I used to love this walk, but since Sheffield's partial renovation – seemingly consisting of mini-roundabouts and traffic lights – it's not the same, although some industrial workers' pubs like The Ship, allegedly haunted by ghosts of flood victims, are still hanging on. The old NUM headquarters have been turned into Lloyds pub. These are the places that should be on *The Full Monty* tourist trail, the real Sheffield with its heart broken and liver swollen.

Still, at least Sheffield's rivers are less polluted today. By the Millennium, when £120 million will have been invested in a Heart Of The City renovation with an indoor garden and, surprise surprise, new council offices as its centre-pieces, there'll be salmon dancing in the Sheaf and Don, while the people of Sheffield will be employed taking each other on Steel City heritage tours. Sometimes I get really frightened and I can't quite understand why ...

77 **Bristol City**

v. Bristol Rovers
DIVISION TWO

14 March

2-0

'There are too many decent followers of both Bristol City and Bristol Rovers who would want this event to run smoothly.'

John Ward

As a city, Bristol is bigger than both its football teams put together. It's not a football place, thus there's no outward sign of today's derby in the city centre. Bigger cities like Sheffield would be consumed on derby days, not here though. Perhaps because it's such a mismatch: Bristol City will almost certainly gain automatic promotion, their only long-term way is up and their moneyed sheen adds a veneer of sophistication to what has permanently been a football backwater. Meanwhile, Rovers (The Gas) haven't even got a ground, their set-up wouldn't be blinked at in the Vauxhall Conference, but they still have fleeting hopes of a play-off slot. This afternoon might yet go down in history as the last Bristol derby.

I've been here before of course. Central Bristol, infested with pink buses, looks as beautiful in sober March daylight as it did in drunken December darkness. Magical things happen. David Withers had his pager stolen: yesterday he paged the thief telling him he'd won £500 in a church fete. Justin Clark turned up to collect the prize and was arrested and fined £150 instead.

I stand alongside the monument to John Cabot and his son Sebastian – who sailed from Bristol in 1497 and 'discovered the continent of America,' a shock no doubt to those who had lived there for centuries – and watch nothing going on. There are no police and none of the city centre pubs have bouncers. I watch the climax of Manchester United v. Arsenal in a pub along the canal. Everyone roars with laughter when Peter Schmiechel injures himself in the last minute, the red-faced (is it a medical or social condition?) fool.

It's quiet on the way to Ashton Gate, City's imposing ground in south-west Bristol. I don't understand any of this, for a game which last season culminated in a mini-riot and Rovers players getting punched by City fans, eleven of whom were arrested. I'm there by the time the crowd starts really building. Nobody is wearing Rovers colours and not just because they're those revolting blue and white quarters. Rovers have turned up in an L-reg Wessex of Bristol coach with many tables but no lamps, the sort of coach Bristol schoolchildren might be ferried to municipal swimming pools in, only a little older.

I'm disappointed inside too. I'm so high up in the Dolman Stand I can see the heat haze on the distant Mendips, but amazingly in a ground with a capacity of under 22,000, there are rows of unsold seats, suggesting that City aren't as big a club as they'd like to suggest. The kid I'm next to is wearing a Tottenham shirt and his father has a moustache; the chicken and mushroom pie I didn't ask for in the first place is suspiciously uncooked and any tea City don't sell – there will be gallons of it – could always be stored underneath Colston Hall as an anthrax-style deterrent. Just in case.

Had they not given Rovers only 1700 tickets in a childish tit-for-tat gesture (Rovers have a small ground, ergo City receive a small allocation of tickets there), the house would have been well-and-truly full. Presumably the sawing sound I can hear in the background is City chairman Scott Davidson (once in Bros's backing band and thirty-five today) cutting off his nose, mightily spiting his face in the process.

There are glamorous dancers to be wolf-whistled at (this is the West Country where City's floodlights are powered by a farmhand on a bicycle with a piece of grass stuck between his teeth and it's always 1975), but the robin mascot is lazy and ineffective. Still the teams enter to Republica's 'Ready To Go' and some West Country ditty. City fans finally find a voice when they jeer peevishly as Rovers go into their pre-match huddle, rattling seats so loudly that the Rovers team changes are inaudible. Opposite me, in the corner of the Database Computers Stand (ah, sweet romance) are the Rovers fans. They try their song, 'Goodnight Irene'. This is drowned out by a more rousing 'Fuck off Irene' or 'One team in Bristol, there's only one team in Bristol'. One team there may be, but less than one in fifty City supporters went to York the other week. Bristol has other things than football on its mind.

It's a shapeless, shot-free start. For City, as I know, every match is a war of attrition. Rovers have won fifteen times this season and I cannot comprehend why. They were useless at home to Grimsby and today, with a victory vital to keep in touch with the play-offs, but with talismanic leading scorer Barry Hayles suspended, they are simply inept. They are however unlucky to concede. Scott Murray wriggles free on the right and crosses for City's Shaun Goater and Rovers' David Pritchard to miss it. Referee Lomas gives a penalty, presumably for a gentle push, and deadly Mickey Bell converts.

Luckily for everyone, Rovers fans have to pass next to City fans to reach toilets and food. Under this guise and with a sense of burning injustice, they charge those Citymen in the Main Stand. Intelligently, the police let them fight to the very point Rovers have sweated out their frustration and the City fans, delighted to join in, have stopped gloating and singing 'The Gas are staying down'. Fans' honour sated, the police restore order. Easy.

It's all over bar the police operation shortly after the restart when Murray is fed by Adam Locke for the umpteenth time, works wonders down the right and puts over a teasing low cross which Goater slides in. There's no fighting this time. Dreary but efficient City don't break sweat and nearly score a third when Shaun Taylor's towering header is expertly tipped over by Andy Collett. Scared and humiliated, Rovers fans start to exit long before the finish. The rest of the ground – not me, I've developed a searing headache – stand and wave their arms semaphore-style, singing 'Cheerio, cheerio, cheerio'. The police stop the exodus rather than the goading, in time for everyone to see City substitute Colin Cramb jinx his way through the Rovers rearguard and unleash a sublime chip which Collett performs wonders to push over the bar.

As the final whistle goes, it's announced that Watford haven't beaten Southend United and City are top of the league. The rightly apologetic Rovers players applaud their imprisoned corner of Ashton Gate at length. This dignified gesture is undermined by the rest of the ground, who are singing along to The Wurzels' 'Drink Up Thy Zider', while dancing in a style midway between a leper cured by Christ and an unfunky chicken that the natives of Inbred, Texas would regard as a mite unsophisticated. Surely, I have passed away this warm March day and gone to trailer trash hell by divine error. I'm hallucinating again, too. When I saw over fifty players on the pitch, a mental hamstring snapped on the right side of my brain just behind my ear.

Afterwards, as before the game, Rovers fans melt away. I lose my sense of direction on the way back to the city and fetch up at a pub by Bristol Pool (names fail me, I'm not well), opposite where well-heeled businessmen have flats overlooking the water. I sit outside, legs dangling over the water's edge, ignoring sailor yokels messing about on the water and the City fans in the pub next door chanting 'Going up, going up, going up'. Even this cannot make me happy and I can't finish my only beer of the evening. Right now, all my problems are physical and by the time I reach Bristol Temple Meads, I'm weeping with pain and I can feel all the veins on the side of my head.

v. Sunderland
DIVISION ONE

15 March

1-1

'We all have to work in the realms of reality and cut our cloth accordingly.'

Alan Curbishley

I turn left out of Charlton station and left again, past two mounted policemen, into a courtyard enclosed by smart flats on Troughton Road, backing onto the railway line from Charing Cross, close to the sidings where Joanne Eddison's strangled corpse was discovered in January 1997. As I rest upon my haunches, my headache explodes and although I have not eaten since the Ashton Gate pie, I silently vomit (in the traditional Latin sense). My sick resembles how I've long imagined the contents of a nuclear reactor in meltdown to be. It is lemon coloured, the consistency of runny cream and, to my dizzy, headswimming – I can think of nothing else save ex-Dr Who Patrick Troughton – horror, it is foaming as it trickles towards residents' parking.

As I take wheezy, foul-smelling breaths between spurts of puking, a trainload of Sunderland fans pulls in. It's so full they must queue to exit the station. I am six feet away from them, tears streaming down my face, mixing with the sick dribbling down my chin. We are separated only by a see-through fence. They don't presume I'm a raging alcoholic or ill, oh no. To these 150 Wearsiders bereft of entertainment, I am a weakling. 'Can't take your beer, man,' one of them sneers. I would answer, but my stomach is erupting again, so I settle on retching so violently, my debased humiliation is a mere sideshow. Wearside flees before me: this activity is not, I now know, a spectator sport. There will be no pubs or pies for me this Sunday lunchtime.

When finally, my stomach has emptied itself of bile and lining, the headache returns newly refreshed, accompanied by the dull ache of newly torn muscles. I shuffle towards The Valley like Howard Hughes leaving Las Vegas for the last time. Although it's festooned with parks, the Romans were here and it was mentioned in the *Doomsday Book*, Charlton (from Churl Town, allegedly in the sense of churls being labourers rather than Town Of The Churlish, although I have my doubts) is essentially a housing estate, as soulless as only South London can be: miles of interchangeable terraced houses, punctuated only by fish'n'chip or video hire shops. The Thames Barrier is here too, Charlton's only attraction.

Today, it's taken over by Sunderland fans, beer-bellied, replica shirt (not the dirty-lemon-coloured away one, even The Region That Fashion Forgot spurns that one) and kilt-wearing, chip-scoffing near-Geordies, who bang on the door of The Antigallican pub opposite Troughton Road at opening time, sixty minutes before the Sky-ordained 1 p.m. kickoff. When they're not frying chips, white-socked South Londoners are selling World Cup '98, Agincourt Revisited, T-shirts (the French won't be doing Crecy Revisited ones) and trade is booming. A penny here, a penny there, ducking and diving: it's Liverpool without the pathos and strangeness.

The Valley, which once held 75,000 and now has the most surly turnstile operators in the land, is an all-seated, compact little ground. It's too small for the Premiership, but ideal for a club that normally demands a recount when there's a five-figure attendance. The dressing rooms aren't Portakabins any more and with Michael Grade on the board of Charlton Athletic PLC (not to be confused with the board of Charlton Athletic Football Company), there might be money here. This season is boom time and, as they displayed in that fine game at Maine Road, Athletic have class and steel. They're fourth, one place and seven points behind Sunderland, who're locked in a dogfight with Nottingham Forest and Middlesbrough for the two automatic promotion places.

I'm in the cantilever Jimmy Seed Stand, named after the wily ex-manager and player, against the wishes of the police who preferred East Stand, for reasons which must be clear to them. My view is terrific and I'm almost looking forward to what should be a dingaling game. It's not cold, but I'm shivering. Pre-match entertainment is a pub band – how very South London – singing distorted versions of 'She's Electric' and 'Blockbuster', climaxing with 'Mull Of Kintyre' re-interpreted as Pride Of Floyd Road (The Valley is on Floyd Road) with new lyrics concerning mist rolling in from the Thames. What loyalty Alan Curbishley displays staying here. As soon as they don't make the Premiership, he'd best be off.

Now the bandwagon has started to roll, and in contrast to the game at Sheffield United in August, Sunderland have sold all their tickets; those who didn't make a weekend of it must have left the north east in the middle of the night to get here. To stoke an already tingling atmosphere, the Charlton fans sing a few anti-Palace and anti-Millwall tunes, although nobody in the whole league cares enough to pen an anti-Charlton song.

It's a furious game. Sunderland's Alex Rae, taunted mercilessly for being ex-Millwall, is on a mission to inflict pain and his clattering of Anthony Barness would have made Ron Harris flinch. After Charlton's Clive Mendonca has a goal dubiously disallowed for offside, his team mate Keith Jones appears to kick a prostrate Kevin Phillips in the stomach, unseen by referee Wilkes, and it all promises to turn ugly.

Charlton's fans are more passionate and bitter than I'd thought. They sense that the club's natural status is similar to Port Vale's and that, despite the elected fan on the Football Company's board, there's a faction 'upstairs' that doesn't want promotion, always with the excuse that they're not a big club. They viciously berate centre half Phil Chapple for being slow and clumsy. 'Curbishley's got to go, he hasn't a clue,' says the idiot next to me, who's wearing enough jewellery to suggest he's a secret West Ham fan. He smells of cheap aftershave, the kind worn by feral cats. I'm not well enough for verbal sparring, so I grunt half-agreement. We ignore each other for the remainder of our afternoon together, but he cannot compete with my breath.

Sunderland's Niall Quinn should have scored twice before his team take the lead when little Phillips heads in Darren Holloway's tempting cross. The Sunderland end croons a perfect version of 'Can't Help Falling In Love' and the outcome seems inevitable. Then, Rae follows through on Charlton's Australian-born Yugoslav goalkeeper Sasa Ilic, who collapses as if hit by Croatian snipers. Rae is sent off to the sound of Sunderland fans chorusing 'Cheat, cheat, cheat' at Ilic, who is keeping goal at the other end of the pitch. There's no music for most of half-time, just to calm things down.

As is sometimes the way, Rae's dismissal draws the sting from the game. When the crowd have finished abusing Mark Bright for lack of effort, he pops up to equalise after short-sleeve shirted goalkeeper Lionel Perez couldn't hold Jones's deflected drive. And that's how it stays, but Sunderland are denied a clear penalty when Ilic fouls Alan Johnston. Ilic's frantic waving bamboozles the referee, but the Sunderland bench surround the dozy linesman and travelling Wearside sings that awfully damning 'You don't know what you're doing' to the referee. For the next fifteen minutes, substitute Daniele Dichio will warm up alongside the linesman, attempting to discuss the official's performance. There's fighting in the West Stand opposite me, quelled by heavy handed stewarding and Perez still finds time to save magnificently from Bright and substitute Kevin Lisbie. There's so much going on, not least Peter Reid restraining his livid coach Bobby Saxton, I've even forgotten I'm supposed to be knocking weakly on death's door.

It's two points lost for both teams, but in the streets of drear outside, there are police on overtime, the overpowering smell of chips and the thunder of my body trembling. Back at crammed Charlton station, some home fans travelling south into Kent use an incoming train as cover to lob rocks at northbound Sunderland fans on the opposite platform. A policeman pretends to arrest one of them, but instead – ooh, the paperwork – dumps the smirking youth outside the station. I feel bloated, as though my stomach has been swapped for Luciano Pavarotti's and that there is an air raid siren in my head. By 5 p.m., I shall be in bed, beginning a sleep which will last for fifteen hours.

79 **Wrexham**

v. Millwall
DIVISION TWO

17 March

1-0

'The players are a good and honest set of professionals and will be doing their utmost to get this club into the play-offs.'

Brian Flynn

Oh goody. It is St Patrick's Day. This is taken by the drunken rabble of Wrexham as an excuse to stumble around town: a) shouting and b) wearing a wash-off shamrock tattoo on their right cheek. This is the smallest of small towns, a couple of minutes' walk from end to end. This market town is not thriving and has escaped redecoration since 1974. Ridiculously in a constituency where just 1170 people voted for Plaid Cymru in the last election, signs are in Welsh in addition to English. The terminally pissed are the only ones allowed out at nights, and there is still room for three competing sex shops.

Wrexham (village of Wrekin folk), has always been a weird one: suspicious of strangers; not quite English; not quite Welsh, ignored by everyone from the Romans to the *Luftwaffe*. Indeed, outsiders visited so rarely that Wrexham had its own legal system before Tudor times. An inferiority complex *vis-à-vis* Chester is a result of rarely troubling Britain's history books, save a great fire in 1643; 'Britain's oldest lager brewery' which should date it *circa* 1973 then; an unnatural fascination with cock fighting and bull baiting; a network of squares which would be leased by Yorkshire cloth merchants during the annual March Fair and, in 1931 an unemployment figure of thirty-six per cent. Every day is early closing.

I try to look at the imposing church, but the gates to the graveyard are locked. I'm a sinner before the gates of heaven, but it's not all damnation for eternity, as I'm feeling better, if not quite on a tippermost toppermost high. Tonight Wrexham smells of hops.

In Baghdad, there are a succession of giant arches modelled on the hirsute hands of Saddam Hussein. Wrexham's Lord Street has much the same thing, although only one: a sculpture of two now unemployed miners or steelworkers leaning on an unfinished arc made of piping. It's wholly out of character.

Wrexham's Racecourse Ground is north of the town. It's a dilapidated tip. Outside, the 'R' of the giant WREXHAM FC hoarding that presents the club to the passing world has dropped off. The ground is three sided, the Mold Road Stand long closed and derelict but still standing. If Wrexham are promoted – if they defeat Millwall they're in the play-off positions – this ground could be their downfall. Not tonight though, for mid-table Millwall are accompanied by less than a hundred supporters and Wrexham's attendances haven't risen with the team. When football's balloon goes up, catching Sky and the Premiership with their snouts in the trough, Wrexham will simply plod on, same as they ever were.

Andy Gray (the black one, ex-Crystal Palace and Tottenham) played one game for England, and thus rode in the England team coach just once, officially, to Luton Airport to catch a charter plane for Poznan. As his career has slid to Millwall, he'll have fantasised about that coach. Today, his fantasy, in a roundabout, depressing way, has become real, for Millwall have swapped their standard Blueways for the same firm's garishly liveried P-reg Green Flag Team England charabanc, with windscreen wipers the size of John Prescott's thighs, so huge they obscure, poignantly, the Millwall FC sign. It's a stately vehicle without a coffee machine, but with tables, gold-plated lamps and a full kitchen. It's a tantalising glimpse into the ways of football's upper echelon, the nearest anyone on the coach today will get to playing for England. Brian Flynn, meanwhile, goes one better, for his VW Passat, with the driver's seat pushed forward to accommodate his 5 foot 3 frame, is an R-reg.

Inside, a giant WREXHAM flag cuts off the view from the balcony of the Turf Hotel pub at one corner. The electronic scoreboard is advertising scientology – grim echoes of Gillingham – and I can't believe they had internationals here as recently as 1994. Still, it's only Wales.

I brave a hot dog. It's OK, which, after Bristol, is enough and my iron stomach (as in it feels like there's an iron inside) holds out. The tea is particularly virile. The mascot, Rockin' Robin, is the finest mascot in football. He gets his own Tannoy introduction and comes bounding down the tunnel to throw himself about and shake a tail feather to 'Rockin' Robin' itself. He exhausts himself, so he has to take a breather in the dugout before repeatedly launching himself against the trembling goalposts. He will not be idle during the game either, completing Gray's regret-strewn evening by mimicking him as he takes a throw-in and urging Wrexham on at every turn. The spacious Kop End adores him and he inspires a chant: 'Robin show us yer arse'. He obliges each time, most notably after Millwall's Kim Grant is hauled up for football's offence *du jour*, diving. I'd be an interactive mascot, like Rockin' Robin.

The teams come out to 'Men Of Harlech' (or is it 'Bread Of Heaven'? Or are they the same thing? Some nationalist anthem, anyway) and within five minutes Neil Roberts has cut in from the right, skipped through Millwall's lethargic defence and scored what proves to be the winner. The kop chants to Millwall's on-loan goalkeeper Paul Crossley at the other end: 'You'll never play for Wales', which is factually incorrect or 'Wales's Number 10', which is funny and when Grant handles, 'Same old England, always cheating'. Funny Wrexham haven't signed up for the League Of Wales yet. Still, 'it's just like watching Chile', recent conquerors of England, whenever Wrexham put a decent move together suggests a sense of humour, as does the chant of 'and the rest and the rest', when a suspiciously low attendance is announced.

The England bus hasn't rubbed off on Millwall any more than it did on Andy Gray's forty-five international minutes, but they persevere, like an autistic child attempting to engage a pet budgie in conversation. Wrexham do enough to hang on and a Peter Ward free kick nearly opens the floodgates. When the whistle goes, the cheers are from relief after an oddly thrilling game, rather than triumph: exactly the emotions etched on the players' faces when they and Rockin' Robin, my new hero, come to applaud the Kop End.

Sparsely populated Wrexham, the place that public transport never remembered, is a ghost town this St Patrick's night, watched over by closed-circuit television. Game for a St Patrick's laugh of sorts, I try O'Neill's, the fake Irish pub, and a stomach-lining Guinness. This version of Ireland features Thin Lizzy at full volume and a by-law that every customer must be a grumpy troll.

Odd there's no such thing as a Welsh theme pub, maybe that's because they'd all resemble the harshly lit and poorly decorated Thirsty Scholar, behind the bus station car park, a meeting point where Welsh teenagers can boom car stereos at each other. It's half empty and the empty half is the least sullen. I watch Arsenal dump West Ham out of the FA Cup and as I leave Wrexham, I turn the lights out. I must buy a holiday home here some time.

80 **Brentford**

'We ALL need to pull together as our fate is in our hands. Think doubt and fail.'

Micky Adams

Oh, happy day. I'm properly well now – I've been hanging on a little of late – and I'm not alone. Me and Tony were best man at the other's wedding, but we hardly see each other now. Today, though, he's demanded to accompany me and he's only twenty minutes late. We shake hands like business colleagues.

Brentford, like all West London, is defined by Heathrow and the A4/M4, given tinnitus by aeroplanes and poisoned by the cars. Multinationals, like SmithKline Beecham – but not Samsung who've pulled out since South Korea went belly up – build their headquarters here, but the wealth and jobs don't filter down to the locals.

The Thames forms Brentford's southern border. We walk down Goat Wharf, and, as the tide is out, past a houseboat onto the riverbed across from Kew Gardens, east of where the Grand Union Canal meets the river. Sometimes, London is a peaceful country park, populated by houseboats and couples taking young children for pleasant walks. For some people it is and I'd love to be among them. For a while at least.

Finding special moments in Brentford is otherwise impossible. The High Street, dominated by a giant Somerfield supermarket, cheap Indian restaurants and Goddard's furniture shop ('serving since 1815,' and some of their original stock still appears to be unsold) is a disaster. Nobody has ever backed Brentford, so it's a warm welcome to Brentford Regeneration Partnership's 'action plan for the town centre'. Essentially this involves making the Great West Road more pleasant, getting tourists to the Kew Bridge Steam Museum (I suggest signposts), homes for the well-off, although Anna Ford and Kate Adie already live here (but not together) and a nice new piazza, which there might be room for had not Brentford's soul already been sold to

Somerfield and were not every Brentford day like a winter's Thursday afternoon anywhere else.

Before being swamped by London and apathy, Brentford had a noble history from the time the Britons under Cassivellaunys gave the Romans a sound kicking (the monument we liberate this information from claims Julius Caesar was involved). Later there would be Civil War battles in Syon Park, the painter Turner lived at The White Horse, there was a wholesale fruit and vegetable market long surrendered to Southall and, by chance, Shirley Bassey's victorious court case over a former employee, which the overworked legal system had transferred from Wood Green, took place here.

Now, there's 1920's housing; the Haverfield Estate where pizza delivery men fear to tread and where, on Green Dragon Lane, drug overlord and millionaire Tony Thompson was thrown from a fourteenth floor flat in October 1997. At The Penny Flyer on the other side of the A4 a couple of years ago a burglar killed himself on the job and spent the next fortnight decomposing. The police station still shuts at 6 p.m. Brentford Regeneration Partnership plan to make the moribund dock a toffs' waterfront. I'd give them better odds on turning it into a giraffe sanctuary.

In the midst of this is Brentford FC, always well supported for a success-free team. Uniquely, there is a pub at every corner of their ground Griffin Park, where a notice on the forecourt declares 'Due to complaints from residents, footballs must not be kicked at any time'. We investigate all four pubs. The New Inn is cramped, smells of paint and is full of friendly Northampton fans. The Princess Royal is the sort of place where old people go to die. The Griffin is pleasingly multiracial and the bar staff could hardly be more civil if they'd taken evening classes in politeness. The Royal Oak seems to welcome only locals, but it is run by a man from Northampton.

Tony has two burgers. At first I assume he's bought one for me, but I should know better. All it means is he suffers doubly. My pie is a stunt double for papier mâché. I can't make out what flavour it's supposed to be.

Unreserved seating means we are at the very front of the Braemar Road Stand, in time to see Brentford's kiddie mascot. He is thirty years of age, a business development manager (whatever one of those might be), bespectacled, overweight and lists 'beer' as a hobby. He looks embarrassed, although maybe that's just me, for him. The cheerleaders are pre-pubescent. Creepy ...

It's a crucial game. Brentford lost to Crewe at Wembley in last season's play-offs. This season has been a disaster, inflamed by hatred of ex-manager and current director David Webb, who paid £21,000 for eighty per cent of Brentford Holdings Limited, which in turn owns just over fifty per cent of Brentford Football Club PLC. Webb may sell for around £250,000. The club is losing £13,000 a week, but the ground is worth millions.

For a London club there are few non-white faces in the crowd and 1992's

Community Club Of The Year now has a little fighting force who stand throughout the game in the New Road Stand, next to the Northampton fans at whom they chant 'shit ground, shut up'. Brentford might have won two on the trot, but they're fifth from bottom and will sink three places if everyone wins games in hand. Meanwhile, Northampton Town have brought most of the Nene counties with them and are fourth, in the middle of a horrendous scrap for the play-offs. They've come down in their A-reg Country Lion coach, sponsored by the Commission For The New Towns. It has a coffee machine, no lamps and some sandwiches in foil. Spacious but unimposing.

It's a rotten match. Brentford can't and Northampton won't. We're next to a bespectacled Cockney geezer with a garish ring and plastic shoes, who shouts 'all you got is a bloody great boot' whenever Northampton hoof it away, which in fairness to him, is their entire game. At half-time the managements walk past us. 'All you got is a bloody great boot,' he shrieks at Northampton's nonplussed boss Ian Atkins who stops, mouths a cheery greeting (My money is on 'stupid cunt', Tony plumps for 'fucking cunt') and caries on, chuckling.

The second half is as bad. 'You're fourth and we don't know why,' chant the Brentford mob to the Northampton fans, until lethargy takes over and they watch the jets flying into Heathrow, managing an occasional 'it's only three weeks to Fulham' between jumbos. Two things happen: Northampton should have scored when Carl Hutchings, bored senseless presumably, miskicks to let Chris Freestone through. Freestone's shot is more wayward than Drew Barrymore. In her most wayward period.

Then Brentford introduce substitute Robert Taylor who has scored twice as many goals as any other Brentford player this season. Taylor's dropping speaks only of insanity, an insanity which he, a pit bull in a china shop, has embraced with petrifying gusto. He is booked within thirty seconds for dissent, has a shot (Brentford's first and last) and is rightly sent off within ten minutes for a silly foul. He trots off screaming abuse at the referee, joined by 'bloody great boot' man, who has taken the trouble to learn the official's name and hollers 'You're a bloody great disgrace Wiley' for what seems suspiciously like eternity. Ian Atkins walks the long way round at the final whistle.

81 **Bolton Wanderers**

v. Leicester City
PREMIER LEAGUE

28 March

2-0

> **'If we can get out of trouble – and I admit we still have an awful lot
> to do – we must be looking to emulate clubs like Leicester.'**
>
> Colin Todd

I've been dreading coming to Bolton, but not like Watford or Gillingham,
where I didn't fancy the mundanity. Last time I came here, to the old ground
Burnden Park, was with my friend John Bauldie, Wanderers season ticket
holder. We saw Bolton and Sheffield Wednesday draw 1-1 and had a fine old
time. When John died in the same stupid helicopter crash that killed his chum
Matthew Harding as they flew home from Burnden, I went to the pub, tried
and failed to get drunk, went home and slept for twenty hours. Then, I started
missing him ...

John would have liked Reebok Stadium (not the name, he'd have hated
that). It's no Stadium Of Light, but it is a symbol that Bolton Wanderers are
progressing long term. It's also a future of football, as relentless as cancer:
Bolton Wanderers' ground isn't in Bolton, it's in Horwich, a suburb so distinct
that it has its own twin town (Crowborough in East Sussex admittedly) and is
the site of genuine wealth, once alien to all football ground surroundings.
There are mansions here, set well back from the road, that wouldn't be out of
place in Beverly Hills, plus golf clubs and a Nursery For The Performing Arts.

Reebok (there's no way of getting round using that name) is visible from
and next door to the M61. It has more car parks than an American football
stadium. The message is clear: if you don't have a car, you are not welcome. At
one fell swoop Bolton Wanderers' working class bedrock support has been
excluded. It might return when the middle classes discover how statistically
difficult it is to be a football winner. It might not. I park an hour's trot from the
ground, not even halfway to Bolton. The traffic is jammed solid before and after
the game for the duration of my walk, a walk I'm the only person to make.

It's a pub-free zone, apart from The Beehive, a vile 'family pub', which charges a family-unfriendly £5 to use the car park and doesn't admit away supporters. I take one of the pile of free *Bolton Evening News* ('STANDING UP FOR BOLTON'), sip a beer and fantasise about being in a town.

Reebok Stadium looks fabulous, like an inverted four-legged kitchen table. It dominates the landscape, suggesting that Bolton is a place to be taken seriously and I wish, with heart-wrenching futility, that John were beside me right now, grumbling.

Outside, the police are refusing to let Leicester fans take their blow up dolls into the ground and the *Bolton Evening News* is giving away COME ON YOU WHITES stickers. Wanderers are in desperate trouble, second from bottom. If they fail to defeat mid-table Leicester in this second of three consecutive home games, their season will go Crystal Palace-shaped.

Tension oozes from each of Reebok's new bricks and, for once, supporters are paying attention to the cable television channel as it attempts to put a positive spin on Bolton's plight. The pie'n'pies – served by bug-eyed mutants – aren't bad at all (but no Stockport). As I munch, absorbing everyone's tension myself, I gaze out over car parks which seem to stretch to Wigan, but they're still far from full, despite the traffic chaos. This is football in the next century and Reebok has been built in supplication to its ring of executive boxes – not all of which are finished – which ensure that those who pay the most get the best view.

They certainly haven't spent money on the pitch, which has eschewed the radical notion of being grass, in favour of a beach look. Still, there's ample leg room in my seat in the West Stand and the view is spectacular. There's a funny thing happening too: Reebok's capacity is 25,000 and that's what today's attendance will be announced as. Yet Leicester haven't sold all their allocation and there are more empty home seats dotted around than natural absenteeism would normally provide. Very odd indeed.

Bolton's mascot is Lofty The Lion, 'the most purrrrfect lion in the world!', once given a rough ride by the police after offering to fight Wolverhampton Wanderers' entire travelling support. Bolton have invested much emotional capital in Lofty. He has his own range of merchandise (£14.99 soft toy reduced to £9.99) and next week he's off on an Instant Photo Roadshow so kids can have photographs taken with him, for a fee. Today, even Lofty looks worried and subdued, although he was probably just mortified when the teams came out to a shocking Bryan Adams dirge.

Like The Stadium Of Light, Reebok confirms that seats *per se* don't have to mean lack of atmosphere. Even the band playing '*The Great Escape*' doesn't detract. Leicester, who've travelled up in a magnificent R-reg Hallmark coach, similar to Arsenal's, with tables and a proper kitchen in the back, don't make things easy for themselves. As he was when I saw Leicester at Filbert Street so long ago, Emile Heskey is a great big cry-baby bear, a blatant diver who is jeered as a cheat all match. He has chances, but were there a barn door in the vicinity it would have remained unhit. Still, Heskey is the one whom Bolton captain Gudni Bergsson upends to get himself sent off after half an hour.

The crowd sing 'We only need ten men', but the nervous, twitchy bloke next to me articulates what they're really thinking: 'They're gonna score in a minute, Leicester'. He can barely look, but when Robert Ullathorne loses his rag and starts pummelling Bolton's Per Frandsen, it's ten men apiece. He stomps off mouthing abuse at the linesman, fuelled by Martin O'Neill's hammy fake indignation on the bench.

The second half is calmer. Heskey has already missed a headed chance which I – and I do not claim this lightly – could have scored, when Bolton's previously anonymous Alan Thompson lashes a 25-yard screamer past a stationary Kasey Keller. The sigh of relief is exultant and 'we are staying up' echoes around Reebok. This wakes Leicester up, so they push lumpen centre half Matt Elliott up front and try to clamber back. Indeed, it's Elliott who helps provide the greatest single footballing moment of my season when his powerful downward header is turned over the bar by Bolton's Keith Branagan. Pele–Banks–1970, all that sentimental nonsense. Simply, it's the best save I have ever seen. There's a moment of silence as everyone takes in the enormity of what we've witnessed. Then the whole ground stands – even Leicester fans, not known for anything more civilised than kicking away fans across their city's Nelson Mandela Park – to applaud the goalkeeper.

There's no way back for Leicester after that, despite their animated substitute goalkeeper Pegguy Arphexad urging them on like a surrogate manager. Bolton run like devils, the fear of Division One coursing through their bodies. With virtually the game's last move, they break out of defence at last and Thompson scores, set up by John Sheridan's expert through ball. 2-0. Bolton might yet sneak out of trouble.

There's a certain etiquette in male toilets. No talking (unless you're cottaging, obviously), even with friends. This etiquette is inverted after football matches, where it is perfectly acceptable to discuss the game with a stranger whilst urinating, so long as your eyes do not stray towards your neighbour's penis. 'Ooh, I thought we'd blown it,' sighs a man, who I cannot help but notice is pissing harder and longer than Red Rum in his prime. 'What about that save? Have you seen anything like it?' 'No,' I reply shaking my head and my own penis in one pleasingly swish movement. And I haven't.

I have a mission after the game, after I've sidestepped the scuffles and walked for an hour to my car. I must go to the pub run by former Bolton midfielder Roy Greaves and raise a silent, solo glass to John Bauldie in the last place we drank together. Trouble is, I know it's near Burnden Park, but I cannot for the life of me remember exactly where, or what it was called.

I walk around the centre of Bolton ('fortified settlement'; formerly Bolton-Le-Moors; motto Supera Moras 'overcome delays' and a Latin pun on moors;

now home of Sara Cox, one of those women who is photographed in her bra for a living) in the drizzle. Its wealth originated with 14th-century Flemish weavers who established a textiles centre, but Bolton's look is Victoriana: imposing, if decrepit and echoey. I've walked so long and so far, all the shops have long since shut and anyone with any sense has gone for an evening in Manchester, allegedly hated by the locals. Frustrated, I find the railway station which I know is near Burnden and take the wrong road, Bradford Street instead of Manchester Road. When I finally see the floodlights in the distance, it's so far away I decide to cut back through town and, obsessed now, do my detective work by car.

I stumble across cobbled streets into Bolton's red light area ('stumbling' into a red light area previously seemed a rather implausible notion to me; I live and learn) on Breightmet Street. I'm approached by a prostitute who won't be seeing forty again and who is talking to her younger, more alluring colleague on the street corner opposite about 'doing forty-five' in three hours the other night. 'Are you looking for business love?' she asks.

What I really want to say is 'No, I'm trying to do a dignified tribute to my dead friend, but I'm cold, wet, lonely and I don't know where I am and you should be careful because there are people out there who will kill you as soon as fuck you and what are you going to do when you're seventy, all alone and rewinding endless memories of men smelling of beer and smegma.' Instead, I smile, say 'No thanks love' and scurry off. She's probably heard that speech before.

I drive up and down the A666 past Burnden Park three times, driving myself insane with frustration. Burnden is still standing, but the forecourt has been taken over by a giant gypsy camp. John would have shaken his head, very slowly. Eventually I find the pub, The Monteraze. I'd been deceived by its setting, way back from the road and its country hotel exterior. Roy Greaves is behind the bar. His playing days beard has been shaved off. He's looked after himself too, a snake-hipped, washboard-stomached opposite of the footballer-turned-publican cliché, but he chews gum like only a footballer can.

I have a drink for John and go home. I feel better now.

82 **Blackburn Rovers**

v. Barnsley
PREMIER LEAGUE
31 March

2-1

'It has promised to be a good season for so long.'

Roy Hodgson

She's gorgeous. She's tall and wearing a micro skirt which shows off a slender, beautifully turned pair of ankles at the end of a pair of endless legs. She has a vaguely 70s haircut which falls across her face in manner most becoming and although she looks sixteen, she's holding a baby which is obviously hers. She's also made out of bronze and since 1974 she has stood outside Blackburn's *Clockwork Orange*-style shopping mall to celebrate its erection.

Blackburn is a strange town, populated by strange folk. Lancashire lore portrays it as insular and backward. There is evidence. Blackburn hasn't the grand buildings of every other nearby town, because its cottonmasters were too busy racing whippets and had the vision of partially sighted bats. There's another statue, honouring Harry Hornby, Blackburn's MP for twenty-three years around the turn of the last century. In those twenty-three years he never spoke in the House Of Commons.

Blackburn was a last bastion of good old-fashioned northern British racism. This twenty per cent Asian town (mostly rural cotton workers from Gujarati who soon found there was nothing here for them, certainly not a friendly welcome) is where, in 1975, the newly formed British National Party tried to establish a bridgehead and won two council elections. A year later there was an Action Against Racism march, which the Mayor castigated, claiming it sent shoppers to Accrington for a Saturday afternoon and upon which the Provost noted acidly, 'Blackburn people were conspicuous by their absence'. I bet they were. Eventually the BNP gave up, discovering Blackburn's whites were too apathetic to bother with. Tonight Blackburn Rovers will give a rare outing to their only black player since Richard Brown played two games in 1993–94, the Swede Martin Dahlin.

Blackburn has always attracted ridicule. The Romans hadn't bothered and no outsiders ventured here until the 14th century when brave Flemish weavers (presumably relatives of Bolton's Flemish weavers) taught the locals their industry. Soon, there was a small mill at the end of almost every street and it was known as Deaf Town because of the noise the looms made. Blackburn boomed, aided by being on the Leeds & Liverpool Canal and the cottonmasters waiting until 1900 to give the workers Saturday afternoons off and 1912 before they granted them a week's holiday.

The Luddites were a major force here. Small minds still are: when factory worker Mukhtar Mohidin won the Lottery, he moved out of Blackburn, but kept his semi so he could visit. It's smashed up every time it's vacated, the only house on his estate to suffer so. Even murder is more unpleasant here: when Nicola Grogan, twenty, killed her married lover recently, she then took a chainsaw to his corpse, stopping only when she felt faint trying to saw his second leg off.

In the original Luddites' day, the town was so ill-constructed there was little worthwhile community property for them to smash, so they sensibly stomped off to the wealthy houses on the outskirts of town. The family of Robert Peel had to flee to Bury during a riot and, in 1835, Blackburn's vicar was lamenting his flock's 'gross filthy habits, their ruffian-like behaviour beggars all description'. There were serious riots in 1878 and by 1892 there was an extensive soup kitchen network.

Today's commemorative mountain ash tree in front of the northern hemisphere's naffest town hall 'to launch a campaign of zero tolerance of violence against women and children' suddenly seems like a watershed for Blackburn, rather than political correctness out of control. A banner on the Town Hall trumpets '1 day to go ...' It doesn't bother to say what happens tomorrow.

There's nothing here, only Ewood Park on the way to Bolton, Blackburn's sole claim on national interest, unless having Jack Straw as an MP counts (it doesn't, unlike when Barbara Castle held the seat). Ewood is the vision of one man, Senior Vice-President Jack Walker owner of Walker Steel, whose millions transformed Rovers from a middling old Division Two side managed by Don Mackay and led by Simon Garner, into champions of England, managed by Kenny Dalglish and led by Alan Shearer. Walker rebuilt Ewood, tubular floodlights and all, as a present to the people of Blackburn, the grand construction it's never had. The sort of thing anyone would do in his position. When they won the Premiership in 1994–95, misanthropic Manchester United fans working for Pot, Kettle & Black Ltd, claimed Rovers had bought it. Up in Newcastle, Sir John Hall must chuckle mirthlessly at the irony.

The Walker Steel Stand, not even cantilever, is a flimsier affair than it looks on television and as small as Blackburn itself. I'm in the Jack Walker Stand, an altogether superior affair (we'll let the televised wrestling in the refreshment area pass). The food is not. My pie is pepper flavoured, and pepper masks many things; things of which I must never be told. The tea is less sludgy than sludge, although it's a close call and the service is confused.

From my seat I can see a horrible housing estate, an unkempt cocoon from which punters are crawling, the hills which they're gingerly picking their way down and an endless vista of wasteground where they dump their rubbish. I can't help thinking of all those zombie films I've never seen.

My view of the pitch is excellent, the atmosphere simmers pleasingly, but demographics can't explain where all these Rovers fans – realistic gate, 6000 – have come from. I'm sat next to a man in a flat cap, old Blackburn, but his quality shoes say moneyed too. He curls his top lip at my friendliest smile when I sit next to him. My libido, on sabbatical since before the nastiness at Bristol and Charlton, has returned. I'm sat next to an attractively pockmarked middle-aged blonde woman, smelling of my favourite perfume, ambrosial alcohol'n'fags. Her shoes also suggest money (Ah ha! A theme!) and she raises one eyebrow when I smile at her. She even instigates a conversation about the referee during the game and laughs uproariously when I make a joke of staggering lameness. Luckily she is not a mindreader. She is, however, a new kind of football fan, of which there must be many here: smart, attractive, unafraid to shout and undoubtedly female. And, like everyone here, white.

Blackburn have stalled of late, but should still make Europe. Barnsley are in trouble and newly resentful after three of their players were not unreasonably sent off against Liverpool on Saturday. Their fans were still whingeing about it outside tonight, but as if to undermine their 'We are Premier League' chant and the hysterical screams whenever a decision goes against their dirty, dissent-prone team, they are nowhere near selling out their allocation for this almost-derby.

The public address system is earth shattering, especially when the teams trot out to Europe's still-hilarious 'The Final Countdown'. There are two, headache-inducing, competing fan bands. Blackburn allow theirs to wander around pitchside, which hopefully will prove to be against some Football Association regulation. Barnsley's are simply rubbish, but they cannot ruin an absorbing match.

Barnsley should have scored in the first minute when the Macedonian Georgi Hristov – famous for finding the women of his adopted town un-attractive, the buffoon – is through and unsurprisingly alone. He fluffs the chance and before eight minutes have passed Rovers take the lead. Dahlin links beautifully with Chris Sutton, victim of endless 'You'll never play for England' chants (ironically the same applies to the whole Barnsley team) and slinks through an invisible defence to slot home. Rovers mistakenly rest awhile and Barnsley huff and puff their way back, rueing the fact that their chances fall to Hristov, except for Chris Morgan's towering warning header which slams off the bar and over.

Early in the second half, Rovers goalkeeper Tim Flowers is clattered by a pair of forwards and, holding his shoulder, eventually gives way to Alan Fettis. 'This lad'll let some in,' declares Flat Cap to his mate. 'And we're always second to the ball.' Fettis's first action is to pick the ball from the net after Hristov has streaked through and uncharacteristically failed to make a fool of himself. The Barnsley fans celebrate like they were a proper Premiership team. Ex-miners leap into each other's arms as they scream 'Stand up if you're staying up'.

Rovers bring on Kevin Gallacher. 'We'll see a bit of action now,' muses Flat Cap, uncharitably, but with unnatural prescience. The Scot scores the winner with five minutes to go. The ball zings around the penalty area before coming to him. One touch and it's beyond goalkeeper David Watson. The Blackburn fans sing at last: 'You're going down with the Shearer'. There is no sound sadder than that of ex-miners' hearts breaking.

Afterwards I try to find a pulse in Blackburn. Like Wrexham, it smells of lovely hops when the wind blows in the right direction. Instead, I see my first closed McDonald's. This pulse is not in Gladstone's pub, which promises 'more fun than you can handle'. There are four customers inside, one of whom is not yet collecting a state pension. I stoop to an establishment called The Blob Shop, where a complement of six hardy drinkers ensure it is undeniably more full. Where have 24,179 people, gathered together a mile or so away, gone? Why do they so dislike their town? What can the people of Blackburn do with themselves, other than scheme to move away as Jack Walker did? It's wearying here. Blackburn has given up, but then Blackburn had always given up. Nice statue though.

83 **Peterborough United**

v. Notts County
DIVISION THREE

3 April

1-0

'We need you, the Posh fans, to forget your frustrations.'

Barry Fry

The last ten. I can see the finishing line. I'm skiing downhill, more Franz Carr than Franz Klammer, admittedly, but gravity always takes its course. The loneliness has evaporated as spring has sprung and I walk around Peterborough laughing to myself, thinking of Henry VIII. Before he ran to fat and wives (Catherine Of Aragon is buried in the epic cathedral, her grave is said to have healing powers. I don't tempt fate), the then-prince was a JP here for a spell, learning about his people in the days royals did such things. He had lovely legs apparently. Mary Queen Of Scots was buried here too in 1587, but she didn't linger, being dug up and removed in 1612. Nice.

Henry would be as perplexed as I am about new Peterborough, the first dry land west of The Fens. It's a cold-mannered place, over-pedestrianised, surrounded by ring roads and car parks. The 1968 New Town looks in need of a brush up. Its decline mirrors Peterborough United, elected to the league in 1960, promoted immediately and then stalling forever.

Populated since 4000BC and a Roman centre, there's the legacy of village mentality – undimmed by a camp which held French prisoners of war during the Napoleonic wars; I always assumed they killed them and moved on – which saw riots in 1914 against an unlucky German shopowner. Men wear T-shirts promoting Shit House Rovers FC, town workers go home to change clothes before a Friday night out and the beggars (too many) are as aggressive as those on London's South Bank. It's the sort of place where the next door neighbour of The Fountain pub had a feud with its landlord. The vindictive old sod promptly bought the pub and sacked his nemesis.

A stroke of fortuitous geographical positioning – halfway between London and the north and (more roughly) halfway between the midlands and the east

– meant Peterborough would be a railway city as well as a brick-making centre and home to a large number of Italians. Today, it's a commutable hour to King's Cross and major companies like Peterborough United sponsors Thomas Cook, site their head offices here. Cook, a Derbyshire man himself, had chartered the trains which took 150,000 people to the Great Exhibition in 1851, setting off from York and passing through Peterborough, the potential of which Cook noted. Despite Peterborough's problems, it's part of Britain's growth region, the powerhouse of the new millennium. The fact that it doesn't rain enough here to sustain massive population growth is not something they discuss on these streets, once policed by Geoff Capes.

What they do discuss is Peterborough United. Barry Fry's easily fulfillable promotion dream has turned into a nightmare, in which not only Brighton & Hove Albion, but Doncaster Rovers have won at London Road. A play-off place, once merely a safety net, is uncertain. Notts County don't care, for they have taken fifty-three points out of the last sixty and are champions, nineteen points ahead of Torquay United in second. It's a wonder County bother to bring their kit with them and don't amble on to the pitch wearing sombreros and drinking cocktails after a day spent carousing Peterborough's crack houses and brothels.

London Road is a fine lower leagues ground, more than capable of hosting Division Two football. It lies south of the rubbish, nondescript city centre, at the end of a bridge over the River Nene. It's a rubbish, nondescript bridge. I fear I peaked too early with bridges.

The success of Cambridge United's bacon rolls means that Peterborough must provide the same fare as their hated rivals. They're not quite as good, poorer quality bacon, I reckon. Good tea, though. I'm in the London Road End, covered and somewhat smaller than it appears on television. I don't approve of the mascot at all. Mr Posh is a ghoulish old man dressed in suit and top hat who shuffles around the pitch perimeter shaking hands with frightened children.

Club–fan relations have sunk of late and despite the crucial nature of this game, the initial all-ticket stipulation has been quietly dropped. In the pro-gramme, striker Jimmy Quinn has an inarticulate whinge about 'a lot of negativity from off the field just recently that I find hard to understand'. Sacking assistant manager Phil Neal has probably helped and Fry's recent hospitalisation and heart scare will have earned him the sympathy vote. Then again, perhaps not: midfielder Derek Payne misses an early tackle: 'You're a disgrace Payne, fuck off,' shouts the mild mannered family man next to me. 'Sort 'em out Fry, they're fucking useless.'

United's brilliant young full back Adam Drury will one day play for England (I've always wanted to say that) and their all-out approach – best illustrated when Martin Carruthers chases the referee like a maniac after he doesn't win a penalty – transforms the crowd's latent disapproval into something approaching support. Suitably aroused, they boo County's Steve Finnan over some old grudge and chant 'You're just a bunch of wankers' to the County hoards, who have turned up to sing 'Championi, Championi' all night. Peterborough, not really a proper city, more an agglomeration of townships, breeds fickle, gnarled people, second or third generation New Town dwellers who've seen their home develop into a glorified roundabout. Peterborough United, still the best supported team in Division Three and Chairmanned by the owner of Pizza Express, are their team.

With time running out, Peterborough win it when player-coach Steve Castle powerfully heads in Niall Inman's corner. Everyone rushes to hug Fry, who's putting more strain on his creaking heart by doing a touchline jig. The crowd sings 'going up, going up, going up' with conviction and 'Barry, Barry give us a wave,' followed by a jaunty 'You fat bastard' when he does. It's an epic victory of sorts and a newly optimistic crowd crosses the rubbish, nondescript bridge back into a city which has transformed itself in the last few hours.

It's still cold and unwelcoming and there are police everywhere (not, surely, anything to do with mild mannered Notts County fans), but the bouncered pubs are full, although not unpleasantly so. I go to The Lion close to the cathedral, where I can hear Catherine Of Aragon turning in her grave. It's a pre-club pub, but not large enough for me to melt into the background. I amble around town, alighting on the West Side bar, loud, dark and what passes for swish around here with a drum'n'bass – the sound of confused urban England – soundtrack, Sky TV and overpriced bottled beer. These are not the beautiful people and other places performing exactly the same rituals on Friday evenings do it better.

It's not exactly that there are two Englands, but I can sense the folk memory of an ancient place like, say, Preston or Oldham or Bristol, folk memory upon which current inhabitants – old and new – can feed. It's not like this here: like Catherine Of Aragon, today's Peterborough dwellers hail from elsewhere and there's no shared heritage for incomers to absorb and embrace. That's the Peterborough effect. I must never visit here again.

84 Bury

v. Huddersfield Town
DIVISION ONE
4 April

2-2

'Yet another vital game ...'

Stan Ternant

Bury doesn't really exist. Once proud and alone, now it's an extension of Manchester which doesn't have a railway station any more. Instead, travellers to Bury must take a Metrolink tram from Manchester to the northern end of the line. This means there's no need for breweries, for councils, for anyone, to invest in Bury, or to reassert its identity. Anything anyone wants is a twenty-minute tram ride away.

Bury FC is now the town's only rallying point. Few have noticed exactly what's happened at this least glamorous of clubs and that won't change when Ferguson or Wenger wins the Manager Of The Year award. Under Stan Ternant, with essentially the same team, Bury have won promotion in successive seasons and this season, their first at this level since 1967, they should be safe. There's no money here, indeed the players have twice threatened to strike (as in 'go on', rather than score goals) this season: firstly when they were forced to pay for an overnight stay before the game at faraway Ipswich out of their own pockets and secondly when their babies weren't given nappy-changing facilities. They've weathered a sixteen-game mid-season spell without a victory and they must perform on the worst pitch in the land, hardly aided by Swinton Lions playing rugby league – but also paying rent – on it.

As such, Bury is forgotten, home to the undead and nearly dead. Luckily, I'm not alone. My friend Peter has yet again elected to travel across England with me to a place where it's raining, where for all we know, it may have been raining forever. It's tiny, slightly bigger than Burslem, lost in a world where Victorian buildings have been replaced by what passed in the early 70s for malls. Times have moved on and Bury is essentially a large discount store where everything costs £1, the women are prematurely fat, and men have food in their beards. Children may well be sacrificed here during pagan festivals.

As a reminder of when it wasn't like this, there's a statue of Sir Robert Peel – the family fled from Blackburn as I discovered there: oh, such bliss when it all ties up – pointing to some public toilets. We settle in a pub opposite the bus station on Manchester Road (as in all roads lead to ...), from where police are videoing football fans. It's understaffed but overflowing with a distinctly northern lunchtime mix of football fans and old dears who sup halves and keep their hats on as they eat hearty lunches. 'Come and bust a lung singing along with our live entertainers,' begs a poster. This happens on Wednesday and Friday afternoons: in some places, possibly only Bury, pensioners are in control and they will have their singalongs.

Taking advantage of a break in the rain, we walk south along Manchester Road to a more well-to-do area, handily facing Manchester and separated from North Bury's slums by the town centre. Bury's ground, Gigg Lane, lies off the main drag and suddenly there are thousands of Huddersfield fans, who, no strangers to these sorts of places, find Bury town too depressing to visit.

Inside, Huddersfield have been allocated both ends, one standing and fenced in, one seated. It's like having a goal start. This is an important match for both teams. When I saw Huddersfield lose to Nottingham Forest early on, they looked doomed. They instantly sacked Brian Horton, appointed Peter Jackson and Terry Yorath and although still in the relegation struggle, one point better off than Bury, they should escape, but a defeat today would push them towards the potential abyss. They've arrived in a distinctly average Wallace Arnold coach which has a mini-kitchen, but no table lamps.

Despite the prefabricated, small-windowed executive boxes, identical to the ticket office outside, Gigg Lane has been upgraded of late. We're in the South Stand, in front of a patronising, smug Scotsman – not my first this season – who bangs on remorselessly about his prostate to his disinterested friend. The view is fair, the announcer a candidate for World's Gruffest Man and the atmosphere would be dead, were not the Huddersfield fans manufacturing enough for everyone. Bury take great trouble to ensure the food hutch is impossible to find, presumably because their pies are soggy and peppery, while one cup of their tea would have ensured Robert Peel's family didn't stay for long. The rain becomes torrential in time for kickoff. Old soldiers who fought at the Somme are commenting on how muddy the pitch is.

The pitch dominates the game. Big, strong Bury know they can't play down the centre, so they use the creative hoof. Before Huddersfield have worked this out, Bury have scored, when Peter Swan heads down Gordon Armstong's free kick and Peter Butler lashes it past startled Steve Harper, on loan from Newcastle. The Bury fans, newly used to dizzying success, don't cheer too loudly. There isn't time anyway, because within a minute Huddersfield are level. Marcus Browning proves anything is possible with a splendid run through Bury's defence, backtracking forward Lennie Johnrose trips him and Lee Richardson thumps in the penalty, although he nearly tumbles over as he steps up.

There's a lot of blood (mostly down Swan's shirt), endless endeavour, but little class. In this game for men, Bury take the lead again early in the second half, shortly after I've discovered I'm 15,000 off winning the Gigg Lane (capacity 11,841) Golden Gamble, run by ridiculously named Commercial Manager Neville Neville, father of Gary and Phil. Nick Daws feeds Rod Matthews – the nearest person on display to a winger – who rushes down the right, puts in a low cross and Tony Ellis sweeps in. Huddersfield resort to Bury's strongarm tactics and when Grant Johnson follows through on Bury goalkeeper Dean Kiely, there's a mass brawl and Huddersfield's Wayne Allison isn't sent off despite trading punches with whoever's up for it.

They equalise when Bury can't clear David Phillips's cross and Richardson pounces to drive home from twenty-five yards for the goal of the game. Huddersfield fans sing 'Stand up if you're staying up' and the Bury fans, having nothing to say themselves, join in. Before they built this decent team, Bury's home games must have been played in the silence that gave the Cemetery End its name. By the end of a titanic struggle, the players are throwing themselves into the mud like schoolboys and everyone can live with a draw.

The Huddersfield fans disappear after the game and we go back into town. Every place, even Bury, has its moment of wonder. Bury's is a tiny monument to Robert Whitehead, 1823-1905, overshadowed by an impressive Boer War memorial in a small unremarkable patch of grass close to the centre. He invented the torpedo (how it doesn't say, nor how it came to be called torpedo, not Whitehead or Bury). Moreover, his daughter Agatha was grandmother to the in-no-way romanticised, but most definitely non-fiction *Sound Of Music* children. At least that's what the tiny plaque says. In fact, it seems Agatha was Baron Georg Von Trapp's first wife, the fortune he married into and mother of seven of the singing children before she died of scarlet fever in 1922 and Julie Andrews arrived. Not one to overstate its case, Bury.

Bury looks like drugtown, but it's dead. What few shoppers there were have sped off home and nobody will visit tonight. We try The Clarence, where the music is loud Oasis and the clientele, hard Budweiser-bottle swigging men. We stick out like The Pope visiting a Sao Paulo favela, but without the worshipping angle.

The rain has stopped and the air is chilled. The Two Tubs, built when Charles II was on the throne, is a biker pub. On the walls are advertisements for a National Association For Bikers With A Disability meeting. At this meeting there will be a 'tits contest'. I get the feeling we're not welcome here either, but the juke box plays Devo, Talking Heads and Sepultura, all paid for by the barman. I imagine myself and Peter resemble plain clothes policemen in a certain light. We leave for Manchester, where Piccadilly Square is sealed off by dozens of dog-wielding policemen while Manchester City fans literally chase those of Stockport County from their city. There are no Bury fans involved.

85 Coventry City

v. Aston Villa
PREMIER LEAGUE
11 April

1-2

'Of course, it looks as if we should be all right.'

Gordon Strachan

When National Socialist bombs razed Coventry to the ground on 14 November 1940, it must have felt like the final proof that there was no God, as a tribe of daft-accented Midlanders were cast adrift with the slate wiped clean but rubble-strewn. They could have built Versailles, Moscow, Los Angeles, a smaller version of any great city of the world. Instead they built a forbidding, ugly, monstrosity, where the ring road would be king and muggers would find it easy. Birmingham, by comparison, is an architectural triumph and a city of luscious culture. The philistine, unattractive people of Coventry must not be pitied.

This morning, in one of the cold, shabby malls, close to the estate agents' ghetto on Warwick Road, a band under a Christ In The Precinct banner is playing 'Free Nelson Mandela'. Badly, but with a certain sincerity. These people have not heard a news bulletin since 1990, unlike the hearts-in-the-wrong-place students at Warwick University, whose Mandela Hall is now named after Desmond Lynam. Nobody objected when Warwick gave a Foreign Office-assisted, United Nations-funded postgraduate place (law) to 31-year-old Valentine Strasser, former military dictator of Sierra Leone. Perhaps they could rename their hall after him when he graduates.

Further along, past Coventry Trophy Centre (not much local business) is a busker on accordion doing 'Old Macdonald's Farm'. This is the ghost town The Specials sang about and it hasn't been resurrected.

Funny thing is, they started so well. I walk around Coventry Cathedral, designed by Sir Basil Spence and rebuilt by 1956; a building so beautiful, designed with such heart-stoppingly obvious love of Coventry and its people, I can sense God. Illogically, he did not desert Coventry after all. An organ is playing, there's a Bethlehem boulder and Graham Sutherland's extraordinary

Christ In Glory tapestry. If I were lucky enough to be Roman Catholic, I'd see the tapestry weeping over pre-Millennium Coventry. Tucked away in a corner is a head of Jesus, sculptured in metal from the remains of a crashed car. I can't stop gazing at it. I've long since stopped feeling immortal, but in front of that creation, I die a little more. If my end comes in a car crash, couldn't they just give my body parts to pleasant folk of a different race (that's very important) and sue the vehicle manufacturers? I'm very anxious about that now. I collect my breath outside, feeling slightly foolish. The cathedral – stunning exterior too – calms me down. I hurry away.

Before the bombs, Coventry had been a typical Midlands town, ruled for centuries by guilds (less ritualistic Freemasons), specialising in wool and cloth and hell-bent on promoting the Lady Godiva myth. She did exist, but is remembered less as the canny 11th-century businesswoman she was, than a virtual imbecile who rode naked through Coventry to make her husband (who owned the place) reduce taxes. Miraculously, nobody saw her beautiful body and hubby Leofric did the decent thing. Nice one, Leofric.

Car City they called it and Coventry's rebuilding was seen as a measure of British postwar virility, until the defeated countries of World War 2 won the peace and began to build better, cheaper and more cars. Daimler, Jaguar and Talbot were deposed in Coventry by Peugeot and a daft-accented tribe was cast adrift once more. Car City has long since stalled and it's still ugly. The people are bored to stupefaction, people like Paul Redhead of Earlsdon who, the other year, pretended to be disabled and, in turn became so bored of that he faked a miracle cure in church.

Against this backdrop are Coventry City: mean-spirited, unloved, but beaten at home only by Leicester City this season and so will not get themselves relegated, despite that wretched performance I saw at Arsenal in August. They contribute nothing to the Premier League. Like its city, the football team began to grow after World War 2. They sped through four divisions in less than a decade and with bright young Jimmy Hill as manager, embraced snazz. They were the first to turn their programme into a matchday magazine, the first to have a decent team coach, the first to take supporters to away games on chartered trains, The Sky Blue Express. Now, again like their home, Coventry City are stagnant, but still they cling on to the Premier League.

This should be a big day. For City, there are dark whispers about European qualification, which cannot happen. Aston Villa harbour vague European ambitions of their own. In truth, it's a mid-table local derby but it is happening in a place so dull Mo Mowlam, former head girl at Coundon Court School, left for more exciting Redcar. The match is a sell-out, the weather is cold, but the key is low.

The ground, Highfield Road, casts a literal and metaphorical shadow over the Asian ghetto it lies with, but inside the elderly, cramped Main Stand it's primitive; a reminder that Coventry City are a small club, existing only to avoid relegation. A new stadium, as ever, is planned, this time at grubby Foleshill, where disabled charity worker Helen Johnson has taken out an injunction against her son after he kicked in the stomach as she waited for a hysterectomy.

The pie, served, thrillingly, in CCFC greaseproof paper, would have been nice if I hadn't been given a kid's portion. There is a sign behind the counter reminding served and servers that 'hidden surveillance cameras' are used 'to detect theft, loss and shortage' and have been 'installed without notice'. No wonder the untrusted virtually spit on the food when it arrives and I'm overcharged. Bet the cameras didn't register that. Mean spirits are everywhere and, in sympathy with the recent stormy weather (fourteen-year-old Coventry boy, Carl Giles, was swept away and presumed drowned while delivering milk yesterday), the toilets are blocked and flooding.

My view is excellent, the pre-match music, an odd mixture of drum'n'bass and Iron Maiden, is played at distortion volume and the elephant mascot, Sam, looks old and more plastic than furry, but when the teams emerge to an impossibly loud Electric Light Orchestra's 'Mr Blue Sky' and, simultaneously the sky turns blue, it's a special moment. Here, in the city that shot itself in the foot. It can happen anywhere. What a wonderful thing to have discovered.

The fans of Aston Villa, a proper club lest we forget, decide to make some noise and within three minutes they're one up. City goalkeeper Steve Ogrizovic fails to claim Lee Hendrie's cross after he'd been set free by pocket battleship Alan Wright and Dwight Yorke heads in. 'Easy easy,' chant the Villa fans and a ludicrous mobile security squad is dispatched, probably going 'hup hup hup' to the Main Stand where a few Villains have sneaked in. City have obviously knocked off for the season, apart from Paul Telfer who plays the role of wound-up psychopath with De Niroesque attention to detail, and once Villa's goalkeeper Mark Bosnich beats out Darren Huckerby's drive, it's they who smell Europe.

It's 0-2 shortly after the restart when Julian Joachim crosses and, watched by a static defence, Yorke's smart overhead kick flies past Ogrizovic. 'Easy, easy.' City pull one back when Noel Whelan crashes in a 25-yarder with the defence thinking about their win bonus. City fans even manage swift run-through of their anthem, 'Let's all sing together' to the 'Eton Boating Song' tune, but despite Gordon Strachan's attention-seeking huffing and puffing on the bench – what *can* he be like to have sex with? – they haven't the guile or interest to blow Villa's house down and everything breaks down around midfielder Trond Soltvedt, mercilessly abused by the home crowd all afternoon. Supporting Coventry City must be like this all the time. It can't get any better than this and this is awful.

After I've stopped laughing at the idiotic stewards who, on the final whistle, sprint to the centre circle and stand in formation like a troupe of beer-bellied cheerleaders, I'm relieved not to be crushed to death as I try to leave, skidding along overflowed urine. I might have elbowed a woman in the face, I try to say sorry but she's gone and I'm swept down some stairs to oxygen. Don't they need safety certificates in Coventry?

Outside, along the nauseatingly named Sky Blue Way dual carriageway, there's some fighting. Proper traffic-stopping stuff too: a well planned ambush (everyone speaks identically and don't wear replica shirts, so I can't tell who's who; the important thing is *they* know), ensuring that the police are too late – they make up for this in numbers and brutality though – to halt the groups of hard men, sixty a side. Nobody is seriously hurt and the police, plus dogs and horses, march the Villa fans to the railway station a mile away. Hysterical over-policing was always the only sure way to stop football hooliganism.

I don't want to hang around a city where things are so bad that shops in the main Hertford Street mall are closed down if they're not short-lease cut-price tat vendors. They've banned drinking in the city centre (but not crime, the pair of whites who robbed a petrol station last night used a baseball bat and CS gas spray), so I resist the omnipresent temptation to sit on a bench, drinking canned Special Brew while muttering obscenities to myself. Instead I drink some unpleasant beer at The Varsity, a retarded cousin to the Preston pub of the same name. It's playing a Beatles album very quietly, cutting edge chic in Coventry. This place isn't going to get any better, this or any other Saturday night. Couldn't Britain go to war again? Just to demolish this hole at England's geographical centre?

86 **Torquay United**

v. Rotherham United
DIVISION THREE

13 April

1-2

'It's important that you supporters, however frustrating it may get at times, refrain from venting those frustrations at the players.'

Kevin Hodges

My irrational fear of bank holiday traffic means I must spend Easter Sunday in Torquay for the game on Monday. I imagined platoons of Bristol and Birmingham youth, displaying flesh, snogging and shouting. Instead, it's cold, wet and hardly bustling, long coats all the way. Maybe Britain doesn't have a tourist industry any more, not at the middle and upper ends. Torquay – still selling itself as the birthplace of Agatha Christie, the priest who wrote 'Abide With Me' and the landing site for William Of Orange – hasn't downscaled sufficiently to attract the fairly poor, desperate for respite from Coventry. This is my final fling before the end, only a month away, but also the last time I'll spend an evening trawling streets and pubs solo. I'll never worry about going into a pub on my own again. A practical gain I suppose.

It feels like an ordinary Sunday, not a public holiday with a free day tomorrow. At the cod-Irish pub, Seamus O'Donnell's there's a sign saying 'put an Irishman on a spit and you will find two more to turn him' and the clientele have gone to seed, while Market Place is over-lit and almost empty. There's nothing more lonesome than a solo pub crawl. I am Johnny No Mates.

At Park Lane, everything changes. It's a bouncered bar, drinks are £1 until 10 p.m., it's karaoke night and it's full, but there's room to get to the bar. Here I employ the tricks of the solo drinker in denial. I can move around undetected, if anyone makes eye contact I can look as if I'm waiting for someone and I can block everything out and lose myself in karaoke, which works if the mob wants it to.

This is the bottom of the social pile at play. Immediately, I see my third penis of the season. The song is 'You Sexy Thing' and one of the three karaoke all-stars has seen *The Full Monty* and as the song climaxes, so – in a sense – does he. The compère flies across stage and ushers him off. It was a fine penis and no mistake. Everyone is drunk and I decide the only decent thing to do is to catch up. The evening's last gasp is a gaggle of women doing 'American Pie' with the whole bar howling the chorus. I take leave of my character there and then and sing along. It feels better joining in. This is a great surprise.

Afterwards I sashay back to my hotel where I'm the youngest customer by twenty years. Being drunk, I don't take the direct route and instead trundle through a town which has transformed itself into a proper resort. Everyone, apart from the legions of tramps, is off somewhere, noisily and in search of adventure. I stumble on a German sausage shop, still open and with a mind-boggling array of spectacular sausage products for connoisseur and drunk alike. The owner is from Hamburg, of adorable temperament, tells me about her life (she and her husband holidayed here for decades and loved it so much they came for good, never to return home). She even pretends not to notice my hiccups, and my bratwurst smothered in German mustard, is delicious. I do hope she's not driven out of town by mobile burger vans or that nasty streak of Britishness which separates anti-German feeling from ugly racism.

Eventually, I find the seafront again. The tide is a way out now, but the sea-smell pulls me towards it. In thrall to the logic of the unsober, I decide this is a fine time (i.e. midnight) to pay my respects. I wash my face in the sea and, lit only by the moon, take a piss of thanks on the beach, as I did at Swansea when, like now, I was about to see Torquay United. Thanks for being alive, thanks for being here, thanks for everywhere I've been this season, thanks for my wife for not divorcing me and thanks for my sausage. Then I go to my hotel room, the route I've taken detectable only by the trail of wet sand behind me.

Next morning, there is a mini-beach in bed with me and my ankle hurts. It not only hurts, but it's swollen and has the hue of three-day old grapes. Ah yes. As I went onto the beach last night for my triumphant wee, I fell flat on my face. That'll be why my nose and hands are cut and there's a hole in my trousers then.

I spend the morning hobbling around Torquay harbour/marina against the wind, wondering what people actually do when they go sailing in flimsy yachts, or how they can afford a fifty-foot boat costing £399,000, about ten times more than my estimate. Torquay, hilly as a man with a bruised ankle doesn't need, might look stunning but there's little here for the locals, apart from a heavy bank holiday police presence for the young; jobs in Plymouth or as poop-scoop by-law enforcers for the middle-aged; McJobs at McDonald's for the old (a good thing and proof acne is not a McJob requirement: hats off to the litigious, health-food selling multinational); overpriced tea rooms for the really old and the overpowering smell of petrol for all. That's why there's no identity.

Torquay was originally a fishing town, based around Torre Abbey. Toff tourism developed during the Napoleonic wars when off-duty navy officers built villas for their wives here while Torbay was used as a supply port. Wealthy invalids followed, but the poor were never welcome. Needless to say, Torquay is not a football town, never has been, never will be, but like Scarborough, Blackpool and the rest, football is something that tourists ignore. Torquay United are having their best season since they were last promoted in 1991 and are second, destined at least for the play-offs, although it's tight beneath Champions Notts County and they've won only one of their last five. Rotherham United's form has collapsed since I saw that fluke against Leyton Orient. They've probably blown their play-off chances and only a win today can help them.

The ground, Plainmoor, is well on the way out of town towards Babbacombe, home of John Lee, the man they couldn't hang (three times they tried). I limp up St Marychurch Road, almost as steep as Lincoln's Steep Hill at exactly the moment brisk cold is replaced by bright, warm, sweat-inducing sunshine. This is wealthy Torquay, where people have palm trees (not native, deliberately introduced in the 1820s) in their gardens. Now I grasp why the tourist board call it The English Riviera. It slides into grot around Plainmoor. In fact it's a spiteful little area and the graffiti around the ground does not say TUFC, nor a hip hop tagline. Instead, it repeatedly names a certain unfortunate as a 'grass' and 'police informer'. It might as well have said We Are Scum, Willingly Ruled By Mobs.

I watch the last few minutes of Nottingham Forest trouncing Wolves in O'Connor's faux Irish bar. The barmaid is lovely, maybe she goes for the newly disabled. She looks down on me over her aquiline nose like I'm a vagrant. The cut on my nose starts to weep blood again. I try Strikers Sports Bar. The customers are not sporty.

I'm in the Popular Side. I brave a pasty (Lord knows why, I don't like the things) which seems to be comprised entirely of sweepings from the floor. The tea is made out of fresh seawater, but the serving girl could have a career as a model. My ankle starts to throb. There's a few hundred Rotherham fans making a din on their open Babbacombe End, but on the Popular Side, there's much muttering about part-time fans (although despite the game's vital nature, I still get a front row perch), the club not wanting to go up – ex-chairman and current director Mike Bateson who has £1 million invested won't attend games – and morale is only saved by some anti-Exeter (they're too scared of Plymouth) chanting and a witty 'I Do Like To Be Beside The Seaside' which ends with the brass band playing 'tiddly-om-pom-pom, fuck off back to Roth-er-ham,' at which everybody laughs.

These locals all have Devon Mouth: this means a hooked nose, an oval lower jaw set forward slightly, plus askew teeth. They speak softly, in order to make themselves appear more important. Mutterings mostly. It's like being on the set of *The Wicker Man* and none of these fans were in town last night. There are gulls on the pitch, Torquay's nickname is The Gulls. Devon is like this.

Torquay are so nervous, the prize so close, that they keep giving the ball away, especially overlapping full backs Andy Gurney and Paul Gibbs, Britain's ugliest footballer. Rotherham have nothing to lose, except their composure when Gary Martindale is put clean through and misses badly. All the Rotherham players hold their heads.

I'm next to a screamer. He's outraged at Rotherham's Mark Monington for some imaginary offence 'you wanker you' and he holds his own team, particularly Kevin Hill (aka 'you, boy'), in contempt too, even when Jon Gittens heads against the bar. Inevitably, Rotherham take the lead. Monington flicks on Steve Thompson's corner and big Jason White heads in. 'You're not singing any more,' declare four Rotherham skinheads, displaying their beer bellies as if they were in some mating ritual, which of course they are.

'Bloody pathetic,' screams Screamer, 'they're too fucking fast for you.' He's right, annoyingly this sort often are. Torquay are missing injured inspiration Rodney Jack, the only player to sign a contract for next season. 'Rodney get well soon, Rodney, Rodney get well soon,' the crowd plead. *They* want promotion.

Rotherham score again after the break. Martindale works wonders down the right. His cross is miskicked by White and Gibbs before Andy Roscoe blasts home past goalkeeper Ken Veysey, playing with a broken nose. 'Waste of fucking time,' screams Screamer. 'You're too fucking dainty.' He's right again.

A quintet of Rotherham fans are in the Popular Side and make themselves known. The stewards escort them past a tiny Torquay mob next to the Babbacombe End and they're showered with plastic bottles. This proves to be an honour-satisfying way of settling things. The police film everything.

Torquay substitute Hill. 'Should have done that in the first half, you wankers,' screams Screamer and with his first touch (a cliché, but true) substitute Tony Bedeau volleys past Bobby Mimms after some lucky bobbles. That's how it stays. Torquay apply pressure, but Rotherham are closest when Darren Garner beats Veysey and turns away in triumph, only for Jamie Robinson to clear off the line.

Afterwards, the announcer hopes (rather than expects) 'you've enjoyed the show' and dourly notes that it's Notts County on Saturday and 'anything can happen up there'. In the windowless gents toilets, the lights are out already and it's pitch black. I take this as an omen and hobble towards London.

87 **AFC Bournemouth**

v. Walsall
DIVISION TWO

14 April

1-0

'We thrive on knocking the odds and this season can be seen as one of progression.'

Mel Machin

Lewis Tregonwell had been a soldier all his working life. One day in 1810, he took his wife Henrietta to the scrubland around the mouth of the River Bourne and showed her his old stomping ground, where he'd apprehended countless Dorset smugglers. What if, the old soldier mused, he bought land round here and built villas he could loan out to his choleric but wealthy friends in need of sea air and spa water? And so, on the site of today's Royal Exeter Hotel, Bournemouth was created.

Soon, the rich and fashionable came to the place that reminded Charles Darwin of Patagonia and was described by Thomas Hardy in *Tess Of The D'Urbervilles* as 'pleasure city and glittering novelty'. D.H. Lawrence was a regular; Robert Louis Stevenson wrote *The Strange Case Of Dr Jekyll And Mr Hyde* here while recuperating (he was always recuperating); Disraeli had his gout cured, while Gladstone made his last public appearance here before departing Bournemouth station to go home and die; Tolkien was a regular visitor and Marconi did all sorts of experiments on the cliffs. Mary Woolstonecraft is buried at St Peter's Church, as is her daughter Mary Shelley and the heart of her husband Percy Bysshe Shelley, which Byron had grabbed as the poet was cremated in Italy. The typhoid epidemics of 1905–06 were never spoken of.

During World War 2, the beaches were mined, the piers broken, 15,000 mostly French or American soldiers were billeted in the hotels, and visitors were banned so Dwight D. Eisenhower and Montgomery could mull over D-Day at the Carlton Hotel. Today, Bournemouth is shrinking, a paedophile magnet according to the Children's Society, elbowed aside by expanding Poole and Southampton. The indoor market closed for good at the weekend. Max

Bygraves and what seems like most of his generation live here. They don't get out much, but there's life and money here.

The beach meets EC recommendations, the sea is bluer than it is in Torquay, the people are deliciously handsome and there are squirrels (technically vermin I know, but I'm smitten) in Pine Walk. The locals still take pride in winning the Britain In Bloom competition in 1991 and were I here next week, I could attend the National Information Centre Open Week and if I were really fortunate 'meet a representative from Wilts & Dorset Bus Co'. I might very well come back and do that.

This week, however, Bournemouth is as near to a football town as it's ever been. When AFC Bournemouth have finished with Walsall tonight, their next engagement is at Wembley, where they meet Grimsby Town in the Auto Windscreens Shield Final, a run that as midfielder Steve Robinson admits in tonight's programme, has cost them a play-off place. Unlike their opponents, Grimsby.

The ground is in Boscombe (the team were Bournemouth & Boscombe Athletic until 1971), a lengthy trek from the sea I've touched. My foot is still sore, but I'm in martyrish mood so I limp up Holdenhurst Road, past M&W Mini-Mart with its petition to free an imprisoned character in a soap opera (can't these people be euthanased on the spot for stupidity? M&W Mini-Mart wouldn't, I somehow know, have launched a similar petition for, say, the Guildford Four, but I must march on), past the kosher butcher (boarded up), past several 'adult magazine' shops (boarded up too, but thriving), past the Conservative Party offices, (flourishing: Labour finished third in both local seats in the General Election) where the Union flag is at half mast, perhaps for today's passing of Ian MacGregor, who so enjoyed decimating the coal industry that even some Conservatives found him a little too ideologically driven. I assume he's in hell, but you never know. Tricky business, going to hell.

Tree-lined Dean Court is in King's Park, a 24-hour lorry park, far from homes and the sea, on what must be temptingly saleable land. It's a ramshackle place which the club began to redevelop in the 70s when John Bond was manager and Ted MacDougall and Phil Boyer scored the goals which seemed set to take AFC Bournemouth out of the basement divisions. By 1987, when they finally reached the old Division Two, only the foundations of a new stand behind the Brighton Beach End remained.

Last season, long back to their rightful level, AFC Bournemouth, £5 million in debt, were nearly closed by the Inland Revenue. A town that had always turned its back on football rallied to the cause. Going to Wembley on Sunday seems like fair reward. People do care. A bit. And the receiver bought a season ticket. Now, a true community club, The Cherries are run by a trust and Jim Davidson's brief directorship finished during the 1982–83 season. This, in a less venal world, could be the future of football.

Amazingly, they have sold over 33,000 tickets for Sunday and to the disgruntlement of many, have incompetently sold out of scarves at the club shop. Where do the one-match brigade come from? What will they feel on Sunday when Bournemouth grace Wembley for the first time? As Sky understands so well, spectators want spectacle. They certainly don't fancy a match with lowly Walsall on a wet Tuesday evening and over 28,000 Wembley ticket holders give it a miss. Helpfully the fanzine, *Community Service*, has an article for Virgin Cherries: 'Style Of Play: this can vary. And your local rivals are ... Southampton'.

I like it here. The PA might be hopeless and I spend much of the game trying to secure a decent view through poles the club neglected to remove when the fences came down, but the mascot, Cherry Bear, wears a beret and throws sweets at the same children at the front of the South Stand terrace who summon the players over one by one for autographs. During the warm up, goalkeeper Jimmy Glass shouts 'heads' whenever a wayward shot threatens to knock a pie out of the hands of the unwary. A shame, for my pie is excellent and the tea most masculine. The ignorant servers, straight out of remand home, couldn't have been more rude if they were keenly contesting a rudeness competition.

It's a funny game, bereft of the atmosphere tension brings. Bournemouth's players are trying to avoid injury. The crowd – lots of attractive couples and women of all ages, no blacks, little passion – sing some Wembley and anti-Reading and Portsmouth songs with more effort than the risible version of 'Staying Alive' the team recorded to accompany them to Wembley. The female staff are uncommonly pretty and even some of the stewards are glamorous: why, one of them looks like Marilyn Monroe. As my cuts have almost healed, I feel confident enough to smile at her. She half returns the greeting, with the indulgence of someone who may well have been smiled at before.

Walsall, relaxed after journeying in their white L-reg Hallmark coach with Walsall FC headrests, tinted windows and quality tables, might get themselves relegated if they don't pick up points. Their few fans – they went out of the Auto Windscreens here a few weeks ago at the southern semi-final stage – are stuck on the open end. When the rain becomes torrential, nice Bournemouth move them into the covered seats, except for twenty-three doughty Midlanders (daft Midlands accent: 'It's not *that* wet!'), who refuse to move and thus get soaked. This old working class stubbornness isn't a football future. These people were once the heart of the game, now they're peripheral eccentrics, but they'll have truly enjoyed tonight. Something noble will be lost when they are no longer permitted to stand in the rain. That day is close and I move into the rain myself to salute them. Until I'm too wet.

The second half is better. When he's not mouthing at a linesman and unnerved by a shout of 'You look like my gerbil, goalie', Walsall's Jimmy

Walker, the churl, abuses a far from sloppy ball-boy. His team-mate, glove-wearing centre forward Didier Tholot, adopts a shoot on sight policy which brings out the best in Glass, especially late on when he leaps like the friskiest of panthers to tip a Tholot header over. Immediately afterwards, Bournemouth are denied a blatant penalty when Robinson is bundled over by Gary Porter. Steve Fletcher wins it for the home side with a majestic but unchallenged header from Neil Young's free kick. Walsall stay pretty, but when substitute Michael Ricketts misses an open goal after Jeff Peron shows the most energy of anyone all evening with a fine solo burst, the match fizzles out, to the accompaniment of increasingly forlorn 'Que sera sera' chants. When Bournemouth do get to Wembley it'll be a quiet affair.

As I walk back through the rain, my hobble bravely vanquished, the football crowd disperses instantly and the deathly quiet of early evening has given way to a succession of night clubs, all plying for trade. Pubs are few but cavernous, so the police don't spend high season (if such a thing exists) driving from one small place to another, sirens blaring. At The Littern Tree, where all the drinkers are glamorous except me, they play soft soul of the Luther Vandross ilk. Bournemouth is that sort of place. The beer isn't great.

Outside, I'm halted by four women, drunkish but friendly. Implausible I know, but after twenty minutes indoors, my drowned rat look could be taken for fetching wet-look gel. 'Would you like to come there with us?' the traditionally least-attractive-but-most-talkative flibbertigibbet asks, pointing to a club along the way. They don't seem to be joking.

I wouldn't mind actually, but: a) ouch, my tender ankle; b) I'm wet underneath; c) I'm carrying an AFC Bournemouth programme and d) the car means I'm near the drink-drive limit, so I can't metamorphosise into my youthful drunken alias, Yuri Gregarious (that's unbearably funny around 11 p.m. when you're seventeen, believe me). I politely decline. One of them, the leggy one, says 'but I wore my split skirt tonight,' and so she has, right up to that point at near-gusset level where tights change hue. Gift horses have such attractive looking mouths sometimes.

I finish my last night-time trip of the season at the giant, cold Brasshouse, on my own in a corner, plotting out dance steps with my fingers, deeply disappointed. I don't go on the beach tonight.

88 Cardiff City

v. Macclesfield Town
DIVISION THREE
18 April

1-2

'I am not about to write half a page full of excuses, just to say that we have experienced a long injury list.'

Frank Burrows

I've gone native. No more journeys by car, it's trains to the finish, in no way a result of not taking up those nice Bournemouth women's offer. More worryingly – and this is pitifully late an admission – I'm enjoying this now. I always have really, but now the end feels less a celebratory conclusion of marathon completed, more a dull thud, born of longing for it to continue. When the season comes to an end, something inside me will end with it. I wish I wasn't like this.

Cardiff is a place to dampen even the most ebullient of souls. Despite being a less appealing Bristol, it purports to be the capital of Wales. Like Yorkshire, Durham and Cornwall, Wales already has a capital: London, just one hour fifty-seven minutes away by train. This arrangement suited everyone fine until 20 December 1955 (without overstating the case, this was less than fifty years ago) when for reasons never properly explained, the Welsh, five per cent of Britain's population, decided they needed a capital. Cardiff, rather than historical Caernarvon or Machynlleth where Owain Glyndwr held court, got the nod, for reasons again never properly explained.

Today, Cardiff can only look inward, so there's an internecine war with Swansea which not only surfaces itself in two of the least pleasant groups of football fans clashing with Biafran viciousness (this season is the first in recent memory that away fans have been permitted), but situation-comedy municipal rivalries about which city should host the pretend Welsh 'parliament', which Cardiff voted against anyway and which will chiefly exist to distribute the massive grants and subsidies winging their way from London, without which Wales would be back in the Stone Age.

Cardiff might not be a proper capital then and the irritating signs in Welsh (less than seven per cent of this city speaks the language, the same that speaks Chinese or Urdu, there are no signs in either) suggest boneheaded backwardness (twenty per cent of adult Cardiff has no qualifications), but this is a city where it is culturally acceptable to be a skinhead, although less so to wear a jacket, be non-white or for the council to collect rubbish.

When blacks do go into the city – like Marcus Walters, Francisco Borg and Marcus's five-year-old sister in August 1997 – things happen. They were attacked by some pit-bull-wielding skinheads, arrested by CS-gas-spraying police and charged with violent disorder after the police had whacked Francisco. Their solicitor advised them to plead guilty. The blessed Citizens Advice Bureau suggested the students might have a case, especially as the whole incident had been filmed on closed-circuit television.

It's no fun being a stray cat either: in February B&Q sacked three workers for torturing one. Or being the woman who told Cardiff crown court she was unable to speak while she was forced to have oral sex with a rapist: 'Like going to a dentist and he asks you where you're going on holiday as he's drilling your mouth,' sympathised Judge John Prosser. Without wholly anathematising Cardiff, it stinks.

They're selling world revolution and *Socialist Worker* on Queen Street, brutish women bawl through hand-held loudhailers that Britain has the longest working hours in Europe (chiefly to subsidise Wales, although I don't hear that coda), something unemployed ex-miners might not see as a pressing problem. Little in the centre has changed since 1978, other than the pubs being open for longer. There's even a Wimpy bar, effortlessly upholding the great Wimpy tradition of being nearly empty.

Cardiff had a head start on the rest of Britain. The docks around Butetown imported Spanish iron ore and exported Rhondda coal, so Cardiff grew from a hamlet of 100 people in 1800 to a city of 220,000 by the mid-1930s. There was a catch which meant it could never prosper: Butetown was named after the Bute family. Rechristening the docks Tiger Bay midway through the last century couldn't hide the fact that the Butes owned the area and ploughed little of the profits into Cardiff.

It was a rum locality, a magnet for Irish families fleeing famine, political refugees and all sorts of unusual races: 'Chinks and Dagos, Lascars and Levantines slippered about the faintly evil by-ways that ran off from Bute Street. It was a dirty, smelly, rotten and romantic district, an offence and an inspiration,' wrote Howard Spring. Without a dominant racial group, especially the white working class, race relations were never a problem in Shirley Bassey's Tiger Bay.

Butetown exists today, five minutes from Cardiff centre. A Salvation Army hostel marks the boundary between city and outlaw country. Most of the docks are closed now and Tiger Bay is Cardiff Bay. Old dockers' terraced slums have been replaced by new two-storey slums, with faintly evil alleyways and mugger-friendly precincts. The rubbish is festering, the graffiti says FUCK THE POLICE or INDEPENDENT TROPICAL WALES. Sometimes the drum'n'bass is of night-club decibel levels, sometimes the women are in purdah, but the betting shops are always full.

At the end of the road – an A road with speedbumps – are the former docks, where all is scarily quiet. This is what it sounds like when gulls don't cry. Incongruously, there is a statue of a black couple and their dog, all looking out to sea, the man is holding a copy of the former *Daily Mirror*. This area, still Butetown, is Cardiff's hope for a regeneration which a solitary Harry Ramsden's restaurant does not fulfil.

There'll be a five star hotel; the world's most unnecessary freshwater lake; shopping malls to replace the Welsh Industrial & Maritime Museum which closes tomorrow so people forget their history; the 'parliament' (after Cardiff Council rejected the proper government's £3.5 million offer to have it at the City Hall demanding instead £14.5 million to locate it in Cardiff Bay); and Millennium Centre 'designed to bring the festival atmosphere of Baltimore or Sydney Harbour to Cardiff', all for £120 million. Wankers.

On waste ground I watch two white boys hurling rocks at cars foolishly parked there, now dented and windscreenless. I tread gingerly past adults pushing British Rail trolleys full of nothing; away from the scary wheelchair woman with half a leg missing trying to mow me down and over the broken glass that carpets Butetown. Unless they demolish this festering slum (or spend money on it, obviously a slightly less glamorous proposition than 'the festival atmosphere of Baltimore'), it won't work. Instead, Cardiff's solution is to pretend Butetown isn't there: on the other side of the railway tracks that run parallel with it to the docks, a new road is to be built and so visitors and dignitaries will never see the slum. How very medieval.

Astonished by this last discovery, I brave a drink in the Baltimore Arms where regeneration and woeful neglect merge. The pub has been redone: the customers (drunk late-middle-age women, Butetown blacks, workmen) have not. I don't tarry.

Cardiff City's Ninian Park is the other side of a city bedevilled by roadworks, in a pleasant area, where middle class Cardiff begins and flows north. There's a functional bridge over the River Taff opposite Cardiff Arms Park where the rugby union (Wales's real love, international days here must be hell) team plays, Wales's technically still illegal football team loses there too, but they rarely attract more than 10,000. Possibly solely to create jobs, it's being knocked down and built up again as, wait for it, Millennium Stadium. Maybe they'll keep repeating the process for eternity.

I pass through the Asian ghetto, where there are shop-window appeals over the November 1997 murder of Yazid Yahiaoui asking, 'Do you know anyone who owns or carries an axe?' Only the 58-year-old who went wild with a hammer and meat cleaver during a family barbecue at Ely, Cardiff in June 1996. And, probably, those who battered Cardiff newsagent Philip Saunders to death with a spade in 1987. Yazid's murder happened on the corner of Tudor Road and Clare Road. When I stand where I think it happened, there are no flowers, there's no blood, but hate and fear stain the air. There are still no birds singing.

This season has been a fiasco for Cardiff City, as most of them have been since they tumbled out of the old Division One in 1962, although they're only one off English football's record number of drawn games in a season. Only Hull, Brighton and Doncaster have acquired less points, while Colchester, Torquay and Barnet push for promotion. Attendances are slipping towards 2000 and Ninian Park, once capable of holding 61,000, has a capacity of 14,000 and is beyond repair. As ever a move is mooted, to, surprise surprise, Cardiff Bay. The finances are desperate, despite the appointment of Joan Hill, an unnaturally glamorous granny, as Chief Executive.

In contrast, the league's newest club Macclesfield Town – who've travelled in a fairly impressive P-reg Hallmark with many lampless tables and un-appetising-looking Tupperware containers of unidentifiable food in the kitchen at the back, confirming there's no money there either – will make virtually certain of automatic promotion if they win today.

I'm on the Popular Bank, where the toilets would be more up to date if they were a hole in the ground. It's unreserved seating with an unused standing terrace in front. Having consumed a shockingly poor minced beef pie, leavened slightly by average tea and tarty service, I arrive at 2.40 and sit on the front row at the halfway line with nobody near me, the best seat in the ground. I stretch my legs out, bask in the sun, my morale higher than everyone save the 200 or so Macclesfield fans in the opposite Grandstand, next to the unused Grange End terrace behind the goal. This is football poverty and on the Canton Stand behind the other goal is Cardiff's little hard mob with their handmade CCFC flag and two Welsh flaglets. They're the remnants of Cardiff's still occasionally fearsome Soul Crew. When they sing 'What the fucking hell is that?' to Macclesfield defender Efetobore Sodje and his idiotic white bandanna, it sounds pathetic, the last yelps of a dying clan in a dying city.

The bespectacled Bluebird mascot walks over the empty terracing and shakes his white-gloved hands with everyone at the front of the Popular Side. This means me! Oh yes! I haven't touched a match ball all season, but now I have shaken hands with a mascot. There are curmudgeons who ignore him, but he's a patient bird and waits until they melt, as they inevitably do. I shake his hand vigorously, with a broad grin. He doesn't linger.

Cardiff are disorganised, dispirited and envious. The team likewise. Jason Fowler, star of that fine game at Barnet, is still outstanding but demob happy.

Only trainee Christian Roberts looks truly lively and he puts City in front with a fine goal. Goalkeeper Jon Hallworth rolls the ball to winger Wayne O'Sullivan, who powers forward, feeds it to Roberts who makes a fool of Macclesfield's Steve Payne and slots it past Ryan Price.

The tiny Cardiff mob do their Ayatollah dance. This, impressively, involves them hitting themselves like the mourners at Khomeini's passing in 1989, the funeral of the century. Like Diana's, only serious. Even so, the cheers that greet the news of Newcastle winning at Manchester United are as loud as those for the goal.

Too-tense Macclesfield, who've done all this with only sixteen professionals, have incomprehensibly left Stuart Whittaker, who I saw win their game with Brighton single-handedly, on the bench. By half-time, Cardiff have created enough chances to have blown the promotion scrap wide open.

Early in the second half, Macclesfield bring on Whittaker and from his evil corner, Sodje's bandanna heads in the equaliser. 'Fuck off, blackie,' snarls a voice behind me. Blacks and women don't come to Ninian Park.

When, in the eighty-fifth minute, Neil Sorvel twists through the defence and flicks in Macclesfield's winner, Cardiff fans' anger surfaces. Macclesfield celebrate in front of the tiny mob, who make street-fighting gestures and then go home. The crowd behind me chant 'Kumar out' to the chairman, Britain's ninety-sixth wealthiest Asian with £50 million in the bank. They barrack their players who're having nightmares: uninspiring captain David Penney, 'off, off, off' is the humiliating chant when he's booked; bobbly arsed Lee Phillips and the awful Anthony Carss. More capable players like Chris Beech, who just cannot be bothered as Whittaker sprints past him time after time, are ridiculed. 'Better club next year, Beechy mate,' sneers another lone voice. Fowler's Man Of The Match award is greeted with sustained booing, as is new manager (at least that's his title, Director Of Football Development Kenny Hibbitt's role is unclear) Burrows's weird decision to substitute Roberts. Afterwards, the Macclesfield players party with their fans, are congratulated by the PA announcer and the few Cardiff fans who've stayed to the grisly finale are on their way home in five minutes. Hopeless, in every sense.

As evening falls, Cardiff blossoms. It's a drinking town and a honeypot for employed valley dwellers under thirty, desperate for a good time. Already, the pubs are filling up as afternoon drinkers stumble off home muttering in English. The Hogshead has shown the Manchester United v. Newcastle game live (no wonder nobody watches Cardiff City) and now, loud Oasis competes with England v. West Germany, 1970. At the Market Inn, Welsh rugby (in Welsh, Jesus) is being studiously ignored. I would have left, but my train is delayed by an hour. This means I can visit the cavernous Square, where the smarter set go. A huge, rotating square juke box above the bar plays Joe Jackson's lachrymose 'Steppin' Out' and the crowds are pouring in. They serve amusingly titled cocktails (Sex On the Beach, Slow Comfortable Screw, et bloody cetera). The women start to look better and the men less red of neck. For one tipsy moment I think I could abide it here. Then I remember Yazid Yahiaoui and his axe-wielding murderer. I catch my late train back to London.

89 Scunthorpe United

v. Exeter City
DIVISION THREE
25 April
2-1

'The fans have got to realise that this squad will get there in the end.'

Brian Laws

Scunthorpe's hitherto unheralded marketing people call it The Industrial Garden Town. I'd have plumped for an infinitely more catchy and honest The 70s Recession Town, with a jaunty Nowhere To Go, Bugger All To Do call to action. For my last basement level trip, I'm joined by Mark, one of several friends I thought I'd lost this year. He's always wanted to come to Scunthorpe, which as recently as a century ago was a few farms and some flat views. *Circa* 1860 ironstone deposits brought mines, which in turn brought the steel industry. It's now a town of 70,000 which spawned Carmel, Tony Jacklin and some flat views. After the decimation of British Steel in the 80s, the newly privatised industry shrank and Scunthorpe hit hard times, but it will always be a steel town. The newly trim British Steel is making profits again, but unemployment still soars whenever there's a sales blip.

Between the station and town centre, we pick our way through a trail of Friday night's detritus: half-eaten burgers, burger grouting, burger packaging, orange vomit, blood and condoms (unused). Lager Man was here last night. Scunthorpe is unlike other towns. Its centre is tiny, underdeveloped and uniquely downcast. Scunthorpe is full, but the people aren't buying cheap Durham Pine, the Freeman, Hardy Willis range or even a £1 coffee from El Toro 'coffee lounge'. Chic-free locals loll about, looking poverty stricken and lost. All the benches on the pedestrianised precinct are taken. People sit there with empty plastic bags, smoking and eating junk food like victims of a social control experiment. A busker plays Bob Dylan's 'Mighty Quinn' and nobody has any money to give him. The library, and this encapsulates Scunthorpe in one Kafka-esque moment, has no windows. There's an indoor market where we don't buy ten bars of soap for £1, or cheek of pork for the same amount, nor do we try to find Bella, the lost Staffordshire pup which can apparently read the notice pleading 'Come home soon baby', nor do we book for *A Night On The Tiles* as performed by the Appleby-Frodingham Theatrical Society at the Plowright Theatre (Joan was born here in 1929 and soon left). Like the rest of Scunthorpe, we can only meander.

In The Tavern (they can't even be roused to name their pubs), the beer is gorgeous Ward's and only old men are supping it. We move across the road to The Mint is search of more fun, if such a thing were possible to imagine. The beer is nearly off and the hands of one of the four customers shakes whenever he lifts his drink. He's under forty and he licks the drips of beer off his wrists as they snake towards the dirty table. This is no football town, no anything town. It's a Doncaster postal district where the headline in the local newspaper concerns a scheme to be implemented by North Lincolnshire Council preventing council car park patrons transferring car park tickets.

We take a cab to the giant but virtually deserted Berkeley near the ground. Mark is a taxi maven; I must give and take in a world where I'm excited by team coaches. Our Sheffield-born driver has recently returned from Libya, a foreman over '250 of the black gets', who invented Christian religious holidays to secure time off.

It's Scunthorpe's last home game this season, the final opportunity for the local police to rack up overtime, which is why they and their horses are here in number. United's year was ruined somewhat by eight straight league defeats, including the game I saw at Mansfield around Christmas. If they win today they'll finish close to a (mathematically impossible now) play-off spot. Exeter, The Grecians, have arrived in their handsome Dartline coach, which might be L-reg and have no lamps, but does have tinted windows, tables and a Grecian Lounge where someone cooks long-journey food. They were going up when I saw them sneak past Swansea, but now they're twelfth, all mutterings of promotion long forgotten.

This, then is a game without meaning, an end of season black hole, with only those whose contracts expire after next week needing to show interest. Glanford Park, Scunthorpe United's home since 1988, was the first new ground: a prefabricated tin shed which holds less than 10,000. As would be the way of these stadia, it's literally the last building in Scunthorpe. Out of sight and out of mind. It does, though, have a standing end which Mark and I – through incompetence – fail to get into. Instead, we're in the Glanford Stand, where there isn't a crush, but the pies are flaky and excellent.

There are many presentations before the players run out to Sham 69's yob anthem 'If The Kids Are United'. The sponsorship deal with Pleasure Island (based in Cleethorpes to everyone's embarrassment, save Scunthorpe's business community if there is such a thing) is at an end. They are to be replaced with Belton-based Motek, 'a mobile communications rental company' (i.e. they lend mobile phones to bastards), for £50,000 over two years. Suspiciously cheap if you ask me and Mark, but, hey, what do we know? All four Player Of The Year Awards go to ever-present defender Chris Hope, who must be good. A ball-boy wearing a Manchester United top shows no interest.

It's a weird game, played at a gentle pace, but not without skill. Maybe Laws has a point about his squad. David D'Auria's exquisite chip early on gives Scunthorpe the lead and from that point their nineteen-year-old midfielder Paul Harsley controls the game.

Lucky Exeter equalise when Michael Walsh nudges centre forward Steve Flack, who collapses as if shot by James Earl Ray. Darran Rowbotham does the honours to the delight of the seventy-four Exeter fans, whom stewards maliciously prevent from leaping up and down. There's just enough time for Jamie Forrester to score Scunthorpe's winner after everyone had a go during penalty area ping-pong. At half-time Hope is prevented from leaving the field by Miss Scunthorpe Evening Telegraph, a feisty looking girl if ever there were, 'looking as lovely as ever' smarms PA man, who gives him a fifth award, possibly not the one he'd really like. Another uncaring ball-boy walks past him, this one wearing a Liverpool shirt.

A brace of sulky models parade the new Motek-dominated kit (half claret, half sky blue, all horrible) around the pitch and the healthy looking young woman who does the half-time draw 'has had a bit of chemotherapy' chuckles PA man. Her friend puts a comforting arm round her, as she crestfalls.

Exeter fans – mostly students from northern universities by the look of them, plus a solitary mini-coach from Devon – are there to be bullied, and bullied they will be. They're harmlessly, unthreateningly end-of-season half-pissed, but the stewards spend the second half arresting fifteen per cent of them for standing up and clapping in an end that's a tenth full at best. It's an unpleasant sight but these stewards will run scared when Rotherham bring their 750 visigoths.

The second half fades like both teams' prospects this season, despite Laws's occasional hysterics on the bench. All the younger footballers have Jennifer Aniston haircuts, which means, disappointingly, I'm condemned to a decade of notionally wanting to sleep with them. Hope goes close with a powerful header from D'Auria's corner and during a lull in play, a sixth award for him is announced. His team-mates – except Harsley who won't be here long and knows it – are humiliated.

In the last minute, as if they were a prehistoric tribe confronted by fire for the first time, something shocks the Scunthorpe fans into a brief chant. Referee Jones blows for time and another season is over. Those Exeter fans who haven't been manhandled or ejected circle a policeman, who cannot have expected to be troubled this sleepy afternoon, to make their point. The stewards stand behind the policeman's back making wanker gestures at officer and fans.

We slope back to the town centre along Doncaster Road before turning off to The Honest Lawyer, dark, dingy but friendly and near the station. It's a long straight walk, past posters advertising a Model Engines Festival and Scunthorpe's pleasant district, handily placed for a quick getaway on the M181. We pass United's former home, Old Show Ground, now Safeways. Legend has it that the sky lit up whenever United scored. Everyone knew it was just new lava being poured over steel slag heaps, but they liked the story and it bound the people of Scunthorpe together, around their team, in shared fantasy. It's not the same seeing it from Safeways car park.

Mystically, at the Baths Hall, my friends from High Wycombe, Fleetwood Bac, will be playing, a few days after an Ultimate Fantasy Show, where for £10 rabid local women can watch 'the big boys play'. At Henry Afrikas – perhaps it's for the best there are no real Africans in Scunthorpe – Samantha Fox will be doing some sort of performance on 9 May, possibly the greatest night in the town's history. We're less intimidated by Bettafit Thermals, where, implausibly 'your satisfaction is our future'. They're easily pleased in Scunthorpe.

90 **Burnley**

'Things look like they could be on a knife edge all afternoon.'

Chris Waddle

There's no public sex, but that aside, this lunchtime in Burnley is a rehearsal for those few hours before earth explodes, as one day it will, although please God not before next Sunday. Every pub is packed and every customer is drinking as if there is not only no tomorrow, but no tonight either. Yet, there's no joy in this abandon, not even hubris. Everyone speaks in hushed tones or remains silent, for today all will be resolved. There are mounted police all around Charter Walk shopping centre, where short skirts are in but shapely legs are out. The police are on the same side as the people, who won't be causing trouble before 3 p.m.

There might be shoppers in the centre of this quiet maelstrom, but I can't see any who aren't Asian, the most run down community of a run down milltown. I try to squeeze into Sidewalks, where tough topless lads drink bottled beer outside, but the queue at the bar is ten deep and 'due to the importance of the Burnley game' the bar is all-ticket afterwards. It's better at Yates's but only just and the bouncers nod gravely as I enter, as if I've come to view the body on funeral day. No thanks, I'd like to remember Burnley FC as they were. The skies have suddenly clouded over.

It goes like this. Division Two ends today and Burnley, the club with Britain's largest percentage support from its home town, play Plymouth Argyle. If Burnley lose or draw, they are relegated. If they win, they might still be relegated if Brentford win at play-offs chasing (although I'll never know how) Bristol Rovers. The third team in the triangle of doom is – wow – Plymouth themselves, level on points with Burnley. But, having scored more goals, a draw would secure the Devonians' status, if Brentford lose in Bristol. If Brentford draw, Burnley or Plymouth must win. All Burnley can do is win and hope their victory isn't pyrrhic: Plymouth would be foolish to adopt a different strategy.

At midday the queue for the ticket office stretches for a hundred metres. It passes the club shop, where manager Chris Waddle's biography (written by his agent) is already discounted. 'It should be called *I Am Shit*,' quips the man behind me as we edge forward.

Football is all Burnley has ever had and that makes its desperation all-consuming and poignant. Burnley's cotton weaving industry has declined along with the population, coal has come and gone, the Leeds & Liverpool Canal is no longer important, the immigrants have moved in, and the railway station has one platform and one track. Burnley FC hung on in the top Division from 1947 to 1971, but now they're the symbol of a town that has nothing else to cling to and where the Number 6 bus goes to Bleak House. Even the animal welfare shop, Only Foals & Horses, is in on the act: 'Up The Clarets,' says its window poster, 'we can do it'. Everyone cares, except Burnley's Asians, but they know what result is good for them.

A season that began with the appointment of Chris Waddle, a most unlikely manager but supposed proof the big time was back, ends like this: a silent, drunken town where I'm charged 20p to enter the Miners' Social Club and its Men Only section near the pool table. And that's before boardroom argy bargy and last Tuesday when the team was 3-1 up at ten-man Oldham and still only drew. Burnley FC is Burnley and vice-versa. There is no alternative.

Outside, Ralph Coates, a man with a Shredded Wheat hairdo which he appears to dye a curious orange, a reminder that Burnley once employed current England players, is doing a television interview. He's interrupted when someone shouts 'I hope you've brought your fucking boots'. After he finishes, fans rush to shake his hand. One actually says 'Ralph, I love you'. He spends half an hour holding court. He thinks Burnley will win, but there's stuff that needs sorting out long-term.

Plymouth shouldn't be in a position where Torquay could be a division above them this evening. Since that memorable day when they fought back against Wigan, they've stuttered and stumbled, pausing only to sell Adrian Littlejohn to Oldham in time for him to sink them with two goals at Boundary Park. I wonder if my Cornish chum from that Wigan game is here. Certainly, Argyle fans nearly fill the massive Endsleigh Stand, a sea of green and white.

Turf Moor, Burnley's home since 1882, six years before league football, is close to the town centre. By 2 p.m. all roads and pavements are blocked by a tide of nervy humanity. It was three-sided in the later glory years, but now it's all-seater and far too grand for Blackpool to visit, let alone Hartlepool. I'm high in the North Stand with a fantastic view over the River Brun (why I'm not in Brunley I'll never know), terraced houses, cobbled streets and moors towards the trollopy south. Served by the hard of hearing and stroppy, I've failed to take succour in my too-tough pie and – the horror – unmushy peas coated in scalding pea jissom or to finish my foul tea.

The crush is scary, but everyone is scared about the other thing so it cannot count. It's compulsory to chain smoke and I'm sandwiched between two hard looking men in a state of nervous tension only slightly alleviated by incessant anti-Blackburn chants: 'No nay never ... 'til we play Bastard Rovers no more' and 'Stand up if you hate Bastards'. In front of me is a man with a ring that says DAD, a BFC tattoo between his thumb and forefinger on his right hand and one saying ENGLAND on his left. He keeps shoving his fist in his girlfriend's face in a friendly way. I look around. Everyone is in this heightened state and the women care so much they cannot help but be gorgeous. Between every record played, there's a warning for supporters not to encroach on the pitch.

When the teams come out to Van Halen's stirring 'Jump', my body begins to tingle all over. The noise is so sustained, so hysterical and so terrifying I have to join in with the primal howl. My stomach begins to flutter and I shiver as all my body hair (including the four fine, dark strands on each nipple) stands on end. This is mass hysteria and the Plymouth fans letting off their green and white balloons feel exactly the same way. 'Fucking hell,' whispers the man to my right between deep drags on his Embassy No 1. 'Fucking hell.' I know exactly what he means.

The game begins in madness. Plymouth, prompted by the still excellent Martin Barlow, gain three corners in the first five minutes. Roared on by a quarter of the town who racially abuse Plymouth's Paul Williams as a matter of course (the proportion of Burnley's whites here will be far higher), the home side weather the storm and try to do the right thing. Unfortunately, apart from Glen Little, they're hopeless at it. As is the way sometimes, they score with their first attack. Damian Matthew gives Little the chance to flight an expert cross and Andy Cooke heads in. 'I'm going to get fucking arseholed tonight,' screams the man to my left, when he's let me slip from his bear hug. 'Fucking hell,' I say. 'Fucking hell,' he replies.

The game rattles on, the first 'fucking hell' man's mantra is 'twat it', which he repeats whenever there's a Burnley shooting opportunity. Players of both teams throw themselves at any opposition shot and Barlow skies a chance when all alone in the penalty area. If they'd played like this all season, this would be a promotion battle. 'Chim-chimernee–chim-chim-cheroo, we are those bastards in claret and blue,' sing the Burnley fans when Plymouth's Carlo Corazzin runs clear and screws wide. They don't notice Cooke and his striking partner Andy Payton almost coming to blows when a rare Burnley attack breaks down around them: there's no on-pitch spirit here, not a jot. Everything that happens today is born of desperation. I look across my row, all I can see is a beautifully arranged succession of bottom cracks. We're all tilted forward on the edge of our seats.

Everyone notices the equaliser. Darren Currie (so awful when I saw him for Shrewsbury) crosses craftily. Burnley goalkeeper Chris Woods hesitates and unmarked Mark Saunders nods in. One end of the ground goes wild. Three sides put their heads in their hands.

Then, Burnley string moves together. Paul Weller's rasping drive hits the bar, bounces on the line and trickles away. Little's flying header hits the bar and from the rebound Cooke heads towards goal, but goalkeeper Jon Sheffield picks himself off the floor and claws it wide. Even some Burnley fans clap. In fantasy world, that sort of save keeps teams up. In the real world, Burnley score soon after with a similar goal to the other two. Aided by minimal backlift Matthew crosses and Cooke scores his second with a straight-forward header.

At half-time, the toilet crush is surreal, but all talk is of Bristol. It's announced as 0-0, but the bloke in the urinal next to me says there's been a sending off (he omits to mention who the man played for) and that Brentford keep hitting the bar. 'Never underestimate our ability to cock it up,' is his parting shot, accompanied by a splash of urine on my shoes and the sage nods of those around us.

If it stays like this, Burnley stay up. During the second half, Plymouth, attacking towards their fans, do everything but score, or create any real chances, until substitute Earl Jean, who scored a hat trick for Rotherham when he last played at Turf Moor, tests Woods with some half hit stabs. When Bristol Rovers score at the Memorial Ground, everyone squeals with delight. An equaliser here and Plymouth stay up, without it Burnley do.

Plymouth switch to three at the back, but besieged Burnley always look more dangerous whenever they sneak out of trouble. While the ball is in the Burnley penalty area, the Plymouth fans shriek, trying to suck the ball in. Burnley defenders let the ball hit them. Then they hack it away. The last chance comes when Barry Conlon crosses, everyone miskicks and the ball falls to Jean, who can't beat Woods. Police sprinkle themselves among the Plymouth fans and excellent referee Taylor calls time. Astonishing. My stomach is in shreds and I'm drained and sopping with sweat. I hug and am hugged once more. I shake my fist and go 'yeah' like everyone around me.

Meanwhile, on the pitch, Chris Waddle has sprinted – quicker than he ever did as a player – down the tunnel which lies in the middle of the Plymouth end, without a word and the invasion has begun. In an instant, Burnley fans stop pawing their players and move towards the Plymouth fans, screaming 'Burnley's staying up', although the Brentford result has not been announced. The distraught Plymouth fans, taunted by the newly unarguable 'going down' chant whatever happens in Bristol and mass finger pointing choreographed with Busby Berkeley precision, try to charge their hosts. They're physically held back by the police within. They settle on ripping out seats and hurling them at Burnley fans, who unsurprisingly return them. Right now, I pray the

Cornishman isn't here. The flask we shared tea from would have been the first to be thrown, but not by him. I hope he's OK, wherever he is. Brentford have lost. Burnley fans stand there jigging up and down. Plymouth fans fold their arms and glare.

The sound of locking stable doors can be heard from here to Accrington as police horses bolt onto the pitch. As if governed by its own internal dynamism – and surprise that the Plymouth fans show no intention of giving ground – the Burnley fans scatter before the shitting horses.

It's mini-mayhem outside and the dozy police seem surprised. How soon roughhouse turns to tears and celebration has quickly evolved into vengeance. Burnley haven't won anything, they're merely where they were a year ago and they haven't had a season like this by accident. There are no heroes in this team, no chants for any of them – even two goal Cooke – or their illustrious manager. Everything is geared towards Burnley, the town and the territory. Thus the adrenaline-fuelled men of Burnley wait outside the Endsleigh Stand and ambush the Plymouth fans, who attempt to give as good as they get, but are heavily outnumbered. Police vans, horses, dogs and men charge down Brunshaw Road. A few slaps later order is restored.

It's fortunate for the police at least that Plymouth is too far away for mass travel by train (unlike Preston – which looks like it's been hit by a riot when I pass through – on the station there's a nasty looking, twenty-strong Bristol City mob who've taken a heavy, bloody battering: they're accompanied by police on their service train), so there will be no foreign presence on the streets of Burnley this evening as it parties with relief. A few terrified northern-dwelling Plymouth supporters flee town on a two-carriage train, under the gloating eyes of Burnley jackanapeses rolling joints at the station.

Had Burnley been relegated, the Plymouth fans would have been there now, with the police still pondering how to get them past those who want re-imbursement for some mythical crime, or simply a good punch-up where their territory can be marked. This is real football, a place – like Preston, but more intense – where the circle squares, where football and town are the way they are because of each other. Today is one of the great days in Burnley – town and team of course – history. I'm honoured to have been there.

91 **West Bromwich Albion**

v. Nottingham Forest
DIVISION ONE

3 May

1-1

'Rest assured things will come right with the time the summer gives us.'

Denis Smith

This, then, is what football has come to. West Bromwich Albion are sniffy about selling tickets to anyone who does not live within a stone's throw of their Hawthorns ground, especially for a sell-out like today's game with Nottingham Forest, who secured the Division One Championship in the week, thus rendering this clash meaningless. I have but one option: a box. A treat to close Division One, I tell myself, vigorously over-estimating their competence.

Thus myself and my latest company, Stuart, find ourselves outside The Hawthorns at an unearthly midday for a 1.30 Sky-ordered kickoff on a steaming Sunday morning, dressed 'smart but casual'. We're hungover, grumpy and lost.

This place, Albion's home since 1900, has been bypassed by time. What must once have been a residential area is now light industry wasteland bordering the M5. West Bromwich is a part of Birmingham, no matter how uppity the natives might get about this. Once, it wasn't: named after a broom shrub, mentioned in the *Doomsday Book* and something of a donkey sanctuary, West Bromwich joined the industrial revolution early with its ironworks, was subsumed into Birmingham and stayed there until manufacturing industry died. Now, it's the birthtown of Robert Plant and a place where they burn down Hindu mandirs. There's football tradition here: Albion were in the original Football League, while their away support at Oxford and Tranmere, both night matches, shows there's still something. I won't be able to glean exactly what.

Myself and Stuart have been promised much for our outlay of £152.75. Best seats, 'pre-match luxury buffet', 'complimentary programmes', 'wine reception on arrival' (which we interpret as enough drink to help us commit a serious misdemeanour), a television to help us watch match replays there and then, while checking how Stoke and Manchester City are doing, plus 'tea/coffee and biscuits at half-time'. Efficiently, the club even telephoned my home to ask which team we supported. 'West Brom,' lied my wife, expertly. 'Right, we'll put them in a home supporters' box,' declared nice office lady.

It begins to unravel outside, where Nottingham Forest fans have turned up *en masse*, some dressed as Robin Hood. After being led down more garden paths than Percy Thrower by nincompoop stewards (we're sheepish at being posh football fans and fail to assert ourselves), we find a carpeted, oasis-like box-holders' entrance. 'Good afternoon and welcome,' smiles a charming, smartly dressed man, handing us our programmes. As we're about to enter this pleasure palace, already seeking out handmaidens, he stops us. 'Ah, you're in the Family Stand, the other side of the ground.'

This entrance is different. It is a turnstile. We are greeted by a steward in an orange Motorway-maintenance navvy's jacket, smoking a roll-up, who grunts aggressively into the distance when we ask where to go. Eventually, we find our way through a cramped passageway into our box, which is unventilated and a temperature residents of Riyadh wouldn't stand for. Some glasses of wine have been left out, all night judging by the putrid taste. The television doesn't work properly unless the whole world is now lime-coloured, and Sky is unobtainable. The 'luxury buffet' has been dumped in the fridge. It's overchilled pasta. Some programmes have been left lying around and our fellow box dwellers are Forest fans.

I'm distraught at bringing poor Stuart along, although not as distraught as the businessman trying to impress clients. The boxholders' toilets are in worse condition than the public ones in Birmingham New Street. There's no soap (I think of the food-preparing staff sharing these toilets and take even less of a fancy to the 'luxury buffet') and the hand-drier is hanging off the wall, kaput.

We have a waiter, part servile, part smirking. He brings us some drinks (which we later discover are not free, but the businessman will pay for ours) and leaves, returning only to tell us immediately before the game that we're not supposed to drink alcohol ten minutes before and after the game or during half-time, 'although I have to tell you that,' he grins. I like him. We The Dehydrated, then begin protracted Yalta-style negotiations to secure tea and coffee. Someone has to go to the kitchen to beg for it. The staff are not pleased to be disturbed. Stuart and I gaze longingly over to the Halfords Lane Stand, where things are nicer, or Division Three, where the organisation is more professional.

Football was not meant to be viewed behind glass. There looks to be a rip-roaring atmosphere: the ground is sold out and people's mouths are moving, but our insulated world is soundproofed too. We're next to a father and his two posh, confident, polite children. They're from Bristol but support Forest. The kids have watched Forest in dozens of executive boxes throughout the country.

They can compare them (this is the worst, but Stoke's are nice) and they're part of a new football vanguard.

Midway between those who see everything on Sky and those who go to games properly, are people like this, who don't find it odd to watch football behind a lightly tinted screen. There are many more things they wouldn't mind: crowds comprised solely of executive box holders, indoor football, retractable roofs, plastic grass, eating a meal with the match as a distraction, grounds unserved by public transport, tickets to price out the scum etc. Football could one day soon resemble dog racing. Another football future, for everywhere except Burnley.

The mascot, Baggie Bird ('I live in the Hawthorns Stadium in the week and come out on matchdays,' he helpfully explains in the programme. I'd always wondered ...), looks cute, but he doesn't get up to any tricks, The Hawthorns isn't that kind of place. It all seems friendly and Albion clap out a Forest team which includes lanky eighteen-year-old débutant Marlon Harewood. It's so end of term, the players might have well brought their own clothes and games for the afternoon. Tomorrow West Bromwich Albion go for a club holiday in Magaluf. All the people in our box clap and cheer the pre-match rituals. A pointless exercise, muse me and Stuart, still trying to come to terms with the wine, a subtle blend of Listermint and balsamic vinegar.

There is much to admire after the imperious Pierre Van Hooijdonk misses a gilt-edged early chance. For Albion, Kevin Kilbane is very very fast until he runs out of steam after ten minutes and Lee Hughes is very very ginger. Forest score when Van Hooijdonk and Steve Stone combine in the penalty area and the latter – still responsible for the miss of my season at Reading – slots past Paul Crichton. This changes everything. Albion's closely monitored ticketing arrangements have extended to selling places near the front of the home Birmingham Road End to thirty Forest fighters. Those Forest fans go a gloating but controlled bonkers, Albion fans pile in from all directions and referee Orr halts the game.

Sometimes I can't understand the police. They're late on the case and have two options. Expel them and risk more trouble outside or escort them to the Forest end where there is some disused terracing and let them claim victory. Tony Blair would have been proud of their Third Way. This is to let the Forest fans go to the Forest end in their own time, without escort. Now, these people know exactly what they're doing: they are hard men, with no kids, no replica shirts and no long hair. As the players stand and watch, they swan down both touchlines offering every single home fan out for a fight. The skirmishes are never-ending and the party atmosphere floats off into the ether. They are applauded into the bosom of the away support who are singing 'You're supposed to be at home' to the humiliated home fans. They clamber into that disused terracing next to the less family-orientated patrons of our Family

Stand. The foundering police let this happen for forty minutes before shoving the infiltrators into the away end.

While We The Still Dehydrated are fighting for half-time refreshment – they've run out of lager and beer – some builders wearing visors and welding gear skulk onto the pitch. I can't hear what's going on so I'm confused. Then after some people dressed as £, 1, 6, 9, (a comma), 3, 1 and 4 respectively have paraded themselves, the welders depart looking glum. Being deaf must be like this.

The lime-green television shows Stone's goal again, again and again until we all feel bilious. We prop the door open for air. I had fantasised my Division One would end more gloriously than this. I'm embarrassed to have brought Stuart here, although he is planning to have a BAGGIES SKINZ tattoo across his forehead and, unlike me, has won a succession of bets the fat Labrokes grumpstress reluctantly let us make. This is still terrible.

The second half potters along. Young Harewood has a brilliant first touch allied to a ferocious temper and nearly scores when he lobs Crichton. A woman comes in to do our washing up – loudly – while the game is still on. It all ends well when Brian Quailey, Albion's splendidly named substitute, wriggles free down the left. His cross is handled by Forest substitute Jon-Olav Hjelde and Hughes blasts the penalty past Dave Beasant.

There's no pitch invasion. The Forest players grope each other and celebrate in front of their own fans with champagne and by pulling Andy Johnson's shorts down and spanking his pert bottom. Albion do a lap of honour, although they've sacked full back Shane Nicholson for persistent drug use (he's friends with the Derby Lunatic Fringe, no strangers to drug dealing) and lost all chance of promotion since Smith, who declared in today's programme he supported Stoke as a boy and 'still does', replaced Ray Harford. It's ruined by two fat fans who milk the occasion with egotistical gusto, ignored by the players, mentally in Magaluf anyway. Hughes throws his boots into the crowd. He's a hero. That's that then.

Outside, in the mid-afternoon heat, at least there is air and a garage selling cold drinks. There are gangs wandering around, but nobody seems to know quite what to do at 4 p.m. Stuart and I amble down Birmingham Road. A policeman is trying to control traffic at the M5 junction, overriding the signals. His simple duty is to wave Nottingham-bound coaches through. Unfortunately he does this so badly, that the coaches clog up the whole roundabout. Then, ignoring the chaos he's created around him, he shrugs his shoulders, leaps aboard his motorbike and rides off.

Sometimes, the world is a mystery to me, but in West Bromwich, right here right now, having betrayed myself by going behind glass for the only time, it's probably wise to live by an old Iberian saying: 'There is no path: paths are made by walking'. I'll never again pay my own money to go in an executive box as long as I live. Unless I change my mind.

v. Arsenal
PREMIER LEAGUE
10 May

1-0

> '**Let's get it firmly fixed in our minds that today is not a celebration
> of Arsenal's success, but the chance for one huge final push on our
> part to earn a place in the UEFA Cup ... God bless Bruce Springsteen.**'

John Gregory

So, this is it. The end. Ninety-two matches since 9 August. And what have I
learned? I'm tempted to think of Father Dougal in *Father Ted* and say
'absolutely nothing', but that's not true. I've learned things about myself
(mostly unencouraging) and about other people (sometimes good, sometimes
bad). I've seen some of Britain's past, much of its present and too much of too
many of its futures. I've spoken to my father often and he's always known how
many matches I've seen, so I guess he must be proud, but I feel only emptiness.
I don't want this to end.

Everyone has one talent: maybe finding football grounds, chuckling with
the natives, drinking beer and abusing pies is mine. Not one that would have
gotten me on the *Titanic* lifeboats. Still, as John Gregory (and who'd have
thought he'd be here after Wycombe's capitulation at Northampton in
February? Not me. Or him), so articulately says, one huge final push ... I've
tried especially hard not to get run over this past week. ninety-one out of
ninety-two would be too much to take.

Birmingham Welcomes The World is the slogan draped on banners everywhere. The G8 leaders are summitting here this week and to celebrate, the city
is on terror alert, with special attention to chemical attack. The only terror so
far has been the promotion: a handful of ordinary Brummies were picked to
feature in a poster campaign suggesting Birmingham is great and deserves G8.
One of the 'ordinary' models appeared topless in the *Sun* last week. Capitalism?
Phwar. Furtively, a black woman and white man, both bespectacled, are pasting
posters advertising Marxism '98, a lesser summit, on ring road bus shelters

I was here on a previous Sunday to see Birmingham City, but now there are
television crews doing G8 previews on Chamberlain Square and a sign next to

a statue of steam engine inventor James Watt telling me I'm 3244 miles from Ottawa.

Villa Park is north towards the M6, half an hour's walk through a city not without great beauty. It must have been a sight to behold in Victorian times, when Birmingham ruled the earth and had the architecture to prove it. Today, it's handsome, albeit blighted by slums like Lee Bank, whose residents scaled Town Hall and unfurled a G8 parodying banner, Welcome To Birmingham Home Of The Lee Bank Slum Quarter.

I head through ring roads and subways, past Aston University to Ben Johnson, a pub which has a Student Discount sign outside. Students Hung, Drawn & Quartered might be more accurate. It's a biker pub, empty of students and bikers, but fairly full of hard Villa fans (a rare species), old men at the bar trying to chat up a barmaid who looks if she'd rather be chatted up by George Michael and a nasty weekend father taking his kids for a meal of sorts. 'Decide what you want first or I'll decide you don't want anything,' he snaps. The children look embarrassed for him. I try to smile at them without being branded a paedophile. He must resent his kids so much.

The G8 swarm will doubtless learn that Birmingham has more miles of canals than Venice (although Venice's tend not to be clogged with rusting bikes and supermarket trolleys), ten Labour MPs and no Conservative ones; that arguably the world's finest collection of pre-Raphaelite art is in the Museum & Art Gallery and that the Industrial Revolution, which ultimately brought all G8 leaders to power, probably began here. They might even discover that Birmingham first came into its own when it supplied Roundheads with weapons in the Civil War. The Royalists promptly took the city.

What G8 won't do is go to Aston, where, hemmed in by the Aston Expressway and the M6, they could learn a thing or two. Bill Clinton (staying at the Swallow Hotel: can this be American irony? Or do their civil service hate him? Or are they really, really thick?) would take pleasure in the Aston Christian Centre, a gathering place for beautiful, black, split-skirted women and their dim-witted besuited husbands. All eight leaders would admire the legions of little black and Asian kids demanding to 'mind your car', a capitalist protection racket in action.

They might look too at Aston's downside. Sapphire Tower smells of piss from fifty metres away, the car parks for middle class football fans (how oxymoronic that phrase would have seemed so recently) advertised solely on grounds of vehicle safety and the dangerous wasteland strewn with domestic detritus and the contents of stolen cars.

I visit the White Swan on Victoria Road, the point where black becomes Asian. Although this afternoon's match is a sell-out and the ground is only ten minutes away, it's empty save a black man swigging shorts while furiously playing the gaming machine. Only a small portion of the pub is used, giving it